Qi Zhang · Yingwei Wang · Liang-Jie Zhang (Eds.)

T0214140

Cloud Computing – CLOUD 2020

13th International Conference
Held as Part of the Services Conference Federation, SCF 2020
Honolulu, HI, USA, September 18–20, 2020
Proceedings

Springer

Editors
Qi Zhang
IBM Research – Thomas J. Watson
Research
Yorktown Heights, NY, USA

Yingwei Wang
University of Prince Edward Island
Charlottetown, PE, Canada

Liang-Jie Zhang (ID)
Kingdee International Software
Group Co, Ltd.
Shenzhen, China

ISSN 0302-9743   ISSN 1611-3349 (electronic)
Lecture Notes in Computer Science
ISBN 978-3-030-59634-7   ISBN 978-3-030-59635-4   (eBook)
https://doi.org/10.1007/978-3-030-59635-4

LNCS Sublibrary: SL3 – Information Systems and Applications, incl. Internet/Web, and HCI

This Springer imprint is published by the registered company Springer Nature Switzerland AG
The registered company address is: Gewerbestrasse 11, 6330 Cham, Switzerland

Preface

The International Conference on Cloud Computing (CLOUD) has been a prime international forum for both researchers and industry practitioners to exchange the latest fundamental advances in the state of the art and practice of cloud computing, identifying emerging research topics and defining the future of cloud computing. All topics regarding cloud computing align with the theme of CLOUD.

CLOUD 2020 is a member of the Services Conference Federation (SCF). SCF 2020 had the following 10 collocated service-oriented sister conferences: the International Conference on Web Services (ICWS 2020), the International Conference on Cloud Computing (CLOUD 2020), the International Conference on Services Computing (SCC 2020), the International Conference on Big Data (BigData 2020), the International Conference on AI & Mobile Services (AIMS 2020), the World Congress on Services (SERVICES 2020), the International Conference on Internet of Things (ICIOT 2020), the International Conference on Cognitive Computing (ICCC 2020), the International Conference on Edge Computing (EDGE 2020), and the International Conference on Blockchain (ICBC 2020). As the founding member of SCF, the First International Conference on Web Services (ICWS 2003) was held in June 2003 in Las Vegas, USA. Meanwhile, the First International Conference on Web Services - Europe 2003 (ICWS-Europe 2003) was held in Germany in October 2003. ICWS-Europe 2003 was an extended event of ICWS 2003, and held in Europe. In 2004, ICWS-Europe was changed to the European Conference on Web Services (ECOWS), which was held in Erfurt, Germany.

This volume presents the accepted papers of CLOUD 2020, held virtually during September 18–20, 2020. For this conference, each paper was reviewed by three independent members of the International Program Committee. After carefully evaluating their originality and quality, 22 papers were accepted.

We are pleased to thank the authors whose submissions and participation made this conference possible. We also want to express our thanks to the Program Committee members for their dedication in helping organize the conference and review the submissions.

Finally, we would like to thank operation team members, Dr. Sheng He and Dr. Yishuang Ning, for their excellent work in organizing the conference. We thank all volunteers, authors, and conference participants for their great contributions to the fast-growing worldwide services innovations community.

July 2020

Qi Zhang
Yingwei Wang
Liang-Jie Zhang

Organization

General Chairs

Mudhakar Srivatsa   IBM Thomas J. Watson Research Center, USA
Song Guo   Hong Kong Polytechnic University, Hong Kong
Shi-Jinn Horng (Vice Chair)   National Taiwan University of Science
and Technology, Taiwan

Program Chairs

Qi Zhang   IBM Thomas J. Watson Research Center, USA
Yingwei Wang   University of Prince Edward Island, Canada

Services Conference Federation (SCF 2020)

General Chairs

Yi Pan   Georgia State University, USA
Samee U. Khan   North Dakota State University, USA
Wu Chou   Vice President of Artificial Intelligence & Software at
Essenlix Corporation, USA
Ali Arsanjani   Amazon Web Services (AWS), USA

Program Chair

Liang-Jie Zhang   Kingdee International Software Group Co., Ltd, China

Industry Track Chair

Siva Kantamneni   Principal/Partner at Deloitte Consulting, USA

CFO

Min Luo   Georgia Tech, USA

Industry Exhibit and International Affairs Chair

Zhixiong Chen   Mercy College, USA

Operations Committee

Jing Zeng   Yundee Intelligence Co., Ltd, China
Yishuang Ning   Tsinghua University, China
Sheng He   Tsinghua University, China
Yang Liu   Tsinghua University, China

Steering Committee

Calton Pu (Co-chair)	Georgia Tech, USA
Liang-Jie Zhang (Co-chair)	Kingdee International Software Group Co., Ltd, China

CLOUD 2020 Program Committee

Gerald Baumgartner	Louisiana State University, USA
Feng Chen	Louisiana State University, USA
Haopeng Chen	Shanghai Jiao Tong University, China
Jingshu Chen	Oakland University, USA
Dazhao Cheng	University of North Carolina at Charlotte, USA
Jai Dayal	Intel, USA
Krishna Kant	Temple University, USA
Mukil Kesavan	Google, USA
Yao Liu	SUNY Binghamton, USA
Aziz Mohaisen	University of Central Florida, USA
Supratik Mukhopadhyay	Louisiana State University, USA
Nagendra Kumar Nainar	CISCO, USA
Sanjay Patel	LDRP-ITR, India
Shaolei Ren	University of California, Riverside, USA
Huasong Shan	JD Silicon Valley R&D Center, USA
Jun Shen	University of Wollongong, Australia
Byung Chul Tak	Kyungpook National University, South Korea
Yuzhe Tang	Syracuse University, USA
Wei Wang	The University of Texas at San Antonio, USA
Pengcheng Xiong	Amazon Web Services (AWS), USA
Xiaohua Xu	Kennesaw State University, USA
Feng Yan	University of Nevada, USA
Yifan Zhang	SUNY Binghamton, USA
Ming Zhao	Arizona State University, USA

Conference Sponsor – Services Society

Services Society (S2) is a nonprofit professional organization that has been created to promote worldwide research and technical collaboration in services innovation among academia and industrial professionals. Its members are volunteers from industry and academia with common interests. S2 is registered in the USA as a "501(c) organization," which means that it is an American tax-exempt nonprofit organization. S2 collaborates with other professional organizations to sponsor or co-sponsor conferences and to promote an effective services curriculum in colleges and universities. The S2 initiates and promotes a "Services University" program worldwide to bridge the gap between industrial needs and university instruction.

The services sector accounted for 79.5% of the USA's GDP in 2016. The world's most service-oriented economy, with services sectors accounting for more than 90% of GDP. S2 has formed 10 Special Interest Groups (SIGs) to support technology and domain specific professional activities:

- Special Interest Group on Web Services (SIG-WS)
- Special Interest Group on Services Computing (SIG-SC)
- Special Interest Group on Services Industry (SIG-SI)
- Special Interest Group on Big Data (SIG-BD)
- Special Interest Group on Cloud Computing (SIG-CLOUD)
- Special Interest Group on Artificial Intelligence (SIG-AI)
- Special Interest Group on Edge Computing (SIG-EC)
- Special Interest Group on Cognitive Computing (SIG-CC)
- Special Interest Group on Blockchain (SIG-BC)
- Special Interest Group on Internet of Things (SIG-IOT)

About the Services Conference Federation (SCF)

As the founding member of the Services Conference Federation (SCF), the First International Conference on Web Services (ICWS 2003) was held in June 2003 in Las Vegas, USA. Meanwhile, the First International Conference on Web Services - Europe 2003 (ICWS-Europe 2003) was held in Germany in October 2003. ICWS-Europe 2003 was an extended event of ICWS 2003, and held in Europe. In 2004, ICWS-Europe was changed to the European Conference on Web Services (ECOWS), which was held in Erfurt, Germany. SCF 2019 was held successfully in San Diego, USA. To celebrate its 18th birthday, SCF 2020 was held virtually during September 18–20, 2020.

In the past 17 years, the ICWS community has been expanded from Web engineering innovations to scientific research for the whole services industry. The service delivery platforms have been expanded to mobile platforms, Internet of Things (IoT), cloud computing, and edge computing. The services ecosystem is gradually enabled, value added, and intelligence embedded through enabling technologies such as big data, artificial intelligence (AI), and cognitive computing. In the coming years, all the transactions with multiple parties involved will be transformed to blockchain.

Based on the technology trends and best practices in the field, SCF will continue serving as the conference umbrella's code name for all service-related conferences. SCF 2020 defines the future of New ABCDE (AI, Blockchain, Cloud, big Data, Everything is connected), which enable IoT and enter the 5G for the Services Era. SCF 2020's 10 collocated theme topic conferences all center around "services," while each focusing on exploring different themes (web-based services, cloud-based services, big data-based services, services innovation lifecycle, AI-driven ubiquitous services, blockchain driven trust service-ecosystems, industry-specific services and applications, and emerging service-oriented technologies). SCF includes 10 service-oriented conferences: ICWS, CLOUD, SCC, BigData Congress, AIMS, SERVICES, ICIOT, EDGE, ICCC, and ICBC. The SCF 2020 members are listed as follows:

[1] The International Conference on Web Services (ICWS 2020, http://icws.org/) is the flagship theme-topic conference for Web-based services, featuring Web services modeling, development, publishing, discovery, composition, testing, adaptation, delivery, as well as the latest API standards.

[2] The International Conference on Cloud Computing (CLOUD 2020, http://thecloudcomputing.org/) is the flagship theme-topic conference for modeling, developing, publishing, monitoring, managing, delivering XaaS (Everything as a Service) in the context of various types of cloud environments.

[3] The International Conference on Big Data (BigData 2020, http://bigdatacongress.org/) is the emerging theme-topic conference for the scientific and engineering innovations of big data.

[4] The International Conference on Services Computing (SCC 2020, http://thescc.org/) is the flagship theme-topic conference for services innovation lifecycle that includes enterprise modeling, business consulting, solution creation, services orchestration,

services optimization, services management, services marketing, and business process integration and management.

[5] The International Conference on AI & Mobile Services (AIMS 2020, http://ai1000. org/) is the emerging theme-topic conference for the science and technology of AI, and the development, publication, discovery, orchestration, invocation, testing, delivery, and certification of AI-enabled services and mobile applications.

[6] The World Congress on Services (SERVICES 2020, http://servicescongress.org/) focuses on emerging service-oriented technologies and the industry-specific services and solutions.

[7] The International Conference on Cognitive Computing (ICCC 2020, http:// thecognitivecomputing.org/) focuses on the Sensing Intelligence (SI) as a Service (SIaaS) which makes systems listen, speak, see, smell, taste, understand, interact, and walk in the context of scientific research and engineering solutions.

[8] The International Conference on Internet of Things (ICIOT 2020, http://iciot.org/) focuses on the creation of IoT technologies and development of IoT services.

[9] The International Conference on Edge Computing (EDGE 2020, http:// theedgecomputing.org/) focuses on the state of the art and practice of edge computing including but not limited to localized resource sharing, connections with the cloud, and 5G devices and applications.

[10] The International Conference on Blockchain (ICBC 2020, http://blockchain1000. org/) concentrates on blockchain-based services and enabling technologies.

Some highlights of SCF 2020 are shown below:

– **Bigger Platform:** The 10 collocated conferences (SCF 2020) are sponsored by the Services Society (S2) which is the world-leading nonprofit organization (501 c(3)) dedicated to serving more than 30,000 worldwide services computing researchers and practitioners. Bigger platform means bigger opportunities to all volunteers, authors, and participants. Meanwhile, Springer sponsors the Best Paper Awards and other professional activities. All the 10 conference proceedings of SCF 2020 have been published by Springer and indexed in ISI Conference Proceedings Citation Index (included in Web of Science), Engineering Index EI (Compendex and Inspec databases), DBLP, Google Scholar, IO-Port, MathSciNet, Scopus, and ZBlMath.

– **Brighter Future:** While celebrating the 2020 version of ICWS, SCF 2020 highlights the Third International Conference on Blockchain (ICBC 2020) to build the fundamental infrastructure for enabling secure and trusted service ecosystems. It will also lead our community members to create their own brighter future.

– **Better Model:** SCF 2020 continues to leverage the invented Conference Blockchain Model (CBM) to innovate the organizing practices for all the 10 theme conferences.

Contents

A Replication Study to Explore Network-Based Co-residency of Virtual Machines in the Cloud

Sanchay Gupta[1]([✉]), Robert Miceli[1]([✉]), and Joel Coffman[1,2]([✉])

[1] Engineering for Professionals, Johns Hopkins University, Baltimore, USA
{sgupta72,rmiceli3,joel.coffman}@jhu.edu
[2] Department of Computer and Cyber Sciences, United States Air Force Academy,
Air Force Academy, USA

Abstract. By deploying virtual machines (VMs) on shared infrastructure in the cloud, users gain flexibility, increase scalability, and decrease their operational costs compared to on-premise infrastructure. However, a cloud environment introduces new vulnerabilities, particularly from untrusted users sharing the same physical hardware. In 2009, Ristenpart et al. demonstrated that an attacker could place a VM on the same physical hardware and extract confidential information from a target using a side-channel attack. We replicated this seminal work on cloud cartography and network-based co-residency tests on Amazon Web Services (AWS) and OpenStack cloud infrastructures. Although the Elastic Compute Cloud (EC2) cloud cartography remains similar to prior work, current mitigations deter the network-based co-residency tests. OpenStack's cloud cartography differs from EC2's, and we found that OpenStack was vulnerable to one network-based co-residency test. Our results indicate that co-residency threats remain a concern more than a decade after their initial description.

1 Introduction

Cloud providers leverage virtualization to run multiple workloads concurrently on a physical server. These workloads may use different operating systems or the same operating systems, but at different patch levels [1,2]. The hypervisor ensures that the virtual machines (VMs) are isolated from each other and that one VM cannot access information from another VM. Sharing resources allows cloud providers to maximize the utilization of each physical machine and reduces the cost to cloud consumers, but co-residency also introduces risks and privacy concerns for customers. For example, an attacker may exploit co-residency by extracting sensitive data, such as cryptographic keys, from other VMs running on the same host.

In seminal work, Ristenpart et al. [3] demonstrated that the use of shared physical infrastructure in cloud environments introduces unique vulnerabilities. Their work used *cloud cartography* to map the placement of VMs in the cloud. Armed with this information, an adversary can achieve a 40% chance of placing their own VM on the same physical machine as a target VM, which opens the

© Springer Nature Switzerland AG 2020
Q. Zhang et al. (Eds.): CLOUD 2020, LNCS 12403, pp. 1–16, 2020.
https://doi.org/10.1007/978-3-030-59635-4_1

door for cross-VM attacks. Ristenpart et al. recommend that cloud providers obfuscate the internal structure of their services to inhibit simple co-residency checks. Other researchers [4,5] echo these recommendations.

Later research examined additional types of co-resident attacks. Zhang et al. [6] detailed the construction of an access-driven side-channel attack to extract fine-grained information from a victim VM running on the same physical computer. Irazoqui et al. [7] demonstrated a side-channel attack for multiprocessor systems even when the VMs do not share the same physical CPU. Xu et al. [8] investigated how Virtual Private Cloud (VPC) networking mitigates earlier attacks [3] but develop new placement strategies to sidestep the defenses. Even though Web Services (AWS) Elastic Compute Cloud (EC2), the Google Compute Engine, and Microsoft Azure all implement mitigations against simple co-residency tests, they remain vulnerable to memory probing, and co-residency is correlated with the launch time of VMs in data centers [9].

In addition to extracting sensitive information using side channels, researchers have also studied attacks targeting the degradation of performance of target VMs through the means of (DoS) attacks. For example, a malicious cloud customer can mount low-cost attacks to cause severe performance degradation for a Hadoop application, and 38x delay in response time for an e-commerce website hosted in AWS EC2 [10]. Because there still exists a high possibility of attacks that can affect the performance or security of a VM, ongoing research into co-location is valuable.

In this paper, we investigate whether the co-location techniques tested by Ristenpart et al. [3] can be replicated a decade after the original research. A *cloud cartography* map was re-created for instances on EC2 on the same VPC network. Amazon VPC prevented network-based co-residency tests for instances created from different AWS accounts. The *cloud cartography* map for OpenStack was different than EC2, but several patterns were discovered in the IP address assignment for OpenStack instances. Additionally, network-based tests on OpenStack instances were successful in determining co-residency for several different network and site configurations. Our results indicate that co-residency threats remain a concern more than a decade after their initial description, and we offer recommendations to mitigate such risks.

The remainder of this paper is organized as follows. Section 2 provides an overview of the two services that we evaluated, AWS EC2 and OpenStack, and describes how we used them in our experiments. In Sects. 3 and 4, we replicate the *cloud cartography* and network-based co-residency check on both services. In Sect. 5, we discuss our results, and we conclude in Sect. 6.

2   Experiment Platforms and Methodology

This section provides an overview of AWS EC2 and OpenStack, the two cloud platforms that we evaluated. We chose EC2 to replicate Ristenpart et al.'s original study [3] and OpenStack due to its position as a leading open source cloud platform.

2.1 AWS Elastic Compute Cloud (EC2)

Amazon Web Services (AWS)[1] is a public cloud platform that is used by startups, enterprises, and government agencies. Its Elastic Compute Cloud (EC2) service allows users to manage VMs, referred to as "instances," with virtualized hardware (CPU, memory, storage, etc.) derived from a user-selected "instance type." EC2 is subdivided into 22 geographic regions and 69 availability zones around the world. Each region is separated geographically, and each region consists of isolated availability zones that are connected to each other through low-latency links. Users may select an availability zone within a region, or EC2 will select one automatically when launching an instance.

A Virtual Private Cloud (VPC) is an AWS service that allows users to provision a logically isolated section of AWS to launch resources. A VPC provides networking capabilities similar to a private data center, but comes with the benefits of availability, reliability, and scalability. Additional benefits and features include having complete control over the virtual networking environment, including selection of the IP address range, creation of subnets, and configuration of route tables and network gateways.

Originally, EC2 used a platform that is now referred to as EC2-classic. With this platform, the instances ran in a single, flat network that was shared with other customers. AWS accounts created before December 2013 still support this platform. Newer accounts only support the EC2-VPC platform. The EC2-VPC platform provides capabilities such as the ability to assign static private IPv4 addresses to instances and to assign multiple IP addresses to an instance. The EC2-VPC platform also creates a default VPC in each AWS region so that the user can start quickly without having to configure a custom VPC. The default VPC receives a /16 IPv4 CIDR block and a size /20 default subnet in each availability zone. These default values end up producing up to 65,536 private IPv4 addresses with up to 4,096 addresses per subnet. The default VPC also configures an Internet gateway and security groups. Figure 1 illustrates the architecture of a default VPC that is set up by AWS.

With the introduction the EC2-VPC platform, the internal IP addresses of instances are private to that cloud tenant. This configuration differs from how internal IP addresses were assigned in EC2-classic. To understand the security implications of this, two cloud experiments were created with the EC2 service to determine the cloud cartography and co-residency between VM instances.

2.2 OpenStack

OpenStack[2] is an open source project that provides cloud infrastructure management and control capabilities. For our experiments, OpenStack (Rocky release) was deployed using CloudLab [11], which allows researchers to run cloud software stacks in an isolated environment. CloudLab is a testbed for the design of

---

[1] https://aws.amazon.com/.
[2] https://www.openstack.org/.

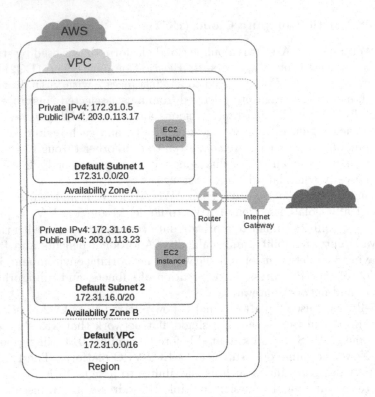

Fig. 1. AWS VPC network architecture

new cloud architectures, testing for vulnerabilities, and learning about deploying clouds. The service is unique because it gives researchers control over their experimental cloud stack, a capability not provided when using commercial cloud offerings.

We created three custom cloud experiments with OpenStack on CloudLab. In the descriptions that follow, we use AWS terminology for consistency across the two cloud platforms.

Simple This configuration had two compute nodes in the same geographic region and were connected on the same LAN. This environment is designed for basic co-residency tests.

Multi-site This configuration had four compute nodes, two nodes in each of two geographic regions that were connected on the same LAN. This environment was used to test if instances on different sites can be distinguished from co-resident instances by analyzing network traffic.

Multi-LAN This configuration had two compute nodes in the same geographic region but each compute node was connected to a different LAN. This environment was used to compare co-resident instances on the same LAN with co-resident instances on different LANs.

OpenStack distinguishes two types of network traffic: north-south and east-west. North-south traffic travels between an instance and external network such as the Internet. East-west traffic travels between instances on the same or different networks. Co-residency detection is only concerned with analyzing east-west traffic. East-west traffic starts at a VM instance, passes through a bridge that maps the virtual Ethernet to physical Ethernet and enforces network security rules, passes through a switch, and finally is sent to the second compute node. Since the traffic passes through a Layer 2 switch, a traceroute will not measure any hops between the two compute nodes. This configuration applies to the simple and multi-site networks.

The multi-LAN experiment places co-resident instances on different LANs. Traffic is routed from one instance to a switch, a router, and back through the switch and to the other instance. Because the traffic passes through a router, a traceroute will measure a single hop between the two instances. Even though these two instances are co-resident, network traffic will take longer to travel between the two instances than two co-resident instances on the same network.

3   Cloud Cartography

Cloud cartography maps a cloud provider's infrastructure (i.e., the location of hardware and physical servers) to identify where a particular VM may reside. In this paper, we replicate the maps previously created for EC2 and create new ones for OpenStack.

3.1   AWS EC2

Before replicating the methodology used by Ristenpart et al. for cloud cartography on EC2, we hypothesized that due to the increase in regions, availability zones, instance types, and IP ranges, an updated map could look significantly different than the original study [3]. To create the map, we collected one data set to fulfill the requirements for two experiments. The first experiment inspected the internal IP addresses associated with EC2 instances that were launched in specific availability zones. The second experiment examined the internal IP addresses assigned to EC2 instances of varying instance types.

Table 1. IPv4 CIDR blocks associated with each EC2 subnet

Region	Availability zone	IPv4 addresses
us-east-1	us-east-1a	172.31.0.0/20
	us-east-1b	172.31.80.0/20
	us-east-1c	172.31.16.0/20
us-west-2	us-west-2a	172.31.32.0/20
	us-west-2b	172.31.16.0/20
	us-west-2c	172.31.0.0/20

We used two regions, us-east-1 (Northern Virginia) and us-west-2 (Oregon), and three availability zones within those regions (see Table 1). Because we used the default VPC, three subnets that are associated with their own respective availability zones were used to provision the instances. The IPv4 CIDR block associated with the different subnets are listed in Table 1. We also used four different instance types: t2.micro, t2.medium, t2.large, and m4.large. AWS sets limits for the number of concurrent EC2 instances and the number of concurrent instance types for each AWS account. By default, AWS limits users to 20 concurrent instances, but not all instance types are allowed to have this number of concurrent instances. The instance types that we used are just a sample of all the instance types that AWS offers, but these instance types are allowed to have the maximum number of concurrent EC2 instances. In addition, not all availability zones within a region have the ability to provision all the instance types. We selected the specific availability zones because other availability zones in the two regions could not launch an instance of one or more of the aforementioned instance types.

For both experiments, 20 instances of 4 different types were launched in 3 availability zones, for a total of 240 instances. For example, 20 t2.micro instances were launched in the us-east-1a region, and the same was repeated for the other two zones in that region. Figure 2 shows the IP addresses that were assigned to the 80 EC2 instances in each availability zone for the us-east-1 and us-west-2 regions, where each colored marker represents an instance in a different availability zone.

Patterns emerge when looking at the IP address assignment in each region and availability zone. Regardless of the instance type, all the instances launched in one availability zone had IP addresses that are clustered together. As a result, if the internal IP address of a VM was exposed, an attacker would be able to launch VMs in the same availability zone as their target to increase the probability of obtaining co-residency. The results shown here exbibit similar patterns as the cloud cartography map from Ristenpart et al. In both cases, VMs were assigned IP addresses clustered with other VMs in the same availability zone. However, the range of IP addresses assigned to each availability zone was approximately 32 times larger in Ristenpart et al. than the ranges shown in Fig. 2.

Our second experiment focused on the internal IP addresses assigned to instances of varying instance types. Figure 3 indicates a lack of a clear pattern for where different instance types are launched in each respective region. The four different instance types are randomly distributed, which suggests that each instance type may be placed anywhere within an availability zone. The results do not display any of the clustered patterns found in Ristenpart et al. and it appears that AWS has since added some randomization to internal IP address assignments.

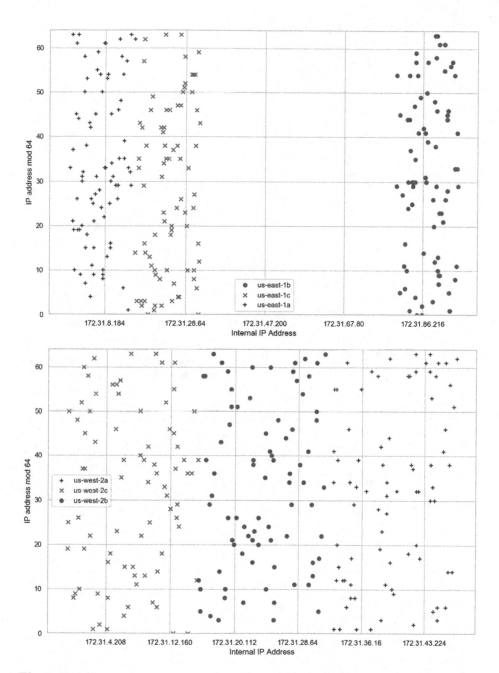

Fig. 2. IP addresses assigned to availability zones in the us-east-1 (top) and us-west-2 (bottom) regions. Each colored marker indicates a different availability zone (Color figure online).

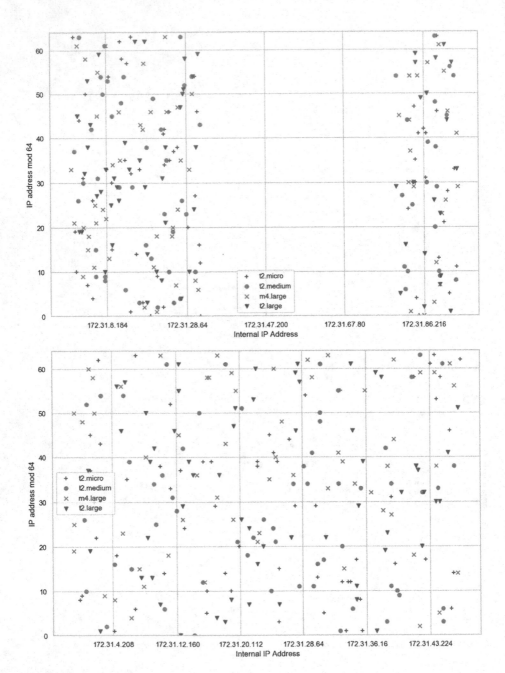

Fig. 3. IP addresses assigned to instance types in the us-east-1 (top) and us-west-2 (bottom) regions. Each colored marker indicates a different instance type (Color figure online).

3.2   OpenStack

We used our multi-site experiment on OpenStack for its cloud cartography. This experiment created two compute nodes in the Clemson region and two compute nodes in the Wisconsin region. We launched 232 m1.small instances, which were placed on a compute node determined by nova, OpenStack's compute service (roughly analogous to EC2).

Each instance receives a private IP address on the local network using Dynamic Host Configuration Protocol (DHCP). The local network was configured to use the 10.254.0.0/16 IP address space. Figure 4 shows the IP addresses assigned to each instance type with the colored markers indicating the two regions. Unfortunately, networking errors prevented any instances from being assigned to the second compute node in the Wisconsin region.

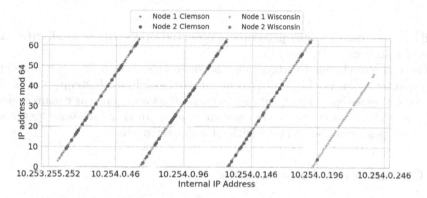

Fig. 4. OpenStack internal IP address allocation across compute nodes. Each colored marker indicates a different compute node and region (Color figure online).

There are several patterns in the IP address allocation process that could potentially be used to determine co-residency. First, the internal IP addresses were assigned somewhat sequentially. For example, six instances were launched with 147, 148, 151, 153, 154, and 178 as the last octet of the internal IP address. An attacker might be able to infer that the instances with numerically-close IP addresses were launched around the same time. Second, 158 of the 232 instances (68%) have a co-resident instance that was assigned a neighboring IP address. For example, the instance assigned 10.254.0.32 is co-resident with the instance assigned 10.254.0.33. Nevertheless, the probability of obtaining co-residency with a neighboring IP address decreases as more compute nodes are added.

Next, we launched 62 instances with four different flavors (comparable to EC2 instance types) on the multi-site configuration to determine if flavors could be used to determine co-residency. The results are shown in Fig. 5. There does not appear to be any patterns for the different flavors. The instances were assigned internal IPs in a somewhat sequential order, but that order is not dependent on

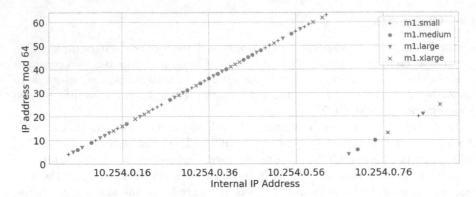

Fig. 5. OpenStack IP address allocation for different flavors. Each colored marker indicates a different flavor (Color figure online).

the flavor because the same pattern was observed previously with all m1.small-flavored instances.

The OpenStack cloud cartography shown in this section does not have any of the patterns observed in the AWS cloud cartography in Ristenpart et al. IP addresses were assigned by OpenStack between the two regions as resources were available on each node and not in separate clusters of IP addresses. OpenStack instance types were also assigned without a cluster pattern.

4   Co-residency Experiments

Ristenpart et al. [3] used two tests to determine co-residency: network-based and cross–VM covert channel based. We replicate the network-based co-residence checks to determine if EC2 and OpenStack have any mitigations in place to deter using them to determine co-residency. The network-based co-residency test asserts that two instances are co-resident if they satisfy any of the following conditions:

- Matching Dom0 IP addresses
- Small packet (RTTs)
- Numerically close internal IP addresses (e.g., within 7)

The remainder of this section explores these checks on EC2 and OpenStack.

4.1   AWS EC2

The first check of matching Dom0 IP addresses did not yield valid results. A TCP SYN traceroute was not able to determine the IP address of the target instance hypervisor. The traceroute produced information for just one hop, which indicates that the two instances are on the same network. There were also multiple

IP addresses for that one hop, which indicates that there are multiple routes through which the instance can reach its destination.

For the second network-based co-residence check (small packet RTTs), we collected data from the 20 t2.micro instances in each availability zone with each instance pinging the other 19 instances in that availability zone 10 times. We used hping3, a network tool that is able to send custom TCP/IP packets and display target replies, to ping the other instances. We collected 190 ping times for each instance. Table 2 shows the mean and median RTTs for each availability zone. The mean and median RTTs between instances provides no clear indication that any two instances are co-resident. That is, no two instances had a significantly lower mean RTT than the mean of the entire availability zone.

Table 2. Round-trip times (RTTs) for 20 t2.micro instances in each availability zone

Availability zone	RTT (ms)	
	Mean	Median
us-east-1a	0.7	0.5
us-east-1b	0.7	0.6
us-east-1c	0.8	0.7
us-west-2a	0.8	0.6
us-west-2b	0.6	0.6
us-west-2c	0.6	0.6

Last, the third co-residence check of numerically close internal IP addresses of two instances was unreliable. As seen in the cloud cartography (Figs. 2 and 3), instances in EC2-VPC are assigned to default subnets within fixed IPv4 CIDR blocks. This assignment results in instances in one availability zone having very similar IP addresses to each other.

4.2 OpenStack

For the OpenStack experiments, the IP address of the hypervisor (Dom0) could not be determined for the target instance using traceroute or other network analysis. Thus, OpenStack is not vulnerable to the first network-based co-residency check. Additionally, OpenStack is not vulnerable to the third network-based co-residency check based on the prior results. OpenStack assigns IP addresses in a somewhat sequential order, and the assignment is not correlated with co-residency. The second network-based co-residency test is the only one that might divulge if two VM instances are co-resident.

To understand how network traffic differs for co-resident and non-coresident instances on OpenStack, RTTs were measured between instances using the simple configuration (see Sect. 2.2). With administrator access to the OpenStack controller instance, co-residency can be determined a priori. This information allows a threshold RTT to be estimated, and this threshold serves as a predictor of co-residency on instances where we do not have administrator access to the controller node. To collect data, 1000 packets were sent between two co-resident instances and then repeated for two non-coresident instances.

A histogram of the round trip times for each measurement is shown in Fig. 6. The mean RTT between co-resident instances was 0.437 ms and the mean RTT for non-coresident instances was 0.515 ms. From the histogram, we observe some separation between the two RTT distributions, which implies that an RTT network-based co-residency check on OpenStack works for this cloud configuration. If the two distributions completely overlapped, it would not be possible to determine co-residency from RTTs. From this data, we set a threshold (RTTs) of 0.476 ms to serve as our co-residency check. This threshold is the midpoint between the two mean RTT from co-resident and non-coresident instances.

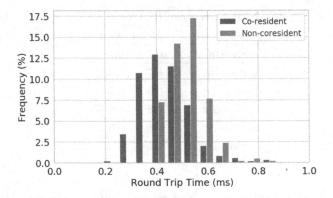

Fig. 6. Histogram of round-trip times (RTTs) for co-resident and non-coresident instances. Co-resident instances have a lower RTT on average.

To determine if this RTT co-residency check could be used on other OpenStack experiment configurations, the same tests were performed on the multi-site and multi-LAN configurations. The results are summarized in Table 3. The first row summarizes the mean RTTs for the simple cloud configuration, where VMs were created on the same LAN in the same region. The second row summarizes the mean RTTs for the multi-LAN configuration, where VMs were created on different LAN in the same region. Here, RTTs are larger than the simple configuration, but there remains a significant difference between the co-resident and non-coresident instances. This difference implies that a RTT co-residency check would still work, as long as the different LANs could be identified. Finally, the last row summarizes the mean RTTs for the multi-site experiment, where VMs were created on the same LAN, but in different regions. VMs in different regions are always located on different hardware. Therefore, it is not possible to have co-resident instances, and the co-resident entry in the table is listed as

"N/A." The largest mean RTT occurs when two instances are located at different regions (25.9 ms). This latency is expected because the traffic is routed through an external network from the Clemson to Wisconsin region.

Table 3. Summary of mean (RTT) in milliseconds for different OpenStack configurations

Configuration	Co-resident	Non-coresident
Simple (same LAN, same region)	0.437	0.515
Multi-LAN (different LAN, same region)	0.656	0.714
Multi-site (same LAN, different region)	N/A	25.908

5   Discussion

In this section, we discuss the results from our cloud cartography and co-residency experiments.

5.1   AWS EC2

The cloud cartography maps produced from the data set collected on the different availability zones and instance types (Figs. 2 and 3) resulted in a very similar map to the original work [3]. There is a clear pattern in the assignment of IP addresses: instances that are launched in one availability zone have very close IP addresses to each other, and instances in other availability zones are clustered in a different IP range. Similarly, the second map that highlights the IP addresses of the different instance types being launched in a region also produced a map similar to the original work.

The cartography maps may have produced similar results but the data sets over which the maps were produced were very different. Ristenpart et al. [3] collected IP addresses from EC2-classic instances, which run in a single, flat network that is shared with other customers. This configuration is different from the one that we used to produce our maps. We collected data from instances on the EC2-VPC platform, meaning instances are run in a VPC which is logically isolated to a single AWS account. Therefore, the cartography maps created and illustrated in this paper only apply to the AWS account where the data was collected and not the entire cloud network. Due to this relatively small sample size, we cannot necessarily generalize our claims and results to the entire AWS cloud network. However, if we are able to replicate these experiments in more VPCs and different AWS accounts and thus, produce the corresponding cartography maps, that will provide the necessary data which could lead us to generalize our claims with a certain degree of confidence for the larger AWS network.

None of the network-based co-residency checks yielded useful results. With the adoption of new technologies such as Amazon VPC, Ristenpart et al.'s network-based co-residency tests are no longer valid. VPC allows EC2 instances that are in the same VPC or different VPC to communicate with each other through a few different means including inter-region VPC peering, public IP addresses, NAT gateway, NAT instances, VPN connections, and Direct Connect connections. The requirement for instances to communicate using public IP addresses ends up causing the routing to happen within the network of the data center instead of going through the hypervisor. Due to this, the prior techniques no longer produce results that can determine if two instances are co-residents.

5.2   OpenStack

The only network-based co-residency test that worked for OpenStack was measuring small packet RTT. We conducted an additional experiment to perform a blind co-residency test across 8 compute nodes. We measured the RTT across instance pairs and used a threshold RTT of 0.437 ms to determine co-residency. This co-residency test was 86% accurate with no false positives and a false negative rate of 33%. For an attacker, these probabilities are very good, especially when considering how quickly and inexpensively one can perform a side-channel attack.

Performance-wise, network-based co-residency tests consume minimal processor, memory, and network resources, making them difficult for a cloud service to detect and restrict. The only significant limitation of these tests is that they consume considerable time for a large number of instances. For large cloud services, there may be thousands of customers using compute nodes in a given availability zone and it might take many days to locate and identify a specific target. For small cloud infrastructures, like the ones that we created with OpenStack on CloudLab, the time investment required to determine co-location is much smaller.

To mitigate these network-based co-residency checks, OpenStack administrators should design their networks to route traffic through a centralized switch regardless of co-residency. Such a configuration increases internal network latency, but for most cases, it would not impact performance significantly, since the additional round trip overhead is only 0.22 ms on average. Nevertheless, when large amounts of data are being transferred internally, this overhead adds up, and administrators must balance the security and performance trade-offs of re-routing network traffic through a centralized switch.

5.3   Legal Issues

Since the experiments were only conducted on AWS accounts that the authors created, we did not violate any terms of AWS's acceptable use policy. The policy prohibits unauthorized access and traffic monitoring, but since we had permission to access instances that we created, these terms were not violated. The OpenStack experiments were run on CloudLab infrastructure, which was explicitly built to test for vulnerabilities in a controlled and isolated environment, and no terms of service were violated during these experiments.

6   Conclusion

Since Ristenpart et al. disclosed the vulnerabilities in AWS EC2 a decade ago, Amazon implemented new security practices and systems, notably Amazon VPC, to prevent network-based co-residency tests. The introduction and continuous innovation of VPC is the primary reason that replicating the prior results is not possible. Repeating the cloud cartography methodology resulted in similar results even though the data sets were different. The original paper was able to create a map that represented a subset of the entire cloud network whereas the data collected in this paper was only for one logically isolated section within one AWS account. The network-based co-residency checks also did not work due to how VPCs changed the behavior of how two instances communicate with each other.

OpenStack is currently vulnerable to network-based co-residency detection when instances are connected to the same or different internal networks. IP addresses for new OpenStack instances are assigned in a somewhat sequential pattern. These vulnerabilities could allow an attacker to co-locate their instance on a target and then conduct side-channel attacks. To mitigate these vulnerabilities, the DHCP server should assign IP addresses randomly, and network traffic for all instances should be sent through a centralized router.

Covert channel co-residency checks are always a potential vulnerability when sharing resources with malicious users. To improve security, further research could examine different co-residency tests based on the shared memory, processor, or storage resources. It is also likely that cloud instances are not allocated to machines completely randomly and future research could try to determine if there are predictable allocation trends that could be used to increase the probability of co-residency. Additional research could also investigate ways to defend against these attacks to either decrease the probability of detection for the attacker or to increase the amount of time and resources required to determine co-residency.

References

1. Smith, J.E., Nair, R.: The architecture of virtual machines. Computer **38**(5), 32–38 (2005)
2. Kotsovinos, E.: Virtualization: blessing or curse? Commun. ACM **54**(1), 61–65 (2011)
3. Ristenpart, T., Tromer, E., Shacham, H., Savage, S.: Hey, you, get off of my cloud: exploring information leakage in third-party compute clouds. In: Proceedings of the 16th ACM Conference on Computer and Communications Security. CCS '09, New York, NY, USA, pp. 199–212. ACM (2009)
4. Vaquero, L.M., Rodero-Merino, L., Morán, D.: Locking the sky: a survey on IaaS cloud security. Computing **91**(1), 93–118 (2011)
5. Hashizume, K., Rosado, D.G., Fernández-Medina, E., Fernandez, E.B.: An analysis of security issues for cloud computing. J. Internet Serv. Appl. 4(1), 25 (2013)

6. Zhang, Y., Juels, A., Reiter, M.K., Ristenpart, T.: Cross-VM side channels and their use to extract private keys. In: Proceedings of the 2012 ACM Conference on Computer and Communications Security. CCS 2012, New York, NY, USA, pp. 305–316. ACM (2012)
7. Irazoqui, G., Eisenbarth, T., Sunar, B.: Cross processor cache attacks. In: Proceedings of the 11th ACM on Asia Conference on Computer and Communications Security - ASIA CCS 2016, Xi'an, China, pp. 353–364. ACM Press (2016)
8. Xu, Z., Wang, H., Wu, Z.: A measurement study on co-residence threat inside the cloud. In: 24th USENIX Security Symposium. USENIX Security 2015, Washington, D.C., USENIX Association, pp. 929–944 (August 2015)
9. Varadarajan, V., Zhang, Y., Ristenpart, T., Swift, M.: A placement vulnerability study in multi-tenant public clouds. In: Proceedings of the 24th USENIX Security Symposium, Washington, D.C., USENIX Association, pp. 913–928, August 2015
10. Zhang, T., Zhang, Y., Lee, R.B.: Memory DoS Attacks in Multi-tenant Clouds: Severity and Mitigation. arXiv:1603.03404 [cs] (March 2016)
11. Duplyakin, D., et al.: The Design and Operation of CloudLab. In: Proceedings of the USENIX Annual Technical Conference. ATC 2019, pp. 1–14 (July 2019)

Leveraging Federated Clouds for Improving Blockchain Performance

R. K. N. Sai Krishna[1], Chandrasekhar Tekur[1], Ravi Mukkamala[2(✉)],
and Pallav Kumar Baruah[3]

[1] Teradata India Pvt Ltd., Hyderabad, India
rkn.sai@gmail.com, t.chandrasekhar@yahoo.com
[2] Old Dominion University, Norfolk, VA, USA
mukka@cs.odu.edu
[3] Sri Sathya Sai Institute of Higher Learning, Puttaparthi, India
pkbaruah@sssihl.edu.in

Abstract. Today, blockchains are popular due to their promise of maintaining a tamper-proof and reliable distributed ledger. As more and more organizations are trying to incorporate this technology within their applications, they are finding the performance and scalability of these systems to be significant bottlenecks. The emerging federated clouds, with a conglomeration of autonomous clouds, could be a solution for this problem. Integrating federated clouds within a blockchain can help overcome these bottlenecks without undermining the autonomy and the peer-to-peer characteristic of the underlying systems. In this paper, we identify a few of the roles in which a federated cloud can play an effective role in a blockchain. In particular, we focus on its role in reducing the communication cost, in cooperation with the miners, incurred in propagating the mined blocks to all the nodes in the system. The proposed integrated approach results in reduced communication cost and improved time for synchronization of the distributed ledger at different nodes. The reduction in network traffic and latency in block synchronization is achieved without deviating from the fundamental autonomous nature of blockchains. The proposed approach results in higher transaction throughputs and lower query response times.

Keywords: Blockchain · Cloud storage · Communication overload · Consensus mechanism · Federated cloud · Latency · Performance · Reliability

1 Introduction

Since the introduction of the peer-to-peer management of cryptocurrencies with an underlying distributed ledger (blockchain) concept by Satoshi Nakomoto [1] in 2008, both blockchain and cryptocurrencies have grown rapidly. Currently, there are more than 1600 cryptocurrencies and hundreds of applications of blockchain technologies in the industry, government, and academia [2]. However, as the usage of these systems is growing rapidly, much more than initially intended by the designers, scalability and performance have become the weaknesses of the systems [3, 4]. For example, as the size

© Springer Nature Switzerland AG 2020
Q. Zhang et al. (Eds.): CLOUD 2020, LNCS 12403, pp. 17–30, 2020.
https://doi.org/10.1007/978-3-030-59635-4_2

of the blockchain is growing, storing and maintaining it on each of the peer nodes has become an issue [5]. Similarly, the communication cost for synchronizing the different blockchains and the delay in doing so have also come under attack. While some solutions such as sharding might address the storage cost aspect, where every node does not have to store the entire blockchain, communication cost is still an issue [4, 6].

At the same time, the use of cloud infrastructures at commercial, academic, and government organization is also becoming a common place [7]. While privacy, security, availability, and trust were the primary concerns of users moving to clouds at the beginning, after a decade of their emergence, trusted clouds have emerged [8]. In particular, federated clouds have overcome most of these obstacles by forming a cloud system that is an integration of several independent and autonomous clouds [9, 10]. They enable interoperability among the individual clouds and offer an integrated cloud interface to the users. When one of the component clouds has been compromised or attacked, the robust federated cloud design prevents the attack spreading to the remaining component clouds [11]. Federated clouds can also be scalable.

In this paper, we look into ways to overcome the scalability, storage, and processing limitations of the current blockchain systems with the help of federated clouds. We do keep in mind the inherently autonomous and decentralized nature of blockchain infrastructure. Here, we consider the federated cloud as an infrastructure that can support the blockchain nodes in the background. We show several roles that a federated cloud could play in the functionality of a blockchain.

The paper is organized as follows. In Sect. 2, we briefly look at some related work in this area. In Sect. 3, we discuss different roles that a federated cloud may play in a blockchain system. In Sect. 4, we summarize mining mechanisms in a blockchain, the focus of our work. Section 5 describes the proposed approach in detail. Section 6 illustrates the proposed approach. Section 7 discusses the implications of including cloud as a node in the blockchain architecture. Finally, in Sect. 8, we provide a summary of our contributions.

2 Related Work

The concept of blockchain started with Nakamoto's proposal [1] for a peer-to-peer network for electronic payments using blockchain consensus protocol. This resulted in the bitcoin network and many more other variants of bitcoin. One of the main problems with the bitcoin protocol is its proof-of-work consensus mechanism which is energy consuming [2]. Thus, there arose a need for cheap and fast block generation. In addition, the risk of majority power owners attacking the network has also become a concern [12–17]. As part of improving bitcoin performance, several proposals have been made [12–14]. These include sharding [4, 6] to reduce the storage at nodes and increase parallelism in the network, directed acyclic graphs [17], etc. Systems such as Byteball offers a decentralized tamper-proof storage system of arbitrary data [23], although it is not basically built on blockchain and is not a solution as much as a substitute of the Blockchain-based currencies. Several attempts are also currently being made to use blockchain as a good provenance or backup mechanism for clouds [24–28].

In [3], Kwon et al. formally prove that with full decentralization, all the promised guarantees of a blockchain are impossible to achieve. This implies that a practical P2P blockchain system must have some degree of centralization.

In [11], Nguyen et al. discuss the means by which Cloud of Things (CoT) could support blockchain platforms. In particular, they show how CoT could support the transaction scalability, security, and fault tolerance featured of blockchains. Similarly, they also show how blockchains could benefit to support CoT networks to enhance their decentralization, network security, and data privacy features.

In this paper, we propose different ways in which federated clouds can support blockchain infrastructure.

3 Role of Federated Clouds in Blockchains

As mentioned above, a federated cloud can play a vital role in improving blockchain's performance without violating the basic tenets of blockchains. Here we describe a few possible roles.

1. **A blockchain miner**. One of the main constraints that is limiting an ordinary person from participating in the blockchain as a data miner is the lack of computing and storage resources [2]. With the resource-intensive consensus mechanisms such as proof-of-work, where a miner that the first miner that successfully mines a block is one who receives the mining reward, it is becoming increasing hard to incentivize common users to become miners. Only the ones with large farms of mining equipment are reaping the mining rewards, and thereby discouraging other nodes to participate in the P2P network. With the introduction of federated clouds, it becomes possible for an ordinary user to obtain computing resources from a cloud and be a competitive miner.

2. **Private blockchains**. While most arguments opposing the use of a cloud in a blockchain are in the context of public blockchains, the arguments may no longer valid in the case of private blockchains. For example, if a consortium of organizations intends to collaborate on some projects and plan to use a private blockchain to record the events. A federated cloud may be a perfect infrastructure to facilitate such a blockchain. Since it is a federated cloud, no individual cloud operator needs to be trusted upon for security or availability. A consortium of collaborators can thus set up a blockchain mechanism where each act as a mining node, where the mining node is either an infrastructure local to the organization or the federated cloud. This relieves the consortium members from incurring additional infrastructural burden for the blockchain. At the same time, it guarantees the same properties as a public blockchain—availability, tamper-proof ledger, and replication. In fact, its performance will be much better than a public chain since the nodes are restricted to the consortium, making the consensus much more efficient and faster.

3. **Storage**. Full nodes and miners in a blockchain are responsible for storing the entire blockchain. As more and more blocks join the blockchain network, with time, the blockchain requires more and more storage. This is forcing some of the peer nodes to drop out of the P2P network, placing the blockchain in the danger of extinction.

With federated cloud, a node can use cloud as a storage. Since federated clouds provide the needed security and availability at a cheaper cost, this is a good alternate for full nodes to continue their participation in the blockchain without undue burden of acquiring additional local storage.

4. **Query capacity**. One of the frequent operations of a node in a blockchain, especially the ones in the high-demand services, is to answer queries from users outside regarding certain records in a blockchain. This operation may require substantial processing and limited processing power at the P2P nodes may limit the query throughput. In such cases, a node, on a federated cloud or with access to it, can achieve higher throughput without itself investing in additional hardware. Of course, it would need to have some mechanism to ensure the legitimacy of the results provided by the cloud (query provenance) [29].

5. **Consensus**. Consensus is a time-consuming and time-sensitive mechanism in the working of a blockchain [2]. The success of a blockchain system does depend on its ability to implement its consensus mechanism efficiently. For example, a proof-of-work consensus mechanism is very much processing-intensive and hence is limited in throughput (e.g., Bitcoin). Some voting mechanisms have lower computing cost but higher communication cost. Federated clouds could come to the rescue of blockchains to overcome the computing and communication bottlenecks.

In this paper, we focus our work on the role of federated cloud in blockchain consensus. Typical public blockchain-based systems such as Bitcoin and Ethereum are purely peer-to-peer systems and avoid depending on any single third-party for decisions such as block validation or blockchain maintenance. So, one may question the validity of introducing a third-party such as a federated cloud violating the very foundation of peer-to-peer concept of a blockchain. However, our inclusion of a federal cloud is for operational efficiency without impacting the other properties such as autonomy guaranteed by the public blockchains based on peer-to-peer network of nodes. This will be evident as we describe the role of the cloud in the blockchain operation.

4 Consensus in a Blockchain

In a distributed environment such as a blockchain, before a block is committed to the blockchain, all the peers need to come to an agreement for which various consensus mechanisms are used by different blockchain applications. For example, bitcoin uses proof of work (where no voting is involved) as a consensus protocol [2]. On the other hand, majority of the consensus protocols that assure Byzantine fault tolerance, such as Tendermint [26], use voting mechanism (using two-thirds majority) for committing a new block. In the rest of the paper, we assume a voting-based consensus where constituent nodes vote on a proposed new block to accept or reject after transaction validation.

Consider a blockchain network, comprising of m nodes n_1, n_2, n_3,..., n_m, and a set of k transactions t_1, t_2, t_3,..., t_k where transactions could be transfer of funds. Let u_1, u_2, u_3,..., u_k be the users initiating transactions t_1, t_2, t_3, ..., t_k respectively. The transactions t_1, t_2, t_3,..., t_k are broadcasted by a user or a node such that a miner n_i i.e., a node trying to create a block b_i, picks up the set of k transactions (or a subset). On creation of block b_i, the miner n_i broadcasts the same to its neighbors, which in turn propagates it further. The broadcast mechanism can be any of the three types— standard block relay, unsolicited block push and direct headers announcement. In standard block relay method, if a node n_i wants to propagate a new block b_i to its neighbor n_j, it first intimates n_j of the block b_i, upon which n_j checks for the existence of b_i in its local storage, and requests n_i for the block header, if the block is absent. Subsequently, the entire block b_i is requested after checking the integrity of the block header. Unsolicited block push happens in the context of a miner n_i, who is the creator of the new block and understands that the block is not possessed by any of its neighbors. So, n_i just pushes the newly generated block to its neighbors without any prior intimation. As a special case to standard block relay, a node can skip the initial step of intimating its neighbors about the new block, and directly broadcast the block header information.

As there could be any number of miners in the P2P network, mining multiple blocks (there could be overlapping transactions), even though only one block is eventually appended to the blockchain, each miner broadcasting the newly generated block increases the network traffic substantially. As a result, there could be a high latency in transmitting a block, which can affect the blockchain synchronization, and thus exposing the network to potential attack. In addition, this can introduce alternate chains resulting in orphan blocks.

We propose a novel approach of introducing federated clouds to blockchain systems to make the voting-based consensus process more efficient.

5 Proposed Approach

The primary innovation of the proposed protocol is to effectively use federated cloud services to reduce the communication overhead involved in the consensus process. In particular, each blockchain subscribes to a federated cloud that acts as an intermediary in performing consensus. In this section, we discuss the details of the resulting architecture (Fig. 1) and the associated algorithms.

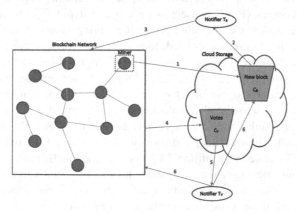

Fig. 1. Blockchain architecture leveraging cloud infrastructure

For a federated cloud to act as an intermediary, to enable efficient consensus, a blockchain performs the following tasks:

- Each blockchain creates containers C_B and C_V in cloud storage. C_B is used to hold a newly mined block on the cloud and C_V is used to maintain any consensus related information. For example, if a blockchain employs voting based consensus to finalize the next block to be added to the blockchain, then C_V maintains the collected votes before a final decision which is taken by the nodes themselves.

- Each blockchain also creates two processes/threads T_B and T_V in the cloud. While T_B is responsible for receiving new proposed blocks from miners and distributing the same to all the nodes, T_V is responsible for soliciting votes from the nodes in cases where voting is used in consensus and distributing the votes received to all the nodes. To facilitate these tasks, both threads are assumed to have a list of all nodes (that maintain a blockchain locally) available. This is achieved by requiring each new node to register with the cloud server. Thus, a cloud server always has the latest list of participating nodes, a master node list. This enables T_B and T_V to communicate with the nodes when needed. Of course, it is quite likely that this list may contain nodes that are no longer active as they have permanently left the blockchain without informing the federated cloud server. Some nodes may be temporarily inactive. One way to weed out the inactive nodes from the master node list is to make the registration valid only for a specific period. When the registration expires, a node must renew its registration. Another way could be to have the nodes send heart beat messages periodically.

- T_B and T_V communicate with the nodes through message passing. The nodes also respond back with the two threads using message passing.

- The federated cloud neither maintains a copy of the blockchain nor does it mine or validate new blocks like a lightweight node. It just holds a newly mined block.

- When a miner mines a block, it sends it to the cloud storage container C_B (as opposed to sending to its neighboring nodes in a P2P system). The cloud storage thread/process (T_B) marks the newly arrived block as uncommitted (since it has not been validated yet) and stores it. The process of turning an uncommitted block to a committed block depends on the consensus protocol followed in the blockchain. Suppose the blockchain follows proof-of-work (PoW) consensus such as in Bitcoin, T_B propagates the new block to all the nodes. On the other hand, if a voting protocol such as a Byzantine/majority voting consensus is used, then the cloud (in particular, T_V) takes the initiative to distribute the new uncommitted block to the nodes in the node list, and solicits their decision (e.g., set of votes, S_V). Obviously, some nodes may not respond as they are not available or no longer members. Some (attacker) nodes may provide incorrect decisions just to disturb the blockchain operations. If the consensus protocol is resilient to such faulty nodes, then T_V will be able to receive the individual node decisions (digitally signed votes) and convey the votes to all the other nodes in the node list. This is unlike in a traditional P2P system such as Bitcoin where each node individually sends messages to its neighbors, they in turn send it to their neighboring nodes, etc. In this case, there is a high likelihood that a node receives multiple copies of the same block from its several neighbors. In the proposed approach, since the cloud knows the list of nodes to be reached, it can send individual messages to each of them. This drastically reduces the message traffic in the system. For example, if there are n nodes in a system, and each node on an average is connected to m other nodes (i.e., degree of node connectivity), then traditional P2P system would require n * m messages to be sent for each piece of information (seeking votes, sending blocks, etc.). On the other hand, the proposed system would only require n such messages. For example, if n = 10,000 and m = 5, propagating a piece of information to all nodes results in 50,000 messages in the traditional system and 10,000 messages in the proposed system. This is a saving of 80%. In general, it results in a cost savings of (m−1)/m * 100% (see Fig. 2).

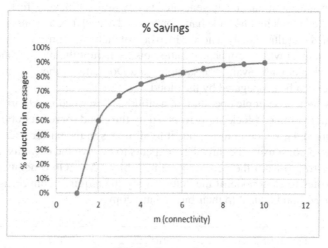

Fig. 2. Cost savings

Let us say we have a rogue or compromised cloud server. It definitely has the potential to disrupt the blockchain operations. First, when a miner sends a newly mined block to the cloud server, it can simply ignore it and not distribute it to other nodes in the node list. This could be a disaster. However, there is a backup plan for such events. When a miner sends a new block to the cloud server for distribution, it waits for certain amount of time to receive the block or information related to it (back from the cloud). If no such information is received within a predefined time, the miner retries sending it to the cloud, since it could have been due to some communication failure or message error. After a fixed number of retries, it assumes either that the cloud is faulty or that the cloud is unavailable or inaccessible. In such a case, it falls back on the traditional scheme where the block is distributed to the peer nodes using the gossip protocol. If in fact the cloud server was unavailable or inaccessible, when it comes back online, it lets its presence known to all the nodes so they can go back to the scheme where cloud server becomes the point of distribution. In case where the cloud server is faulty (e.g., compromised), then the peer nodes should disconnect it from their network (logically) and continue to follow the traditional protocol. But given the high availability and security offered by today's cloud, this occurrence is very unlikely.

In the event when multiple miners propose blocks simultaneously, there are a few options to adopt. First option is to simply have only one not-yet-committed block as the next block in C_B. This option is relevant when miners send their blocks to the cloud for consensus. Once this block is either committed or rejected (by the respective consensus protocol), the new block becomes part of the blockchain copy stored at every node or discarded, respectively. This avoids the problem of having orphan blocks. The next mined block is accepted only after decisions has been taken on the last one. In other words, the cloud sequentializes the process of running the consensus algorithm on new blocks. A second option is for the federated cloud to behave just like any other node in traditional systems—propagate simultaneously generated newly mined blocks as forked siblings to the last committed block in the blockchain copy stored at each node. Consensus for these blocks is initiated simultaneously. Those which do not make the consensus are discarded. This option is helpful when a rogue node attempts to disrupt the blockchain operations by generating blocks with invalid transactions as a DoS attack, thereby preventing the legitimate blocks to be propagated by the cloud.

Let us now look at a simple operation of a cloud as described in Algorithm 1. When a new uncommitted mined block M_B is received by the cloud server, it publishes it as an event to the thread T_B which in turn sends it to all nodes in its master node list. In case of a voting-based consensus, the thread T_V expects to receive the digitally signed votes (to avoid voter fraud) from the nodes on the new block M_B. On timeout, it sends the collection of votes to each node. If the votes satisfy the required consensus, each node commits block M_B and adds it to their blockchain copy.

```
Algorithm 1: Cloud Storage (including T_B, T_V)
```

```
1.    N:= Set of nodes in the blockchain network
2.    t:= threshold, round trip time from cloud to a node
3.    C_B waits for M_B
4.    C_B publishes an event to T_B with M_B as parameter
5.    T_B marks M_B as uncommitted
6.    T_B sends M_B to every node m∈N
7.    if voting based consensus then
8.    |   T_V does the following
9.    |      waits for S_V till time t
10.   |      prepares S_V for M_B
11.   |      sends S_V to every node m∈N
12.   |      clears C_V
13.   else
14.   |   Propagate M_B to every node m∈N
15.   end
```

Now let us look at the operation of the miner as explained in Algorithm 2. After mining a block, a miner sends it to the cloud container C_B, and waits for the block to be published by T_B. Once the block M_B is received, it just appends the block to the local blockchain, in case of non-voting based consensus protocol. Else, the miner publishes its vote to C_V and waits for the set of votes, S_V from T_V. Based on the majority votes, the block is either appended to the local blockchain or discarded. On timeout either while waiting for a new block from T_B (even after retries) or for S_V from T_V it assumes that the cloud server is either compromised or down, and proceeds with the traditional protocol.

```
---------------------------------------------------------------
Algorithm 2: Miner
---------------------------------------------------------------
1.    t:= threshold, round trip time from a node to cloud
2.    send M_B to C_B
3.    wait for T_B to notify about M_B
4.    if not notified within t even after retries then
5.    |   use existing gossip mechanism
6.    |   return
7.    end
8.    if voting based consensus then
9.    |   vote yes for M_B
10.   |   wait for T_V to send S_V
11.   |   if not notified within time t then
12.   |   |   initiate existing gossip mechanism
13.   |   |   return
14.   |   end
15.   |   if S_V is received then
16.   |   |   if majority of S_V approves M_B then
17.   |   |   |   append M_B to local blockchain
18.   |   |   else
19.   |   |   |   drop M_B
20.   |   |   end
21.   |   end
22.   else
23.   |   append M_B to local blockchain
24.   end
---------------------------------------------------------------
```

The primary responsibility of a node is like that of a miner except proposing a new block to the cloud server as explained in Algorithm 3.

```
------------------------------------------------------------
Algorithm 3: Node
------------------------------------------------------------
1.     t:= threshold, round trip time from a node to cloud
2.     wait for T_B to notify about M_B
3.     validate M_B
4.     if voting based consensus then
5.     |   if M_B is valid then
6.     |   |   vote yes for M_B
7.     |   else
8.     |   |   vote no for M_B
9.     |   end
10.    |   wait for T_V to send S_V
11.    |   if not notified within time t then
12.    |   |   wait for miner to initiate gossip
13.    |   |   return
14.    |   end
15.    |   if S_V is received and majority approves M_B then
16.    |   |   append M_B to local blockchain
17.    |   else
18.    |   |   drop M_B
19.    |   end
20.    else
21.    |   if M_B is valid then
22.    |   |   append M_B to local blockchain
23.    |   else
24.    |   |   drop M_B
25.    |   end
26.    end
------------------------------------------------------------
```

6 Illustration

For illustration consider a blockchain network with 11 nodes n_1, n_2, ..., n_{11} as shown in Fig. 3. Let n_3 and n_9 be two miners and b_3 and b_9 be the blocks mined respectively.

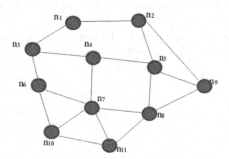

Fig. 3. Sample blockchain network.

With the state-of-the-art approach, the block b_3 is broadcasted by n_3 to its neighbors n_1, n_4, n_6 initially. Each of these nodes further propagate to their neighbors and so on using direct headers announcement as a broadcast mechanism. Also, all the 11 nodes in the network receive the newly generated blocks b_3 and b_9 from all their neighbors (redundant copies of a block). Based on the degree of connectivity, 36 messages are sent for the propagation of a newly mined block. Since there are two miners, the number of messages sent increases to 72. If the consensus protocol requires voting, another 72 messages are sent across for propagating the votes. Thus, a total of 144 messages are sent.

With the proposed approach, both miners n_3 and n_9, try to append the newly generated blocks b_3 and b_9 to the cloud container C_B, only one of the two blocks can be appended though. Let b_3 be the block considered by C_B. 13 messages are sent across the network for the propagation of b3 i.e., one message from both the miners n_3 and n_9 to cloud and 11 messages from T_B to all the 11 nodes. If voting is required, another 22 messages are sent across (11 messages from each node to T_V and subsequently 11 messages from T_V to all the nodes). Thus, a total of 35 messages are sent.

We consider the following parameters to compare the performance of the proposed approach with the state-of-the-art mechanism.

Network Load: Totally 144 messages are sent across the network with the existing approach as compared to 35 messages (~75% savings) with the proposed approach, for a newly mined block to be committed or dropped using voting-based consensus. Even if there is no second block mined in parallel, there would be a saving of ~50%. On the other hand, the savings would increase if more than two blocks are mined in parallel.

Degree of Consistency: With most of the existing consensus mechanisms, the block b_9 mined (parallelly) by n_9, becomes an orphan block introducing a degree of inconsistency at some nodes temporarily. With the proposed approach, the possibility of orphan blocks can be drastically reduced.

Fault Tolerance: Responsibility of block propagation is shifted to cloud, instead of nodes in the blockchain network. For example, if the miner n_9 publishes b_9 before miner n_3, and nodes n_2 and n_3 are malicious (refuse to propagate any block other than theirs), then n_1 would never receive b_9. This situation arises because it is the nodes' responsibility to propagate new blocks. Also, it is very difficult to detect malicious nodes in such a context. By shifting this responsibility to cloud, the proposed approach ensures that every node receives a new block even if there are malicious nodes in the network. In addition, any malicious activity on the cloud infrastructure can be easily detected by the nodes at any stage (be it block propagation or voting process).

If there exists another node n_{12}, which shares an edge with n_{11} alone, failure of the node n_{11} forcing n_{12} into unreachable state. Also, failure of nodes such as n_2, results in delayed block propagation of b_9 to n_1, with the state-of-the-art approach. With the proposed approach, node failure does not result in any delay of block propagation.

7 Implications

Today, there are several ideas on using a blockchain to improve the security, accountability, and provenance of clouds [14, 16–20, 22]. All these ideas have come up in the last two years. However, our proposal is to improve the performance of the blockchain systems and the cryptocurrencies. While there will be no opposition to adding blockchains to federated cloud infrastructure to improve its correctness properties, our idea of adding federated cloud to blockchain P2P network seems somewhat radical. Critics may object to its addition claiming that it is against the fundamental principle of P2P networks—no trusted third-party. However, just like the impossibility of distributed consensus in distributed systems under several conditions (e.g., asynchronous systems), it is also shown that full decentralization in permission less blockchains is impossible [23]. This is also evident from the current permission less, fully distributed P2P networks such as bitcoin which are suffering from performance issues. In fact, several such systems have also undergone attacks. While there are several attempts to improve the performance, and especially the scalability and throughput, these are only a patchwork and do not address the real problem—impossibility of achieving ideal systems under fully distributed and permission less systems.

What we are proposing is a middle ground in this battle—improve performance without undue centralization. Adding a federated cloud with special role in the consensus process in a blockchain not only reduces the communication cost but also removes the notion of *impossibility* label from the permission less P2P blockchains. In fact, the several choices of roles that we have proposed for the new cloud opens up several options for these blockchains. Depending on the roles that a specific application domain can assign to the cloud node, several of the current performance bottlenecks in blockchains may be removed, and better performance achieved. In fact, in our opinion, it is much riskier for an organization to completely trust a permission less blockchains for its business operations than adopting the proposed architecture where much more trusted cloud is a node with special role. In fact, the organization itself may decide to add its own cloud or its subscribed federated cloud as a node to enhance its trust of the system.

8 Summary and Future Work

In this paper, we have proposed a way to introduce federated cloud storage and computing platforms into blockchain infrastructure. We have identified different roles that a federated cloud can play in a blockchain system to improve its performance without unduly compromising the security and the autonomy properties. In particular, a federated cloud acts as a special lightweight node that is more reliable, available, and cost-effective offering high-performance. In addition, it can aid in answering user queries. The cloud platform's large storage, high computing power, and high availability to its distributed nature aligns with the nature and needs of today's blockchain and cryptocurrency systems. The paper primarily focused on the role of a federated computing in consensus and in distributing the mined blocks across the P2P nodes in an efficient and timely manner.

We are currently working on implementing the proposed scheme, at least at a prototype level, and observe the actual performance gains. In addition, we intend to investigate the role cloud could play under different consensus mechanisms.

References

1. Nakamoto, S.: Bitcoin: a peer-to-peer electronic cash system (2008). https://bitcoin.org/bitcoin.pdf
2. Narayanan, A., Bonneau, J., Felten, E., Miller, A., Goldfeder, S.: Bitcoin and Cryptocurrency Technologies: A Comprehensive Introduction. Priceton University Press, Princeton (2016)
3. Kwon, Y., Liu, J., Kim, M., Dong, D., Kim, Y.: Impossibility of full decentralization in permissionless blockchains. In: ACM Advances in Financial Technologies (AFT 2019), Zurich, Switzerland, 21–23 October 2019 (2019, to appear)
4. Luu, L., Narayanan,V., Zheng, C., Baweja, K., Gilbert, S., Saxena, P.: A secure sharding protocol for open blockchains. In: Proceedings 2016 ACM SIGSAC Conference on Computer and Communications Security (CCS 2016), pp. 17–30 (2016)
5. Eyal, I., Gencer, A.E, Sirer, E.G., Renesse, R.V., Bitcoin, N.G.: A scalable blockchain protocol. In: Proceedings of the 13th USENIX Symposium on Networked Systems Design and Implementation (NSDI 2016), Santa Clara, CA, 16–18 March 2016, pp. 45–59 (2016)
6. Kokoris-Kogias, E., Jovanovic, P., Gasser, L., Gailly, N., Syta, E., Ford, B.: OmniLedger: a secure, scale-out, decentralized ledger via sharding. In: IEEE Symposium on Security and Privacy, San Francisco, CA, 21–23 May 2018, pp. 583–598 (2018)
7. Varghese, B., Buyya, R.: Next generation cloud computing: new trends and research directions. Future Gener. Comput. Sys. **79**, 849–861 (2018)
8. El-Yahyaoui, A., Dafir, M., Kettani, E.-C.: Data privacy in cloud computing. In: IEEE 4th International Conference on Computer and Technology Applications, Istanbul, Turkey, 3–5 May 2018, pp. 25–28 (2018)
9. Attardi, G., Martino, B., Esposito, A., Matroianni, M.: Using federated cloud platform to implement academia services for research and administration. In: 32nd International Conference on Advanced Information Networking and Applications Workshops, Krakow, Poland, 16–18 May 2018, pp. 413–418 (2018)
10. Malomo, O., Rawat, D.B., Garuba, M.: A federal cloud computing framework for adaptive cyber defense and distributed computing. In: IEEE Conference Communication Workshops (INFOCOM), Atlanta, GA, 1–4 May 2017, p. 6 (2017)
11. Nguyen, D.C., Pathirana, P.N., Ding, M., Senevirtane, A.: Integration of blockchain and cloud of things: architecture, applications and challenges, IEEE Commun. Surv. Tutori. (2019, to appear)
12. Donet Donet, J.A., Pérez-Solà, C., Herrera-Joancomartí, J.: The bitcoin P2P network. In: Böhme, R., Brenner, M., Moore, T., Smith, M. (eds.) FC 2014. LNCS, vol. 8438, pp. 87–102. Springer, Heidelberg (2014). https://doi.org/10.1007/978-3-662-44774-1_7
13. Decker, C., Wattenhofer, R.: Information propagation in the bitcoin network. In: IEEE P2P Conference, Trento, Italy, 9–11 September 2013, pp. 1–10 (2013)
14. Decker, C., Wattenhofer, R.: A fast and scalable payment network with bitcoin duplex micropayment channels. In: Pelc, A., Schwarzmann, A.A. (eds.) SSS 2015. LNCS, vol. 9212, pp. 3–18. Springer, Cham (2015). https://doi.org/10.1007/978-3-319-21741-3_1
15. Eyal, I., Sirer, E.G.: Majority is not enough: bitcoin mining is vulnerable. Commun. ACM **61**(7), 95–102 (2018)
16. Fischer, M., Lynch, N., Merritt, M.: Easy impossibility proofs for distributed consensus problems. Distrib. Comput. **1**, 26–39 (1986)
17. Garay, J., Kiayias, A., Leonardos, N.: The bitcoin backbone protocol: analysis and applications. In: Oswald, E., Fischlin, M. (eds.) EUROCRYPT 2015. LNCS, vol. 9057, pp. 281–310. Springer, Heidelberg (2015). https://doi.org/10.1007/978-3-662-46803-6_10
18. Churyumov, A.: Byteball: a decentralized system for storage and transfer of value (2016). https://byteball.org/Byteball.pdf

19. Ho, Y.H., Cheng, Z., Ho, P.M.F., Chan, H.C.B.: Mobile intercloud system with blockchain. In: Proceedings of the International Multiconference of Engineers and Computer Scientists, IMECS 2018, 14–16 March 2018, Hong Kong, p. 6 (2018)
20. Ren, Y., Liu, Y., Ji, S., Sangaiah, A.K., Wang, J.: Incentive mechanism of data storage based on blockchain for wireless sensor networks. In: Mobile Information Systems, Hindwai (2018). 10 pages
21. Shafagh, H., Burkhalter, L., Hithnawi, A., Duquennoy, S.: Towards blockchain-based auditable storage and sharing of IoT data. In: ACM CCSW 2017, Proceedings 2017 Conference on Cloud Computing Security Workshop, Dallas, Texas, pp. 45–50 (2017)
22. Tosh, D.K., Shetty, S., Liang, X., Kamhoua, C.A., Kwiat, K.A., Njilla, L.: Security implications of blockchain cloud with analysis of block withholding attack. In: 17th IEEE/ACM International. Symposium Cluster, Cloud and Grid Computing (CCGRID), Madrid, Spain, 14–17 May 2017, pp. 458–467 (2017)
23. Tosh, D.K., Shetty, S., Liang, X., Kamhoua, C.A., Kwiat, K.A., Njilla, L.: ProvChain: a blockchain-based data provenance architecture in cloud environment with enhanced privacy and availability. In: 17th IEEE/ACM International Symposium Cluster, Cloud and Grid Computing (CCGRID), Madrid, Spain, 14–17 May 2017, pp. 468–477 (2017)
24. Tosh, D.K., Shetty, Foytik, P., Kamhoua, C., Njilla, L., CloudPos: a proof-of-stake consensus design for blockchain integarted cloud. In: IEEE 11th International Conference on Cloud Computing, CLOUD 2018, San Francisco, CA, 2–7 July 2018, pp. 302–309 (2018)
25. Zhu, L., Wu, Y., Gai, K., Choo, K.R.: Controllable and trustworthy blockchain-based cloud data management. Fut. Gen. Comput. Syst. **91**, 527–535 (2019)
26. Amousssou-Guenou, Y., Pozzo, A.D., Potop-Butucaru, M., Tucci-Piergiovanni, S.: Correctness and fairness of Tendermint-core Blockchains (2018). https://eprint.iacr.org/2018/574. pdf
27. D'Angelo, G., Ferretti, S.: Marzolla, a blockchain-based flight data recorder for cloud accountability. In: Proceedings of the ACM CryBlock 2018 1st Workshop on Cryptocurrencies and Blockchains for Distributed Systems, 15 June 2018, Munich, Germany, pp. 93–98 (2018)
28. Gencer, A.E., Basu, S., Eyal, I., van Renesse, R., Sirer, E.G.: Decentralization in bitcoin and ethereum networks. In: Meiklejohn, S., Sako, K. (eds.) FC 2018. LNCS, vol. 10957, pp. 439–457. Springer, Heidelberg (2018). https://doi.org/10.1007/978-3-662-58387-6_24
29. Li, Y., Mukkamala, R., Mascagni, M.: Validating the correctness of outsourced computational tasks using pseudorandom number generators. In: 15th International Digital Avionics Systems Conference, Orlando, FL, November 2017, pp. 391–398 (2017)

A Resource Trend Analysis from a Business Perspective Based on a Component Decomposition Approach

Yuji Saitoh$^{(\boxtimes)}$, Tetsuya Uchiumi, and Yukihiro Watanabe

Fujitsu Laboratories Ltd., 4-1-1 Kamikodanaka, Nakahara-ku, Kawasaki 211-8588, Japan
{saitoh.yuji,uchiumi.tetsuya,watanabe.y}@fujitsu.com

Abstract. To ensure reliability for information and communication technology (ICT) systems, it is important to analyze resource usage for the purpose of provisioning resources, detecting failures, and so on. It is more useful to understand the resource usage trends for each business process because generally multiple business processes run on an ICT system. For example, we can detect an increase in resource usage for a specific business process. However, conventional methods have not been able to analyze such trends because resource usage data is usually mixed and cannot be separated. Therefore, in the previous work, we proposed an analysis method that decomposes the data into components of each business process. The method successfully analyzed only single sources of data. However, an actual system consists of multiple resources and multiple devices. Therefore, in this paper, we enhance this method so that it is able to analyze multiple sources of data by incorporating a technique for unifying multiple sources of data into a single sources of data on the basis of a workload dependency model. In addition, the proposed method can also analyze the relationship between resources and application workloads. Therefore, it can identify specific applications that cause resource usage to increase. We evaluated the proposed method by using the data of on-premise and actual commercial systems, and we show that it can extract useful business trends. The method could extract system-wide processes, such as file-copy between two servers, and identify a business event corresponding to a resource usage increase.

Keywords: Non-negative matrix factorization · Capacity provisioning · Resource management · IT operations management · Business semantics

1 Introduction

To ensure reliability for information and communication technology (ICT) systems, it is important to analyze trends of resource usage, such as CPU usage, memory usage, disk IOs, and disk capacity, for the purpose of provisioning resources, detecting failures, and so on. Therefore, system operators acquire data on resource usage and analyze these sources of data to find trends, such as increasing and periodic trends. The analysis results are often used to improve system configurations.

© Springer Nature Switzerland AG 2020
Q. Zhang et al. (Eds.): CLOUD 2020, LNCS 12403, pp. 31–48, 2020.
https://doi.org/10.1007/978-3-030-59635-4_3

Various business processes, such as online transaction processing and batch processing, run simultaneously on a system. In this paper, a business process is defined as a series of processes executed for a common business purpose. For example, the business process of reservation for store visitors consists of a process for searching for an available day, a process for inputting the reservation information, and a process for confirming the reservation. Each business process has a different resource usage trend, such as a long-term increase or periodically appearing pattern. It is more useful to understand such trends for each business process because we can detect an increase in resource usage for a specific business process. However, the acquired resource usage data is usually mixed and cannot be separated by business process since this data is acquired generally for each resource but not each process. Therefore, it is not possible to analyze the resource usage trends of each business process with the conventional resource analysis methods. Figure 1 shows the basic target problem and advantage of our approach. To solve this problem, we previously proposed an analysis method for decomposing resource usage into components of each business process by applying a decomposition method used for the sound signal separation problem [1]. In our method, resource usage is represented by a linear combination of basis vectors and weights. Here, a basis vector corresponds to a component of each business process, and a weight corresponds to the degree of occurrence of each business process. Then, by finding basis vectors and weights, resource usage trends of each business process are estimated. This problem is formulated as a matrix factorization problem, and non-negative matrix factorization (NMF) [2, 3] is applied to solve this problem.

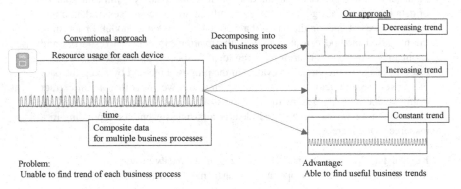

Fig. 1. Basic target problem and advantage of our approach.

The previous method successfully analyzed data for only single resources but not multiple ones. In other words, it could analyze only the CPU usage of one server. However, an actual business process consumes multiple resources, such as through CPU usage, memory usage, and disk IOs. Moreover, an actual business process is a series of processes executed on multiple devices. For example, processing for a web service consists of multiple processes executed on web, application, and database servers. In other examples, data transfer processing is a processing performed between multiple servers. Therefore, an analysis method from a business process perspective must be able to handle multiple sources of data. In this paper, we propose a method for analyzing such data.

In addition, our previous method had an issue with business semantic analysis. It was difficult to understand business semantics corresponding to estimated components because the analysis results were only on resource usage. Therefore, business knowledge was required for understanding business semantics with the previous method. For example, analysts had to infer that an estimated component corresponded to virus-scan processing since it appeared every Sunday as with the virus-scan schedule. To solve this problem, we propose an analysis method that relates resource usage data to application workload data, such as the number of HTTP requests. This is achieved by analyzing multiple sources of data as mentioned above. This approach can identify a specific application that causes resource usage to increase.

We evaluated the proposed method by using data acquired from actual commercial systems, and we show that the method can extract useful business characteristics. The proposed method could extract system-wide processes, such as file-copy between two servers, and identify a business event corresponding to a resource usage increase.

2 Related Work

In this section, we discuss the differences between the conventional and proposed approaches from three points of view.

First, there is lots of research on the categorization and characterization of workloads [4]. Zhang et al. [5] designed an intelligent workload factoring service for proactive workload management. It segregated the base workload and flash crowd workload, two naturally different components composing a workload, with a data item detection algorithm. Gmach et al. [6] decomposed a workload into trend and periodic components based on a spectral and autocorrelation analysis. However, these pieces of research were categorizations based on only behavior, such as flash or periodic, but not business characteristics. In addition, trends in long-term workload data were difficult to understand from the analysis results since they were based on only the decomposition of each behavior component, not a linear combination of basis vectors and weights.

Second, the relationship between multiple resource usages [7] is well-studied area. These studies were based on a clustering algorithm. They grouped the similar trends in the same clusters and predicted the future trend of each cluster. In Xu et al. [8], subsequences are extracted from an entire workload by a sliding window, and these are clustered. A predictive model is created for each cluster by using a hidden Markov model. In Khan et al. [9], VMs that show the similar behavior were grouped by using a co-clustering technique which captured common workload patterns along both temporal and spatial dimensions. However, the studies did not consider the decomposing of resource usage that consists of multiple trends. In addition, they were based on the correlation between multiple resource usages. Therefore, simultaneously appearing but differently shaped patterns, i.e., not correlated, across multiple resource usages could not be extracted as a relationship.

Third, there is research on the relationship between resource usages and application workloads [7]. Kousiouris et al. [10, 11] proposed an approach that estimated high level information of applications from low level workload attributes by using a neural network. This approach considered the application workloads and resource usages as input and predicted QoS of the application. However, conventional approaches did not consider decomposing a mixed workload caused by various applications.

3   Previous Method

3.1   Component Decomposition Approach

Generally, business processes on ICT systems have daily periodical workload patterns. Therefore, our previous method assumes that a frequently appearing daily workload pattern corresponds to the workload for a particular business process. Figure 2 shows a representation of resource usage data with this approach. According to this assumption, the daily resource usage $\mathbf{v}_m$ on the m-th day is represented in $\mathbf{v}_m = \sum_k h_{km}\mathbf{w}_k$ with the frequently appearing daily workload pattern $\mathbf{w}_k$ and the weight h_{km}. The weight indicates the degree of daily occurrence for the frequently appearing workload pattern, i.e., the workload for a business process.

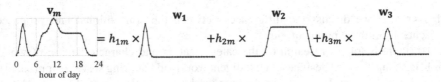

Fig. 2.   Representation of resource usage data with component decomposition approach.

3.2   Non-negative Matrix Factorization (NMF)

To extract frequently appearing daily workload patterns, we apply non-negative matrix factorization (NMF). NMF has constraints in that basis vectors and weights are non-negative. Because of these constraints, it is known that NMF is able to extract frequent patterns in input data as basis vectors [2, 3]. Figure 3 is a diagram for the matrix factorization of a data matrix.

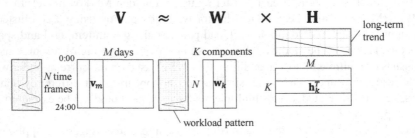

Fig. 3.   Diagram for matrix factorization of data matrix.

Beforehand, the acquired resource usage data for M days is divided into N time frames per day, and the aggregated value for each time frame, such as the average or sum value for each frame, is used as input data to NMF. v_m is defined as a vector of one day's worth of resource usage (N dimensions and non-negative value), and a data matrix V is defined as $V = [v_1, v_2, \ldots, v_M]$ [matrix size of (N, M)]. In NMF, assuming that vector v_m is represented by a linear combination of K basis vectors, the basis vectors and weight vectors are estimated. That is, this estimation problem is formulated by matrix factorization $V \approx WH$, where W is a component matrix $W = [w_1, w_2, \ldots, w_K]$[matrix size of (N, K)] containing non-negative basis vectors w_k, and H is a weight matrix $H = [h_1, h_2, \ldots, h_K]^T$ [matrix size of (K, M)] containing non-negative weight vectors h_k.

One of the most useful properties of NMF is producing sparse representations of input data. However, depending on the input data, it is difficult to produce these representations. Therefore, explicitly incorporating sparseness constraints has been proposed in order to positively obtain sparse representations [12, 13]. We utilize sparseness constraints to extract daily workload patterns more efficiently.

$$\left(W^*, H^*\right) = \underset{W, H}{\text{argmin}}\, D(W, H) \quad s.t. \quad W, H \geq 0 \tag{1}$$

$$D(W, H) = \|V - WH\|_F^2 + \alpha \|W\|_1 + \beta \|H\|_1 \tag{2}$$

$$\|A\|_F^2 \stackrel{\text{def}}{=} \sum_n \sum_m a_{n,m}^2 \tag{3}$$

In NMF, non-negative matrices W^* and H^* are estimated by minimizing the cost function as the Frobenius norm of the error matrix $V - WH$. This problem is formulated as Eq. (1). Equation (2) shows this cost function with sparseness constraints as L1 norm regularization terms of W and H, where α and β are parameters that control the sparseness of matrices W and H, respectively. Equation (3) shows the definition of the Frobenius norm, where $a_{n,m}$ is an element of matrix A.

The parameters are determined as follows in this paper. The number of components K is set to $K = \min(N, M)$. For coefficients α and β, we set $\alpha = \beta$ for simplicity and find the maximum α with $\|V - WH\|_1 \leq \mu \|V\|_1$, where μ is a parameter to control the upper limit relative to the data matrix V. μ is determined depending on the specific experiment. For details, see our previous paper [1].

4 Proposed Method

In this paper, we propose a decomposition method that is able to handle multiple sources of data by expanding the previous method. By handling multiple sources of data, the proposed method can analyze multiple resources, multiple devices, and the relationship between resource usages and application workloads. Details on the proposed method are given below.

4.1 Approach to Handling Multiple Sources of Data

To handle multiple sources of data, we assume that each business process has a business workload as a latent variable. Executing a business process increases resource consumption of multiple resources on multiple devices and application workloads, such as the number of web requests to a URL. In this case, we assume that these observed workloads, such as resource usages and application workloads, are proportional to the common business workload. Figure 4 shows this dependency between observed and business workloads.

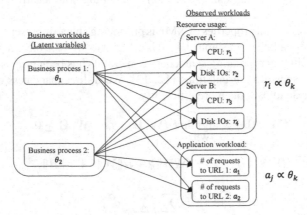

Fig. 4. Dependency between observed and business workloads.

Each observed workload depends on the common business workload. By finding the business workload, the proposed method makes it possible to extract a workload pattern that appears simultaneously across multiple sources of data as a system-wide business process. Furthermore, the proposed method can extract the relationship between resource usages and application workloads. Figure 5 shows an example result of analyzing the relationship between resource usages and application workloads.

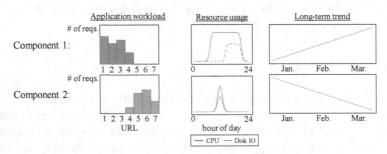

Fig. 5. Result of analyzing relationship between resource usages and application workloads. Note that Disk IO increase occurs later than CPU usage for resource usage of component 1.

By identifying a set of web requests that corresponds to a resource usage component, it is easier to understand business semantics corresponding to resource usage components. This also makes it possible to find which set of web requests is causing resource usage to increase.

Next, we describe benefits of the proposed approach. First, the approach does not employ the correlation between multiple sources of data. Thus, the approach can extract relationships between multiple sources of data based on only behaviors appearing simultaneously. In general, resource consumption caused by a particular business process does not always have the same tendency among multiple resources. For example, Disk IO increase may occur later than CPU usage shown as Fig. 5. The approach can extract a behavior with difference in time. Second, it is reasonable to assume that multiple workloads are proportional to a common business workload even if this assumption hold for not all of business processes because it is easy to understand workload characteristics from an analysis result.

4.2 Procedure of Proposed Method

In this section, we show the procedure of the proposed method. We enhance the previous method by incorporating a technique for unifying multiple sources of data into a single sources of data based on the workload dependency model. This allows the method to analyze multiple sources of data. Figure 6 shows an overview. The method consists of the following steps.

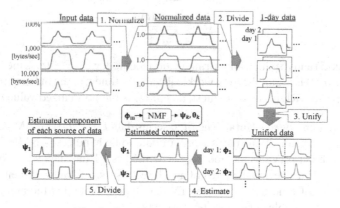

Fig. 6. Overview of proposed method.

Normalizes Multiple Sources of Input Data. The scale of data values depends on the type of data. For example, CPU usage is measured by "percentage," and disk IOs are measured in "bytes/sec." Therefore, these values have different ranges. This causes a problem in that the cost function value for large-scale data types is unintentionally emphasized in NMF. To solve this problem, the proposed method normalizes the scale of values between multiple types of data.

Two methods are used: normalization between different resource usages and normalization between resource usages and application workloads. First, we describe normalization between different resource usages. We convert the average of each resource usage value to 1. That is, the normalized value indicates the difference from the usual state. Note that percentiles and thresholds can also be used instead of averages. The normalization by percentiles is more robust to outliers than averages. The normalization by thresholds aligns values that indicate a high workload between different resource usages.

$$r_i'(t) = \frac{r_i(t)}{c_i} \tag{4}$$

Equation (4) shows this normalization method, where $r_i(t)$ is a resource usage value at time t, i is an index of the resource type, such as CPU usage, $r_i'(t)$ is the normalized value of $r_i(t)$, and c_i is the normalization factor, such as the average, percentile, or threshold for $r_i(t)$.

Next, we describe normalization between resource usages and application workloads. We convert the sum of multiple resource usage values to 1. Similarly, we convert the sum of application workload values to 1. These resource usage values were normalized by the above method beforehand. Thus, this enables NMF to handle resource usages and application workloads equally.

$$r_i''(t) = \frac{r_i'(t)}{\sum_{i,t} r_i'(t)} \tag{5}$$

$$a_j'(t) = \frac{a_j(t)}{\sum_{j,t} a_j(t)} \tag{6}$$

Equations (5) and (6) show this normalization method, where $r_i''(t)$ is the normalized value of $r_i'(t)$, $a_j(t)$ is the application workload value at time t, j is an index of the function name, such as the URL of a web request, and $a_j'(t)$ is the normalized value of $a_j(t)$.

Divides Input Time Series Data. The time series data $r_i''(t)$, $a_j'(t)$ for M days have to be divided into a vector of one day's worth of data to be handled by NMF. This step is the same as with our previous method. $\mathbf{v}_{m,l}$ is defined as a 1-day data vector of data type l, such as the CPU usage and the URL of a web request. $\mathbf{v}_{m,l}$ is an N_l dimension vector. N_l is the number of time frames per day for data type l. Note that the number of time frames per day is variable depending on the data type.

Unifies Multiple Sources of Data. The proposed method unifies multiple sources of data, i.e., multiple vectors, into one vector so that it can be handled by NMF.

$$\phi_m = \begin{bmatrix} \mathbf{v}_{m,1} \\ \vdots \\ \mathbf{v}_{m,L} \end{bmatrix} \tag{7}$$

$$\Phi = [\phi_1, \phi_2, \ldots, \phi_M] \tag{8}$$

A unified 1-day data vector ϕ_m is defined as Eq. (7). The dimension of vector ϕ_m is $\sum_{l=1}^{L} N_l$, where L is the number of data types. A unified data matrix Φ is defined as Eq. (8). The size of matrix Φ is $(\sum_{l=1}^{L} N_l, M)$. Thus, this makes it easy to handle multiple sources of data with the same framework as our previous method.

Estimates Components and Weights. We estimate components and weights for a unified data matrix Φ by NMF with sparseness constraints as with our previous method.

$$\left(\Psi^*, \Theta^*\right) = \underset{\Psi, \Theta}{\arg\min}\, D(\Psi, \Theta) \quad s.t. \quad \Psi, \Theta \geq 0 \tag{9}$$

$$D(\Psi, \Theta) = \|\Phi - \Psi\Theta\|_F^2 + \alpha\|\Psi\|_1 + \beta\|\Theta\|_1 \tag{10}$$

This problem is formulated as Eqs. (9) and (10), where Ψ is a unified component matrix $\Psi = [\psi_1, \psi_2, \ldots, \psi_K]$ containing non-negative basis vectors ψ_k, and Θ is a unified weight matrix $\Theta = [\theta_1, \theta_2, \ldots, \theta_K]^T$ containing non-negative weight vectors θ_k. The size of matrix Ψ is $(\sum_{l=1}^{L} N_l, K)$. The size of matrix Θ is (K, M). The matrices Ψ^* and Θ^* are estimated results.

$$\psi_k = \begin{bmatrix} \mathbf{w}_{k,1} \\ \vdots \\ \mathbf{w}_{k,L} \end{bmatrix} \tag{11}$$

Note that the estimated component ψ_k is a vector that unifies the components of each source of data shown as Eq. (11), where $\mathbf{w}_{k,l}$ is a component for data type l (N_l dimension vector). This property is the main difference from our previous method.

Divides Estimated Components. We divide ψ_k to obtain a final estimated component $\mathbf{w}_{k,l}$. However, we do not have to divide estimated weights because the weight is shared by each source of data. We explain this later.

Here, we explain what it means to handle unified 1-day data vectors by NMF. This approach is based on the workload dependency model described in Sect. 4.1. Each source of data in the same component is proportional to a common weight. That is, an estimated weight corresponds to a business workload in the workload dependency model. Thus, an estimated component corresponds to a workload pattern that appears simultaneously across multiple sources of data on the same day.

5   Evaluation

In this section, we describe the results of evaluating the proposed method with actual commercial data. We carried out two types of analysis. The first was an analysis with multiple resources on multiple devices. The second was an analysis of the relationship between resource usages and application workloads.

5.1 Experiment with Multiple Resources on Multiple Devices

In this experiment, we used resource usage data acquired from two file servers that were practical-use systems (fileserv14 and fileserv41). We evaluated whether the proposed method could extract a workload pattern that appeared simultaneously across multiple resource usages as a system-wide business process. We performed the evaluation by comparing the results with the resource usage data acquired for each process.

The resource usage data used in this experiment were disk read [bytes/sec], disk write [bytes/sec], memory usage [bytes], network received [bytes/sec], network sent [bytes/sec], and the processor time for the two servers. These data were an average value for 30 min, with the number of time frames per day $N_l = 48$. The number of days of data M was 102 (data period was from 9/2/18 to 12/16/18, excluding data-loss days). The number of data types L was 12, which was the 6 resources multiplied by 2 servers. The normalization factor c_i was the average of each piece of resource usage data. The NMF parameter was $K = 102$, $\mu = 0.05$.

Next, we describe the results of the experiment. A total of 100 components were extracted, but only characteristic components are described here. Figure 7 shows the estimated components for each resource of each server. The component values were normalized so that the maximum value for all resources was 1. However, the component values were insignificant because the normalized values have little meaning. Therefore, the vertical axis is omitted. Figure 8 shows the estimated weights. We interpreted the estimated components and weights as follows.

- **Component 1:** Typical workload pattern

  - **Component trend:** This component mainly consisted of two business characteristics. The first characteristic was a peak workload from 9:00 to 21:00 every 2 h across multiple resource usages excluding memory usage. The second characteristic was constant memory consumption.
  - **Weight trend:** This indicated that this component occurred every day and decreased sharply at the end of each month.
  - **Interpretation:** This component indicates the typical workload pattern for this system because it occurred every day. According to the information from the system operator, the first characteristic corresponds to a daily backup process from the behavior of the peak workload. Moreover, according to that information, unnecessary memory consumption by resident programs was stopped at the end of each month. The sharp decrease in this weight corresponds to this business process for the following reasons. Figure 9 shows that this weight trend was similar to the trend of minimum memory usage for each day. We think that the minimum memory usage roughly corresponds to memory usage by resident programs.

- **Component 2:** Virus-scan process

  - **Component trend:** This indicates that multiple resource usages on fileserv41 increased simultaneously from 0:00 to 9:00.
  - **Weight trend:** This indicates that this component occurred every Saturday.

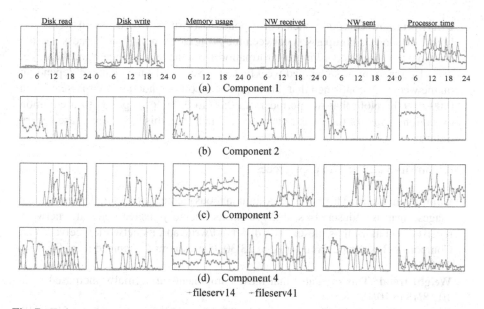

Fig. 7. Estimated components for multiple resources on multiple devices. Vertical axis is component value but is omitted here. Horizontal axis is hour of day.

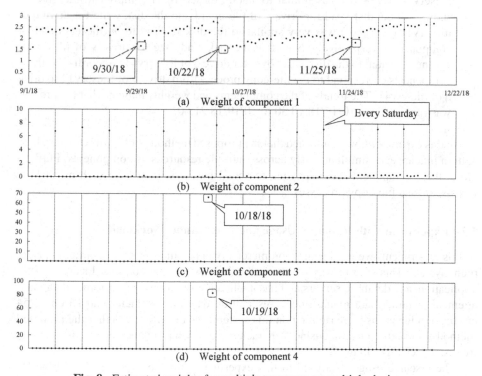

Fig. 8. Estimated weights for multiple resources on multiple devices.

- **Interpretation:** This component corresponds to a virus-scan process on fileserv41. Figure 10 shows a comparison between the processor time for the process and the component value. According to information from the system operator, the target drive for scanning was changed weekly, so the scan end time changed depending on the week. We confirmed that this component corresponded to a virus-scan from 0:00 to 9:00. Note that the period from 0:00 to 9:00 corresponds to a common execution period for the virus-scan process. Therefore, this weight increased every Saturday.

- **Components 3 and 4:** File-copy process

  - **Component trend:** This indicates a simultaneous increase across multiple resource usages, that is, fileserv14's disk read, its memory usage, and its network received/sent as well as fileserv41's disk read/write and its network received/sent. Component 3 occurred from 10:30 to 23:30. Component 4 occurred from 00:00 to 21:00.
  - **Weight trend:** This indicates that these components abnormally increased from 10/18/18 to 10/19/18.
  - **Interpretation:** These components correspond to the file-copy process from fileserv14 to fileserv41. Figure 11 shows that the memory usage of the process on fileserv14 (10/18/18) was similar to that on fileserv14 of component 3. Figure 12 shows that the disk read for drive v of fileserv14 and the disk write for drive q of fileserv41 (10/18/18) was very similar to the disk read/write on fileserv14/41 of component 3, respectively. Note that the disk read byte for drive v of fileserv14 was nearly equal to the disk write byte for drive q of fileserv41. Accordingly, these components correspond to the file-copy process from drive v of fileserv14 to drive q of fileserv41. The trends of the components and weights indicate that the process was running from 10/18/18 10:30 to 10/19/18 21:00.

In this experiment, we confirmed that the proposed method could extract a workload pattern that appears simultaneously across multiple resources as components. Furthermore, these components corresponded to actual business processes, such as backup, virus-scan, and file-copy processes.

5.2   Experiment with Resource Usage and Application Workload

In this experiment, we used actual commercial data acquired from a contract management system. This system was a web application system that consists dozens of web, application, and database servers and has application functions for customer data management, contract data management, reservation data management, and so on. 1254 application functions were running on this system. We evaluated whether the proposed method could extract useful business characteristics, such as increasing trends, monthly trends, and changes in trend.

The resource usage data used in this experiment was the average CPU usage for these servers. This data was sampled hourly with the number of time frames per day $N_{cpu} = 24$. The application workload data used was the number of application function requests per day, with the number of time frames per day $N_{app} = 1$. The number of days of data M was 514 (data period was from 1/3/18 to 5/31/19, excluding data-loss days). The number of data types L was 1255, which was the sum of 1 resource and 1254 application functions. The normalization factor c_i was the average of the CPU usage. The NMF parameter was $K = 514$, $\mu = 0.05$.

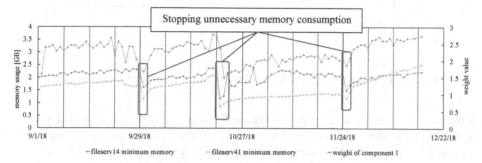

Fig. 9. Comparison between memory usage and weight of component 1.

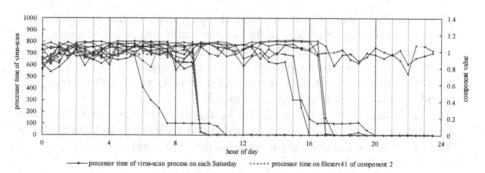

Fig. 10. Comparison between processor time of virus-scan process and component 2.

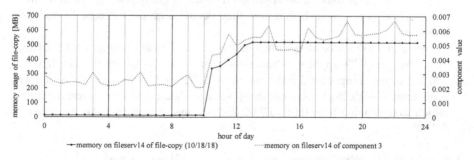

Fig. 11. Comparison between memory usage of file-copy process and component 3.

Next, we describe the results of the experiment. A total of 27 components were extracted, but only characteristic components are described here. Figure 13 shows the

44   Y. Saitoh et al.

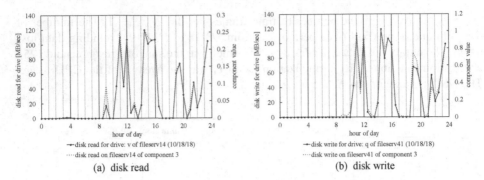

(a) disk read   (b) disk write

Fig. 12. Comparison between disk read/write for each drive and component 3.

estimated components, which consist of an application workload and a resource usage. Figure 14 shows the estimated weights that indicate the tendency for each component to appear. We interpreted the estimated components and weights as follows.

- **Component 1:** Typical workload pattern

  – This component indicates the typical workload pattern for this system because it occurred every day according to this weight. According to this resource usage component, it increased from 10:00 to 20:00. Thus, we can see that the business hours of this system were around 10:00–20:00 every day.
  – According to this weight, this system had a monthly trend with an increasing workload at the end or beginning of the month.
  – The weight value increased from 5/23/19. According to information from the system operator, the number of accesses increased due to a sales campaign from 5/23/19. Thus, we estimate that this campaign caused this high workload.

- **Components 2 and 3:** Change of application functions on 5/1/18

  – These components indicate an application function group that was running from 0:00 to 7:00 in common. In addition, they occurred on days except Thursday in common.
  – Component 2's resource usage component was very similar to component 3's. However, component 2's application functions were entirely different from component 3's. Moreover, component 2 was running from 5/2/18. However, component 3 was running until 4/30/18. Thus, these components indicate that application functions, which were running from 0:00 to 7:00 and on days except Thursday, changed on 5/1/18.

- **Component 4:** Application functions at beginning of business hours

  – This component indicates an application function group that was running at 10:00, i.e., the beginning of business hours.
  – According to this weight, this group had an increasing trend in the long term.

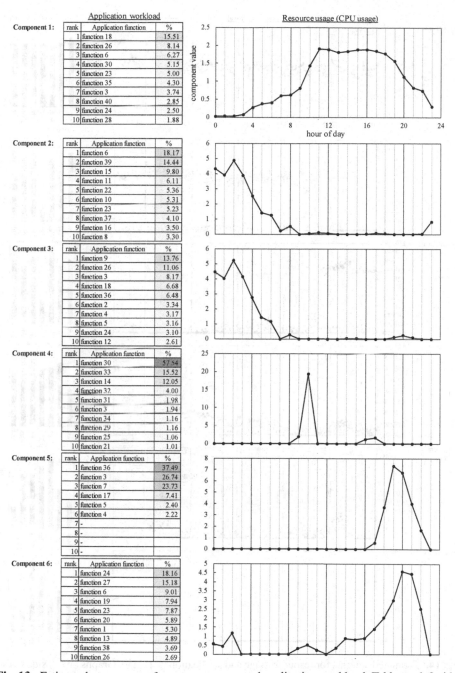

Fig. 13. Estimated components for resource usage and application workload. Tables on left side show percentage of each application function request, showing only top 10 application functions. Graphs on right side show daily resource usage trend. Component value was normalized so that its average value was 1.

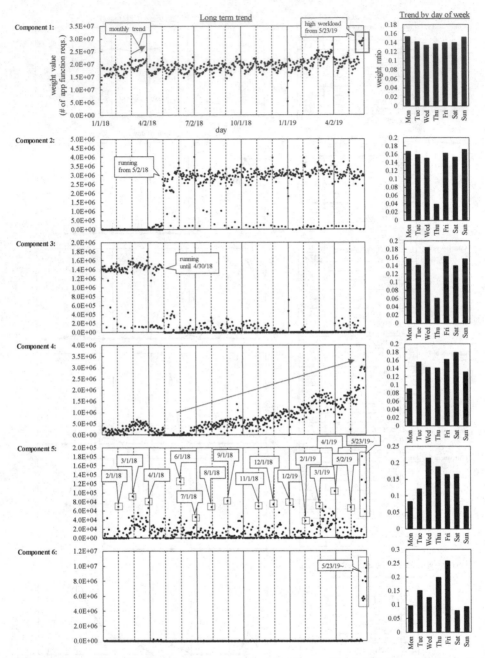

Fig. 14. Estimated weights for resource usage and application workload. Graphs on left side indicate daily occurrence of each component. Weight value corresponds to the number of application function requests. Graphs on right side indicate weight value ratio by day of week.

- **Component 5:** Trend change caused by the sales campaign

  - This component indicates an application function group that was running from 18:00 to 22:00.
  - Until 5/22/19, this group was mainly running on the 1st of every month. However, from 5/23/19, it was running almost every day. Thus, this component indicates that the business hours of this system had changed from 10:00–20:00 to 10:00–22:00 after 5/23/19 through combination with component 1. We estimate that this trend change was caused by the sales campaign from 5/23/19.

- **Component 6:** Application functions for the sales campaign

  - According to this weight, this component occurred just from 5/23/19. Thus, this component indicates an application function group due to the sales campaign from 5/23/19.
  - It indicates that the business hours had changed from 10:00–20:00 to 10:00–22:00 after 5/23/19 similar to component 5.

In this experiment, we confirmed that the proposed method could extract actual business characteristics such as increasing trends, monthly trends, and changes in trends. In particular, it could extract a change corresponding to a sales campaign from 5/23/19, which was a business event in this system.

6 Conclusion

In this paper, we proposed an analysis method that decomposes multiple sources of data into components of each business process. By incorporating a technique for unifying multiple sources of data into a single sources of data on the basis of the workload dependency model, the proposed method can analyze multiple resources and the relationship between resource usage data and application workload data.

In an experiment with multiple resources, we confirmed that the proposed method could extract workload patterns that appear simultaneously across multiple resources. These patterns corresponded to actual business processes, such as backup, virus-scan, and file-copy processes. In an experiment with resource usage and application workloads, we confirmed that the proposed method could extract actual business characteristics, such as increasing trends, monthly trends, and changes in trends. In particular, the method could identify a business event that caused resource usage to increase. Therefore, we conclude that the proposed method is very useful for analyzing multiple resource usages from a business perspective.

References

1. Saitoh, Y., Uchiumi, T., Watanabe, Y.: IT resource trend analysis by component decomposition based on non-negative matrix factorization. In: 20th Asia-Pacific Network Operations and Management Symposium (APNOMS). IEEE (2019)

2. Cichocki, A., Zdunek, R., Phan, A. H., Amari, S. I.: Nonnegative Matrix and Tensor Factorizations: Applications to Exploratory Multi-way Data Analysis and Blind Source Separation. John Wiley & Sons (2009)
3. Kameoka, H.: Non-negative matrix factorization and its variants for audio signal processing. In: Applied Matrix and Tensor Variate Data Analysis, pp. 23–50 (2016)
4. Calzarossa, M.C., Massari, L., Tessera, D.: Workload characterization: a survey revisited. ACM Comput. Surv. (CSUR) **48**(3), 1–43 (2016)
5. Zhang, H., Jiang, G., Yoshihira, K., Chen, H.: Proactive workload management in hybrid cloud computing. IEEE Trans. Network Serv. Manag. **11**(1), 90–100 (2014)
6. Gmach, D., Rolia, J., Cherkasova, L., Kemper, A.: Workload analysis and demand prediction of enterprise data center applications. In: IEEE 10th International Symposium on Workload Characterization, pp. 171–180. IEEE (2007)
7. Amiri, M., Mohammad-Khanli, L.: Survey on prediction models of applications for resources provisioning in cloud. J. Network Comput. Appl. **82**, 93–113 (2017)
8. Xu, D.Y., Yang, S.-L., Liu, R.-P.: A mixture of HMM, GA, and Elman network for load prediction in cloud-oriented data centers. J. Zhejiang Univ. Sci. C **14**(11), 845–858 (2013). https://doi.org/10.1631/jzus.C1300109
9. Khan, A., Yan, X., Tao, S., Anerousis, N.: Workload characterization and prediction in the cloud: a multiple time series approach. In: IEEE Network Operations and Management Symposium, pp. 1287–1294. IEEE (2012)
10. Kousiouris, G., Menychtas, A., Kyriazis, D., Gogouvitis, S., Varvarigou, T.: Dynamic, behavioral-based estimation of resource provisioning based on high-level application terms in cloud platforms. Fut. Gen. Comput. Syst. **32**, 27–40 (2014)
11. Bouras, I., et al.: Mapping of quality of service requirements to resource demands for IaaS. In: The 9th International Conference on Cloud Computing and Services Science (CLOSER), pp. 263–270 (2019)
12. Hoyer, P.O.: Non-negative matrix factorization with sparseness constraints. J. Mach. Learn. Res. **5**, 1457–1469 (2004)
13. Andrzej, C., Phan, A.H.: Fast local algorithms for large scale nonnegative matrix and tensor factorizations. IEICE Trans. Fund. Electr. Commun. Comput. Sci. **92**(3), 708–721 (2009)

A Utility-Based Fault Handling Approach for Efficient Job Rescue in Clouds

Fei Xie$^{(\boxtimes)}$, Jun Yan, and Jun Shen

School of Computing and IT, University of Wollongong, Wollongong, NSW 2522, Australia
fx439@uowmail.edu.au, {jyan,jshen}@uow.edu.au

Abstract. In recent years, many organizations face challenges when managing large amount of data and data-intensive computing tasks. Cloud computing technology has been widely-used to alleviate these challenges with its on-demand services and distributed architecture. Data replication is one of the most significant strategies to decrease the access latency and improve data availability, data reliability and resource utilization by creating multiple data copies to geographically-distributed data centers. When a fault occurs at a data center, existing jobs that require data access in this data center can be redirected to other data centers, where data replicas are available. This paper proposes a utility-based fault handling (UBFH) approach to rescue the jobs at the faulty data center. Then a fault handling algorithm is developed to determine the direction of job redirection by considering the network performance and job attributes. Our main objective is to achieve better repairability, job rescue utility and job operation profit. The simulation results show that our UBFH approach outperforms HDFS, RR and JSQ approaches in all these aspects.

Keywords: Fault handling · Data replication · Cloud computing · Job rescue utility · Job redirection and migration

1 Introduction

In recent years, many organizations face challenges when managing large amount of data generated from various business activities inside and outside the organization. Massive data storage and access might cause issues such as network overloading, low working efficiency and effectiveness, high data management cost, and low data management efficiency. The cloud computing technology has been widely used to alleviate these disadvantages based on its on-demand services and distributed architecture [1]. It allows heterogeneous cloud environments to satisfy the user requirements and helps users minimize the data loss risks and downtime. To obtain better data management performance in the cloud environment, data replication has been proposed to create and store multiple data copies in multiple sites [2]. There are many benefits gained from data replication such as cost reduction, response time saving, data availability improvement and reliability enhancement [3, 4]. Particularly, fault tolerance is one of the benefits by the implementation of data replication [5]. In the cloud environment, a variety of faults may

Q. Zhang et al. (Eds.): CLOUD 2020, LNCS 12403, pp. 49–63, 2020.
https://doi.org/10.1007/978-3-030-59635-4_4

occur to a data center, such as disasters, artificial accidents, information loss, data corruptions, software engineering faults and miscellaneous faults, etc. [1, 6]. These faults might significantly disrupt the job executions that require accessing the massive data stored in the faulty data center [7]. As one of the advantages of data replication, jobs can be redirected to other data centers where data replicas are available, known as backup data centers. Replication itself is also one of the proactive fault tolerance approaches. However, existing approaches such as Hadoop have not taken sufficient consideration to the characteristics of the jobs to be rescued as well as the overall performance of the cloud environment when handling faults. This might result in job rescue failure or performance deterioration.

In this paper, we propose a utility-based fault handling (UBFH) approach for more efficient job rescue at the faulty data center. This approach focuses on developing fault handling strategies based on common network performance measurements such as network latency, bandwidth consumption and error rate and job attributes including job deadline constraint, job urgency and job operation profit. A utility function is developed to prioritize the jobs to be rescued, in other words, to be relocated. For each job redirection operation, network performance is evaluated to find the optimal route so that the job can be migrated out the faulty data center to access a selected data replica. By doing so, our approach aims at achieving better repairability, job rescue utility and job operation profit. The simulation results show that our approach has better repairability, job rescue utility and job operation profit than HDFS, RR and JSQ approaches.

The remainder of the paper is organized as follows. Section 2 reviews the related work. Then Sect. 3 discusses the system modelling. Section 4 describes the replica selection mechanism of our UBFH approach. Section 5 illustrates our fault handling approach and algorithms followed by the simulation results in Sect. 6. Finally, Sect. 7 concludes our paper and pinpoints our future works.

2   Related Work

The cloud environment is subject to many types of faults, which might lead to a data center or the network links to a data center being unavailable [1, 6]. When such a fault occurs, the jobs that require data access from the faulty data center might be seriously impacted resulting in deteriorated performance or access disruption [7]. Hence, it is critical to a data center to own the ability to handle unexpected faults to a large extent [8]. Fault tolerance techniques are typically divided into two categories, proactive fault tolerance techniques and reactive fault tolerance techniques [9]. Proactive fault tolerance techniques try to proactively predict and manage the faults to avoid the faults from occurring while reactive fault tolerance techniques reduce the influence of faults when they already occurred [10]. For example, MapReduce uses self-healing and preemptive migration as its proactive fault tolerance approaches [9]. Besides, the examples of reactive fault tolerance approaches include checkpoint, retry, rescue workflow, user defined exception handling, task resubmission and job migration, etc. [5].

Many contemporary fault tolerance approaches focus on resolving the faulty problem. In [1], a proactive fault tolerance approach is proposed by considering the coordination among multiple virtual machines to jointly complete the parallel application execution. The authors use CPU temperature to detect the deteriorating physical machine in the data center and migrate the VMs on the deteriorating physical machine by deploying an improved particle swarm optimization algorithm. In [11], the authors propose an offloading system by considering the dependency relationships among multiple services to optimize execution time and energy consumption, which aims to make robust offloading decisions for mobile cloud services when faults occur. In [12], authors propose a redundant VM placement optimization approach with three employed algorithms to improve the service reliability.

There are situations in which a fault cannot be handled within a data center. For example, a data center might be temporarily closed due to a natural disaster, or it might have temporary limited connectivity to the outside due to a network problem, or the data stored in a data center might be corrupted accidently. In such situations, all job requests requiring massive data access to a faulty data center might be completely disrupted. Data replication has become a promising approach to handle such situations.

Several static and dynamic replication approaches have been proposed in the past years. In [6], authors propose a software-based selective replication to address silent data corruptions and fail-stop errors for HPC applications by aligning redundant computation with checkpoint/restart method. To evaluate the extent of reliability enhancement, authors develop a reliability model based on Markov chains. In [13], an HDFS framework with erasure coded replication scheme is proposed to provide space-optimal data redundancy with the least storage space consumption and good storage space utilization in order to protect against data loss, and the data distribution is based on consistent hashing. In [14], authors propose a threshold-based file replication mechanism to make the creation of file, file popularity based dynamic file replication and the file request processing in case of node failure without user intervention. The threshold-based file replication approaches carry out the file replication when the total number of access requests for a particular file reaches the threshold value. Specifically, Hadoop uses the typical three-replica strategy to replicate each file to three blocks to improve read bandwidth for upper-layer applications. When a fault occurs on a specific data node, Hadoop will generally redirect the data access request to another replica that meets certain criteria.

Unfortunately, most of these approaches took insufficient consideration to both common network performance measurements and the attributes of affected jobs such as their size, service delivery deadline, and job operation profit, which can be shown in Table 1. When the data access requests are redirected to other replica sites or when new data replicas are created, the impact to the overall cloud environment performance has been largely overlooked. If a system executes many redirection or re-replication operations, it will significantly increase the storage and network load on certain data centers [15]. In some cases, the redirection of data access requests from a faulty data center may even deplete resources of another data center. In addition, some jobs may miss the deadline even if they have been redirected to access the data replicas without considering the attributes of the affected jobs. This may result in user dissatisfaction, reputation damage, and compensation. Therefore, the insufficient consideration of both common network performance measurements and job attributes may largely degrade the overall performance [16]. Thus, it is desirable to have a novel replication based fault handling approach that fully considers both common network performance measurements and the attributes of the affected jobs.

Table 1. The comparison of fault tolerance approaches.

Approaches	Year	Common Network Performance Measurements				Job Attributes				Other Measurements
		Bandwidth	Latency	Error Rate	Job Size	Service Delivery Deadline	Job Execution Time	Job Dependency	Job Operation Profit	
PCFT [1]	2018	✓	✗	✗	✗	✗	✗	✗	✗	CPU temperature, CPU idle capacity, memory
Software-based selective replication technique for HPC applications [6]	2017	✗	✗	✗	✗	✗	✓	✗	✗	Failure probability, current workload, Reliability
Computation offloading strategy [11]	2015	✗	✗	✗	✗	✗	✓	✓	✗	Queue waiting time, energy consumption, current workload
Redundant VM placement optimization approach [12]	2017	✗	✓	✗	✗	✗	✗	✗	✗	Available host servers, current workload, strategy cost
HDFS framework with erasure coded replication scheme [13]	2014	✗	✗	✗	✗	✗	✗	✗	✗	Storage load
TBFR [14]	2012	✗	✗	✗	✗	✗	✗	✗	✗	Job request count
Location-aware data block allocation strategy [16]	2016	✓	✗	✗	✗	✗	✗	✗	✗	Data block location, write cost

3 System Modelling

3.1 Definitions

We define the following terms in our system. A data center is used to house computer systems and associated components such as air conditioning systems, fire protection systems and electrical power systems. In our paper, there are multiple data centers DC: $\{dc_1, dc_2, ..., dc_n\}$ and multiple users with the corresponding multiple jobs J: $\{j_1, j_2, ..., j_m\}$. We consider the job as independent job without the consideration of its inner workflow structure in this paper. We consider an independent replica as a dataset which is required to support the execution of the job.

The repairability refers to the ability to rescue jobs when a fault occurs at a data center. It is measured as the ratio of the number of the rescued jobs to the total number of the jobs to be rescued.

The job utility refers to the modelled value of the jobs and the job rescue utility is the sum of job utilities of those jobs that have been rescued from the faulty data center. The job operation profit is directly proportional to revenue, and it is also inversely proportional to cost. The job operation profit refers to the subtracting result between the revenue and the cost.

3.2 Job Urgency and Operation Profit Model

Each job j in J is associated with a service delivery deadline requirement $T_{Dead}(j)$. If such a requirement is not specified, the job has infinite deadline. But in our paper, we only consider the jobs with the service delivery deadline because the jobs with infinite service delivery deadline always do not have negative influences on cloud service providers.

Each job j also has a total completion time $TCT(j)$ which is determined by the nature of the job j. Besides, the past processing time in its original execution location $T_{Past}(j)$ should be considered if j has been selected to migrate or redirect out of its initial location. $T_{Past}(j)$ equals to 0 if the job has not been executed. Internodal communication delay $T_{IC}(j)$ is another factor to be considered because the extra time will be generated when the job is migrated or the data is transmitted across multiple network nodes between users and the host nodes. In some cases, the input scheduling delay $T_{IS}(j)$ is the extra time generated by scheduling the data input or the task execution. We assume that all jobs will be re-executed if the job is migrated out of its initial location. To ensure the quality of services, all migrated jobs should satisfy their own service delivery deadline constraint, otherwise the migration operation will be deterred.

We use job urgency (UR) to evaluate the time buffer of the job. The higher the job urgency value, the more time buffer the job has. The job urgency is formulated as in (1), where $UR(j)$ is the job urgency value of the job j.

$$UR(j) = T_{Dead}(j) - (TCT(j) + T_{Past}(j) + T_{IC}(j) + T_{IS}(j)) \tag{1}$$

Each job j in J is also associated with the value of job operation profit, $PRO(j)$, which is the subtracting result between the revenue and the cost of the job j.

3.3 Evaluation Metrics

The replica selection in this paper is primarily based on the cloud performance and service delivery performance in the overall cloud environment. To evaluate the cloud performance, we consider the bandwidth, the network latency, and the error rate as three major evaluation metrics. The bandwidth consumption of a specific data center dc_x in DC, $BC(dc_x)$, can be calculated using the equation in (2), where J^x is the set of jobs accessing this data center, $Size(j^x)$ is the size of the dataset that is requested by a job j^x, and $TCT(j^x)$ denotes the total completion time of the job j^x.

$$BC(dc_x) = \sum_{j^x \in J^x} \frac{Size(j^x)}{TCT(j^x)} \tag{2}$$

Then the available bandwidth of this data center $AB(dc_x)$ is the difference between the maximum bandwidth of this data center $maxB(dc_x)$, which can be presented as in (3).

$$AB(dc_x) = maxB(dc_x) - BC(dc_x) \tag{3}$$

Besides, the network latency is usually measured as either one-way delay or round-trip delay. Round-trip delay is quoted by network managers more for the reason that it can be measured from a single point. Ping value has been widely used to measure the round-trip delay. It depends on a variety of factors including the data transmission speed, the nature of the transmission medium, the physical distance between two locations, the size of the transferred data, and the number of other data transmission requests being handled concurrently, etc. To simplify the problem, the network latency of a data center dc_x, $NL(dc_x)$, is modelled as a constant value.

The error rate of a data center dc_x, $ER(dc_x)$, refers to the ratio of the total number of transmitted data units in error to the total number of transmitted data units, which can be represented as in (4).

$$ER(dc_x) = \frac{Total\ number\ of\ transmitted\ data\ units\ in\ error}{Total\ number\ of\ transmitted\ data\ units} \tag{4}$$

3.4 Job Rescue Utility

The utility function is often used to compare objects with multiple requirements and attributes. In this research, the utility value is used to prioritize jobs when they need to be redirected or migrated when handling fault in order to avoid the negative influence. Generally speaking, a data center prefers to rescue the jobs as many jobs as possible to fit their deadline requirements. In this case, the fault handling of the jobs should have priority assignment based on their job urgency. At the same time, a data center always tries to maximize its profit. In this case, jobs that bring more profits to the data center should have higher priority. Therefore, we propose a job utility based on both job urgency and job operation profit to prioritize the jobs.

For the job j_y^x at the faulty data center dc_x, the general expression of job utility function $U\left(j_y^x\right)$ is shown in (5) and should satisfy the condition in (6), where $U_{UR}\left(j_y^x\right)$ and $U_{PRO}\left(j_y^x\right)$ denote the utility value of the job urgency and the job operation profit for job j_y^x, respectively. W_{UR} and W_{PRO} denote the corresponding weight of the job urgency and the job operation profit.

$$U\left(j_y^x\right) = W_{UR} * U_{UR}\left(j_y^x\right) + W_{PRO} * U_{PRO}\left(j_y^x\right), \ j_y^x \in J^x \tag{5}$$

$$W_{UR} + W_{PRO} = 1 \tag{6}$$

The utility value of the job urgency for a specific job j_y^x at a faulty location dc_x is calculated as follows in (7).

$$U_{UR}\left(j_y^x\right) = \frac{max(UR(j^x)) - UR\left(j_y^x\right)}{max(UR(j^x)) - min(UR(j^x))}; \ j_y^x, \ j^x \in J^x \tag{7}$$

The utility value of the job operation profit for a specific job j_y^x at a faulty location dc_x is calculated as follows in (8).

$$U_{PRO}\left(j_y^x\right) = \frac{PRO\left(j_y^x\right) - min(UR(j^x))}{max(PRO(j^x)) - min(PRO(j^x))}; \ j_y^x, \ j^x \in J^x \tag{8}$$

Then the job rescue utility of a faulty data center dc_x, $U_R(dc_x)$, can be calculated using the equation in (9), where ϑ is a variable parameter to judge the job rescue situation. If the job is rescued from the faulty data center, ϑ will be 1, otherwise 0.

$$U_R(dc_x) = \sum_{j_y^x \in J^x} \vartheta * U\left(j_y^x\right), \ j_y^x \in J^x \tag{9}$$

4 The Replica Selection Schema

Our replica selection schema is an evaluation method based on overall cloud performance by applying three network evaluation metrics to select the best replica site to access. Three weighted parameters are developed to configure evaluation metrics and generate different replica selection decisions. W_{AB}^x denotes the weight of the available bandwidth metric of dc_x, W_{NL}^x denotes the weight of the network latency metric of dc_x, and W_{ER}^x denotes the weight of the error rate metric of dc_x. The expression of the final weight of a specific data center $FW(dc_x)$ can be summarized in (10), where NC_{AB}^x denotes the normalization component of the available bandwidth metric of dc_x, NC_{NL}^x denotes the normalization component of the network latency metric of dc_x, and NC_{ER}^x denotes the normalization component of the error rate metric of dc_x. For a request to access a dataset that has replicas at multiple sites, the data center with the maximum $FW(dc_x)$ value will be selected as the optimal access route for the request.

$$\begin{cases} FW(dc_x) = W_{AB}^x * NC_{AB}^x + W_{NL}^x * NC_{NL}^x + W_{ER}^x * NC_{ER}^x, dc_x \in DC \\ W_{AB}^x + W_{NL}^x + W_{ER}^x = 1 \end{cases} \tag{10}$$

Different evaluation metrics should be treated in different ways depending on their own nature. The available bandwidth metric with the highest value should be the best case while the network latency metric and error rate metric with that should be the worst case. Hence, the normalization processes of three evaluation metrics can be formulated as follows in (11), (12), and (13) respectively. If $FW(dc_x)$ is the same among two or more locations, the location with the least network latency will be selected as the optimal route. Furthermore, if $NL(dc_x)$ is also the same among two or more locations, the location with the lower error rate will be recognized as the optimal route.

$$NC_{AB}^x = \frac{AB(dc_x) - min\{AB(dc)\}}{max\{AB(dc)\} - min\{AB(dc)\}}; \ dc_x, dc \in DC \tag{11}$$

$$NC_{NL}^x = \frac{max\{NL(dc)\} - NL(dc_x)}{max\{NL(dc)\} - min\{NL(dc)\}}; \ dc_x, dc \in DC \tag{12}$$

$$NC_{ER}^x = \frac{max\{ER(dc)\} - ER(dc_x)}{max\{ER(dc)\} - min\{ER(dc)\}}; \ dc_x, dc \in DC \tag{13}$$

5 UBFH Fault Handling Approach and Algorithms

Put simply, our UBFH fault handling approach tries to migrate jobs out of the faulty data center and redirect them to backup replica sites. The migration not only considers the performance of accessing backup replicas, but also strives to satisfy the service delivery deadline constraints. To achieve these goals, the algorithm uses two functions *Redirection*() and *Migration*() to find fault handling solutions under different scenarios for a job at the faulty data center. The algorithm uses utility-based ranking to evaluate the job priority for redirection or migration. The job utility should be treated in different ways depending on the fault circumstances in different data centers. The job with lower utility has higher migration priority at a backup data center while the job with higher utility has higher migration priority at faulty data centers.

Algorithm1: UBFH Algorithm

Input: Bandwidth consumption, available bandwidth, data centers, job set, job rescue utility
Output: Fault handling solution (*FHS*)

1. Quicksort j in J based on $U(j)$ at the faulty data center and add into $ranklist[]$
2.   for j_i in $ranklist[]$, $i = 0$ to $sizeof(ranklist[])$ do
3. $j_i \rightarrow j_{fault}$
4. $RedirectionResult = \{dc_{red}, dc_{mig}\}$
5. $RedirectionResult = Redirection(j_{fault})$
6.   generate FHS
7.   end for
8.   do FHS {
9.   move j_{fault} to dc_{red}
10.   move j_{mov} to dc_{mig}
11.   }
12. end

The UBFH algorithm includes two major parts, faulting handling solution generation and implementation. Firstly, the jobs at the faulty data center will be ranked in a descending order based on their $U(j)$ in Line 1 and then add into rank list $ranklist[]$. Then a fault handling solution (*FHS*) will be worked out based on the *Redirection*() function for each job in the $ranklist[]$ from Line 2 to 7. The input parameter of the *Redirection*() function are the job at the faulty data center which is desired to be rescued. The generation of the *FHS* is based on the *RedirectionResult* which includes a set of data center information, the redirection destination dc_{red} and the migration destination dc_{mig}. Finally, after the *FHS* is generated, job moving activities will be done from Line 8 to 12.

Function 1: Redirection Function *Redirection*()

Input: Bandwidth consumption, available bandwidth, data centers, job set, j_{fault}
Output: *RedirectionResult*

1. map $dc_{backup} \rightarrow j_{fault}$
2.   compare $BC(j_{fault})$ with $AB(dc_{backup})$
3.   select dc_{backup} where $BC(j_{fault}) \leq AB(dc_{backup})$ and add into $red\_des\_dc[]$
4. $FW(red\_des\_dc[])$
5. $dc_{red} \leftarrow max(FW(red\_des\_dc[]))$ //select the optimal destination dc in $red\_des\_dc[]$
6.   return $\{dc_{red}, null\} \rightarrow RedirectionResult$
7.   else
8. $RedirectionResult = Migration(j_{fault})$
9. end

If the job redirection function *Redirection()* is called, the backup replica-ready data centers will be firstly mapped to the input job in Line 1. A comparison between the bandwidth consumption of the input job and the available bandwidth of the backup replica-ready data centers is created to find out the optimal job redirection route from Line 2 to Line 6. If the available bandwidth in the backup replica-ready data centers are all insufficient to receive the redirected job from the faulty data center, a migration function *Migration()* will be initiated in Line 8.

Function 2: Migration Function *Migration()*

Input: Bandwidth consumption, available bandwidth, data centers, job set, job rescue utility, j_{fault}

Output: *RedirectionResult*

1. collect the running jobs J_{mig} on dc_{backup} in Function 1
2. for each j_{mig} in J_{mig}
3.   map $dc_{backup} \rightarrow j_{mig}$
4.   compare $BC(j_{fault})$ with $AB(dc_{backup}) + BC(j_{mig})$
5.   select j_{mig} which $BC(j_{fault}) \leq AB(dc_{backup}) + BC(j_{mig})$ and $U(j_{mig}) <$ $U(j_{fault})$
6.   add into *movable_job[]*
7.   Reverse Quicksort *movable_job[]* based on the job rescue utility
8.   for each j_{mov} in *movable_job[]*, *mov* = 0 to *sizeof*(*movable_job[]*) do
9.   select dc_{backup} where $BC(j_{mov}) \leq AB(dc_{backup})$
10.   add into *mov_des_dc[]*
11. $FW(mov\_des\_dc[])$
12. $dc_{mig} \leftarrow max(FW(mov\_des\_dc[]))$
13.   return {the original data center of j_{mov}, dc_{mig}} $\rightarrow$ *RedirectionResult*
14.   else
15.   return {*null, null*} $\rightarrow$ *RedirectionResult*
16.   end for
17. end for
18. end

In case that all the backup data centers do not have capacity to support a job to be rescued, the migration function *Migration()* is to migrate an existing job out of a replica-ready backup data center to release some resources for that job. Firstly, Line 1 collects the running jobs on the backup data centers and create a new group of jobs j_{mig}. Then based on the new group of jobs j_{mig}, backup data centers will be mapped in Line 3 for each job in the group. A bandwidth comparison between the bandwidth consumption of the redirected job at the faulty data center and the sum of the bandwidth consumption of j_{mig} and the available bandwidth in its backup replica-ready data centers will be conducted in Line 4, and a new group of migratable jobs *movable_job[]* will be further created in Line 6 based on the movable job selection rule in Line 5. A reverse Quicksort algorithm will be applied on the new group of migratable jobs to rank the job in the *movable_job*[] in an ascending order based on the job rescue utility in Line 7. A comparison between the bandwidth consumption of the movable job and the available bandwidth of its backup replica-ready data centers is conducted in Line 9 to find the eligible migratable data centers for the movable job in *movable_job*[]. Then based on our replica selection schema, the optimal job redirection route for rescuing the job at the faulty data center and the optimal job migration route for the movable job at the backup data centers will be finalized from Line 11 to Line 15.

6 Simulation Results

To evaluate the fault handling effectiveness and efficiency, we performed a series of simulations on OMNeT++ 5.4.1. The OMNeT++ application is an extensible, modular, component-based C++ simulation library and framework, primarily for building network and cloud communication simulators [17, 18]. To reduce the simulation uncertainty and present a clear result, we assume the following conditions in our simulations:

- The data centers in the cloud environment has same speed and resources.
- The storage resource is large enough.
- The routes between the data centers have no overlap.
- The transfer latency keeps stable between each pair of data centers.
- The job consumes the bandwidth resource at a constant rate when executing.

A cloud environment including 5 data centers with 250 circuits of 100 Gbps optical-fiber network integrated at each data center site was implemented. The maximum bandwidth from dc_1 to dc_5 is all set to 25000 Gbps. The network latency from dc_1 to dc_5 is set to 20, 60, 40, 60, and 100 respectively. The error rate from dc_1 to dc_5 is set to 0.1%, 0.2%, 0.5%, 0.1% and 0.4% respectively. To avoid the fluctuation of uncertain internodal latency, input scheduling time and network latency between users and data centers, we set the $T_{IC}(j)$ and $T_{IS}(j)$ as 5 ms and adopt a single user with multiple requested jobs to access the datasets at different data centers in the simulated environment. A fault is set to occur at 10 ms system running time ($T_{Past}(j) = 10$ ms) in dc_2, which leads to the closing down of dc_2. The job deadline $T_{Dead}(j)$ and the total completion time of the jobs $TCT(j)$ are randomly set in the range of 0 ms and 1000 ms. The size of a job is randomly selected in the range of 0 GB to 5 GB, the same with that of many current data-intensive workflow jobs, such as Epigenomics. Each dataset has 3 replicas that are randomly placed in 5 data centers. To simply the problem, the weights W_{AB}^x, W_{NL}^x and W_{ER}^x are all set to 1/3.

We compared our fault handling approach with the typical HDFS robustness approach applied in the HDFS system, the RR approach [19] applied in SQL server 2016 and the JSQ approach applied in the Cisco Local Director, IBM Network Dispatcher, and Microsoft Sharepoint [20–22]. All four approaches were implemented under a single-fault scenario. They were evaluated the job rescue performance in terms of the repairability, job rescue utility and job operation profit as we mentioned above. The utility weights were changed in all 3 simulations under equivalent utility weight scenario, urgency-heavy utility weight scenario and profit-heavy utility weight scenario to test the effectiveness of our approach.

6.1   Simulation 1 – Equivalent Utility Weights

In the Simulation 1, the weights of the job urgency and the job operation profit are both set to 0.5. The simulation results are shown in Fig. 1. The weights of the job rescue utility are set to equivalent utility scenario which both W_{UR} and W_{PRO} are set to 0.5.

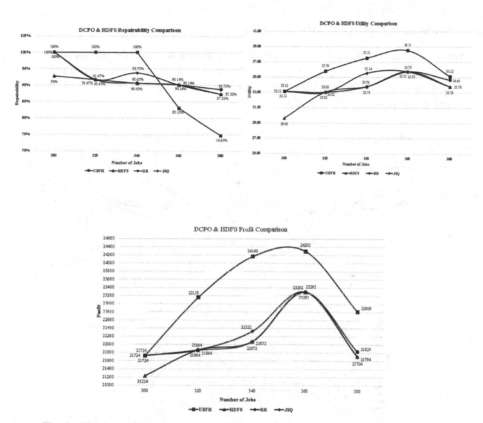

Fig. 1. The repairability, job rescue utility and job operation profit of simulation 1.

In Fig. 1, it is obvious that our UBFH approach is better from both job rescue utility and job operation profit perspectives in both situations when the environment has sufficient and insufficient resources than all other three approaches. For example, when the environment has sufficient resources at 340 jobs, our UBFH approach achieves higher job rescue utility by maximum 11.89% increase and more job operation profit by maximum 9.46% increase than the HDFS and RR approaches. As the number of jobs increases, when the environment has insufficient resources at 380 jobs, our UBFH approach still achieves higher job rescue utility by maximum 11.04% increase and more job operation profit by maximum 5.09% increase than the HDFS and RR approaches.

From the repairability perspective, our UBFH approach also has better repairability when the resource is sufficient to support the job execution than all other three approaches. When the resource becomes limited, our UBFH approach aims to migrate the lower-utility jobs in the backup data center in order to release resources for higher-utility jobs from the faulty data center. By adopting this operation, the higher-utility job saving from the faulty data center may increase the resource pressure to other data centers. Therefore, some lower-utility jobs might be sacrificed. This leads a repairability decrease when the resource becomes insufficient.

6.2 Simulation 2 – Urgency-Heavy Utility

In Simulation 2, we increase the weight of the job urgency to 0.67 and decrease the weight of the job operation profit to 0.33. The simulation 2 results are shown in Fig. 3. The weights of the job rescue utility are set to urgency-heavy scenario which W_{UR} is 0.67 and W_{PRO} is 0.33.

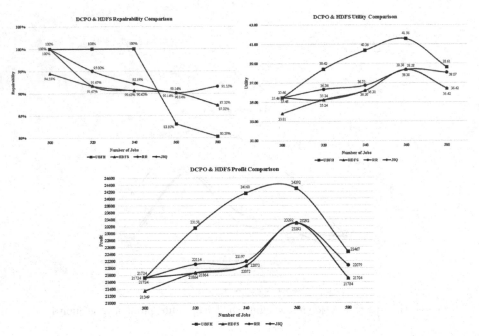

Fig. 2. The repairability, job rescue utility and job operation profit of simulation 2.

In Fig. 2, our UBFH approach remains the similar trend in the simulation 1. For example, when the environment has sufficient resources at 340 jobs, our UBFH approach achieves higher job rescue utility by maximum 11.49% job rescue utility increase and maximum 9.46% job operation profit increase than the HDFS and JSQ approaches when the utility weight has been set to urgency-heavy. As the number of jobs increases, when the environment has insufficient resources at 360 jobs, our UBFH approach still achieves higher job rescue utility by maximum 8.29% increase and more job operation profit by maximum 4.29% increase than the HDFS and JSQ approaches.

The repairability is also divided into sufficient and insufficient resource scenarios. Our UBFH approach remains higher repairability to compare with all other three approaches when the resource is sufficient. But when the resource becomes limited, our UBFH operations still have a certain degree of repairability decrease due to the same reason in the simulation 1.

6.3 Simulation 3 – Profit-Heavy Utility Weights

In Simulation 3, we decrease the weight of the job urgency to 0.33 and increase the weight of the job operation profit to 0.67. The simulation 3 results are shown in Fig. 3. The weights of the job rescue utility are set to profit-heavy scenario which W_{UR} is 0.33 and W_{PRO} is 0.67.

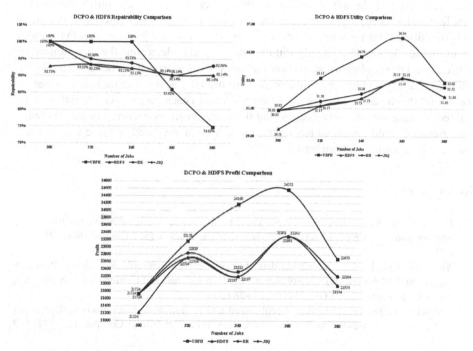

Fig. 3. The repairability, job rescue utility and job operation profit of simulation 3.

In Fig. 3, it proves that our UBFH approach still maintains higher job rescue utility and job operation profit to compare with all other three approaches when the utility weight has been set to profit-heavy in both sufficient and insufficient resource scenarios. We still achieve maximum 9.36% job rescue utility increase and maximum 8.84% job operation profit increase than the HDFS and JSQ approaches when the number of jobs arrives 340 in a resource-sufficient scenario. The job rescue utility and job operation profit also remain higher than all other three approaches under resource-insufficient scenario, for example, 3.14% higher job rescue utility and 3.26% more job operation profit than the HDFS and JSQ approaches.

The repairability still experiences a decrease when the resource becomes limited. In contrast, the repairability remains higher than all other three approaches with a maximum 7.88% repairability increase at 340 jobs under sufficient resource scenarios.

7 Conclusions and Future Works

Data replication is a common method to achieve a proactive fault tolerance approach by creating multiple data copies to geographically-distributed locations. But sometimes, there are a variety of faults occurred in the cloud environments. Most of common replication approaches have insufficient considerations to the common network performance measurements and the job attributes. In this paper, we propose a utility-based fault handling (UBFH) approach to rescue the jobs at the faulty data center with the major considerations of the network performance measurements and job attributes in the cloud environment. A fault handling algorithm is developed to determine the direction of job redirection. The simulation results show that our UBFH approach has better repairability, job rescue utility and job operation profit than the HDFS, RR and JSQ approaches. In the future, the uncertain influences of the error rate in each data center site will be considered because we currently assume that there are no errors occurred in each network link. Besides, multi-packaged job migration will be investigated because we currently only consider a single-job migration.

References

1. Liu, J., Wang, S., Zhou, A., Kumar, S., Yang, F., Buyya, R.: Using proactive fault-tolerance approach to enhance cloud service reliability. IEEE Trans. Cloud Comput. 6(4), 915–928 (2016)
2. Yuan, D., Cui, L., Liu, X.: Cloud data management for scientific workflows: Research issues, methodologies, and state-of-the-art. In: 10th International Conference on Semantics, Knowledge and Grids (SKG) 2014, pp. 21–28 (2014)
3. Mansouri, Y., Buyya, R.: Dynamic replication and migration of data objects with hot-spot and cold-spot statuses across storage data centers. J. Parallel Distrib. Comput. 126, 121–133 (2019)
4. Lin, J.-W., Chen, C.-H., Chang, J.M.: QoS-aware data replication for data-intensive applications in cloud computing systems. IEEE Trans. Cloud Comput. 1(1), 101–115 (2013)
5. Prathiba, S., Sowvarnica, S.: Survey of failures and fault tolerance in cloud. In: 2nd International Conference on Computing and Communications Technologies (ICCCT), pp. 167–172 (2017)
6. Subasi, O., Yalcin, G., Zyulkyarov, F., Unsal, O., Labarta, J.: Designing and modelling selective replication for fault-tolerant hpc applications. In: 17th IEEE/ACM International Symposium on Cluster, Cloud and Grid Computing (CCGRID), pp. 452–457 (2017)
7. Schwarzkopf, M., Murray, D.G., Hand, S.: The seven deadly sins of cloud computing research. In: Hotcloud 2012, p. 1 (2012)
8. Jhawar, R., Piuri, V.: Fault Tolerance and Resilience in Cloud Computing Environments, 2nd edn. Morgan Kaufmann, Burlington (2013)
9. Cheraghlou, M.N., Khadem-Zadeh, A., Haghparast, M.: A survey of fault tolerance architecture in cloud computing. J. Network Comput. Appl. 61, 81–92 (2016)

10. Kalanirnika, G.R., Sivagami, V.M.: Fault tolerance in cloud using reactive and proactive techniques. Int. J. Computer Sci. Eng. Commun. **3**(3), 1159–1164 (2015)
11. Deng, S., Huang, L., Taheri, J., Zomaya, A.Y.: Computation offloading for service workflow in mobile cloud computing. IEEE Trans. Parallel Distrib. Syst. **26**(12), 3317–3329 (2014)
12. Zhou, A., et al.: Cloud service reliability enhancement via virtual machine placement optimization. IEEE Trans. Serv. Comput. **10**(6), 902–913 (2017)
13. Ko, A.C., Zaw, W.T.: Fault tolerant erasure coded replication for HDFS based cloud storage. In: IEEE Fourth International Conference on Big Data and Cloud Computing, pp. 104–109 (2014)
14. Vardhan, M., Goel, A., Verma, A., Kushwaha, D.S.: A dynamic fault tolerant threshold based replication mechanism in distributed environment. Procedia Technol. **6**, 188–195 (2012)
15. Shwe, T., Aritsugi, M.: PRTuner: proactive-reactive re-replication tuning in HDFS-based cloud data center. IEEE Cloud Comput. **5**(6), 48–57 (2018)
16. Xu, H., Liu, W., Shu, G., Li, J.: Location-aware data block allocation strategy for HDFS-based applications in the cloud. In: IEEE 9th International Conference on Cloud Computing (CLOUD) 2016, pp. 252–259
17. Jiang, J., Li, Y., Hong, S. H., Xu, A., Wang, K.: A Time-sensitive Networking (TSN) simulation model based on OMNET++. In: IEEE International Conference on Mechatronics and Automation (ICMA), pp. 643–648 (2018)
18. Oujezsky, V., Horvath, T.: Case study and comparison of SimPy 3 and OMNeT++ Simulation. In: 39th International Conference on Telecommunications and Signal Processing (TSP), pp. 15–19 (2016)
19. Jiang, W., Xie, H., Zhou, X., Fang, L., Wang, J.: Performance analysis and improvement of replica selection algorithms for key-value stores. In: 2017 IEEE 10th International Conference on Cloud Computing (CLOUD), pp. 786–789 (2017)
20. ElYamany, H.F., Mohamed, M.F., Grolinger, K., Capretz, M.A.: A generalized service replication process in distributed environments. In: Proceedings of the 5th International Conference on Cloud Computing and Services Science, pp. 186–193 (2015)
21. Thorsen, S.: Replica selection in Apache Cassandra: reducing the tail latency for reads using the C3 algorithm. Unpublished (2015)
22. Gupta, V., Balter, M.H., Sigman, K., Whitt, W.: Analysis of join-the-shortest-queue routing for web server farms. Perform. Eval. **64**(9–12), 1062–1081 (2007)

Analyzing CNN Based Behavioural Malware Detection Techniques on Cloud IaaS

Andrew McDole[1](✉), Mahmoud Abdelsalam[2](✉), Maanak Gupta[1](✉), and Sudip Mittal[3](✉)

[1] Tennessee Technological University, Cookeville, TN, USA
amcdole42@students.tntech.edu, mgupta@tntech.edu
[2] Manhattan College, Riverdale, NY, USA
mabdelsalam01@manhattan.edu
[3] University of North Carolina at Wilmington, Wilmington, NC, USA
mittals@uncw.edu

Abstract. Cloud Infrastructure as a Service (IaaS) is vulnerable to malware due to its exposure to external adversaries, making it a lucrative attack vector for malicious actors. A datacenter infected with malware can cause data loss and/or major disruptions to service for its users. This paper analyzes and compares various Convolutional Neural Networks (CNNs) for online detection of malware in cloud IaaS. The detection is performed based on behavioural data using process level performance metrics including cpu usage, memory usage, disk usage etc. We have used the state of the art DenseNets and ResNets in effectively detecting malware in online cloud system. These CNNs are designed to extract features from data gathered from live malware running on a real cloud environment. Experiments are performed on OpenStack (a cloud IaaS software) testbed designed to replicate a typical 3-tier web architecture. Comparative analysis is performed for different CNN models.

Keywords: Deep learning · Convolutional Neural Network · Cloud IaaS · Residual networks · Dense networks

1 Introduction and Motivation

Cloud has become a popular platform due to its characteristics of on-demand services, infinite resources, ubiquitous availability and pay-as-you go business model [1]. Infrastructure as a Service (IaaS) is the most widely offered service model where the resources of a large data center can be purchased by clients to perform computing tasks. Since user clients can utilize any number of virtual machines, ranging from a couple to thousands, automatic monitoring of these virtual machines is necessary to ensure the security of the cloud provider and its clients. While there are several risks associated with IaaS, one of the greatest risks is the possibility of a virtual machine becoming infected with malware and

Q. Zhang et al. (Eds.): CLOUD 2020, LNCS 12403, pp. 64–79, 2020.
https://doi.org/10.1007/978-3-030-59635-4_5

spreading the malware to other virtual machines in the data center. This would put cloud providers and their customers at risk as well as end users whose data is stored or transferred on these infected virtual machines. As cloud providers increase their client base, the potential for loss also increases and so does the responsibility of cloud providers to invest in security mechanisms for their customers. The scale of an attack is multiplied due to similar configuration and automatic provisioning of the virtual machines (VMs) hosted by a cloud service provider. Identical configurations for these virtual machines make attacks repeatable and allow them to more likely spread within the data center once a single machine is infected.

Static malware analysis technique is widely used, in which the files are scanned before they can be executed on the systems. In such case, file is disassembled by disasssemblers to obtain the source code which can then be examined using different tools. Although the method is fast and efficient, it can easily be bypassed by malware writers who can trick the disassemblers into generating incorrect code. This is done by inserting errors which lead to the actual code execution path being hidden or obfuscated. The binary file can also be worked on directly. An example of this is extracting n-grams of the binary file as features and then using machine learning techniques to locate known malicious patterns. Static analysis generally fails in the case of cloud as malware is injected into an application that was already scanned and deemed safe. Such an attack in cloud IaaS is referred to as a cloud malware injection [2]. In this case, if the application is not re-scanned at a later time, the newly injected malware will not be detected. Therefore, the need to constantly monitor these applications running in cloud environments is essential.

While there are several works in the domain of malware detection, few research papers [3–9] deal with *online* malware detection specifically and in particular provide solutions using machine learning based approach. This process consists of a typical machine learning approach i.e. building a machine learning model, training the model with relevant captured dataset, and using the trained model to determine if a malware exists in the system or not. In the case of building the model, features must first be selected to determine what data will be used as input. This is no different for cloud based detection methods except that the features to be chosen are limited to the information that can be gained through the hypervisor. Through careful selection of features, machine learning can be used to provide dynamic malware analysis to detect whether machines have been infected by adversaries in the data centers. This kind of dynamic analysis fulfills the need for constant surveillance in cloud IaaS for malware detection.

The most unique characteristics of cloud computing include resource pooling, on-demand self-service, and rapid elasticity, can be fulfilled by an auto-scaling architecture. In this paper, we focus on auto-scaling wherein the machines are spawned based on the demand and usually these VMs are of similar type, resulting in similar behaviour. It is likely that an injected malware will result in behaviour deviation on a VM at some point. In this work, we seek to detect such malicious behaviour and compare state-of-the-art deep learning models (i.e.

CNN models). We are focused on detecting a single infected VM ignoring the fact that malware can easily propagate to similarly configured VMs in a more sophisticated attack. We plan to address this problem in future work.

This work is an extension to our earlier work where only one kind of CNN model was used, with the prime goal that such techniques can be effectively used malware analysis. In this work, we compare and contrast several CNN models using the same data as [3–5] and six other deep learning models to determine possible use cases within a cloud IaaS scenario.

The paper is organized as follows. Section 2 discusses related work in cloud online malware detection. Section 3 provide an overview of the key intuition and methodology for the experiments. Section 4 covers evaluation metrics and experimental results whereas Sect. 5 presents comparative analysis among different CNN models used. Section 6 covers certain limitations of our approach along with discussion on future work. Finally, Sect. 7 summarizes this paper.

2   Related Work

Several works have been done in malware detection which focus on different aspects. The first step in developing a machine learning based model for online malware detection is to determine which features are most relevant and are to be extracted. Research papers [10–12] focus on API calls whereas [7,13,14] primarily utilize system calls. Other features such as performance counters [15] or memory features [16,17] have also been used. Although several existing resilience frameworks exist [9,18–20], it is highly likely that novel attacks and new techniques will defeat existing detection methods.

Most of the algorithms for detecting malware, such as support vector machines (SVM) [9], all-nearest-neighbor (ANN) classifier [21], and naïve bayes [10,22], work for examining a single VM in the cloud. Although, using a single VM is not the most common use case of cloud environments, generally, there is no substantial difference between a single VM and a standalone host except that, in cloud, the hypervisor plays a vital role in gathering information about the VMs. Consequentially, most works [7,10–17] are restricted to the features that can be extracted through the hypervisor. Dawson et al. [7] collect system calls for features and are primarily concerned with rootkits. A non linear phase-space algorithm is used in their analysis of system calls to detect anomalies. The results are evaluated on the phase-space graph dissimilarities.

Entropy based Anomaly Testing (EbAT) was introduced in [8]. EbAT analyzed multiple metrics such as CPU and memory utilization for the purposes of anomaly detection. This paper analyzed these metrics based upon distribution instead of a flat threshold. This approach yielded accurate results for detection and the ability to scale to keep up with metric processing. However, the evaluation did not demonstrate usefulness in practical and realistic cloud environment scenarios. Azmandian et al. [23] utilize performance metrics such as disk and network input-output gathered from the hypervisor to form a new anomaly detection approach. K-NN and Local Outlier Factor are utilized in this work.

Work by Abdelsalam et al. [4] showed that a black box approach can be used to detect malware. This paper used VM level performance and resource utilization metrics. This approach worked well in detecting highly active malware which showed up in the resource utilization metrics, but was not as effective in detecting malware that hide itself with low utilization. Similarly, in [3] the authors introduce a detection method which uses a CNN model with the goal of identifying low profile malware. This method achieved 90% accuracy using resource metrics and was able to identify multiple low-profile malware. While these results are good, it is limited in that it targeted only a single virtual machine like many other related works without considering cases like auto-scaling in cloud.

3 Key Intuition and Methodology

In this section, we discuss the key intuition behind our approach and describe our methodology in detail.

3.1 Key Intuition

For online malware detection using process-level information, we train a model on a dataset that contains benign and malicious samples. Each sample consists of information about a collection of processes running at a particular time, and the task is to classify the input sample as benign or malicious. To build up our dataset, we run a VM through a benign phase, where the VM is clean, followed by a malicious phase, where a malware is injected into the VM.

Different malware are used for different runs of the experiment to create the dataset. We then partition our dataset into training, validation, and testing datasets. In other words, the model is trained on samples from different experiments which contained different malware. This way, the model can achieve better generalization to detect the malware by learning the various ways they utilize processes metrics/features. A model's ability to generalize and predict new samples is dependent on its internal architecture. More complex models may achieve higher accuracy by adding more hidden layers or by connecting those hidden layers in a novel manner. Metrics used also affect performance of different models. Some process level features used in this paper include CPU usage, number of context switches, and network information such as the number of bytes sent and received by the target virtual machine, as elaborated in [5].

3.2 Methodology

Convolutional Neural Networks (CNN) have been commonly used in various visual imagery tasks. A basic flowchart of a neural network is shown in Fig. 1. CNNs generally take two dimensional data as an input, in our case, the process level data is represented as a two dimensional array. A sample consists of rows of processes with columns of process features. Assuming p_i is a process, f_n is a

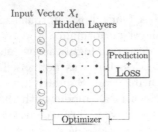

Input Vector X_t

Hidden Layers

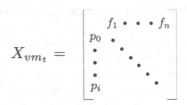

$$X_{vm_t} = \begin{bmatrix} & f_1 & \cdots & f_n \\ p_0 & & & \\ \vdots & & \ddots & \\ \vdots & & & \ddots \\ p_i & & & \end{bmatrix}$$

Fig. 1. Neural network flow

Fig. 2. Sample at time t consisting of process level information

process metric, vm is a virtual machine ID, then X_{vm_t} is a sample at time t as shown in Fig. 2.

Each sample represents a single virtual machine at a given time interval so the models learn what an infected machine "looks like" over time. During the course of time in an operating system, processes get created and destroyed and as these IDs can be assigned/re-assigned to different processes, they provide no useful information for the task at hand. For this reason, we focus on *unique process* defined as a tuple that contains a process ID, the command used to run the process, and a hash of the binary executable. This *unique process* will be referred to as a process in this work. Once the training dataset has been used to train the model, it is used for generating predictions on an unseen test dataset that the model did not use during the training process.

We used Openstack[1], a popular cloud computing platform to replicate a standard 3-tier web architecture consisting of web servers, application servers, and a database. Auto-scaling was enabled on the web and application servers and was configured with a CPU utilization based policy. As per the policy, if the average CPU utilization is above 70%, the architecture scales out and it scales in if the utilization is below 30%. We spawned between 2 and 10 servers in each tier depending on the traffic load. An ON/OFF Pareto distribution with the default NS2[2] tool parameters was used to generate the traffic load.

Figure 3, shows the data collection process. Each experiment was 1 h long, consisting of a 30 min clean phase and a 30 min infected phase. During the infected phase, malware was injected into a virtual machine at some time after the infected phase started. We introduced 113 different malwares to collect our dataset. These malwares were obtained from VirusTotal[3]. The VMs were configured with full internet access and all firewalls were disabled. This was done so that the malware could operate without any interference. After every 10 s, a sample was collected from the infected virtual machine in the experiment resulting in 360 samples over the course of each experiment.

---

[1] Openstack. https://www.openstack.org/.
[2] NS2 Manual. http://www.isi.edu/nsnam/ns/doc/node509.html.
[3] VirusTotal Website. https://www.virustotal.com.

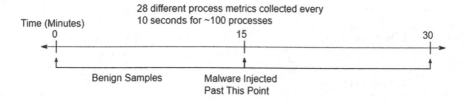

Fig. 3. Data collection overview

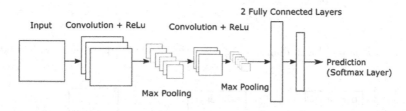

Fig. 4. LeNet-5 model

3.3   Convolutional Neural Network Models

LeNet-5 [24]: It is a shallow CNN with few layers so the gradients can be computed quickly. Figure 4, shows the model architecture. Note that the architecture is simple and straightforward where the output of each layer serves as the input to the next layer.

The input to the model is a two dimensional matrix of 120×45 representing a sample with a maximum of 120 processes and 45 features of these processes. Each process that was not active at the time the sample was taken, but would become active during the course of the experiment was padded with zeroes. The first layer of LeNet-5 consists of a convolutional layer with 32 kernels, each with a size of 5×5. The output of this layer is 32 feature maps with the same input shape of 120×45. The max pooling layer of size 2×2 downsizes these feature maps to become 60×23. The second convolutional layer has 64 kernels with the shape of the output from the previous max pooling layer, 60×23. This convolutional layer is followed by another max pooling layer of size 2×2 which results in 64 feature maps of size 30×12. The final layers of LeNet-5 are fully connected with sizes 1024, 512, and 2 respectively. The final layer has an output of size 2 since it represents a binary prediction of malicious or benign sample.

All of the activation functions used Rectified Linear Units (ReLU) [25] which were placed after every convolution and fully connected layer excluding the final layer. We used the Adam Optimizer [26], which is a stochastic gradient descent algorithm with automatic learning rate adaptation. The optimizer trains the weights of the model after every min-batch. The learning rate controls how drastically the weights of the model are changed in response to the backpropagation. A higher learning rate leads to faster training but can result in unstable gradient descent and can inhibit convergence. A learning rate that is too slow can cause the model not to achieve higher accuracy results.

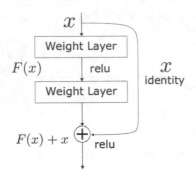

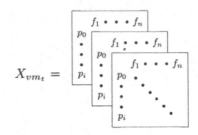

Fig. 5. Residual block diagram

Fig. 6. Data input shape with window size 3

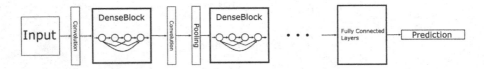

Fig. 7. Dense networks

Residual Networks: One problem with models with a large number of layers is degradation [27]. Adding more layers to the network can lead to optimization problems and therefore lower accuracy. This degradation is caused by the backpropagation not being able to reach the initial layers of the model. Residual networks (ResNets) solve this issue by adding skip-connections or residual connections. By adding these shortcut paths between layers, the gradient is allowed to flow better through the model, and deeper models are able to be trained without degradation.

Residual blocks as shown in Fig. 5, are used in *ResNets* [27]. The *identity* is the shortcut connection that allows the back propagation to affect the initial layers and, in turn, help these layers to learn as quickly as the final layers in the model. Three ResNets were used in our work: ResNet-50, ResNet-101, and ResNet-121. ResNets use a three channel data samples, however our samples are represented in 2d matrices. Consequentially, we replicated the samples to build three dimensional data samples. A representation of this data is shown in Fig. 6. At the end of each model, global average pooling was added.

Dense Networks: While ResNets seek to resolve the gradient degradation problem, DenseNets [28] attempt to alleviate the vanishing gradient problem [29]. A generic DenseNet model is shown in Fig. 7. DenseNets are different from ResNets because instead of having an identity mapping from one layer to the next, DenseNets pass the outputs of each layer to all subsequent layers. This way, each layer has collective knowledge from all the preceding layers. This causes the feature maps to be 'reused' by latter layers. This helps in reducing the number of feature maps required as input due to the compounding nature of DenseNets.

Each dense block makes use of these identity mappings and feature reuse. Between each dense block, there are transition layers that are comprised of a convolution and pooling layer. These are meant to reduce the feature map size between dense blocks. Similar to the ResNets, all DenseNets models received the same input shape as the ResNet models, $120 \times 45 \times 3$. The batch size used was 64 for all models to maintain consistency.

4 Experimental Evaluation and Results

4.1 Evaluation Metrics

For our comparative analysis, we have used four evaluation metrics:

$$Accuracy = \frac{TP + TN}{TP + TN + FP + FN}$$

$$Precision = \frac{TP}{TP + FP}$$

$$Recall = \frac{TP}{TP + FN}$$

$$F1\ Score = 2 \times \frac{Precision \times Recall}{Precision + Recall}$$

True Positives (TP) is the number of correctly identified malicious samples. True Negatives (TN) is the number of correctly identified benign samples. False Positives (FP) is the number of samples that were benign but identified as malicious. False Negatives (FN) are the samples that were malicious but not identified correctly by the model.

Accuracy is a measure of correct classification. Precision is a measure of accurate positive predictions over the total amount of positive predictions. Recall is a measure of true positive over total actual positive. The F1 score shows the balance between precision and recall.

We also include the Receiver Operating Characteristic (ROC) analysis [30] which is used for comparing models at different thresholds. The ROC measures a models ability to distinguish between classes so in our experiments, it measures the models' abilities to detect malware. If the ROC curve for a model is close to representing $f(x) = x$, then the model lacks the ability to differentiate between classes. A common way to analyze the ROC curve is to measure the area-under-curve (AUC) value. Higher AUC indicates higher correct predictions.

4.2 Experiment Results

Our dataset consists of 113 data collection experiments which were split up into the following: training dataset (60%), validation data (20%), and testing data (20%). The training dataset was randomly shuffled. Each CNN model is trained for a total of 100 epochs. To choose the best set of trained parameters, the model

Table 1. Results for different evaluation metrics

Model	Accuracy	Precision	Recall	F1
LeNet-5	89.2	94.7	80.9	87.2
ResNet-50	88.4	86.0	88.9	87.4
ResNet-101	86.6	82.3	89.7	85.9
ResNet-152	89.5	89.0	87.8	88.4
DenseNet-121	92.9	100	84.6	91.5
DenseNet-169	92.8	99.7	84.4	91.4
DenseNet-201	92.8	99.5	84.6	91.5

was periodically tested against the validation set after each epoch. The set of parameters that yielded the highest steady validation accuracy was chosen.

Table 1 shows the results of the CNN models considered in this research. DenseNets reached the highest accuracy at almost 93% and precision at ≃100%. Additionally, DenseNets had the highest F1 score at ≃91.5%, while ResNet-101 had the highest recall score at 89.7%.

5   Comparative Analysis and Discussion

As stated in Sect. 4.1, the comparative analysis is performed using four metrics. We discuss each of the metrics along with the ROC curves. Additionally, we provide training and performance cost analysis of the models. Finally, we provide an overall analysis discussion and take away which sheds the light on the importance of finding the balance in choosing right models based on the use case and intention. Results for all performance metrics are show in Fig. 8.

5.1   Performance Analysis

The base model LeNet-5 reaches an accuracy of ≃89%. Since LeNet-5 is a shallow model, it lacks the ability to capture enough features. The DenseNet-121 model has the highest accuracy of ≃93%, with a very negligible difference compared to DenseNet-169 and DenseNet-201. This indicates that adding more layers did not improve the accuracy. One reason might lie in the fact that our dataset is limited (i.e., 40k samples) and deeper networks need more data.

ResNet-152 has a slightly better accuracy than LeNet-5. Considering the substantially longer training time for ResNet-152, such slight accuracy increase might not be worthwhile in some cases. Note that ResNets perform better considering other metrics and, in turn, can work in different scenarios. ResNet-50 and ResNet-101 have the lowest accuracy. The DenseNets performed better than the other models likely due to the feature reuse property of the dense blocks. Additionally, DenseNet models are more feature efficient than the other models.

The DenseNet models highly outperformed the other models in precision. DenseNet-121 achieved a precision of 100%, meaning that every sample classified as infected was indeed infected. DenseNet-169 also achieved a high precision of 99.7% followed by DenseNet-201 with a precision of 99.5%.

The ResNet models have noticeable lower precision than all the other models, indicating that they are incorrectly classifying benign samples as malicious. LeNet-5 achieved a high precision score so it would be more appealing than the ResNet models when some false positives can be tolerated. The high precision achieved by all the DenseNet models indicates that they correctly identified the benign samples more often and were less likely to classify samples as malicious unless they had a high confidence.

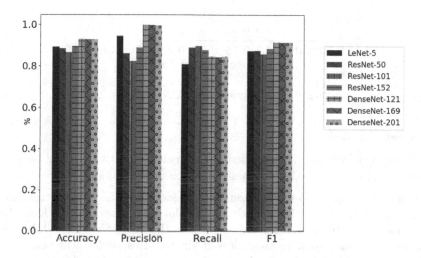

Fig. 8. Metrics comparison for used CNN Models

Recall is the only metric where ResNet models performed better than the other models, with ResNet-101 achieving the highest recall rate. The DenseNets performed worse than the ResNets and LeNet-5 performed the worst by far. Since recall is a measure of how many infected samples were missed by the models, ResNets seem to be effective at identifying most infected samples. LeNet-5's low recall rate suggests that the model is weak at identifying less obvious malicious samples. This can be a substantial problem in datacenters where the samples taken represent an unbalanced dataset. Typically, there would be an overwhelming amount of benign samples before machines are infected and malicious samples begin to arise. Low recall rate models would be less reliable in predicting the malware as soon as it appears. The higher recall rate demonstrated by the ResNet models are due to the high sensitivity of the model to classifying samples as malicious, meaning that the model correctly predicted the malicious samples.

F1 Score shows the balance of precision and recall. In that regard, the DenseNet models scored the highest. Furthermore, the ROC curves, shown in Fig. 9, illustrate that the best performing models were the DenseNet models due to their high precision scores which involve both TP and FP values.

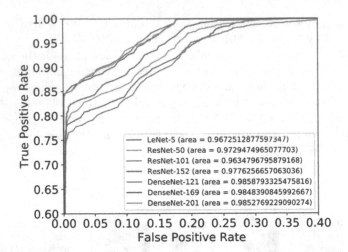

Fig. 9. ROC curves of the CNN models

5.2   Cost Analysis

Table 2 shows the training time needed to reach the respective models' accuracy. It also shows the time needed to classify a given data sample.

Training Time. LeNet-5 trained ten times faster than the next fastest model making it viable as a model to quickly process large volumes of data. DenseNet-201 and DenseNet-169 took much longer to train than DenseNet-121 while reaching similar accuracy making them less desirable. ResNet-50 achieved a high (90%) accuracy after 1815 s but ResNet-101 and ResNet-152 did not achieve better accuracy even with longer training times. In the case of ResNet-152, the model reached its highest accuracy at the end of testing so it is possible the model could have achieved better a higher accuracy if tested longer.

Detection Time. Detection time is used to show how long each model took to produce a prediction for any given sample. The results are unsurprising, more layers in a model cause it to take longer to feed the input through the model. This is important to include, however, because samples in a data center may be getting collected faster than a given model process a prediction. The detection time differences may also indicate that some models may not be suited for lower specification hardware. Since the detection time is dependent on how quickly the model can process the input, increasing the input size or the volume of inputs could prevent some models from scaling with large data center operations. In these cases, the models with lower detection times may be preferable.

5.3   Overall Analysis

Highly tightening a model causes many false alarms while loosening a model causes malware to slip through. Finding the right balance is a critical and daunting task. Our analysis suggests that the DenseNet models are the most accurate

Table 2. Training and detection time

Model	Validation accuracy	Epoch reached	Elapsed time (s)	Detection time (ms)
LeNet-5	89.9	29	170	54
ResNet-50	90.7	67	1815	96
ResNet-101	87.0	60	2940	130
ResNet-152	88.7	99	7029	165
DenseNet-121	92.1	32	1683	164
DenseNet-169	91.9	81	5848	209
DenseNet-201	91.5	36	3060	249

models with the best balance between precision and recall. However, depending on the use case, other models might prove to be more useful. For example, DenseNets has lower recall rates than ResNets which might be an issue for a use case where allowing malicious samples to slip through could be disastrous.

DenseNets proved to be more accurate than the other models mainly due to their better ability to generalize. Figure 10 shows the binary cross-entropy loss of the models during training and validation phases. DenseNets validation losses are mostly lower than their training losses, which indicates that DeneNets are better at generalization than the other models. It is also worth noting that while most of the models had stable validation loss, ResNet-101 and ResNet-152 had substantial fluctuations.

Another important aspect to determine the most desirable model in a real world scenario is training time. Table 2 shows the training epochs where the models reached their highest validation accuracy along with their corresponding time elapsed. For example, DenseNet-121 reached its highest accuracy after 32 training epochs in 1683 s. This shows that DenseNet-121 could be trained for less time than DenseNet-169 or DenseNet-201 and attain higher accuracy.

6   Limitations and Challenges

Although, our results provide good understanding of which CNN model works best in what kind of scenario, there are some limitations we would like to highlight based on our experience. One limitation of using CNN on our data is that it fails to capture a time correlation in the dataset. When detecting malware in an already running virtual machine, it is important for a model to have some knowledge about existing samples and the behavior of the machine over time. One such scenario is when a machine begins to experience more traffic and due to some constraint on scaling, the samples generated from that machine begin to resemble some malicious samples. In this case, if the model does not learn that process features can be scaled according to valid demands on the machine, the false positive rate might increase. Another scenario is when the model detects

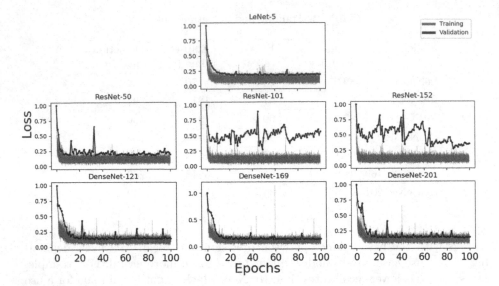

Fig. 10. Binary cross-entropy loss for trained CNN Models

an infected sample, but the malware immediately becomes dormant as to hide itself. If the model does not take into account the previous sample when the malware was detected, it may increase false negatives where the model doesn't detect a malware even if it is hidden.

Some of these limitations can be mitigated by using Recurrent Neural Networks (RNN). RNNs are comprised of cells that have a memory mechanism and can learn relationships among data with respect to time. Such models are used to process sequences of data such as audio or text. RNNs can be used to solve these limitations by lowering false positives and false negatives in certain scenarios.

Another limitation of this paper is the number of malware samples used. We used 113 malware samples, however, we believe with more samples CNN models could have performed better. The deeper networks such as DenseNet-201 and ResNet-152 may perform better on low-active malware that barely affect the system, and the complexity of those networks may be trained on those samples better than a shallower model. By increasing the amount of malware available, the models also gain a broader dataset that could be used to better generalize their predictive power. Further, once a malware is injected, there are no guarantees that the malware is exhibiting malicious behavior at any given time without knowing what code was being executed at that same moment a sample was recorded. This can lead to a problem where samples are mislabeled as malicious or benign. This problem was addressed in [3], but without writing custom malware that will beacon when malicious activity begins and ends, it is unlikely that all samples will be labeled properly.

7 Conclusion and Future Work

In this paper, we analyzed seven CNN models to determine which one is better suited for malware detection in cloud IaaS. Our analysis shows that LeNet-5 model is quick but sacrifices accuracy. The model is still useful as it attains a 90% accuracy and can be used in situations where a quick prediction is needed but incorrectness is not too costly. It can also be used when early predictions can be made with LeNet-5 which can be rechecked with more complex models. Additionally, our analysis suggest that while the ResNets performed well averaging $\simeq$86 accuracy, the DenseNet models performed the best at 93% accuracy. The ResNet models have higher recall scores indicating that they are more suited for cases where not identifying the malware posing a great security risk. DenseNet models have higher accuracy and precision which indicates they are less likely to generate false positives which are useful in cloud IaaS environments where service availability is extremely important. For future work, we plan to examine more malware samples including Windows malware as well as examine other architectures such as Hadoop and Containers. We also plan to analyze and propose new deep learning techniques by infecting multiple VMs to replicate more sophisticated attack scenarios.

Acknowledgment. This work is partially supported by NSF SFS Grant DGE-1565562.

References

1. Mell, P., Grance, T., et al.: The NIST definition of cloud computing (2011)
2. Gruschka, N., et al.: Attack surfaces: a taxonomy for attacks on cloud services. In: Proceedings of IEEE International Conference on Cloud Computing, pp. 276–279 (2010)
3. Abdelsalam, M., et al.: Malware detection in cloud infrastructures using convolutional neural networks. In: Proceedings of IEEE International Conference on Cloud Computing (CLOUD), pp. 162–169 (2018)
4. Abdelsalam, M., Krishnan, R., Sandhu, R.: Clustering-based IaaS cloud monitoring. In: Proceedings of IEEE International Conference on Cloud Computing (CLOUD), pp. 672–679 (2017)
5. Abdelsalam, M., Krishnan, R., Sandhu, R.: Online malware detection in cloud auto-scaling systems using shallow convolutional neural networks. In: Foley, S.N. (ed.) DBSec 2019. LNCS, vol. 11559, pp. 381–397. Springer, Cham (2019). https://doi.org/10.1007/978-3-030-22479-0_20
6. Pannu, H.S. Liu, J., Fu, S.: Aad: adaptive anomaly detection system for cloud computing infrastructures. In: Proceedings of IEEE Symposium on Reliable Distributed Systems, pp. 396–397 (2012)
7. Dawson, J.A., et al.: Phase space detection of virtual machine cyber events through hypervisor-level system call analysis. In: Proceedings of IEEE International Conference on Data Intelligence and Security (ICDIS), pp. 159–167 (2018)
8. Wang, C.: Ebat: online methods for detecting utility cloud anomalies. In: Proceedings of the Middleware Doctoral Symposium, pp. 1–6 (2009)

9. Watson, M.R., et al.: Malware detection in cloud computing infrastructures. IEEE Trans. Dependable Secure Comput. **13**(2), 192–205 (2015)
10. Alazab, M., et al.: Zero-day malware detection based on supervised learning algorithms of API call signatures. In: Proceedings of the Australasian Data Mining Conference, pp. 171–182. Australian Computer Society Inc. (2011)
11. Pirscoveanu, R.S., et al.: Analysis of malware behavior: type classification using machine learning. In: Proceedings of IEEE International Conference on Cyber Situational Awareness, Data Analytics and Assessment, pp. 1–7 (2015)
12. Tobiyama, S., et al.: Malware detection with deep neural network using process behavior. In: Proceedings of IEEE Annual Computer Software and Applications Conference, vol. 2, pp. 577–582 (2016)
13. Luckett, P., et al.: Neural network analysis of system call timing for rootkit detection. In: Proceedings of Cybersecurity Symposium (CYBERSEC), pp. 1–6, April 2016
14. Dini, G., Martinelli, F., Saracino, A., Sgandurra, D.: MADAM: a multi-level anomaly detector for android malware. In: Kotenko, I., Skormin, V. (eds.) MMM-ACNS 2012. LNCS, vol. 7531, pp. 240–253. Springer, Heidelberg (2012). https://doi.org/10.1007/978-3-642-33704-8_21
15. Demme, J., et al.: On the feasibility of online malware detection with performance counters. ACM SIGARCH Comput. Archit. News **41**(3), 559–570 (2013)
16. Khasawneh, K.N., Ozsoy, M., Donovick, C., Abu-Ghazaleh, N., Ponomarev, D.: Ensemble learning for low-level hardware-supported malware detection. In: Bos, H., Monrose, F., Blanc, G. (eds.) RAID 2015. LNCS, vol. 9404, pp. 3–25. Springer, Cham (2015). https://doi.org/10.1007/978-3-319-26362-5_1
17. Xu, Z., et al.: Malware detection using machine learning based analysis of virtual memory access patterns. In: Proceedings of IEEE Design, Automation & Test in Europe Conference & Exhibition, pp. 169–174 (2017)
18. Sterbenz, J.P.G., et al.: Resilience and survivability in communication networks: Strategies, principles, and survey of disciplines. Comput. Networks **54**(8), 1245–1265 (2010)
19. Watson, M.R., Shirazi, N.-H., Marnerides, A.K., Mauthe, A., Hutchison, D.: Towards a distributed, self-organising approach to malware detection in cloud computing. In: Elmenreich, W., Dressler, F., Loreto, V. (eds.) IWSOS 2013. LNCS, vol. 8221, pp. 182–185. Springer, Heidelberg (2014). https://doi.org/10.1007/978-3-642-54140-7_19
20. Marnerides, A.K., et al.: A multi-level resilience framework for unified networked environments. In: Proceedings of IFIP/IEEE International Symposium on Integrated Network Management (IM), pp. 1369–1372 (2015)
21. Fan, Y., Ye, Y., Chen, L.: Malicious sequential pattern mining for automatic malware detection. Expert Syst. Appl. **52**, 16–25 (2016)
22. Firdausi, I., et al.: Analysis of machine learning techniques used in behavior-based malware detection. In: Proceedings of IEEE International Conference on Advances in Computing, Control, and Telecommunication Technologies, pp. 201–203 (2010)
23. Azmandian, F., et al.: Virtual machine monitor-based lightweight intrusion detection. ACM SIGOPS Oper. Syst. Rev. **45**(2), 38–53 (2011)
24. LeCun, Y., et al.: Gradient-based learning applied to document recognition. Proc. IEEE **86**(11), 2278–2324 (1998)
25. Agarap, A.F.: Deep learning using rectified linear units (relu). arXiv preprint arXiv:1803.08375 (2018)
26. Kingma, D.P., Ba, J.: Adam: a method for stochastic optimization. arXiv preprint arXiv:1412.6980 (2014)

27. He, K., Zhang, X., Ren, S., Sun, J.: Deep residual learning for image recognition. arXiv preprint arXiv:1512.03385 (2015)
28. Huang, G., Liu, Z., Weinberger, K.Q.: Densely connected convolutional networks. CoRR, abs/1608.06993 (2016)
29. Pascanu, R., Mikolov, T., Bengio, Y.: Understanding the exploding gradient problem. CoRR, abs/1211.5063 (2012)
30. Metz, C.E.: Receiver operating characteristic analysis: a tool for the quantitative evaluation of observer performance and imaging systems. J. Am. College Radiol. **3**(6), 413–422 (2006)

NLC: An Efficient Caching Algorithm Based on Non-critical Path Least Counts for In-Memory Computing

Jingya Lv[1,2], Yang Wang[1(✉)], Tianhui Meng[1], and Cheng-zhong Xu[3]

[1] Shenzhen Institutes of Advanced Technology, Chinese Academy of Sciences,
Shenzhen, China
yang.wang1@siat.ac.cn
[2] University of Chinese Academy of Sciences, Beijing, China
[3] State Key Lab of IoTSC, University of Macau, Taipa, Macau

Abstract. The explosion of applications in data-parallel systems and ever-growing high-efficiency needs for data analysis have made parallel systems under enormous memory pressure when dealing with large datasets. Out-of-memory errors and excessive garbage collection can seriously affect system performance. Generally, for those data-flow tasks with intensive in-memory computing requirements, how to achieve efficient memory caching algorithms is a primary measure to make a trade-off between performance and memory overhead. By taking advantage of the latest research findings on the DAG-based task scheduling, we design a new caching algorithm for in-memory computing by exploiting the critical path information of DAG, called *Non-critical path least reference count* (NLC). The strategy is distinct from the existing ones in that it applies the global information of the critical path to the caching replacements rather than the task scheduling as most existing works do. Through empirical studies, we demonstrated that NLC can not only effectively enhance the parallel execution efficiency, but also reduce the number of evictions, improve the hit ratio, and memory utilization rate as well. Our comprehensive evaluations based on the selected benchmark graphs indicate that our strategy can not only fulfill the parallel system requirements but also reduce the costs by as much as 19%, compared with the most advanced LRC algorithm.

1 Introduction

The explosion of bigdata applications has led to many research and development systems to support ultra-low latency services and real-time data analysis [10,13,17,26]. For example, the clusters for data analysis are moving from disk-centric processing to memory-centric computing for performance consideration [4]. Additionally, we witness a revolution in the design of database systems that use main memory as the data storage layer for database efficiency [13]. As a consequence, the demands on the memory resources in the current stage are dramatically increasing, which renders the memory a highly constrained resource.

© Springer Nature Switzerland AG 2020
Q. Zhang et al. (Eds.): CLOUD 2020, LNCS 12403, pp. 80–95, 2020.
https://doi.org/10.1007/978-3-030-59635-4_6

In in-memory computing, the inefficiency of garbage collection (GC) – a common used automatic memory management technique [5,6] and the high cost of data movements are the underlying reasons for the bottlenecks of parallel system performance, due to the accompanied high latency and meaningless consumption of CPU and memory resources. On the other hand, improper scheduling strategies may even negate the benefits of parallel computation.

To address these issues, the caching technology, as one of the effective solutions to traditional parallel computing, has been extensively studied and widely deployed. However, the existing caching algorithms in the currently accessible data analysis systems are relatively inefficient for in-memory computing [1,12,24,25]. This is because of the inherent structure and data access pattern of parallel programs. Specifically, a parallel program is often modeled as a task graph, which is controlled by a set of accessed data and dependent subtasks to form a directed acyclic graph (DAG), to carry out a complex computation process [14,20], where the nodes in the graph represent sub-tasks (such as an executable file or a script), and the current requests for interactive and iterative data processing are usually accompanied by a precise data relies on application-specific semantics [25]. However, most existing caching strategies, such as LRU, LFU, and LRU-K, have not made the best use of dependency information between data items [7]. Rather, they optimize the caching strategies by mostly predicting the application-specific data access patterns based on the historical information, such as the frequency and reference recency, which often result in low hit ratio and long response time in certain cases [28].

According to this problem, Mao et al. [19] use reinforcement learning and neural networks to learn workload-specific scheduling algorithm to facilitate the caching. However, its complexity is much higher than the above strategies. LRC [28] is a most recent caching algorithm proposed for the Spark-based in-memory computing, it makes use of data dependency information of subtasks by continuously expunging the data block with the smallest reference count, and thus it realizes an efficient memory caching strategy with low overhead. However, the optimization strategy of LRC is myopic, lacking the notion of the global information of the task graph, especially when the memory resources are not sufficient.

In this paper, motivated by the caching problem in in-memory parallel computing and inspired by the algorithm of LRC and the concepts of narrow and wide RDD dependency in Spark [29], we propose a new caching algorithm for in-memory computing by exploiting the critical path information of DAG to direct the caching replacement, called *Non-critical path least reference count* (NLC). Of course, leveraging the critical path information to optimize the performance of program execution is not new. However, our algorithm is distinct from the existing ones in that it applies the global information of the critical path to the caching replacements rather than the task scheduling as most existing works do.

Through an empirical study, we showed that NLC can not only effectively reduce the number of evictions but also improve the hit ratio and memory utilization without increasing the dynamic response time. As such, it effectively improves the efficiency of in-memory parallel execution. Our test efficiency increased by an average of 20% compared to the most efficient LRU.

The remainder of the paper is organized as follows: Sect. 2 briefly discusses the related work of caching algorithms and highlights their limitations. Then the NLC algorithm is described in Sect. 3. Afterward, a detailed discussion and analysis of the experiment results and performance evaluation appear in Sect. 4 and the conclusions and future work are presented in Sect. 5.

2   Related Work

The studies on caching have a long-standing history, during which people put forward a lot of algorithms and strategies for diverse applications. They are widely applied in the storage system, database, file system, and processor, each with different purposes. Here we will mainly focus on some typical principles and algorithms that are highly related to our research.

LRU is a classic caching replacement algorithm widely used in different computing systems. In reality, it is often reduced to an implementation of a linked list. New data will be inserted into the header of the linked list. While there is a cache hit, the data will be moved to the head of the linked list. If the list is full, the data item at the end of the list will be evicted. When the accessed data item is hit, it requires checking the linked list first to find out the index and then moving the data to the header. Since LRU is in favor of preserving the data recently used, the hit ratio is very low for occasional and periodic applications, and thus it could lead to persistent excessive pollution of the cache. As opposed to LRU, as a variant of LRU, LRU-K is proposed based on the kth-to-last reference [7]. In LRU-K, the referenced page is moved to the linked list only after it has been accessed K times. As such, LRU-K replaces the page with the least reference frequency and the least reference recency as well.

Unlike foregoing strategies, LFU (Least Frequently Used) [7] evicts the data in cache that has been accessed the least frequently over a while. It often uses a binomial heap to select the least frequently accessed data blocks for elimination. The strategy is inefficient since it accumulates the useless old data with a high probability. In contrast to LFU, CRPF [18] is proposed to combine LRU and LFU by self-tuning to switch between different caching algorithms in an adaptive and dynamical way as a response to the access pattern changes.

LRC (Least Reference Count) [28] is a most recent caching algorithm proposed to facilitate Spark-based in-memory computing. It evicts the data block whose reference count is the smallest. For recurring applications, the LRC-Online strategy extracts its entire data dependency DAGs from previous runs. For the non-recurring applications, it should be noted that LRC updates the data dependency information of the application whenever a new job is submitted. Although LRC is effective to Spark-based in-memory computing to some extents, its optimization strategy is myopic, lacking the notion of the global information of task graph, especially when the memory resources are not sufficient.

In addition to the discussed strategies, many other caching strategies evict or prefetch blocks of data with hints from the application provided by programmer

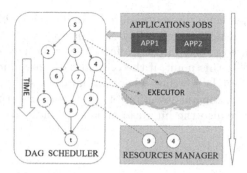

Fig. 1. The architecture of our scheduler.

that indicate what data will be referenced again and when [8,21,28]. However, inserting such hints is difficult for programmers as they must carefully examine the underlying data access patterns.

In summary, the aforementioned strategies are all based on either reference recency and frequency or other local information. They all have their own limitations and do not perform well for all the situations. We wonder whether there are other factors worth considering besides the reference recency and frequency in the case of maintaining the same cost and easy to implement. Motivated by this, we propose the NLC caching algorithm in the paper.

3   Description of NLC

In this section, we elaborate on the proposed caching algorithm, called *Non-critical path Least reference count* (NLC). Figure 1 depicts the architecture of our scheduler including the context of the caching algorithm. We will focus on the "DAG scheduling" module where a DAG-based task graph is accepted to be scheduled, the edges in the DAG represent sub-tasks, and the nodes represent data blocks.

3.1   A Motivation Example

Unlike LRC, we try to develop the caching algorithm from a global perspective by considering the critical path of the task graph. For I/O intensive recurrent applications, NLC could take advantage of their entire data dependencies information, which can be extracted from the historical runs. Concretely, a critical path (CP) of DAG–an essential structure in the DAG–is the logical path with the longest delay from the input to the output. Optimizing the critical path is an effective method to improve the speed of program execution [16]. In reality, a parallel program may have multiple critical paths.

As NLC is designed to improve LRC, we first leverage an example as shown in Fig. 2 to demonstrate that the problem with LRC. In the figure, nodes A, B, C, and D represent data blocks, with reference count $A > B > C > D = 1$. As shown in Fig. 2(a), when the memory resources are limited to three blocks, LRC firstly evicts data block D. Unfortunately block D is on critical path. Whether data block D can be prepared timely directly affects the smooth execution of the task on the critical path. At this point, if the critical path introduced by data block D is in the form of a single pipeline, where all data blocks have reference count equal to 1, then the continuous eviction of the them appearing on the critical path will ultimately reduce the hit ratio and delay the entire parallel working time.

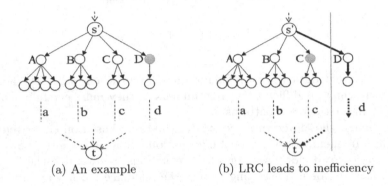

(a) An example   (b) LRC leads to inefficiency

Fig. 2. Each node represents a data block. Block A, B, C, and D are data blocks that are already cached in memory. The following nodes depend on them.

In order to alleviate the memory pressure and make the task map execute smoothly, data block D will be removed from the memory. This is a greedy strategy. To make matters worse, more blocks are generated in downstream because their fathers with higher reference counts are retained preferentially. Therefore, the next step of memory competition pressure will be intensified. However, according to NLC, the retaining priority shifts to those data blocks on critical paths. When there are multiple critical paths, they are preferentially moved into the earliest starting data block. On the other hand, when the beginning block of the critical path only has one reference, it will not be evicted. In contrast, data blocks with less reference count have more eviction possibilities. As shown in Fig. 2(b), $1 < C.lrc = 2 < B.lrc < A.lrc$.

Therefore, block C will be evicted. Relevant definitions are shown in Table 1. Data block D that satisfies both the critical path and the reference count of 1 will remain in the cache in a single pipeline operation. By sacrificing fewer subsequent data blocks, the priority of the critical path is preserved, while mitigating the high memory requirements of the more massive subsequent dependent block.

The advantages of NLC comes from its capability of improving the above problem. The blocks with a dependency of 1 can be kept in memory in a pipeline manner, while other eviction operations of LRC can be performed. This strategy is enlightened by the narrow and wide dependencies pattern in Spark's RDD. Simultaneously, NLC prioritizes the processing tasks along the critical path.

Table 1. Definitions of notations

Symbol	Definition
n_i	Sub-node number in a parallel task DAG (Directed Acyclic Graph)
$w(n_i)$	The I/O cost of node n_i
$t(n_{i,j})$	The computation cost of n_i to n_j
$e_{i,j}$	An edge from n_i to n_j
$E_{i,j}$	1: The edge from n_i to n_j is the only entry edge of n_j; 0: no edges between n_i and n_j or the entry edge of n_j is greater than 1
v	The total number of nodes in the task graph
e	The total number of edges in the task graph
$N.cri$	Critical level of critical path node
$N.lrc$	Lrc level: the number of reference count derived from node N

3.2   NLC Design

NLC is designed to cope with the recurring I/O intensive application tasks. Its advantage over the previous caching algorithms is the ability to adaptively adjust the priority ranks of data node at runtime from a global perspective of task DAGs. As a consequence, it can enhance the program performance significantly and promptly. NLC achieves these merits by using *replaces queues*, whose priorities depend on the reference counts, and the simplified HLFET (Highest level first with estimate Times) scheduling algorithm [2]–a scheduling algorithm in BNP [3].

Place Queue

The priority of each block in place queue depends on its "Critical Level" calculated in Eq. 1. We simplify the heuristic HLFET. The concept of critical level of $V_{i,pp}$ is the costs of all nodes and edges along the critical path from block i (i.e., the concept of those whose parent nodes have all been prepared) to exit one. Back to the example in Fig. 2, we use bold lines to indicate more considerable costs. The critical level of node D is higher than that of A, B, and C.

$$V_{i,pp} = \max\{\sum_{j=i}^{end}(t(n_j) + w(n_j))\} \tag{1}$$

Replace Queue

Similar to the place queue, the NLC replacement level priority of block depends on the number of not-yet generated blocks derived from it, which is calculated in Eq. 1, with additional conditions: If the block with the smallest reference count $V_{i,rp}$ has the highest critical level $V_{i,pp}$ that calculated in Eq. 1, we update its value to the maximum number. At the same time, the block with the second smallest reference count will be evicted. For the task DAG shown in Fig. 2(b), when memory are limited, we give the priority for retaining the single pipeline with higher critical level: retaining block D, even thought its reference count is the smallest one in A, B, C, D and preferentially evicting block C, whose critical level is lower than that of D. The relevant formulas are shown below as Eq. (2) and (4).

$$E(i, j) = \begin{cases} 1 & e_{i,j} = 1 \text{ and } e_{i,j} \text{ is the only indegree of } n_j \\ 0 & e_{i,j} = 0 \text{ or indegree of } n_j > 1 \end{cases} \tag{2}$$

$$V'_{i,rp} = \sum_{j=i+1}^{end} E(i, j) \tag{3}$$

$$V_{i,rp} = \begin{cases} V'_{i,rp} & V_{i,rp} > 1 \\ n & V'_{i,rp} = 1 \text{ and } V_{i,pp} \text{ is the biggest} \end{cases} \tag{4}$$

NLC Algorithm

Our algorithm is illustrated in Algorithm 1, which performs in two major relatively straight-forward operations: *Replace* and *Place*. The basic idea is that in a DAG, $cri\_level(n_i)$ refers to all the computational cost along the longest path from i to the exit node. In a similar way, $lrc\_level(n_j)$ refers to the n_j node subsequent reference counts. n_i and n_j are two independent nodes, if $cri\_level(A) > cri\_level(B)$, node A's execution priority is higher than B. If $lrc\_level(B) < lrc\_level(B)$, node A has higher priority than node B when the resources are limited. Overall, in NLC, the two operations–place and replace–are in two separate processes that run independently and interact with each other by producing and consuming the resources (via sub-task allocation and deallocation).

So, with constraint conditions, NLC ensures that every eviction would win more memory resources in the next layer by sacrificing blocks with more references (When memory resources are abundant, prioritizing D's dependencies frees up more resources than prioritizing C's.) and each step to minimize the length of a critical path (Each step assigns a value of zero to the initial node on the longest side of the critical path). The essential of this design is to achieve the goal task parallelism maximization and procedure parallel execution time minimization.

NLC-Online

NLC-Online is designed to handle a wide range of application situations. We note that NLC needs to extract the DAG information for the entire data in the application. Naturally, recurring applications can extract task maps efficiently. However, on the one hand, though the studies of production traces reveal that a large portion of cluster workloads are recurring applications [11], in systems such as Spark and Tez [22], only the DAGs information of the calculated jobs are available when the job is submitted. Generally, data dependencies between most tasks are unavailable at run time. They could be very complicated if the job is executed iteratively. On the other hand, even if the task appears in cycles [9, 23] the running time and memory consumption of each sub-task in the new cycle could be fine-tuned. In order to deal with those kinds of the phenomenon we have the following countermeasures:

Algorithm 1. Scheduling Algorithm using NLC caching algorithm

---

1 **procedure** NLC(G) Initialization: each node is not yet accessed;
2 $cp\_level \leftarrow DP\_CPval\_list(G)$;
3 $place\_queue \leftarrow PriorityQueue < Node > (com1)$;
   $//Com1 < Node > a.cri\_level - b.cri\_level$;
4 $replace\_queue \leftarrow PriorityQueue < Node > (com2)$;
   $//Com2 < Node > b.lrc\_level - a.lrc\_level$;
5 **Repeat:**
6 **if** *exit node has been done* **then**
7 ⌊ return;

8 **forall the** v_i *that* $v \in Activatedgather$ **do**
9 ⌊ $place\_queue.add(v_i)$;
10 ⌊ **if** *memory available* **then**
11 ⌊ ⌊ reserve it for $v \leftarrow place\_queue.pop()$; $replace\_queue.add(v_i)$;
12 ⌊ **else**
13 ⌊ ⌊ $v \leftarrow replace\_queue.pop()$;
14 ⌊ ⌊ **if** *node v has not been done* **then**
15 ⌊ ⌊ ⌊ $place\_queue.pop()$;
16 ⌊ ⌊ ⌊ Put the data node back to the ready-to-use sub-nodes priority queue;

17 **End Repeat: Return**

---

a) *For recurring tasks with state-fine-tuning:* NLC-Online is illustrated in Algorithm 2. We can reduce the overhead of DAG chart tuning through relying on LRC-replace queue information by synchronizing the fine-tuning in real-time. As for CP-place queues, we have to target the node to be executed in order to reduce complexity. If the execution time of a subtask is much different from that of the previous cycle, only the cost information of the current subtask is updated, and the subsequent dependencies are not considered.

b) *For non-recurring applications:* As with LRC, we propose that online updating the data dependency DAG of the application is performed whenever a new job is submitted. As for small DAGs, the computational complexity is relatively low while for complex task graphs, the time overload is negligible relative to the overall execution time.

3.3   Overhead Analysis

Excellent performance is usually accompanied by the considerable time and space overhead. The goal of this paper is to make a compromise between performance and overhead by proposing a caching algorithm with low complexity (practical application) and high performance. For time complexity, HLFET is one of the simplest BNP scheduling algorithms. Though the time-complexity of the HLFET algorithm is $O(n^2)$ (n is the number of tasks), for cyclic tasks, only once the computation is required in the very beginning. The computation of node cri_level queue can be ignored for periodic tasks.

Algorithm 2. Algorithm for NLC-Online

---

1 **procedure** NLC-Online()
2 //For recurring tasks
3 NLC(G)
4 //G is the historical topology
5 Initialization: each node is not yet accessed;
6 //Think of a change in block size as a change in the number of blocks.
7 **if** *A mismatch is detected* **then**
8   **if** *A block of data becomes larger* **then**
9   The single stream is then separated to update the topology sequence with a simple insert; $Uplist \leftarrow$ Topological_Sorting of G;
10   DP_CPval_list(G);
11   //Update the Place information generated after dynamic planning of the topology.
12   **if** *A new node is detected to be inserted or deleted* **then**
13   Update the topology sequence in time; DP_CPval_list(G);
14   //Update the Replace information generated after dynamic planning of the topology
15 For non-recurring tasks, waiting until the topology is submitted and execute NLC(G)
16 **Return**

As for the space complexity, NLC only needs to maintain two dynamic priority queues and the relevant operations of the replace queue and place queue just need a constant time complexity. As such, NLC is as complicated as LRU but performs better than LRC.

4   Performance Studies

In this section, we evaluated the performance of NLC by comparing it with LRC and LRU for parallel programs. To this end, we measured the difference between the actual parallel execution times of different benchmark graphs with the same DAG size and memory constraints.

In the process of evaluation, we also studied the execution effects of the periodic loop parallel programs under the condition of DAG fine-tuning in NLC-Online, and investigated the aforementioned caching algorithms in terms of execution time, hit and miss times through the empirical research.

4.1 Experimental Setup

To validate the effectiveness of NLC, we developed a small evaluation system in Java language, where a task graph scheduler is built according to the model in Sect. 3 and a thread pool is maintained to simulate the processor kernels as shown in Fig. 3. The system accepts as inputs three kinds of benchmark task graphs and random task graphs in different sizes, and uses the task DAG and its estimated memory resources and execution time to measure the scheduling length. The scheduler dispatches the subtasks to threads in the pool for execution, according to the scheduling algorithm. The execution of the subtask is performed by the associated thread to allocate the required memory and then sleep for a period of time in function of the estimated execution time.

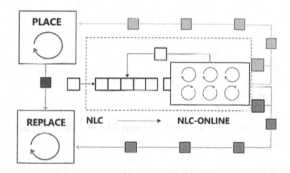

Fig. 3. The DAG scheduler where the place and replace of two priority queue scheduling modules are included.

4.2 Experimental Results

In this section, we presented and discussed the performance of NLC by comparing it with LRC and LRU–two typical caching algorithms. For testing NLC, we performed a series of experimental studies on the cases with extreme constrained memory[1] to demonstrate the performance of our algorithm for two suites of representative benchmark graphs: regular graphs and irregular graphs, including Gaussian elimination [27], Cholesky factorization [15], Fast Fourier Transformation task graph [3], and graphs with randomly generated structures for the task graphs in general forms.

---

[1] It refers to the minimum available resource in the sense that if the current resource volume is fewer than that, the seleced tasks graphs cannot be performed simultaneously.

Comparing with LRC and LRU, we tracked the access flow of NLC under random workload. Figure 4(a) shows part of the data blocks' time-state sequence in a random graph, with parallel processing branch being neglected. In contrast experiments, the different caching strategies produce the different topological orders. The orange data block represents they have high critical level, which have large retention priority under NLC. However, the myopia of LRC and LRU would lead to the ineffective replacement of some critical data blocks, resulting in delay or repeated I/O operations.

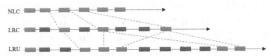

(a) A sequence of accessed states of partial data blocks.

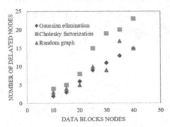

(b) The number of data blocks that satisfy Eq. 5 in benchmark graph experiments at different scales.

Fig. 4. The running trace information of the random task graph

Assuming that the cost from the beginning to the last use of data block i is C_i, the execution cost along the critical path from data block i being discarded to the end is S_i, and the total execution time is SUM. If there exists at least one data block in the critical path that has least reference count and is preferentially evicted by LRC.

$$C_i^{LRC} - C_i^{NLC} > 0 \qquad (5)$$

Figure 4(b) shows the number of data blocks that satisfying Eq. 5 in the three benchmark graphs of different sizes. During the execution of the tasks, the critical paths change continually. However, the constraint phenomenon of untreated critical path data blocks will be more obvious in the subsequent processing. Caching of non-critical data blocks in advance is of little significance for the completion time of the whole work. Predictably, compared with NLC, the more critical path data blocks that LRC delays processing, the more significant the delay will be.

In the initial state, there are apparent critical paths in both the Gaussian elimination and Cholesky factorization graphs. However, in contrast, the number of sub-task dependencies on those nodes along the critical path of the Gaussian

26. Wilmanns, P.S., Hausmans, J.P.H.M., Geuns, S.J., Bekooij, M.J.G.: Accuracy improvement of dataflow analysis for cyclic stream processing applications scheduled by static priority preemptive schedulers. In: Digital System Design (2014)
27. Wu, M., Gajski, D.: Hypertool: a programming aid for message-passing systems. IEEE Trans. Parallel Distrib. Syst. **1**(3), 330–343 (1990)
28. Yu, Y., Wei, W., Zhang, J., Letaief, K.B.: LRC: dependency-aware cache management for data analytics clusters. In: IEEE INFOCOM-IEEE Conference on Computer Communications (2017)
29. Zaharia, M., et al.: Resilient distributed datasets: a fault-tolerant abstraction for in-memory cluster computing. In: USENIX Conference on Networked Systems Design and Implementation (2012)

Job Completion Time in Dynamic Vehicular Cloud Under Multiple Access Points

Aida Ghazizadeh[1(✉)], Puya Ghazizadeh[2(✉)], and Stephan Olariu[1]

[1] Old Dominion University, Norfolk, VA 23529, USA
aghaziza@cs.odu.edu, olariu@cs.odu.edu
[2] St. John's University, Queens, NY 11439, USA
ghazizap@stjohns.edu
http://www.ghazizadehphd.github.io

Abstract. Vehicular cloud is a group of vehicles whose corporate computing, sensing, communication and physical resources can be coordinated and dynamically allocated to authorized users. One of the attributes that set vehicular clouds apart from conventional clouds is resource volatility. As vehicles enter and leave the cloud, new compute resources become available while others depart, creating a volatile environment where the task of reasoning about fundamental performance metrics such as job completion time becomes very challenging. In general, predicting job completion time requires full knowledge of the probability distributions of the intervening random variables. However, the datacenter manager does not know these distribution functions. Instead, using accumulated empirical data, she may be able to estimate the first moments of these random variables. In this work we offer approximations of job completion time in a dynamic vehicular cloud model involving vehicles on a highway where jobs can be downloaded under multiple stations.

Keywords: Cloud computing · Vehicular cloud · Edge computing · Internet of vehicles · Connected cars

1 Introduction

Cloud Computing (CC), a catchy metaphor for utility computing, implemented through the provisioning of various types of hosted services over the Internet, has seen a phenomenal growth in the past decade [1,2]. A few years ago, inspired by the success and promise of conventional CC, a number of papers have introduced the concept of a *Vehicular Cloud*, (VC), a non-trivial extension of the conventional CC paradigm [3,4]. VCs were motivated by the realization that present-day vehicles are endowed with powerful on-board computers, powerful transceivers and an impressive array of sensing devices. Most of the time the computing, storage and communication resources available in present-day vehicles

© Springer Nature Switzerland AG 2020
Q. Zhang et al. (Eds.): CLOUD 2020, LNCS 12403, pp. 96–110, 2020.
https://doi.org/10.1007/978-3-030-59635-4_7

are chronically under-utilized. Putting these resources to work in a meaningful way is poised to have a significant challenges [5–8] and societal impacts [9].

Back in 2010, Eltoweissy *et al.* [10] have argued that in the near future the vehicles on our roads and city streets will self-organize into VCs utilizing their corporate resources on-demand and largely in real-time for resolving critical problems that may occur unexpectedly. Although [10] have envisioned from the start VCs set up on moving vehicles, it is interesting to note that the first papers discussing VCs considered the simpler case of parked vehicles [9,11]. Thus, it has become customary in the VC literature to distinguish between *static* VCs involving stationary (e.g. parked) vehicles and *dynamic* VCs that are harnessing the compute resources of moving vehicles. We believe that this distinction is largely artificial and that, with the advent of ubiquitous network coverage available in the Smart Cities of the (near) future, connectivity will be pervasive and the on-board compute resources of vehicles will be available whether they are stationed or not.

2   The VC Model

This work is based on our previous work [12], in which we envision a *dynamic* VC that is harnessing the compute power of vehicles moving on a highway. In order to implement this idea, the VC controller is connected by optical fiber to pre-installed *access points* (APs, for short) deployed along the highway. Referring to Fig. 1, the access points are placed d meters apart along the highway and are numbered consecutively as $AP_0, AP_1, \cdots, AP_n, \cdots$. As illustrated in Fig. 1, each AP has a radio coverage area of c meters.

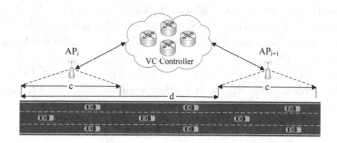

Fig. 1. Illustrating two consecutive APs and their coverage areas.

A vehicle can communicate with an AP only when it is in its coverage area. We assume that the APs are placed at the entry and exit ramps along the highway. This assumption implies that a vehicle entering the highway is under the coverage area of an AP. Similarly, a vehicle exits the highway under the coverage area of an AP.

Upon entering the highway, each vehicle is assigned a job for processing. Consider a vehicle that just entered the highway at AP_i. The vehicle informs

AP_i of the access point AP_j at which it will exit. Given this information, and the average speed on the highway between AP_i and AP_j, the VC controller can estimate the amount of time the vehicle will spend on the highway. This helps determine the workload that can be allocated to the vehicle for processing.

Jobs are encapsulated as container images. The vehicle will begin by downloading the corresponding container image, will execute the job and, upon termination, will upload the results to the first available AP. Each job can be downloaded under one or several APs. In case the vehicle leaves the highway before completing job execution, the corresponding container will have to be migrated to another vehicle, using one of several migration strategies [13,14]. In this work, we assume workloads that, with high probability, do not deal with migration.

2.1   Communication Model

The communication between APs and passing vehicles is supported by a variant of DSRC [15] that we discuss below.[1] Since each coverage area may contain several vehicles, the communication between the APs and the vehicles in their coverage area is, necessarily, contention-based.

Specifically, the APs continuously send out frames of size F bits containing a fixed length payload of b bits as illustrated in Fig. 2. In each frame, vehicles that are under the coverage area and wish to communicate with the AP compete with each other to secure a communication slot in that frame. As in [16–18], we assume that each frame has two adjacent contention periods of M minislots each. In each contention slot a vehicle that wishes to communicate with the AP picks a random number between 1 and M and transmits its identity in the corresponding minislot. This is repeated in the second contention period. If two vehicles transmit in the same minislot a collision occurs and the AP receives a garbled message. Vehicles whose message gets to the AP ungarbled in at least one contention period are considered successful and are allocated one data slot in the frame.

We let p_{k+1} denote the conditional probability of successful slot allocation given that the vehicle competes with k other vehicles in a given frame. It is easy to see that p_{k+1} can be computed as

$$p_{k+1} = 2\left(1 - \tfrac{1}{M}\right)^k - \left(1 - \tfrac{1}{M}\right)^{2k}. \tag{1}$$

From the standpoint of a given vehicle, a frame is *successful* if the vehicle has secured a communication slot in that frame. In each frame, the payload of b bits is partitioned evenly among the successful vehicles in that frame. We assume a communication bandwidth of $B = 27$ MBps which is the maximum data transmission rate in DSRC.

---

[1] The Dedicated Short Range Communications (DSRC) is the wireless communication standard for vehicular communications designed to facilitate vehicle-to-infrastructure (V2I) and vehicle-to-vehicle (V2V) communications. DSRC provides high data transfer rates (i.e. 27 MBps) with minimized latency, which is convenient for the highly mobile nature of vehicles and transportation systems.

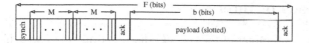

Fig. 2. General structure of a communication frame.

3 Virtualization

The past decade has witnessed the large-scale adoption of different virtualization techniques such as hypervisor-based and container-based virtualization. Container-based virtualization, which has gained popularity in the recent years, is a lightweight and agile alternative to the traditional hypervisor-based virtualization [2]. Containers are standard units of software that run on top of the host operating system and are isolated from each other [19]. An executable application and its dependencies and everything needed to run the application such as the code, runtime, system tools, system libraries and settings are packaged into a lightweight executable package of software called the container image [20].

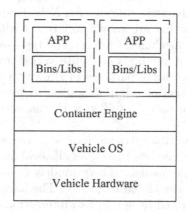

Fig. 3. Container based virtualization model for VCs

In a container image, layers or intermediate images can be created on top of the existing images by adding a layer that contains the filesystem differences between the images [2]. The basic image on which layers are added to create a final image is called a base image. See Fig. 3.

In our proposed VC, vehicles are assumed to be preloaded with the Linux operating system and a container engine such as LXC (Linux Container) or Docker. These images can be downloaded from the APs at the time the vehicle owner decides to join the vehicular cloud and participate in the computation service.

4   Workloads of Interest

The workloads contemplated for the VC discussed in this paper have a number of defining features in common:

- they are all delay-tolerant, not constrained by real-time requirements;
- the processing time is relatively short;
- they are, as a rule, cpu-bound and do not require inter-processor communication.

Examples of such workloads include:

- *Machine translation* of short documents, say, from English to Spanish or vice-versa. These types of documents include all sorts of memoranda, personal and business letters, job applications, newsletters, sundry legal documents, resumes, and the like. As pointed out by [21], context-based machine translation (CBMT) is a new paradigm for corpus-based translation that requires no parallel text. CBMT relies on a light-weight translation model utilizing a full-form bilingual dictionary and a sophisticated decoder using long-range context via long n-grams and cascaded overlapping;
- *N-body simulation* of dynamic systems. An N-body simulation approximates the motion of particles that are known to interact with one another through some type of (electro)-mechanical forces. The types of particles that can be simulated using N-body methods are quite varied, ranging from vehicles in dense traffic, to trajectories of particles in Brownian motion applications, to predicting the interaction of celestial bodies, to predicting the diffusion of individual atoms in an enclosure filled with gas, among many similar ones [22];
- *Molecular simulations:* Molecular mechanics is a growing area of interdisciplinary research and it involves the use of classical mechanics to describe the physical basis molecular models. These models typically describe atoms as point charges with an associated mass [23]. The interactions between neighboring atoms are described by spring-like interactions [24];
- *Monte Carlo simulations:* Monte Carlo simulations are very important in computational physics, chemistry and related applied fields. Monte Carlo simulations are also very widely used in engineering for sensitivity analysis and in the study of various "what if" scenarios [25];
- *Strategic Planning for Emergency Evacuations:* As pointed out by [26,27] and others, traditional evacuation schemes utilize predetermined routes that work reasonably well for hurricanes and other similar planned events. However, these routes are likely infeasible for unplanned evacuation such as in the wake of a terrorist attack or a HAZMAT spill. Raw *et al.* [28] argued that dynamic VCs will be able to suggest dynamic clustering of vehicles over large areas to improve the efficiency of unplanned evacuations such as earthquakes and other similar natural or man-made disasters;
- *Vehicular crowdsourcing applications:* It has been suggested that there is a need to push cloud computation towards the edge of the network, closer to

where the data sources are [29]. The vehicles on our highways and city streets are witnessing all sorts of traffic-related events and can be tasked with logging and reporting such events [30].

5   Approximating Job Completion Time

In this section we study the job completion time for cases in which the download of a job may be completed under the coverage of one or more Access Points (AP). We offer easy-to-compute approximations of job completion time in a VC model involving vehicles on a highway. We assume estimates of the first moment of the time it takes the job to execute in the absence of any overhead attributable to the working of the VC.

Table 1 summarizes a list of the symbols and parameters used in this paper. Let the random variable N_{k+1} keep track of the number of (complete) frames a vehicle sees while in the coverage area of an arbitrary AP. It is easy to confirm that

Table 1. A summary of notation and terminology

Symbol	Description
l	Number of lanes of traffic
B	Available bandwidth in bps
W	Size of the container image encapsulating the user job in bits
b	Payload per frame in bits
F	Frame length in bits
M	Number of available slots per contention period
p_{k+1}	Conditional probability that a frame is successful for a vehicle, given that k other vehicles are also competing for slots
N_{k+1}	Number of (complete) frames a vehicle sees while in the coverage area of an arbitrary AP, given that k other vehicles are also competing for slots
c	Size of access point coverage area in meters
d	Distance between two consecutive APs in meters
v_{k+1}	Vehicle's speed given a density of $k + 1$ vehicles per coverage area
T	Execution time time of a job in the absence of any overhead attributable to the VC. Only $E[T]$ is assumed known
J	Job completion time, including all overhead attributable to the VC
r_{k+1}	Number of successful frames necessary to download the job given a density of $k + 1$ vehicles per coverage area
D_{k+1}	Total number of frames necessary to download the job given a density of $k + 1$ vehicles per coverage area
U_{k+1}	Total number of frames necessary to upload the results given a density of $k + 1$ vehicles per coverage area

$$E[N_{k+1}] = \frac{cB}{Fv_{k+1}} - 1. \tag{2}$$

Let W be the size of the job (in bits) and let the random variable r_{k+1} denote the number of successful frames necessary to download (or upload) the corresponding job. Clearly,

$$r_{k+1} = \frac{W}{\frac{b}{(k+1)p_{k+1}}} = \frac{(k+1)Wp_{k+1}}{b}. \tag{3}$$

For all k, $(k \geq 0)$, let the random variables D_{k+1} (resp. U_{k+1}) represent the *total number of frames* in which the vehicle has to compete, in order to complete the download (resp. upload) of a job, given that in each frame k other vehicles are also competing for a slot. It is easy to see that D_{k+1} and U_{k+1} have a negative binomial distribution with parameters r_{k+1} and p_{k+1}. It follows that for an arbitrary non-negative integer m,

$$\Pr[D_{k+1} = m] = \binom{m-1}{r_{k+1}-1}p_{k+1}^{r_{k+1}}(1-p_{k+1})^{m-r_{k+1}}, \tag{4}$$

Since D_{k+1} and U_{k+1} are identically distributed, $\Pr[U_{k+1} = m]$ has the same expression. By (4) and (3) it follows that the expectations $E[D_{k+1}]$ and $E[U_{k+1}]$ are

$$E[D_{k+1}] = E[U_{k+1}] = \frac{r_{k+1}}{p_{k+1}} = \frac{W(k+1)}{b} \tag{5}$$

It is interesting to note that $E[D_{k+1}]$ is independent of the success probability p_{k+1} and only depends on the size W of the job to download, the payload b, and the traffic density $k + 1$.

Let G_D be the random variable that keeps track of the number of APs that the full coverage is used to download the job. It is clear that:

$$G_D = \lfloor \frac{D_{k+1}}{N_{k+1}} \rfloor \tag{6}$$

And, the probability of G_D is obtained as:

$$\begin{aligned}
\Pr[G_D = i] &= \Pr[\lfloor \frac{D_{k+1}}{N_{k+1}} \rfloor = i] \\
&= \Pr[i \leq \frac{D_{k+1}}{N_{k+1}} < i + 1] \\
&= \Pr[N_{k+1}i \leq D_{k+1} < N_{k+1}(i+1)] \tag{7}
\end{aligned}$$

Since D_{k+1} is an integer, we then obtain:

$$\begin{aligned}
\Pr[G_D = i] &= \Pr[\lceil N_{k+1}i \rceil \leq D_{k+1} < \lfloor N_{k+1}(i+1) \rfloor] \\
&= \sum_{j=\lceil N_{k+1}i \rceil}^{\lfloor N_{k+1}(i+1) \rfloor} \Pr[D_{k+1} = j] \tag{8}
\end{aligned}$$

Applying the expectation operator to (8), $E[G_D]$ is then obtained as:

$$E[G_D] = E[\lfloor \frac{D_{k+1}}{N_{k+1}} \rfloor] = \sum_{i \geq 0}^{\infty} i \sum_{j=\lceil N_{k+1}i \rceil}^{\lfloor N_{k+1}(i+1) \rfloor} \Pr[D_{k+1} = j] \tag{9}$$

D_{k+1} has a negative binomial distribution with parameters r_{k+1} and p_{k+1}. It follows that for an arbitrary non-negative integer j,

$$\Pr[D_{k+1} = j] = \binom{j-1}{r_{k+1}-1} p_{k+1}^{r_{k+1}} (1 - p_{k+1})^{j-r_{k+1}} \tag{10}$$

Using (10) in (9), we then obtain:

$$E[G_D] = E[\lfloor \frac{D_{k+1}}{N_{k+1}} \rfloor]$$

$$= \sum_{i \geq 0}^{\infty} i \sum_{j=\lceil N_{k+1}i \rceil}^{\lfloor N_{k+1}(i+1) \rfloor} \binom{j-1}{r_{k+1}-1} p_{k+1}^{r_{k+1}}$$

$$(1 - p_{k+1})^{j-r_{k+1}} \tag{11}$$

This Eq. (11) shows the expectation of the number of APs that the full coverage is used to download the job.

Table 2 shows the values of $E[G_D]$ obtained using (11) for jobs of size 10 MB and k 1 to 12.

Table 2. $E[G_D]$ for jobs of size 10 MB and k 1 to 12

k	$E[G_D]$
1	0.999999999999841
2	2.00000000000011000
3	2.99999999999946000
4	3.99999999999983000
5	4.00000086614947000
6	4.99999999999889000
7	4.99999999955399000
8	4.64672659954036000
9	4.00000000000181000
10	4.00000000000261000
11	4.00000000000070000
12	4.00000000000309000

Let G_U be the random variable that keeps track of the number of APs that the full coverage is used to upload the job. Since D_{k+1} and U_{k+1} have similar distribution, t is clear that $E[G_U]$ can be obtained in a similar way to $E[G_D]$.

We define G_T as the random variable that keeps track of the number APs that the full coverage is used to execute the job. We obtain:

$$G_T = \lfloor \frac{T}{\frac{d}{v_{k+1}}} \rfloor \tag{12}$$

Applying the expectation operator to (12), $E[G_T]$ is then obtained as:

$$E[G_T] = \lfloor \frac{E[T]}{\frac{d}{v_{k+1}}} \rfloor \tag{13}$$

We define δ_D, δ_U and δ_T, respectively as the remaining of the frames needed to download, upload and execute the job.

$$\delta_D = D_{k+1} - \lfloor \frac{D_{k+1}}{N_{k+1}} \rfloor N_{k+1} \tag{14}$$

$$\delta_U = U_{k+1} - \lfloor \frac{U_{k+1}}{N_{k+1}} \rfloor N_{k+1} \tag{15}$$

$$\delta_T = T - \lfloor \frac{T}{\frac{d}{v_{k+1}}} \rfloor \frac{d}{v_{k+1}} \tag{16}$$

Applying the expectation operator to (14), (15), and (16), and by replacing (6) we then obtained:

$$E[\delta_D] = E[D_{k+1}] - E[G_D]N_{k+1} \tag{17}$$

$$E[\delta_U] = E[U_{k+1}] - E[G_U]N_{k+1} \tag{18}$$

$$E[\delta_T] = E[T] - \lfloor \frac{E[T]}{\frac{d}{v_{k+1}}} \rfloor \frac{d}{v_{k+1}} \tag{19}$$

To find the job completion time, we distinguish between the two cases below:

Case 1: *Job execution terminates under the coverage of some AP.*

In this case, $\frac{F}{B}\delta_D + \delta_T \leq \frac{c}{v_{k+1}}$ or $\frac{F}{B}\delta_D + \delta_T \geq \frac{d}{v_{k+1}}$. Upload starts immediately under the same coverage area that the job execution terminated and therefore there is no delay.

The expected download time is obtained as the time it takes to travel to the number of APs that the full coverage is used to download the job plus the time it takes to download the remainder of the frames needed to download the job ($\frac{F}{B}E[D_{k+1}] + \frac{(d-c)}{v_{k+1}}E[G_D]$). We obtain the expected job completion time as:

$$E[J_1] = E[T] + \frac{F}{B}E[D_{k+1}] + \frac{(d-c)}{v_{k+1}}E[G_D]$$
$$+ \frac{F}{B}E[U_{k+1}] + \frac{(d-c)}{v_{k+1}}E[G_U] \tag{20}$$

By algebraic manipulations we then obtain:

$$E[J_1] = E[T] + \frac{F}{B}(E[D_{k+1}] + E[U_{k+1}])$$
$$+ \frac{(d-c)}{v_{k+1}}(E[G_D] + E[G_U]) \tag{21}$$

Case 2: *Job execution terminates between the coverage areas of two adjacent APs.*

In this case, $\frac{c}{v_{k+1}} < \frac{F}{B}\delta_D + \delta_T < \frac{d}{v_{k+1}}$, and upload starts after some delay at the next available AP.

The minimum delay occurs when the upload starts almost immediately after the job execution terminates, meaning that the delay is close to 0, and the maximum delay occurs when the vehicle travels the entire distance between two adjacent APs which is obtained as $\frac{d-c}{v_{k+1}}$. Therefore the average delay is calculated as $\frac{d-c}{2v_{k+1}}$.

Considering the download time, upload time, execution time and the delay, the job completion time is obtained as:

$$J_2 = G_D\frac{d}{v_{k+1}} + \frac{F}{B}\delta_D + G_U\frac{d}{v_{k+1}} + \frac{F}{B}\delta_U + T + \frac{d-c}{2v_{k+1}} \tag{22}$$

By algebraic manipulations and applying expectation to 22, we then obtain:

$$E[J_2] = \frac{d}{v_{k+1}}(E[G_D] + E[G_U]) + \frac{F}{B}(\delta_D + \delta_U) + E[T] + \frac{d-c}{2v_{k+1}} \tag{23}$$

5.1   Combining the Two Cases

The goal of this subsection is to combine the two cases discussed above into a coherent approximation of the job completion time. Let π_1 and π_2 be, respectively, the *limiting* probabilities of Case 1 and Case 2 occurring. Using the Law of Total Expectation, the expectation $E[J]$ of job completion time can be computed as

$$E[J] = \pi_1 E[J_1] + \pi_2 E[J_2]. \tag{24}$$

To evaluate the limiting probabilities π_1, π_2, consider the time interval of length I of length $\frac{d}{v_{k+1}}$. Since the probability distribution of T is not known, to a first approximation, we assume that job execution terminates, uniformly at random in the time interval I. In turn, this assumption implies that π_1, π_2 are given by the expressions

$$\pi_1 = 1 - \pi_2; \quad \pi_2 = \frac{d-c}{d}. \tag{25}$$

Considering $\pi_1 = 1 - \pi_2$, $\pi_2 = \frac{d-c}{d}$ the overall job completion time is obtained as:

$$E[J] = \pi_1 E[J_1] + \pi_2 E[J_2]. \tag{26}$$

6   Simulation Model

We have evaluated the accuracy of our predictions with the help of simulations. We have simulated a three-lane highway with APs placed every 2000 m. Each AP has a coverage area of 100 m in which the vehicles driving along the highway can transmit or receive messages. The APs continuously send out frames of length 56624 bits with a payload of 53792 bits. We have implemented the different necessary fields in the frame, such as the Start of frame (SOF), end of frame (EOF), communication period, recognition period, transmission period and acknowledge (ACK), the detailed discussion of which is out of the scope of this paper. The speed of each vehicle is determined by the traffic density. In our simulation, we have used the five-parameter logistic speed-density function in [31] to determine the vehicle's speed based on the number of the vehicles in the coverage area. When a vehicle enters the coverage area of an AP and receives the beginning of the frame, it competes with the other vehicles in the same coverage area. For this purpose, it chooses at random one of the 20 slots in the first contention period and the same procedure is repeated in the second contention period. Vehicles that select a unique slot in either contention periods are *successful*. The available payload is then divided equally among the successful vehicles. A vehicle that contacts the AP for the first time is assigned a job with a processing time exponentially distributed with a common parameter λ. The vehicle then starts the download of the job and continues to compete in the next frames until the job is fully downloaded. The job execution starts immediately after the download of the job and once the job execution is completed, the vehicle immediately attempts to upload the results. The process of uploading of the results is similar to download, in terms of competing for transmission slots. If a vehicle is not under the coverage area at the time that the job execution is completed, then it attempts to upload the results at the next AP. We record the job completion time from the moment that the job is assigned to a vehicle until the results are uploaded. In this paper we have assumed that the residency time of a vehicle is larger than the job completion time. Our simulations were developed in house with each experiment repeated 10^4 times.

7   Simulation Results

This section presents our simulation results performed in order to validate the analytical results obtained in Sects. 5. We have performed several sets of experiments that we now describe.

In the first set of experiments, the model has been set up in such a way that jobs processing times are exponentially distributed with a common parameter λ. The simulation and prediction results of job completion times for k values of 1 to 12 are shown in Table 4.

In the second set of experiments we considered jobs with processing times that are uniformly distributed on the interval from $\lambda - a$ to $\lambda + a$. Table 5 shows the simulation and prediction results for k values of 1 to 12. The maximum relative error is less than 0.31%, with an average of 0.16% for uniform distribution, and less than 0.26%, with an average of 0.15% for exponential distribution. The comparison of simulation results and analytical results confirms the accuracy of the theoretical predictions.

Table 3. Simulation parameters

Symbol and description	Value
l (number of lanes)	3
B (available bandwidth)	27×10^6 bps
W (size of the job)	8×10^6 bits
b (payload in one frame)	53792 bits
F (frame length in bits)	56624 bits
F_s (frame length in seconds)	0.002 s
M (number of available slots for competing)	20
c (access point coverage range)	100 m
d (distance between two consecutive APs)	2000 m
a (parameter used for intervals of job processing time)	600 s
v_{k+1} (vehicle's speed when k other vehicles are in the area)	(10, 30) m/s
v_b (average travel speed at stop and go condition)	9 kph
v_f (free flow speed)	107.44 kph
k_t (turning point for the speed-density curve)	17.53
θ_1 (scale parameter for speed-density function)	1.8768
θ_2 (parameter which controls the lopsidedness of the curve)	0.0871

Table 4. Simulated and predicted job completion times for jobs of size 10 MB for exponentially distributed job processing times with parameter $\lambda = 1200$ (20 min).

k	Simulated	Predicted	%Error
1	1372.971177	1370.085158	0.210202446
2	1506.602746	1504.023341	0.17120671
3	1642.814903	1640.536782	0.1386718
4	1793.948394	1792.201082	0.097400349
5	1851.216304	1847.766624	0.186346673
6	2098.006361	2097.589206	0.0198834
7	2227.232571	2226.370874	0.038689134
8	2299.213903	2297.220068	0.086718117
9	2298.473231	2292.467841	0.261277352
10	2445.785379	2439.69165	0.249152238
11	2607.28175	2601.495095	0.221942067
12	2783.440482	2778.096422	0.191994765

Table 5. Simulated and predicted job completion times for jobs of size 10 MB with job processing times uniformly distributed on the interval from $\lambda - a$ to $\lambda + a$, where $a = 600$ s and $\lambda = 1200$.

k	Simulated	Predicted	%Error
1	1373.45613	1370.085158	0.2454372
2	1507.096864	1504.023341	0.2039367
3	1643.080926	1640.536782	0.1548398
4	1794.929018	1792.201082	0.1519802
5	1851.925975	1847.766624	0.224596
6	2098.557275	2097.589206	0.0461302
7	2227.832187	2226.370874	0.0655935
8	2301.024405	2297.220068	0.1653323
9	2299.763016	2292.467841	0.3172142
10	2446.058988	2439.69165	0.2603101
11	2602.666214	2601.495095	0.0449969
12	2779.290042	2778.096422	0.0429469

8   Concluding Remarks and Future Work

Vehicular cloud is an extension of cloud computing where a network of vehicles interact using different communications devices. This model has several challenges that should be address by researchers in the field including job completion time. Job completion time is one of the basic performance figures of merit both in CCs and in VCs. In general, predicting job completion time requires full knowledge of the probability distributions of the intervening random variables. In practice, the datacenter manager does not know these distribution functions. Instead, she may have an estimate of the first moment of job execution time, in the absence of any overhead attributable to the VC. The main contribution of this work was to offer easy-to-compute approximations of job completion time in a VC model involving vehicles on a highway for cases that jobs can be downloaded under one or several APs.

In future work, we will look at other scenarios involving short vehicular residency times, where VMs (or containers) need to be migrated to other vehicles.

References

1. Buyya, R., Vecchiola, C., Thamarai Selvi, S.: Mastering Cloud Computing: Foundations and Applications Programming. Morgan Kaufman, Elsevier (2013)
2. Marinescu, D.C.: Cloud Computing, Theory and Applications, 2nd edn. Morgan Kaufman, Elsevier (2017)
3. Ghazizadeh, P.: Resource allocation in vehicular cloud computing, Ph.D. Thesis, Old Dominion University, July 2014
4. Ghazizadeh, P., Olariu, S., Ghazi Zadeh, A., El-Tawab, S.: Towards fault-tolerant job assignment in vehicular cloud Proceecings IEEE SCC, pp. 17–24, June 2015

5. Ghazizadeh, P., Florin, R., Ghazi Zadeh, A., Olariu, S.: Reasoning about the mean time to failure in vehicular clouds, IEEE Trans. Intell. Transport. Syst. **17**(3), 751–761 (2016)
6. Florin, R., Ghazi Zadeh, A., Ghazizadeh, P., Olariu, S.: Towards approximating the mean time to failure in vehicular clouds. IEEE Trans. Intell. Transport. Syst. **19**(7), 2045–2054 (2018)
7. Florin, R., Ghazizadeh, P., Ghazi Zadeh, A., Mukkamala, R., Olariu, S.: A tight estimate of job completion time in vehicular clouds. IEEE Trans. Cloud Comput. 1, 1 (2018)
8. Florin, R., Ghazizadeh, A., Ghazizadeh, P., Olariu, S., Marinescu, D.C.: Enhancing reliability and availability through redundancy in vehicular clouds. IEEE Trans. Cloud Comput. 1, 1 (2019)
9. Whaiduzzaman, M., Sookhak, M., Gani, A., Buyya, R.: A survey of vehicular cloud computing. J. Netw. Comput. Appl. **40**, 325–344 (2014)
10. Eltoweissy, M., Olariu, S., Younis, M.: Towards autonomous vehicular clouds. In: Proceedings of AdHocNets'2010. Victoria, BC, Canada, August 2010
11. Ghazizadeh, P., Mukkamala, R., El-Tawab, S.: Scheduling in vehicular cloud using mixed integer linear programming. In: Proceedings of the First International Workshop on Mobile Sensing, Computing and Communication, ser. MSCC 2014. New York, NY, USA: Association for Computing Machinery, 2014, p. 7–12. https://doi.org/10.1145/2633675.2633681
12. Ghazizadeh, A., Ghazizadeh, P., Mukkamala, R., Olariu, S.: Towards approximating expected job completion time in dynamic vehicular clouds. In: 2019 IEEE 12th International Conference on Cloud Computing (CLOUD), pp. 481–483 (2019)
13. Refaat, T.K., Kantarci, B., Mouftah, H.T.: Dynamic virtual machine migration in a vehicular cloud. In: 2014 IEEE Symposium on Computers and Communications (ISCC), vol. Workshops, pp. 1–6 June 2014
14. Kumar, N., Zeadally, S., Chilamkurti, N., Vinel, A.: Performance analysis of bayesian coalition game-based energy-aware virtual machine migration in vehicular mobile cloud, vol. 29, no. 2, pp. 62–69, March 2015
15. US Department of Transportation, "Standard Specification for Telecommunications and Information Exchange Between Roadside and Vehicle Systems - 5 GHz Band Dedicated Short Range Communications (DSRC) Medium Access Control (MAC) and Physical Layer (PHY) Specifications," ASTM E2213–03, August 2003
16. Ghazizadeh, P., Fathi, R.: A propagation based model for communication in vehicular cloud. In: IEEE International Conference on Pervasive Computing and Communications Workshops (PerCom Workshops) **2018**, 295–299 (2018)
17. Ghazizadeh, A., Ghazizadeh, P.: Design and analysis of a communication protocol for dynamic vehicular clouds in smart cities. In: 2018 21st International Conference on Intelligent Transportation Systems (ITSC), pp. 1–6, November 2018
18. Ghazizadeh, A., Ghazizadeh, P., Olariu, S.: Reasoning about a communication protocol for vehicular cloud computing systems. In: 2019 IEEE International Conference on Pervasive Computing and Communications Workshops (PerCom Workshops), pp. 214–219, March 2019
19. Pahl, C., Brogi, A., Soldani, J., Jamshidi, P.: Cloud container technologies: a state-of-the-art review. IEEE Trans. Cloud Comput. **2017**, 1–14(05) (2018). https://doi.org/10.1109/TCC.2017.2702586
20. "Docker containers" (2019). https://www.docker.com/resources/what-container/
21. Carbonell, J., Klein, S., Miller, D., Steinbaum, M. , Grassiany, T., Frey, J.: Context-based machine translation. In: Proceedings 7th Conference of the Association for Machine Traslation in the Americas, Cambridge, pp. 19–28, August 2006

22. Callahan, P.B., Kosaraju, R.: A decomposition of multidimensional point sets with applications to k-nearest neighbors and n-body potential fields. J. ACM **42**, 67–90 (1995)
23. Schlick, T.: Molecular Modeling and Simulation, 2nd edn. Springer, Berlin (2010). https://doi.org/10.1007/978-0-387-22464-0
24. Leach, A.R.: Molecular Modeling: Principles and Simulation, 2nd ed. Pearson Education (2009)
25. Fishman, G.S.: A First Course in Monte Carlo. Thomson Brooks/Cole, Belmont, CA (2006)
26. Lindell, M.K., Prater, C.S.: Critical behavioral assumptions in evacuation time estimate analysis for private vehicles: examples from hurricane research and planning. J. Urban Plan. Dev. **133**(1), 18–29 (2007)
27. Murray-Tuite, P., Mahmassani, H.: Transportation network evacuation planning with household activity interactions. Transport. Res. Record: J. Transport. Res. Board **1894**, 150–159 (2004)
28. Raw, R.S., Loveleen, L., Kumar, A., Kadam, A., Singh, N.: Analysis of message propagation for intelligent disaster management through vehicular cloud network. In: Proceddings 2nd ACM International Conference on Information and Communication Technology for Competitive Strategies, (ICTCS'2016), March 2016
29. Satyanarayanan, M., Bahl, P., Caceres, R., Davies, N.: The case for VM-based cloudlets in mobile computing. IEEE Pervasive Comput. **8**(4), 14–23 (2009)
30. Boukerche, A., De Grande, R.E.: Vehicular cloud computing: architectures, applications, and mobility. Comput. Netw. **135**, 171–189 (2018)
31. Wang, H., Chen, Q.-Y., Ni, D.: Logistic modeling of the equilibrium speed-density relationship. Transport. Res. Part A: Policy Pract. **45**(6), 554–566 (2011)

PLMSys: A Cloud Monitoring System Based on Cluster Performance and Container Logs

Yongzhong Sun[1], Kejiang Ye[1(✉)], and Cheng-Zhong Xu[2]

[1] Shenzhen Institutes of Advanced Technology, Chinese Academy of Sciences,
Shenzhen 518055, China
{yz.sun1,kj.ye}@siat.ac.cn
[2] State Key Laboratory of IoT for Smart City, University of Macau,
Macau SAR, China
czxu@um.edu.mo

Abstract. Docker, a kind of lightweight virtualization technology which has the characteristics of resource isolation, rapid deployment and low cost, is widely used in the construction of the cloud services. Docker-based containers has become the important basis of core cloud businesses. In order to manage the large-scale cloud cluster and enforce the quality of cloud services for consumers, monitoring mechanism for the container-based clouds are indispensable. In this paper, we design and implement a cloud monitoring system - PLMSys based on cluster performance and container logs. It provides the following functions: i) Multi-dimensional resources monitoring. PLMSys can monitor the running states of the cluster hosts and containers, including the utilization of CPU, memory, disk and other resources. ii) Container log collection. PLMSys can centrally collect the logs generated by all containers of the cluster. iii) Rule-based exception alerts. PLMSys allows users to define the abnormal state of the hosts and containers by creating rules, and provides multiple alerting methods. iv) Workload analysis and prediction. PLMSys extracts the descriptive statistics from the cluster workloads and uses the time series models to predict the future workloads. v) Data monitoring visualization. The system uses rich visual charts to reflect the running states of cluster hosts and containers. By using PLMSys, users can better manage cluster hosts and containers.

Keywords: Cloud monitoring · Log collection · Rule-based alerts · Workload analysis · Data visualization

1 Introduction

In order to meet the computing demand brought by the rapid growth of business, enterprises need to purchase various hardware equipments and software services. Therefore, the enterprises' IT infrastructure construction is facing the bottleneck

© Springer Nature Switzerland AG 2020
Q. Zhang et al. (Eds.): CLOUD 2020, LNCS 12403, pp. 111–125, 2020.
https://doi.org/10.1007/978-3-030-59635-4_8

caused by the high cost of funds. Cloud computing, a new computing paradigm, has appeared as the excellent solution to the problem. Because the cloud computing has the advantages of high scalability, high reliability, and low cost, it has been supported by many cloud service providers such as Alibaba, Google, and Microsoft. Users can order the computing services provided by cloud platforms on-demand at any time [12]. So that it saves the investment in hardware facilities, software development and system maintenance.

Virtualization is the foundation of cloud computing [18]. Docker, a kind of light-weight virtualization technology which has the characteristics of resource isolation, rapid deployment and near-native performance [16], is widely used in the construction of the cloud services. Due to the dynamic changes of user demand and the huge complexity of cloud tasks, the failures of cluster hosts and containers will cause huge losses for service providers and users. Therefore, designing a monitoring system for cluster hosts and containers is a crucial task. On one side, it is a key tool for controlling and managing hardware and software infrastructures; on the other side, it provides information and Key Performance Indicators (KPIs) for cloud platforms [1].

In this paper, we design and implement a cloud monitoring system - PLMSys based on cluster performance and container logs. The main contributions of this paper are as follows:

- **Multi-dimensional resources monitoring.** PLMSys can monitor the running state of the cluster hosts and containers, including the utilization of CPU, memory, disk and other resources.
- **Container log collection.** PLMSys can centrally collect the logs generated by all containers of the cluster.
- **Rule-based exception alerts.** PLMSys allows users to define the abnormal state of the host and container by creating rules, and provides multiple alerting methods such as e-mail and instant messaging applications.
- **Workload analysis and prediction.** PLMSys extracts the descriptive statistics from the cluster workloads and uses the time series models to predict the future workloads.
- **Data monitoring visualization.** PLMSys uses rich visual charts such as histogram, heat map, and line chart to reflect the running states of cluster hosts and containers.

The rest of the paper is organized as follows: Sect. 2 of this paper introduces existing monitoring tools and related researches. Section 3 describes the system architecture and function modules of PLMSys. Section 4 verifies the effectiveness and usability of PLMSys. Section 5 summarizes the whole paper.

2   Related Work

With the wide application of Docker technology in cloud computing, monitoring schemes for Docker are also emerging. Docker stats [4] is a built-in Docker command that provides monitoring function for the containers. Administrators can obtain the container resource utilization statistics such as CPU, memory, and disk utilization. It is of limited use because it has no visual interface and data storage function. cAdvisor [5] is an open source project developed by Google which provides users the resource utilization of the running containers. Users can browse the charts of performance characteristics from query interface provided by cAdvisor. But it can only monitor one Docker host like Docker stats and keep metrics for 1 min, unless linking to an external database. Prometheus [13] is a free monitoring application which supports pulling performance metrics from the cluster. It provides short-term storage, flexible queries, and real-time monitoring but lacks dashboard and logging solution. DataDog [3] is a commercial monitoring service that aggregates performance metrics and log data from cluster hosts and containers. It can also create alerts and dashboards based on these metrics. However, it has a higher economic cost compared to the above scheme, requiring $15 per host.

Many researchers have proposed specific solutions for cloud monitoring. Wang et al. proposed a self-adaptive monitoring approach for cloud computing systems to improve the anomaly detection accuracy and lower the monitoring overheads [15]. The approach conducts correlation analysis to select key metrics representing others. Principal component analysis is proposed to characterize running status and predict the possibility of faults. Jiménez et al. present CoMA [9], a container monitoring agent, that oversees resource consumption of operating system level virtualization platforms. Liu et al. addressed the monitoring overheads problem by presenting an adaptive cloud monitoring framework [10]. In the proposed framework, a traffic prediction model is designed to estimate short-term traffic overheads based on historical monitored data, which is then used to dynamically change the sampling frequency of low-level sensors. Ji et al. designed a monitoring and alarming platform - CMonitor [8], which is built upon the interfaces provided by Docker containers. It has some new features, such as integrated monitoring services, global topology view, and intelligent alarming mechanism.

On the basis of performance metrics monitoring, PLMSys also supports log collection, workload analysis and other functions. PLMSys complements existing monitoring solutions and help users better manage cluster hosts and containers.

3   System Architecture

The system architecture of PLMSys is shown in Fig. 1. The whole system consists of 6 modules, including metrics acquisition module, container logging module, exception alerting module, workload analysis module, permission verification module and data storage module. The permission verification module adds common security mechanisms to the monitoring platform, including login control, CSRF protection, and role access control. The functions of the other modules are described as follows.

3.1   Metrics Acquisition Module

Cloud cluster contains multiple hosts, and multiple docker containers running on a single host. The metrics acquisition module is installed on each host, which

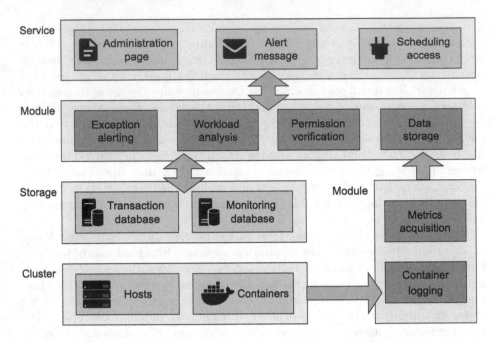

Fig. 1. The system architecture of PLMSys.

is responsible for regularly collecting the performance metrics of each host in the cluster and all containers deployed on it, such as CPU and memory utilization, disk and network I/O speed, etc. The performance metrics will be sent to the data storage module through the message queuing mechanism, and then saved to the monitoring database. The specific performance metrics collected by PLMSys are shown in the Table 1.

Table 1. The specific performance metrics

Source	Category	Metrics
Host	CPU	utilization_guest/idle/iowait/irq/nice/softirq/steal/system/user
	Disk	free, inodes_free/total/used, total, used, used_percent
	Disk I/O	io_time, read_bytes/time, reads, write_bytes/time, writes
	Memory	active, available, buffered, cached, dirty, free, total, used
	Network	Bytes_sent/recv, packets_sent/recv, err_in/out, drop_in
	Swap	free, in, out, total, used, used_percent
	System	load1, load5, load15, n_users, n_cpus, uptime.
Container	CPU	utilization_in_kernelmode/in_usermode/system/total/percent
	Memory	cache, failcnt, pgpgout, rss, unevictable, utilization, writeback
	Blkio	io_service_bytes_recursive_async/read/sync/total/write
	Network	rx/tx_bytes/dropped/errors/packets
	Status	exitcode, finished_at, oomkilled, pid, started_at, uptime_ns

3.2   Container Logging Module

Docker supports logging function to record various events which occur when containers arc running. These container logs are widely used in system anomaly detection [6] and task dynamic migration [17], effectively reducing the failure time of cloud services. Because the container logs are stored on the disk of each host, it is not convenient for users to browse and manage. Therefore, the container logging module implements the structuralization for the container logs, and then sends them to the monitoring database through the message queuing mechanism for centralized preservation. The structured log contains the following fields:

- Container_id. The full 64-character container ID.
- Container_name. The container name at the time it was started.
- Source. stdout or stderr.
- Log. The container log.
- Host. The hostname of the host which the container is deployed on.
- Time. The timestamp at which the container event occurs.

3.3   Exception Alerting Module

According to the sampling period set by the users, this module regularly takes performance metrics from the monitoring database for anomaly detection. The users can add alert rules for hosts and containers through this module, and set security thresholds for specific performance metrics. If the performance metrics of the hosts or containers hit the alert rules in the sampling period, the module will send the alert message to the users automatically. The configuration items of alert rules are as follows:

- Rule name. Customize the descriptive name of the rule.
- Emergency degree. General or urgent.
- Hitting condition. Set the safety threshold of performance metrics.
- Alert methods. Set the notification mode of alert event when the rule hits.
- Statistical rules. Set a time range and a count. Within this time range, the alert is triggered when the number of hits to an associated rule exceeds the count.

This module provides multiple alerting methods, such as email and IM applications which surpport webhook interface. Due to the limited sending frequency of email and IM applications, this module adopts different warning message sending strategies according to the emergency degree of alert rules: the messages marked as "urgent" will be sent immediately; the messages marked as "generic" are consolidated by this module every five minutes and sent as summaries.

3.4   Workload Analysis Module

Due to the miscellaneous performance metrics obtained from the cluster hosts and containers, it is necessary to summarize them to extract the relevant descriptive statistics. The descriptive statistics include statistical indicators such as mean, range and standard deviation, which is convenient for analyzing the central tendency and dispersion degree of the cluster overall workload. In addition to the descriptive statistics, this module also draws various charts to reflect the overall operation of the cluster, providing intuitive reference for the users.

The workloads of cluster hosts and containers have a significant impact on QoS and resource allocation in cloud environment. On one hand, a sudden or continuous increase in workload can lead to QoS degradation or even application failure; On the other hand, reduced workload means that the allocated computing resources are not fully utilized. Therefore, how to accurately predict the workload of hosts and containers has become a hot topic for cluster administrators. Based on accurate workload prediction, task scheduling and load balancing can be implemented more effectively to ensure quality of services and improve resource utilization. This module provides users with workload predictions for servers and containers through the time series model - Prophet [14].

Through the query interface provided by this module, the scheduling system can obtain statistics data and predictions information of the cluster workloads.

3.5   Data Transfer and Storage Design

In order to satisfy the demand of users to monitor the whole cluster, the performance metrics and container logs of each host need to be processed centrally. In addition, with the increasing number of Docker container instances, the cluster generates a large amount of monitoring data at any time. In order to reduce the flow pressure caused by the large amount of monitoring data, PLMSys adopts the message queuing mechanism for data transfer. Message queue can ensure the reliability and efficiency of data transfer with the function of data caching and flow smoothing.

The message queue is composed of message producer, message consumer and message broker. The transfer architecture of PLMSys based on message queue is shown in the Fig. 2.

- Producer. Metrics acquisition module and Container logging module are deployed as producers for each host in the cluster. The producer periodically creates and pushes messages to the broker based on the performance metrics and container logs.
- Broker. When the producer pushes the messages to the broker, the exchange will route the messages to the corresponding queue. When the broker receives the request from the consumer, it will fetch the messages from the corresponding queue and send them to the consumer in accordance with the FIFO rule.

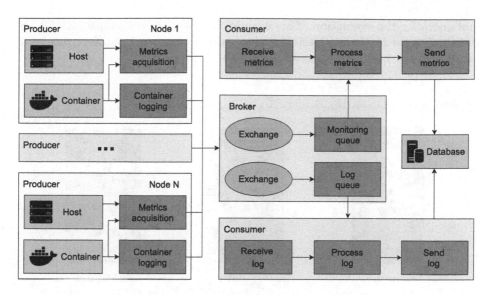

Fig. 2. The data transfer architecture of PLMSys.

– Consumer. The consumer's task flow includes receiving, processing and sending messages. The messages will be processed by data filtering and format encapsulation after they are received by the consumer from the broker. Finally the messages will be sent to the database for storage.

Performance metrics and container logs are typical time series data, which have the characteristics of fast frequency, high correlation with time and large amount of information. Time series data is not characterized by many relationships, it is usually unchangeable, and the same data is often repeated over time in the sampling period. That makes it very inefficient for relational databases to process them. Therefore, PLMSys adopts temporal database OpenTSDB as monitoring database to store performance metrics and container logs, and MySQL as transaction database to store user information and platform settings.

4   Experimental Evaluation

The objective of the evaluate is to assess the validity of the preformance metrics gathered by PLMSys, the throughputs of data transmission, the correctness of the exception alerting, and the accuracy of the prediction models.

4.1   Validity of the Preformance Metrics

The validity of the preformance metrics means that for the metrics reported by PLMSys, whether the measured values reflect the real values. In consideration of the numerous performance metrics, we choose the CPU utilization from various containers for the evaluation. This evaluation is based on Ubuntu 18.04 LTS and the Docker platform v1.40. The physical host runs on Intel Xeon E5-2630 v3 processor × 2 with 16 cores 32 threads totally.

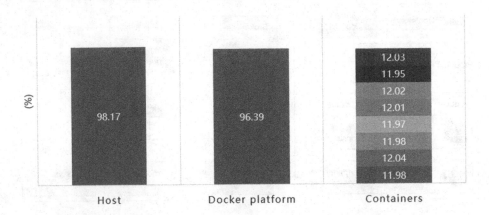

Fig. 3. Each container runs the same stress-ng process, generating the same CPU workload across all 8 containers. PLMSys reports the total CPU utilization of the 8 containers and the value of the Docker platform. Glances reports the value for the host.

Table 2. CPU utilization and standard deviations (SD) of 8 containers running the same stress-ng process

Host(%)		Docker platform(%)		Containers(%)		
User CPU	SD User CPU	Total CPU	SD Total CPU	Name	Total CPU	SD Total CPU
98.17	3.36	96.39	1.81	A	11.98	0.21
				B	12.04	0.26
				C	11.98	0.18
				D	11.97	0.23
				E	12.01	0.17
				F	12.02	0.22
				G	11.95	0.21
				H	12.03	0.19

We run stress-ng [2] on the Docker platform through containerization to generate the workloads. In the absence of workloads, the idle CPU utilization of the host is maintained at around 99%. And we record the CPU utilization of the host using system monitoring tool Glances [7]. To assess the validity of the CPU utilization from Docker platform reported by PLMSys, we compare it with the host-specific CPU metrics collected by Glances in two scenarios. For each scenario, we repeated the experiment 6 times, each time for 1 h.

In Scenario 1, 8 containers execute the same stress-ng process to generate workload on the CPU, with each process occupying 4 logical CPU cores. PLMSys reports the total CPU utilization for the containers and for the Docker platform and Glances reports the user CPU utilization for the host. According to the Completely Fair Scheduler (CFS) [11] of Linux kernel, the expected outcome is the same CPU utilization observed from each container. The CPU utilization statistics are shown in Table 2 and Fig. 3, each container is granted an average of around 12% of the CPU. And the total CPU utilization of each container adds up to 95.98%, which is very close to the docker platform CPU utilization and the user CPU utilization.

Table 3. CPU utilization and standard deviations (SD) of 4 containers running the different stress-ng process

Time period	Host(%)		Docker platform(%)		Containers(%)		
	User CPU	SD User CPU	Total CPU	SD Total CPU	Name	Total CPU	SD Total CPU
0–10 min	26.2	3.14	25.21	1.64	A	25.07	0.32
10–20 min	77.34	2.77	75.12	2.12	A	25.04	0.21
					B	49.97	0.19
20–30 min	52.27	3.34	51.13	1.17	B	50.01	0.22
30–40 min	99.92	0.58	99.67	0.77	C	99.05	0.23
40–50 min	64.92	2.83	64.01	2.03	D	62.60	0.18
50–60 min	90.34	4.05	87.12	1.83	A	24.99	0.26
					D	62.61	0.23

In Scenario 2, 4 containers execute the difference stress-ng process to generate workload on the CPU in 6 time periods, with each process occupying 4, 6, 20 or 32 logical CPU cores. As shown in Table 3, the aggregation of all containers' total CPU utilization in each time period is very consistent with the docker platform CPU utilization and the user CPU utilization. Figure 4 shows that the metrics collected by PLMSys matches the dynamic changes of the container CPU utilization for each time period.

4.2 The Correctness of the Exception Alerting

In order to verify the correctness of the exception alerting, we prepare a series of test cases. Test metrics include CPU utilization, network traffic, container running status, as shown in the Table 4. For each test case, we build two groups of 10 datasets each. One group contains exception measures for the corresponding metrics, while the other does not. In addition, we set the emergency degree of all test cases as "urgent" to facilitate the detection of the alert sending time.

The test result is shown in Table 5. It confirms that the monitoring platform identifies exceptions in the workload correctly, and notifies users in time.

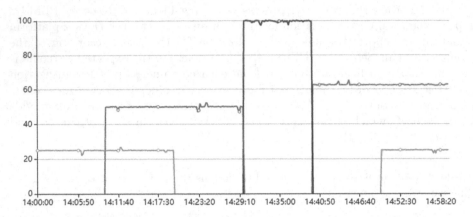

Fig. 4. The CPU utilization of 4 containers in 6 time periods

Table 4. The test cases for the exception alerting

Case	Hitting condition	Statistical rule
A	No data returned by the metrics acquisition module	4 hits / 1min
B	The container is in a state other than "Running"	Not set
C	Total CPU utilization is greater than 70%	100 hits / 30 min
D	Total memory utilization is greater than 80%	100 hits / 30 min
E	The remaining disk space is less than 20 GB	Not set
F	Rx_dropped value exceeds 2000	Not set

One of the test datasets for case D contains a large number of data points that exceed the threshold. Figure 5 is the monitoring view attached to the alert message generated by case D based on the test dataset. From this figure, we can see that the monitoring platform accurately marks all outliers.

4.3   The Throughputs of Data Transmission

When the sampling cycle is reached, the metrics acquisition module deployed on each host will generate a large amount of monitoring data, which will put great pressure on the processing and storage of these data. Therefore, we introduces the message queuing mechanism for the monitoring platform to smooth the workload during the peak data transmission period. To verify the throughputs of the message queue, we prepare three hosts with Intel Xeon E5-2630 v3 processor and 64 GB memory. The three hosts deploy producer client, broker and consumer client respectively. We keep the consumer client inactive and start the producer client to send messages to the borker. After the messages in the queue accumulate to a certain size, we stop the producer client and start the consumer client to receive the messages.

Table 5. The test result for the exception alerting

Case	Number of positives	Number of false/missing positives	Sending time
A	10	0/0	7.52 s
B	10	0/0	9.45 s
C	10	0/0	7.78 s
D	10	0/0	8.93 s
E	10	0/0	8.41 s
F	10	0/0	10.62 s

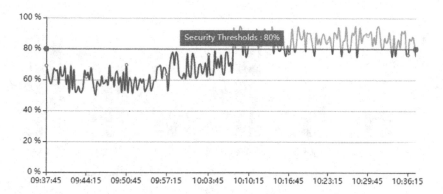

Fig. 5. The monitoring view attached to the alert message generated by case D

We repeat the test three times and the result is shown in the Table 6 and Fig. 6. The test result shows that with the increase of the data size of a single message, the throughput increases accordingly, and the data transmission speed is kept around 12000 messages / s. The performance of message queue can meet the needs of data transmission.

4.4   The Accuracy of the Prediction Models

The monitoring platform provides users with workload prediction for hosts and containers through the time series models Prophet. Prophet provides the following configuration options:

– Cap. Prophet allows users to make prediction using a logistic growth model or a linear model. The logistic growth model needs to specify the carrying capacity named cap. Cap is the upper bound of the predicted value.
– Changepoint. Time series have abrupt changes in their trajectories frequently. Prophet provides two ways to detect the changepoints: one is manually specified; The other is selected automatically. Option changepoint_range sets the detection range of the change point on the time series. Option changepoint_prior_scale adjusts flexibility of the trend changes.

Table 6. The test result for the throughputs of data transmission

	Message size	Expt. 1 (MB/s)	Expt. 2 (MB/s)	Expt. 3 (MB/s)	average (MB/s)
Producer	1 KB	12.97	13.16	13.64	13.26
	2 KB	25.14	24.77	25.59	25.17
	4 KB	45.16	47.11	44.42	45.56
Consumer	1 KB	11.23	10.54	13.22	11.66
	2 KB	23.85	24.69	25.01	24.52
	4 KB	44.95	44.73	44.99	44.89

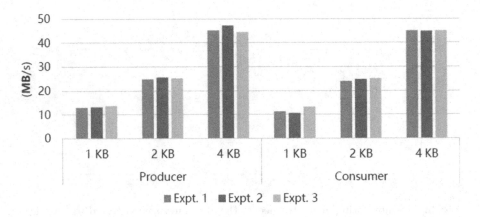

Fig. 6. The comparison of the throughputs between the producer and the consumer

We collect the workload of 5 hosts for 12 h as the test dataset. We adopt sliding window mechanism to predict the workload. The length of the window is set to 8, that is, the last 8 pieces of historical data are used to predict the load values of machines in the next period. When a sampling period is reached, the predicted values of machine load will be compared with the actual values to detect the prediction effect, and then the sliding window will be moved to the next sampling period to realize the rolling prediction.

We use the logistic growth model of Prophet for prediction. Option cap is 100%, changepoint_range is 100%, change_point_prior_scale is 0.2, and the changepoints is detected by Prophet automatically.

Figure 7 and Fig. 8 shows the actual workload and the predicted workload of the specified host in the sampling period. The two figures show that the prediction which obtained by Prophet can fit the fluctuation of the host workload very well.

We use Success Rate and Root Mean Square Error (RMSE) to evaluate the prediction accuracy. The Success Rate is the ratio of the number of successful predictions to the total number of predictions. We define the prediction as a success, if the difference between the predicted load value and the actual load value is within $[-6\%, 6\%]$. In general, a higher Success Rate and lower RMSE

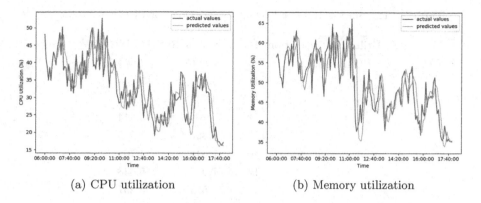

(a) CPU utilization   (b) Memory utilization

Fig. 7. The comparison of the actual and the predicted workload of Host A

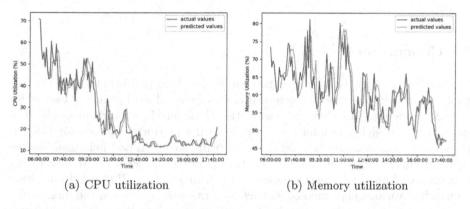

(a) CPU utilization   (b) Memory utilization

Fig. 8. The comparison of the actual and the predicted workload of Host B

means a better prediction. Within the sampling cycle, the Success Rate and RMSE of load prediction for 5 hosts are shown in Table 7. The success rate is maintained above 70%, and RMSE less than 6. The result shows that Prophet model has enough accuracy to predict the workload.

Table 7. The Success Rate and RMSE of workload prediction for 5 hosts

Utilization prediction	Host	Success Rate	RMSE
CPU utilization	A	77.206%	4.864
	B	73.529%	5.234
	C	76.744%	4.985
	D	77.206%	5.044
	E	81.395%	4.515
Memory utilization	A	81.618%	4.764
	B	77.941%	5.088
	C	75.581%	5.257
	D	76.471%	4.662
	E	73.256%	4.981

5   Conclusion

Docker is widely used in the construction of the cloud platform so that Docker-based containers become the technical basis of core cloud businesses except for virtual machines. Therefore, to ensure the cloud platform work properly, it is necessary to design and implement a monitoring platform software for Docker. In order to complement the existing monitoring solutions and help users better manage cluster hosts and containers, this paper proposes a cloud monitoring system based on cluster performance and container logs - PLMSys. In addition to monitor various performance metrics of containers and hosts, the monitoring system integrates various modules to achieve container log collection, cluster workload analysis and other functions. In the experiment, we evaluate the validity of the preformance metrics gathered by PLMSys, the throughputs of data transmission, the correctness of the exception alerting, and the accuracy of the workload prediction. The evaluation demonstrates the feasibility of PLMSys as a cloud monitoring solution.

Acknowledgment. This work is supported by Key-Area Research and Development Program of Guangdong Province (NO.2020B010164003), National Natural Science Foundation of China (No. 61702492), Science and Technology Development Fund of Macao S.A.R (FDCT) under number 0015/2019/AKP, Shenzhen Basic Research Program (No. JCYJ20170818153016513), Shenzhen Discipline Construction Project for Urban Computing and Data Intelligence, and Youth Innovation Promotion Association CAS.

References

1. Aceto, G., Botta, A., De Donato, W., Pescapè, A.: Cloud monitoring: a survey. Comput. Netw. **57**(9), 2093–2115 (2013)
2. ColinIanKing: Stress-ng. https://kernel.ubuntu.com/~cking/stress-ng/

3. Datadog: Datadog. https://www.datadoghq.com/
4. Docker: docker stats. https://docs.docker.com/engine/reference/commandline/stats/
5. Google: cadvisor. https://github.com/google/cadvisor
6. He, S., Zhu, J., He, P., Lyu, M.R.: Experience report: system log analysis for anomaly detection. In: 2016 IEEE 27th International Symposium on Software Reliability Engineering (ISSRE), pp. 207–218. IEEE (2016)
7. Hennion, N.: Glances. https://nicolargo.github.io/glances/
8. Ji, S., Ye, K., Xu, C.-Z.: CMonitor: a monitoring and alarming platform for container-based clouds. In: Da Silva, D., Wang, Q., Zhang, L.-J. (eds.) CLOUD 2019. LNCS, vol. 11513, pp. 324–339. Springer, Cham (2019). https://doi.org/10.1007/978-3-030-23502-4_23
9. Jiménez, L.L., Simón, M.G., Schelén, O., Kristiansson, J., Synnes, K., Åhlund, C.: Coma: Resource monitoring of docker containers. In: CLOSER, pp. 145–154 (2015)
10. Liu, D., Liu, Z.: An adaptive cloud monitoring framework based on sampling frequency adjusting. Int. J. e-Collaboration (IJeC) 16(2), 12–26 (2020)
11. Molnar, I.: Cfs scheduler. https://www.kernel.org/doc/html/latest/scheduler/sched-design-CFS.html
12. Patidar, S., Rane, D., Jain, P.: A survey paper on cloud computing. In: 2012 Second International Conference on Advanced Computing & Communication Technologies, pp. 394–398. IEEE (2012)
13. Prometheus.io: Prometheus. https://github.com/prometheus
14. Taylor, S.J., Benjamin, L.: Forecasting at scale. Am. Stat. (2018)
15. Wang, T., Xu, J., Zhang, W., Gu, Z., Zhong, H.: Self-adaptive cloud monitoring with online anomaly detection. Fut. Generation Comput. Syst. 80, 89–101 (2018)
16. Xavier, M.G., Neves, M.V., Rossi, F.D., Ferreto, T.C., Lange, T., De Rose, C.A.: Performance evaluation of container-based virtualization for high performance computing environments. In: 2013 21st Euromicro International Conference on Parallel, Distributed, and Network-Based Processing, pp. 233–240. IEEE (2013)
17. Yu, C., Huan, F.: Live migration of docker containers through logging and replay. In: 2015 3rd International Conference on Mechatronics and Industrial Informatics (ICMII 2015). Atlantis Press (2015)
18. Zhang, Q., Cheng, L., Boutaba, R.: Cloud computing: state-of-the-art and research challenges. J. Internet Serv. Appl. 1(1), 7–18 (2010). https://doi.org/10.1007/s13174-010-0007-6

A Network Intrusion Detection Approach Based on Asymmetric Convolutional Autoencoder

Shujian Ji[1,2], Kejiang Ye[1(✉)], and Cheng-Zhong Xu[3]

[1] Shenzhen Institutes of Advanced Technology, Chinese Academy of Sciences, Shenzhen 518055, China
{sj.ji,kj.ye}@siat.ac.cn
[2] University of Chinese Academy of Sciences, Beijing 100049, China
[3] State Key Laboratory of IoT for Smart City, University of Macau, Macau SAR, China
czxu@um.edu.mo

Abstract. Network intrusion detection is an important way to protect cyberspace security. However, it still faces many challenges. The network traffic and intrusion behaviors are always very complex and changeable. Deep learning is a potential method for network intrusion detection. In this paper, we first propose an asymmetric convolutional autoencoder (ACAE) for feature learning. Then, we propose a network intrusion detection model by combining asymmetric convolutional autoencoder and random forest. This approach can well combine the advantages of deep learning and shallow learning. Our proposed approach is evaluated on KDD99 and NSL-KDD dataset, and is also compared with other intrusion detection approaches. Our model can effectively improve the classification accuracy of network abnormal traffic. Furthermore, it has strong robustness and scalability.

Keywords: Deep learning · Anomaly detection · Asymmetric convolutional autoencoder · Random forest

1 Introduction

With the rapid development of computer network and information technology, people are very convenient to get all kinds of information they need from the Internet. According to Symantec's Internet security threat report [1], cyber attacks increased by 25% in 2018 compared with 2017, with an average of more than 4800 different websites being attacked every month around the world. The Internet has brought convenience to people's daily work and life, but at the same time it has also caused a variety of security risks.

In order to protect network security, network intrusion detection system (NIDS) is proposed and becomes an active security defense method. However,

© Springer Nature Switzerland AG 2020
Q. Zhang et al. (Eds.): CLOUD 2020, LNCS 12403, pp. 126–140, 2020.
https://doi.org/10.1007/978-3-030-59635-4_9

there are still many challenges to protect cyberspace security in the modern network environment. First, the data of Internet network traffic is too large and keeps changing. It is difficult to detect these attacks from large amount of network traffic data in a timely and efficient manner. Second, there are many types of network intrusion. It is very challenging to detect all those intrusions with a high accuracy.

In recent years, many shallow machine learning algorithms such as k-nearest neighbor (KNN) [20], support vector machine (SVM) [9], naive bayes (NB) [25] are widely used in intrusion detection, and show good performance. The shallow learning algorithm needs more complex data feature engineering, and the parameters of the algorithm training process need to be adjusted. With the rapid development of modern network technology, many protocols have been added to network traffic, leading to poor scalability of traditional shallow machine learning algorithms in intrusion detection. However, in the high-dimensional feature space, the shallow learning algorithm has a powerful classification ability for some non-linear features and can also learn some small samples of data. The advantage of deep network is to process large samples and high-dimensional data, and it has a good ability for learning abstract features of data and a strong generalization ability. Recently, some researchers have proved that hierarchical deep learning algorithms can learn more essential features from network data than shallow learning classifiers [15].

In this paper, we propose a network anomaly intrusion detection method based on asymmetric convolutional autoencoder (ACAE) and random forest (RF) classification algorithm. The ACAE is used as a feature extractor which can learn the better features of data through unsupervised learning, and the RF algorithm can decide on the newly generated data features and classify them by mapping on the multi-dimensional space. The approach can combine the advantages of deep learning and shallow learning, and can effectively analyze and identify network data. We perform experiments by using the classic KDD99 [2] and NSL-KDD [3] dataset, which can effectively improve the accuracy and detection efficiency of abnormal intrusion detection.

The main contributions of this paper are as follows:

- We propose a novel unsupervised learning ACAE method, which is different from traditional autoencoder technology. It solves the shortcomings of convolutional neural network and autoencoder. Compared with deep belief network (DBN) and stacked nonsymmetric deep autoencoder (S-NDAE), it can improve the classification performance.
- We combine ACAE and RF classification algorithm in the final anomaly detection model. The combination of deep learning and shallow learning technology can improve the classification performance of anomaly detection model and reduce detection overheads.
- Our proposed asymmetric convolutional autoencoder (ACAE) can be used as a feature extractor, which can well adapt to the input of high-dimensional features and improve the classification performance of small samples of data.

The rest of the paper is organized as follows. Section 2 presents the related work in the intrusion detection field. Section 3 introduces the background of autoencoder. Section 4 describes our proposed intrusion detection model. Section 5 discusses the findings from evaluation on different datasets. Finally, Sect. 5.3 concludes the paper.

2   Related Work

Distributed intrusion detection and intelligent intrusion detection are the two key technologies in the field of intrusion detection.

Tsai *et al.* [28] introduced the development of intelligent intrusion detection methods from 1990s to 2009. In the 1990s, intrusion detection methods adopted some shallow perceptron models, including SVM, KNN, decision tree, bayes network and hidden markov. SVM adopted at the beginning of this century was also a shallow perceptron model, which had a better classification effect in processing small sample size and low-dimensional datasets.

Deep learning is a kind of machine learning method, which effectively overcomes the training difficulties of multi-layer neural networks [14]. Deep learning has made progress in image detection and natural language processing [7]. The advantage of deep network is to deal with large amount of data.

Zhao *et al.* [32] proposed a new study on deep learning applications in the literature. They compared traditional machine learning methods with four common deep learning methods such as autoencoder (AE), restricted boltzmann machines (RBM), convolutional neural networks (CNN), and recurrent neural networks (RNN). Their research concluded that deep learning methods are better than traditional machine learning methods.

Salama *et al.* [26] proposed an intrusion detection method which combines DBN and SVM. Their proposed method was tested on NSL-KDD [3] dataset, using deep belief network to reduce the dimension of dataset, and using support vector machine to classify attack categories of intrusion data into four categories. The experimental results showed that the overall accuracy of the proposed method was relatively high.

Niyazi *et al.* [16] proposed a detection method based on deep learning for network intrusion detection system. They used self-taught learning (STL) technology and experimented with NSL-KDD. In the experiment, the performance of the proposed method, such as accuracy, precision, recall and so on, was more effective than some current work.

KIM *et al.* [19] used deep neural network to improve the detection accuracy of abnormal traffic in intrusion detection system. The depth neural network proposed by the author used 100 hidden neurons and used adam algorithm to optimize the depth model. The method was tested on KDD99 data set and 99% accuracy was achieved. At the same time, the author also pointed out that recurrent neural network (RNN) and long short-term memory (LSTM) models were the defensive needs of future networks.

Yin *et al.* [30] used the recurrent neural network intrusion detection system (RNN IDS), which improved the accuracy of intrusion detection, and its performance was superior to the traditional machine learning two-classification and multi-classification methods, which provided a new research method for network intrusion detection.

Cui *et al.* [12] compared convolution neural network and recursive neural network in Intrusion detection, in order to provide basic guidance for intrusion detection system. The results showed that CNN had better recognition ability in binary classification tasks, and RNN could detect complex attacks better in multi-classification tasks.

Cordero *et al.* [11] used unsupervised method to utilize the network flow features characterized by entropy, and combined with the extended region of the original replicator neural network (RNN) to learn the normality model. By testing the actual network data, their proposed method could accurately detect different categories of network attacks.

Shone *et al.* [27] proposed a deep learning method for anomaly detection. A nonsymmetric stacked autoencoder was used to learn the features of the data, and random forest was used to classify the data. In addition, KDD99 and NSL-KDD datasets were used to carry out experiments. Five and thirteen classifications of the model were tested respectively. The authors showed that the combination of deep neural network and shallow classifier was more effective.

Our group has also proposed several methods for network anomaly/intrusion detection [17,21,22,24], and also developed several tools for fault/anomaly/intrusion detection [18,23,29].

3   Background

3.1   Autoencoder

Autoencoder is one of the deep learning algorithms. Different from traditional linear dimensionality reduction methods such as PCA, autoencoder overcomes these limitations with inherent nonlinear neural network structure. It can learn the essential characteristics of data from many unlabeled original data. Since Rumelhart proposed autoencoder in 1986, many improved algorithms have shown excellent performance in classification tasks [4,13]. As shown in the Fig. 1, the autoencoder consists mainly of an encoder and a decoder that generates the reconstruction. Encoder compresses the input data into potential spatial representation using the encoding function $h = f(x)$, and decoder reconstructs the compressed spatial representation using the decoding function $r = g(h)$. Autoencoder automatically selects the important features for learning, so it is suitable for feature learning of data.

3.2   Convolutional Autoencoder

Convolutional autoencoder has been applied in image recognition [8] and network intrusion detection [31]. Convolutional autoencoder is proposed on the basis of

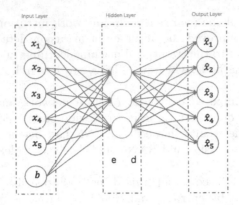

Fig. 1. Autoencoder

autoencoder. It adds convolution operation on the basis of autoencoder. Convolutional autoencoder combines the advantages of convolutional neural network and autoencoder, and solves the sensitivity of convolutional neural network to weight and the dependence of large-scale data with labels. Autoencoder and deep neural networks have some drawbacks, and there must be a large number of training parameters between layer and adjacent layer. The convolution kernel in the convolutional neural network can effectively extract the optimal features in the data, construct the model structure using deep training, and convert high-dimensional data into low-dimensional data. Convolutional autoencoder implements depth model by using multiple hidden layers. Each hidden layer added to the model can produce more complex features, which can reduce the cost of calculation and the amount of training data needed. The structure of convolutional autoencoder is shown in Fig. 2. The training method of convolutional autoencoder is similar to the classic autoencoder.

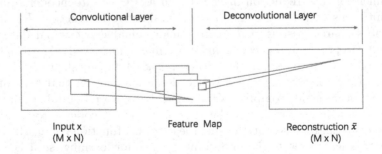

Fig. 2. Structure of convolutional autoencoder

4   Methodology

In this section, we first introduce our deep learning approach in detail. Finally, we present our model based on the proposed approach for network intrusion detection.

4.1   Asymmetric Convolutional Autoencoder

The goal of modern network intrusion detection systems is to improve the accuracy of intrusion classification and improve detection efficiency. Hinton [14] uses a multi-layer stacked deep autoencoder to reduce the dimensionality of the data, and the data generates more abstract features under the pre-trained deep autoencoder model. Deep autoencoders work better for data dimensionality reducing than PCA. The deep autoencoder is a multi-layers deep neural network that includes many encoders that can learn more advanced abstract features, and many decoders that reconstruct data. A deep autoencoder can produce less reconstruction error than a shallow autoencoder, but has the disadvantage of generating a large number of training parameters.

Compared with the deep symmetric autoencoder with encoders and decoders, our proposed asymmetric convolutional autoencoder just uses the encoder phase and is an asymmetric multi-layer deep network model. The reason we propose asymmetric convolutional autoencoder is that ACAE combines the advantages of convolutional neural networks and deep autoencoders. ACAE's convolution operation has two advantages: local perception and parameter sharing. Local perception allows the network model structure to perceive local data, and then combines these local information at a higher level to obtain all the characterization information of the data. The weight parameter sharing makes the network structure similar to the biological neural network, which reduces the complexity of the model and reduces the number of weights. It avoids the problem of training parameters among neurons in each layer of deep autoencoder, and effectively improves the efficiency of data feature extraction.

The input vector of ACAE is assumed to be $x \in R^l$, and the coding mapping after the hidden layer learns the input layer is $x_i \in R^l$. The encoding function can be determined as (1). Here, l denotes the dimension of vector.

$$h_i = \sigma(w_i h_i + b_i), i = 1, 2..., n \tag{1}$$

The proposed ACAE does not retain the decoder. After the conversion of the n-layer hidden layer and the sigmoid activation function, the output data can be shown in (2)

$$h_n = \sigma(w_n h_{n-i} + b_n) \tag{2}$$

The proposed model uses backpropagation for error adjustment during unsupervised training. Finally, the reconstruction error generated by ACAE can be shown in (3).

$$E(\theta) = \frac{1}{2m} \sum_{i=1}^{m} (x_i - y_i)^2 \tag{3}$$

4.2   Intrusion Detection Model Based on ACAE-RF

In Sect. 4.1, we introduce the reason and motivation for designing asymmetric convolutional autoencoder. However, compared with shallow classification, the accuracy of single asymmetric convolution automatic encoder has not been greatly improved. Softmax classifier is less effective than other machine learning classification models. Therefore, we combine the deep learning model with the shallow classification learning model to improve the accuracy of classification detection.

We use the ACAE as a layered feature extractor, which can be used to scale and adapt to high dimensional data. We use multiple hidden layers to construct the depth structure of ACAE, and the model can learn the abstract features of each layer as the number of layers increases. In addition, the ACAE model uses an unsupervised way to learn the characteristics of the data. This has great advantages for a large number of unmarked network traffic data, and the network anomaly detection model has strong adaptability to unknown intrusion events. RF is one of the popular ensemble learning algorithms. RF is a classifier containing multiple decision trees, and the final output is determined by the classification results of all decision trees. The advantage of a RF is that it can process high-dimensional data and can be processed in parallel to improve efficiency of classification, with good anti-interference ability and is not easy to over-fitting. Some research have proved that RF is one of the best algorithms for network anomaly detection [6,10]. We use the combination of ACAE and RF as our final anomaly detection model.

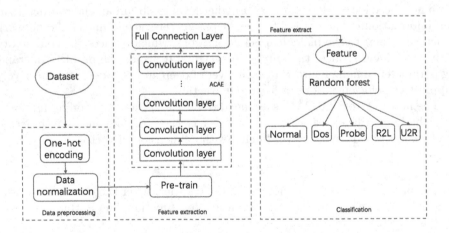

Fig. 3. Structure of intrusion model based on ACAE-RF

As shown in the Fig. 3, ACAE is used to extract features from preprocessed data, and RF is used to classify network traffic data into normal and abnormal categories. There are some unavoidable problems in current traffic data and intrusion models, such as the scarcity of data with labels and the problem of vanishing gradient in deep neural networks. Therefore, the problem can be avoided by using unsupervised ACAE.

5 Experimental Results and Analysis

In this section, we will conduct an experimental evaluation of our proposed ACAE-RF model. Similar to other anomaly detection work, we use the KDD99 and NSL-KDD dataset for evaluations. Next we will introduce the performance metrics and experimental data we evaluated.

5.1 Performance Metrics

In this section, we will introduce the defined metrics we have evaluated below:

- True Positive (TP) - Intrusion data is correctly classified as an intrusion.
- False Positive (FP) - Normal data is incorrectly classified as an intrusion.
- True Negative (TN) - Normal data is correctly classified as normal.
- False Negative (FN) - Intrusion data is incorrectly classified as normal.

- Accuracy: It is the ratio of the number of correctly classified samples by the classifier to the total number of samples, which is calculated as follows.

$$Accuarcy = \frac{TP + TN}{TP + TN + FP + FN} \tag{4}$$

- Recall: It measures how many of the positive samples are predicted correctly. We can understand it as sensitivity.

$$Recall = \frac{TP}{TP + FN} \tag{5}$$

- Precision: It measures the number of correct classified samples penalised by the number of incorrect classified samples.

$$Precision = \frac{TP}{TP + FP} \tag{6}$$

- $F_1 - score$: This metric is a weighted harmonic mean of precision and recall, which is often used to evaluate the quality of a classification model.

$$F_1 - score = 2 * \frac{Precision * Recall}{Precision + Recall} \tag{7}$$

- False Alarm: This metric the proportion of the number of false classification detected by the classifier.

$$FalseAlarm = \frac{FP}{FP + TN} \tag{8}$$

5.2 Dataset

KDD99 dataset is a well-recognized test dataset in the field of network intrusion detection, which has made great contributions to the research of network intrusion detection. This dataset has five categories: Nomal, Dos, R2L, U2R, Probe. The total number of attack categories is 39. Each category contains data for different labels. NSL-KDD dataset solves the inherent problems existing in KDD99 dataset and is an improvement of KDD99 dataset. Each data in KDD99 and NSL-KDD dataset consists of 41 features, which contain many non-numeric data and useless features.

We first preprocess the dataset and replace it with features that can be accepted by the model. We use numerical features and normalized processing. The numerical feature is the conversion of non-numeric features in the dataset to numerical features during the pre-processing phase. We use one-hot coding method to map the corresponding values. There are some discrete or continuous values in the KDD99 and NSL-KDD dataset. We use a normalized method to convert the features into the range of [0,1] because ACAE can only be applied to the 2D shape data. For dimensional data $x = (x_1, x_2, x_3, ..., x_d)$, We construct data into 2D data through zero-padding operations. Finally, we can get the 8×8 size matrix for each 1D vector. Table 1 show the parameters of ACAE network structure we designed. The learning rate of each layer is 0.001 and the stride is 1.

Table 1. The structure of ACAE

Layer	Type	Filter	Output Size
L1	Convolution	3×3	$8 \times 8 \times 64$
L2	MaxPooling	3×3	$4 \times 4 \times 64$
L3	Convolution	3×3	$4 \times 4 \times 32$
L4	MaxPooling	3×3	$2 \times 2 \times 32$
L5	UpSampling	3×3	$4 \times 4 \times 32$
L6	Convolution	3×3	$4 \times 4 \times 32$
L7	MaxPooling	3×3	$2 \times 2 \times 32$

5.3 Evaluation

Model Structure. First, we study the influence of the layers of analytical models on the accuracy of model detection. In this part of the experiment, we use the accuracy and false alarm to evaluate detection. We have designed six different hidden layers of asymmetric convolutional autoencoder, which are 4, 5, 6, 7, 8 and 9 layers respectively. Because the number of convolution layers is increasing, the accuracy and false alarm of the final anomaly detection model will be affected to some extent.

As shown in the Fig. 4(a), as the number of hidden layers increases, the accuracy increases and the false alarm decreases. The main reason is that with the increase of the number of hidden layers, the non-linear fitting ability of the model becomes stronger, so the detection accuracy will increase. We find that the detection results are optimal in the 7-layer network structure, with accuracy reaches 98.39% and false alarm reaches 2.87%. When the number of model layers is more than 9 layers, the accuracy will decrease and the false alarm will increase slightly. This also shows that the depth of the neural network is not as deep as possible. If the number of layers is too large, the accuracy will be reduced and the parameter adjustment will be more complicated.

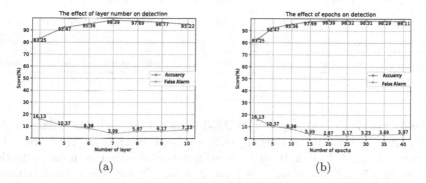

Fig. 4. The effect of model structure and training epochs on accuracy and false alarm

The training epochs of the model determines whether the model can learn the features in the data. We also use experiments to constantly adjust the appropriate parameters to find the best number of epoch. The effect of the epoch on accuracy and false alarm can be seen in the Fig. 4(b). When the epoch is within 10 rounds, the false alarm is still high and the accuracy is under 90%. Because the neural network model do not learn all the features. When the epoch reaches 20, the false alarm is the smallest and the accuracy is the highest. This result shows that the neural network can basically learn all the features of the data. When the epoch is greater than 20, the false alarm increases. This is because the model has been over-fitting. So we use 20 epochs to let the model learn the features and ensure that the model does not overfit.

Performance Metric. After our survey, we compare the detection model with the model of other papers in this experiment. In first paper, the author proposes a DBN [5] stacked with RBM as anomaly detection model, and the evaluation on the KDD99 and NSL-KDD dataset has achieved good results. In another paper, the author proposes a S-NDAE [27] method to classify KDD99 and NSL-KDD traffic data. We compare the two researches using the same evaluation standard, which are based on accuracy, accuracy, recall and $F_1-score$. As shown in Table 2 and Table 3, we compare our proposed model performance with the detection model mentioned in the other two researches.

Table 2. Performance metrics on KDD99 compared with other researches

Category	Accuracy			Precision			Recall			$F_1 - score$		
	S-NDAE	DBN	ACAE-RF	S-NDAE	DBN	ACAE-RF	S-NDAE	DBN	ACAE-RF	S-NDAE	DBN	ACAE-RF
Normal	99.49%	99.49%	**99.58%**	100%	94.51%	**100%**	99.49%	99.49%	**99.64%**	99.75%	96.94%	**99.82%**
DoS	99.79%	99.65%	99.76%	100%	99.74%	**100%**	99.79%	99.65%	**99.81%**	99.89%	99.19%	**99.90%**
Probe	99.74%	14.19%	**99.81%**	100%	86.66%	**100%**	98.74%	14.19%	**99.23%**	99.36%	24.38%	**99.61%**
R2L	9.31%	89.25%	24.36%	100%	100%	**100%**	9.31%	89.25%	88.36%	17.04%	94.32%	**93.83%**
U2L	0%	7.14%	**10.17%**	0%	38.46%	**41.32%**	0%	7.14%	**47.23%**	0%	12.05%	**44.08%**
Total	97.85%	97.90%	**98.39%**	99.99%	97.81%	**99.99%**	97.85%	97.91%	**98.26%**	98.15%	97.47%	**99.12%**

We first evaluate our proposed ACAE-RF model on the KDD99 dataset. We classify the network data of Normal, DoS, Probe, R2L and U2L categories. The results are shown in Table 2. It can be seen from the table that in the classification of large sample categories such as DoS, Normal, Probe, the detection model proposed in this paper is better than S-NDAE in accuracy, precision, and $F_1 - score$. Similarly, S-NDAE and ACAE-RF also use the proposed autoencoder to extract the data features, and then use the random forest to classify the network anomaly categories.

The experimental results show that the proposed model is better than the S-NDAE. It is worth noting that on small sample classifications such as R2L and U2L, ACAE-RF results are better than the other two models. In the classification results of ACAE-RF, recall and $F_1 - score$ on R2L are 88.36% and 93.83% respectively, which is significantly improved compared with the classification of S-NDAE model on R2L. In the classification of U2L, the detection performance of ACAE-RF has been significantly improved. Compared with S-NDAE, precision increase from 0% to 41.32%, recall and $F_1 - score$ increase from 0% to 47.23% and 44.08%, respectively. This result shows that our proposed model method has obvious advantages on small samples. In addition, ACAE-RF is not as good as DBN in R2L accuracy, which is related to the small number of training data in KDD99 dataset, which results in the accuracy of detection is not very stable. It shows that ACAE-RF needs more balanced data to learn. However, compared with the S-NDAE which also uses the autoencoder for feature extraction, the accuracy score is improved. In a large amount of network traffic, some special attack traffic often occupies a small amount of traffic in the total amount. If it cannot be detected in time, it will pose a huge threat to network security. We plot the total performance metrics in Fig. 5(a).

Table 3. Performance metrics on NSL-KDD compared with other researches

Category	Accuracy			Precision			Recall			$F_1 - score$		
	S-NDAE	DBN	ACAE-RF	S-NDAE	DBN	ACAE-RF	S-NDAE	DBN	ACAE-RF	S-NDAE	DBN	ACAE-RF
Normal	99.49%	99.49%	**99.58%**	100%	94.51%	**100%**	99.49%	99.49%	**99.64%**	99.75%	96.94%	**99.82%**
DoS	99.79%	99.65%	99.76%	100%	99.74%	**100%**	99.79%	99.65%	**99.81%**	99.89%	99.19%	**99.90%**
Probe	99.74%	14.19%	**99.81%**	100%	86.66%	**100%**	98.74%	14.19%	**99.23%**	99.36%	24.38%	**99.61%**
R2L	9.31%	89.25%	24.36%	100%	100%	**100%**	9.31%	89.25%	88.36%	17.04%	94.32%	**93.83%**
U2L	0%	7.14%	**10.17%**	0%	38.46%	**41.32%**	0%	7.14%	**47.23%**	0%	12.05%	**44.08%**
Total	97.85%	97.90%	**98.39%**	99.99%	97.81%	**99.99%**	97.85%	97.91%	**98.26%**	98.15%	97.47%	**99.12%**

Similarly, we also evaluate the ACAE-RF model on the NSL-KDD dataset. Table 3 shows the results of performance metrics of different anomaly classifications. In the NSL-KDD dataset, the total accuracy, precision, recall and $F_1 - score$ of ACAE-RF metrics have been improved compared with the other two models proposed by the research work. In the classification of Probe, ACAE-RF accuracy is improved from 14.19% to 99.81% compared with DBN. And each performance metrics of ACAE-RF have been significantly improved in the classification of R2L. In particular, recall and $F_1 - score$ reach 47.23% and 44.08% respectively, which shows that our proposed ACAE-RF detection model can effectively detect different network anomaly categories on different datasets, with certain robustness. Figure 5(b) shows the total performance metrics of ACAE-RF in the experiment of NSL-KDD.

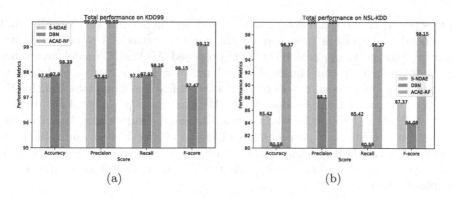

(a)   (b)

Fig. 5. The performance metrics on KDD99 and NSL-KDD compared with other researches

In the final evaluation, we test the performance of our proposed ACAE-RF model for multi-classification. We process the NSL-KDD training set and retain more than 100 network event categories. The purpose of this experiment is to test the stability and effectiveness of ACAE-RF when the number of attack categories increases. In NIDSs, the ability to effectively classify multiple categories of anomalies is a measure of an anomaly detection model. As shown in the Table 4, ACAE-RF can detect network event categories more effectively when the detection categories increases. This shows that our proposed model can still maintain a high level of detection in the case of multiple classifications.

Table 4. Multi-classification on NSL-KDD

Label	Accuracy	Precision	Recall	$F_1 - score$
back	97.11%	97.71%	97.08%	97.39%
neptune	97.23%	97.95%	99.29%	98.62%
pod	100%	100%	100%	100%
smurf	97.98%	98.96%	99.22%	99.09%
teardrop	99.04%	99.16%	97.52%	98.33%
ipsweep	91.32%	85.41%	92.90%	89.00%
nmap	81.33%	80.17%	60.60%	69.02%
portsweep	92.27%	93.87%	86.83%	90.21%
satan	89.34%	88.47%	79.17%	83.56%
warezclient	94.11%	90.27%	93.4%	91.81%
Normal	98.39%	99.27%	99.53%	99.40%
Total	98.72%	98.66%	98.72%	98.69%

6   Conclusion

In this paper, an intrusion detection system based on asymmetric convolutional autoencoder (ACAE) is proposed for the current status of the network environment and the future scalability. Our proposed ACAE-RF model overcomes the shortcomings of convolutional neural network and autoencoder by using asymmetric convolutional autoencoder to extract features from data and classify abnormal events by using random forest. We perform experimental evaluations on the KDD99 and NSL-KDD datasets and achieved good results. And from the experimental results, our proposed model has good effectiveness and robustness in network anomaly detection. In the future, we will conduct in-depth research on the existing work and further improve the classification performance on small samples of data.

Acknowledgment. This work is supported by Key-Area Research and Development Program of Guangdong Province (NO.2020B010164003), National Natural Science Foundation of China (No. 61702492), Shenzhen Basic Research Program (No. JCYJ20170818153016513), Shenzhen Discipline Construction Project for Urban Computing and Data Intelligence, Science and Technology Development Fund of Macao S.A.R (FDCT) under number 0015/2019/AKP, and Youth Innovation Promotion Association CAS.

References

1. internet security threat report. https://www.symantec.com/security-center/threat-report (2019)
2. Kdd99. http://kdd.ics.uci.edu/databases/kddcup99/kddcup99.html (2019)
3. Nsl-kdd dataset. https://www.unb.ca/cic/datasets/nsl.html (2019)
4. Alain, G., Bengio, Y., Rifai, S.: Regularized auto-encoders estimate local statistics. In: ICLR (2013)
5. Alrawashdeh, K., Purdy, C.: Toward an online anomaly intrusion detection system based on deep learning. In: 2016 15th IEEE International Conference on Machine Learning and Applications (ICMLA), pp. 195–200. IEEE (2016)
6. Anbar, M., Abdullah, R., Hasbullah, I.H., Chong, Y.W., Elejla, O.E.: Comparative performance analysis of classification algorithms for intrusion detection system. In: 2016 14th Annual Conference on Privacy, Security and Trust (PST), pp. 282–288. IEEE (2016)
7. Bengio, Y., et al.: Learning deep architectures for AI. Found. Trends® Machine Learn. 2(1), 1–127 (2009)
8. Chen, M., Shi, X., Zhang, Y., Wu, D., Guizani, M.: Deep features learning for medical image analysis with convolutional autoencoder neural network. IEEE Transactions on Big Data (2017)
9. Chen, W.H., Hsu, S.H., Shen, H.P.: Application of svm and ann for intrusion detection. Comput. Oper. Res. 32(10), 2617–2634 (2005)
10. Choudhury, S., Bhowal, A.: Comparative analysis of machine learning algorithms along with classifiers for network intrusion detection. In: 2015 International Conference on Smart Technologies and Management for Computing, Communication, Controls, Energy and Materials (ICSTM), pp. 89–95. IEEE (2015)
11. Cordero, C.G., Hauke, S., Mühlhäuser, M., Fischer, M.: Analyzing flow-based anomaly intrusion detection using replicator neural networks. In: 2016 14th Annual Conference on Privacy, Security and Trust (PST), pp. 317–324. IEEE (2016)
12. Cui, J., Long, J., Min, E., Liu, Q., Li, Q.: Comparative study of CNN and RNN for deep learning based intrusion detection system. In: Sun, X., Pan, Z., Bertino, E. (eds.) ICCCS 2018. LNCS, vol. 11067, pp. 159–170. Springer, Cham (2018). https://doi.org/10.1007/978-3-030-00018-9_15
13. Goroshin, R., LeCun, Y.: Saturating auto-encoders. arXiv preprint arXiv:1301.3577 (2013)
14. Hinton, G.E., Salakhutdinov, R.R.: Reducing the dimensionality of data with neural networks. Science 313(5786), 504–507 (2006)
15. Hou, S., Saas, A., Chen, L., Ye, Y.: Deep4maldroid: a deep learning framework for android malware detection based on linux kernel system call graphs. In: 2016 IEEE/WIC/ACM International Conference on Web Intelligence Workshops (WIW), pp. 104–111. IEEE (2016)
16. Javaid, A., Niyaz, Q., Sun, W., Alam, M.: A deep learning approach for network intrusion detection system. In: Proceedings of the 9th EAI International Conference on Bio-inspired Information and Communications Technologies (formerly BIONETICS), pp. 21–26. ICST (Institute for Computer Sciences, Social-Informatics and ... (2016)
17. Ji, S., Sun, T., Ye, K., Wang, W., Xu, C.-Z.: DAFL: deep adaptive feature learning for network anomaly detection. In: Tang, X., Chen, Q., Bose, P., Zheng, W., Gaudiot, J.-L. (eds.) NPC 2019. LNCS, vol. 11783, pp. 350–354. Springer, Cham (2019). https://doi.org/10.1007/978-3-030-30709-7_32

18. Ji, S., Ye, K., Xu, C.-Z.: CMonitor: a monitoring and alarming platform for container-based clouds. In: Da Silva, D., Wang, Q., Zhang, L.-J. (eds.) CLOUD 2019. LNCS, vol. 11513, pp. 324–339. Springer, Cham (2019). https://doi.org/10.1007/978-3-030-23502-4_23

19. Kim, J., Shin, N., Jo, S.Y., Kim, S.H.: Method of intrusion detection using deep neural network. In: 2017 IEEE International Conference on Big Data and Smart Computing (BigComp), pp. 313–316. IEEE (2017)

20. Liao, Y., Vemuri, V.R.: Use of k-nearest neighbor classifier for intrusion detection. Comput. Secur. **21**(5), 439–448 (2002)

21. Lin, P., Ye, K., Chen, M., Xu, C.Z.: Dcsa: Using density-based clustering and sequential association analysis to predict alarms in telecommunication networks. In: 2019 IEEE 25th International Conference on Parallel and Distributed Systems (ICPADS), pp. 1–8. IEEE (2019)

22. Lin, P., Ye, K., Xu, C.-Z.: Dynamic network anomaly detection system by using deep learning techniques. In: Da Silva, D., Wang, Q., Zhang, L.-J. (eds.) CLOUD 2019. LNCS, vol. 11513, pp. 161–176. Springer, Cham (2019). https://doi.org/10.1007/978-3-030-23502-4_12

23. Lin, P., Ye, K., Xu, C.Z.: Netdetector: an anomaly detection platform for networked systems. In: 2019 IEEE International Conference on Real-time Computing and Robotics (RCAR), pp. 69–74. IEEE (2019)

24. Lu, C., Ye, K., Chen, W., Xu, C.Z.: ADGS: anomaly detection and localization based on graph similarity in container-based clouds. In: 2019 IEEE 25th International Conference on Parallel and Distributed Systems (ICPADS), pp. 53–60. IEEE (2019)

25. Panda, M., Patra, M.R.: Network intrusion detection using naive bayes. Int. J. Comput. Sci. Network Secur. **7**(12), 258–263 (2007)

26. Salama, M.A., Eid, H.F., Ramadan, R.A., Darwish, A., Hassanien, A.E.: Hybrid intelligent intrusion detection scheme. In: Soft computing in industrial applications, pp. 293–303. Springer, Heidelberg (2011). https://doi.org/10.1007/978-3-642-20505-7_26

27. Shone, N., Ngoc, T.N., Phai, V.D., Shi, Q.: A deep learning approach to network intrusion detection. IEEE Trans. Emerg. Top. Computat. Intell. **2**(1), 41–50 (2018)

28. Tsai, C.F., Hsu, Y.F., Lin, C.Y., Lin, W.Y.: Intrusion detection by machine learning: a review. Expert Syst. Appl. Int. J. **36**(10), 11994–12000 (2009)

29. Ye, K., Liu, Y., Xu, G., Xu, C.-Z.: Fault injection and detection for artificial intelligence applications in container-based clouds. In: Luo, M., Zhang, L.-J. (eds.) CLOUD 2018. LNCS, vol. 10967, pp. 112–127. Springer, Cham (2018). https://doi.org/10.1007/978-3-319-94295-7_8

30. Yin, C., Zhu, Y., Fei, J., He, X.: A deep learning approach for intrusion detection using recurrent neural networks. IEEE Access **5**, 21954–21961 (2017)

31. Yu, Y., Long, J., Cai, Z.: Network intrusion detection through stacking dilated convolutional autoencoders. Secur. Commun. Netw. **2017**, 56 (2017)

32. Zhao, R., Yan, R., Chen, Z., Mao, K., Wang, P., Gao, R.X.: Deep learning and its applications to machine health monitoring. Mech. Syst. Signal Process. **115**, 213–237 (2019)

Post-cloud Computing Models and Their Comparisons

Yingwei Wang[1(✉)] and Parimala Thulasiraman[2]

[1] University of Prince Edward Island, Charlottetown, Canada
`ywang@upei.ca`
[2] University of Manitoba, Winnipeg, Canada
`thulasir@cs.umanitoba.ca`

Abstract. In this paper, four computing models, CDEF (Cloudlet, Dew computing, Edge computing, and Fog computing), were portrayed and compared; the concept of post-cloud computing was examined and defined. This paper tries to clarify the connotation and denotation of each post-cloud computing model and to help users to choose the proper one for further exploration.

1 Introduction

Th widely acceptance of cloud computing made some people believe that cloud computing would be the model that replaces traditional on-site computing equipment and IT departments. While this kind of replacement has been going on, some new computing models came into existence in the last few years. Among these new computing models are cloudlet, dew computing, edge computing, and fog computing. These computing models caused much confusion: What are they? What are their features? Are they similar to each other? Can some of the them replace others? Which one should I use?

This paper is devoted to clarify these confusions. This paper is not a complete survey of the progress in the areas of cloudlet, dew computing, edge computing, and fog computing. Instead, it provides a portrait for each of these computing models, compares and distinguishes them, provides a unified framework to observe them so that they can be used properly. The rest of the paper is organized in the following way: in Sect. 2, we describe the origins, definitions, basic principles, and applications of these computing models; in Sect. 3, the concepts of CDEF and post-cloud computing are discussed; in Sect. 4, we compare these models and discuss their similarities and differences; Sect. 5 presents conclusions.

2 Overview of New Computing Models

In this section, we would like to provide a portrait for each of the four computing models: cloudlet, dew computing, edge computing, and fog computing. The

---

Partial content of this paper has been presented in workshops and kept as preprints [12,20,23,24]. No content of this paper has been officially published anywhere.

© Springer Nature Switzerland AG 2020
Q. Zhang et al. (Eds.): CLOUD 2020, LNCS 12403, pp. 141–151, 2020.
https://doi.org/10.1007/978-3-030-59635-4_10

goals of these portrait introductions are to help readers to master the connotation/denotation of each model and to choose the proper one for further exploration. We do not intent to perform a full survey to these computing models. Instead, we concentrate on the following aspects of each model:

1. the origin: when did it start and how it was started?
2. the definition: what is it?;
3. the principles and applications: how does it work and how could it be used?
4. a commercial application example: how is it used in real world?

We would like to explain our considerations regarding to the origins and definitions of these models.

For origins, in our understanding, every computing model goes through the following steps in its origination:

1. Before the concept was proposed, some concrete technical approaches that are very similar to the new concept or exactly the same with the new concept were proposed as research ideas and/or applied in products or services;
2. The new concept was proposed after technical accumulation;
3. After the concept was proposed, technical approaches based on the new concept were widely and quickly spread; existing approaches were interpreted with the new concept; new approaches were proposed according to the new concept.

No computing model can be proposed without technical accumulation described in Step 1. A long-term accumulation process is necessary for the establishment of a computing model.

The origination of a new concept is a significant event because the new concept leads researchers to explore solutions to wide range of problems using a paradigm or a framework that comes with the new concept. Thus, we would like to identify the origin of each computing model.

For definitions, each computing model may have more than one definition. Different researchers may have different opinions toward these definitions. For each computing model, we try to find a definition that, we believe, accurately describe this model.

2.1   Cloudlet

Origin. Although the word *cloudlet* existed long time ago with different meanings, it was started being used in the meaning of a computing arrangement in 2009 [10,17].

Definition. The following is a definition of a cloudlet [17]:

A cloudlet is a trusted, resource-rich computer or cluster of computers that is well-connected to the Internet and is available for use by nearby mobile devices.

Principles and Applications. The cloudlet model promotes to put small-scale cloud data centers at the edge of the Internet. A cloudlet is the middle tier of a 3-tier hierarchy: mobile device - cloudlet - cloud. A cloudlet is close to a mobile device but not on the mobile device.

A Commercial Application Example. Akamai is a major content delivery network (CDN) provider. It operates a geographically distributed network of proxy servers and their data centers. Its goal is to provide high availability and high performance by distributing the service spatially relative to end-users. Akamai provides cloudlet services [1] to its customers. Currently, ten kinds of cloudlets are available. We just introduce one kind of cloudlets, Request Control Cloudlet, to illustrate the way it works.

Access control is an important part of managing visitor access to website or application. In today's connected world, having control over who can, or can't, access web properties is critical to protecting customer organization's content and information. It's important to ensure customer's resources remain available for intended audience and are not hindered by unwanted traffic that could be driving up costs. Often times these access control policy changes need to be made quickly and frequently creating a challenge to customer web operations.

Suppose a customer is operating a website through Akamai's CDN. This customer could also use Akamai's Request Control Cloudlet. The customer may use the control panel to create some rules. These rules could specify that requests from a specific CIDR, a specific continent, or a specific country will be given/or not given access. If this kind of request control is provided by the data center, the latency would be longer and load of the server and the network would be much higher. The cloudlet is running in an edge device in the CDN called Akamai Intelligent Platform; this device is geographically closer to the Web client, but is not in the cloud server where the website is running. The above feature is a key feature of cloudlet paradigm.

2.2 Dew Computing

Origin. *Dew Computing* was proposed in 2015 [19,23,27]. The first paper became online in January 2015.

Definition. The definition of dew computing can be found in [28]:

Dew computing is an on-premises computer software-hardware organization paradigm in the cloud computing environment where the on-premises computer provides functionality that is independent of cloud services and is also collaborative with cloud services. The goal of dew computing is to fully realize the potentials of on-premises computers and cloud services.

Principles and Applications. Dew computing is a computing model appeared after the wide acceptance of cloud computing. While cloud computing uses centralized servers to provide various services, dew computing uses on-premises computers to provide decentralized, cloud-friendly, and collaborative micro services to end-users.

Dew computing is complementary to cloud computing. The key features of dew computing are that on-premises computers provide functionality independent of cloud services and they also collaborate with cloud services.

A Commercial Application Example. We use a well-known application, Dropbox [5], to illustrate dew computing. Dropbox works in the following ways: when the local host is online, the local copy of files are synchronized with the cloud copy of the files automatically; when the local host is offline, the local copy can still be used in whatever way the user wants to use them; when the local host get back online again later, the synchronization will be performed without any human intervention.

The above example is only one category of dew computing: Storage as Dew (SaD). Other categories of dew computing can be found in [28]. Although one example cannot reflect the whole landscape of dew computing, it showed the two major features of dew computing: independent and collaboration.

2.3 Edge Computing

Origin. The term *edge cluster* was used in a paper in August 2015 [13]. *Edge Computing* was proposed for the first time in October 2015 [8]. Some work has been done before this time. As discussed in the beginning of Sect. 2, we consider those work as the accumulation work before the concept was proposed.

A paper used the term "computing on the edge" in 2004 [14], but it is an "early flavor of edge computing" and the new vision of edge computing was "far beyond this initial approach" [8]. The fact that the accumulation work did not use this term also indicates that this paper was not the origin of edge computing.

Many research papers about edge computing appeared after 2015. It is reasonable to say that edge computing was originated in 2015.

Definition. The following is a definition of edge computing [18]:

Edge computing refers to the enabling technologies allowing computation to be performed at the edge of the network, on downstream data on behalf of cloud services and upstream data on behalf of IoT services. Here we define "edge" as any computing and network resources along the path between data sources and cloud data centers.

Principles and Applications. Edge computing pushes applications, data, and services away from central servers (core) to the edge of a network; it is based on the core-edge topology [16, 18].

Cloud offloading, video analytics, smart home/smart city are some examples where edge computing can be actively applied [3, 7].

A Commercial Application Example. Amazon Web Services (AWS) is a major cloud computing provider. Besides the well-known service Elastic Compute Cloud (EC2), Lambda@Edge [2] is a feature of another AWS Service: Amazon CloudFront. Lambda@Edge provides edge computing service.

Lambda@Edge lets you run code closer to users of your application, which improves performance and reduces latency. With Lambda@Edge, you don't have to provision or manage infrastructure in multiple locations around the world. You pay only for the compute time you consume - there is no charge when your code is not running.

With Lambda@Edge, you can enrich your web applications by making them globally distributed and improving their performance—all with zero server administration. Lambda@Edge runs your code in response to events generated by the Amazon CloudFront content delivery network (CDN). Just upload your code to AWS Lambda, which takes care of everything required to run and scale your code with high availability at an AWS location closest to your end user.

2.4   Fog Computing

Origin. *Fog Computing* was proposed by Cisco. It was first proposed by Flavio Bonomi, Vice President of Cisco Systems, in a keynote presentation at a conference in Sept. 2011 [4,6].

Definition. The following is a definition of fog computing [22]:

Fog computing is a scenario where a huge number of heterogeneous (wireless and sometimes autonomous) ubiquitous and decentralised devices communicate and potentially cooperate among them and with the network to perform storage and processing tasks without the intervention of third-parties. These tasks can be for supporting basic network functions or new services and applications that run in a sandboxed environment. Users leasing part of their devices to host these services get incentives for doing so.

Principles and Applications. Fog computing extends cloud computing and services to devices such as routers, routing switches, multiplexers, and so on. It mainly involves automation devices because fog computing was proposed with Internet of Things (IoT) as its background.

A Commercial Application Example. SONM [20] is a decentralized fog computing platform. It provides cloud services based on distributed customer level hardware including PCs, mining equipment, and servers. You can either rent out your hardware or use someone's computing power for your needs.

This example illustrates that fog computing is different from cloud computing. In cloud computing, computing power exists in data centers; in fog computing, computing power exists everywhere. Fog computing provides some incentive to those who provide computing power. Such a financial model was proposed together with the fog computing concept.

3   CDEF and Post-cloud Computing

The new computing models, Cloudlet, Dew computing, Edge computing, Fog computing, can be expressed in an easy-to-remember way: **CDEF**, where C represents Cloudlet, D represents Dew computing, E represents Edge computing, and F represents Fog computing [24].

CDEF computing models originated from different background, proposed to solve different problems, related to diffcrent disciplines/industries, involved different devices, and have different methodologies. All CDEF models were proposed to provide some features that cloud computing cannot provide. They share one common feature: they all perform computing tasks at devices that are closer to users[12,21].

CDEF summarizes these computing models, but we still need a concept to conveniently describe the common features of these computing models. *Post-cloud computing* can serve this role [9,12,21,24,25,29,30].

Literally speaking, post-cloud computing is the computing paradigm appears after the cloud computing era. This concept should be inclusive. Here we provide a definition for post-cloud computing: *Post-cloud computing is an umbrella concept that covers computing models that extend cloud computing and work together with cloud computing.*

Post-cloud computing is not a specific computing model; instead, it covers a few computing models that are related to cloud computing and remedial to cloud computing. Apparently, CDEF are post-cloud computing models.

Cloud computing obtained widely acceptance in the past decade, but the trend is changing. With the quick development of Internet of Things, wireless devices, and artificial intelligence, new computing models play more and more important roles. We are confident that the post-cloud computing era is coming.

4   Comparison of Post-cloud Computing Models

4.1   Similarities

All these computing models share a common feature: they all perform computing tasks at devices that are closer to users. It is hard to determine the exact differences among these models by checking their definitions. The reasons are:

- Normally a computing model was proposed to solve a specific problem with a narrow definition. With the progress of research, researchers tend to expand the definition to cover a wider range of area. Thus the definitions of these post-cloud computing models have much similarity. Such definition expansion reflects researchers' eagerness and excitement in exploring new technologies.
- Even if differences among these models were found in definitions, some researchers may have different opinions to these definitions.

To understand the underlying reasons of these similar computing model definitions, we had better take a bird's view position to observe the general trend in the history of computer science. Dr. Mahadev Satyanarayanan [16] summarized the past history in the following quote:

"Since the 1960s, computing has alternated between centralization and decentralization. The centralized approaches of batch processing and timesharing prevailed in the 1960s and 1970s. The 1980s and 1990s saw decentralization through the rise of personal computing. By the mid-2000s, the centralized approach of cloud computing began its ascent to the preeminent position that it holds today. Edge computing represents the latest phase of this ongoing dialectic."

After the widely acceptance and huge success of cloud computing, some researchers discovered the limitations of cloud computing and proposed remedial solutions from different perspectives. CDEF post-cloud computing models were proposed as the result of this trend.

4.2   Differences

Although these computing models reflect the same trend in response to cloud computing's limitations, these models were quite different because:

- they originated from different background;
- they were proposed to solve different problems;
- they are related to different disciplines or industries;
- they deal with different types of devices and environment;
- they have different methodologies.

Here we would like to point out some differences among these models.

Cloudlet features micro data centers; it is related to mobile services. Micro data centers could be set up by mobile service providers, application providers, or even users.

Dew computing is more closely related to software design; its strong point is to inspire novice applications. Dew computing was proposed to solve the data availability problem when an Internet connection is not available. Dew computing's features, categories, and architecture are helpful for new applications be developed. Dew computing normally does not involve edge devices such as routers and switches.

Edge computing's rational is that computing should happen at the proximity of data sources [18]. Edge computing is tightly related to IoT [15].

Fog computing is also tightly related to Internet of Things. Fog computing emphasizes proximity to end-users and client objectives, dense geographical distribution and local resource pooling, latency reduction and backbone bandwidth savings.

Sometimes, the difference is quite clear. For example, if cloudlet model is introduced in mobile applications, a 3-tier hierarchy: mobile device - cloudlet - cloud would be established. A cloudlet is close to a mobile device but not on the mobile device. If dew computing is introduced, the dew component would be on the mobile devices.

Different models may work together. For example: A hierarchy was proposed [19] for cloud computing, fog computing, and dew computing to work together.

Different models may obtain similar results. For example, an edge computing idea about cloud/edge applications [11] has similar ideas with the cloud-dew architecture proposed in dew computing [23].

Each model may have its special strength. For example, the Dewblock system [26], that small-data-size blockchain clients with full node features, can hardly be classified into cloudlet, fog computing, or edge computing applications; it is only possible under the computing model of dew computing.

4.3   Choice Suggestions

If someone is interested in these post-cloud computing models, which one should he/she choose? What should be considered in making a choice? Here we give some suggestions.

If you are interested in improving mobile services, from services providers' viewpoint or from application developer's viewpoint, cloudlet model is the suitable model for you to work on.

If you are interested in the design of novice distributed applications, dew computing could bring you with inspirations and architectural assistance. Dew computing normally does not involve edge devices, such as routers and switches; Dew computing is not restricted by network topology.

If you are interested in infrastructure design, such as smart home/smart city, or are interested in cloud offloading for improved efficiency, edge computing could be a suitable choice.

If you are related to IoT research or IoT industry, fog computing is the area you should pay attention to. With the development of IoT, huge amount of sensors will be deployed everywhere. The best place for computing powers to process data from these sensors should not be far away cloud servers or low-capacity sensors. Devices such as routers and switches are a better choice.

4.4   Post-cloud Computing Models Summary

Here we would like to present the features of CDEF post-cloud models in a summarized, convenient way. Table 1 contains key information discussed in Sect. 2 and Sect. 4.3.

Table 1. Features of post-cloud computing models

	Cloudlet	Dew computing	Edge computing	Fog computing
Origin year	2009	2015	2015	2011
Definition	A cloudlet is a trusted, resource-rich computer or cluster of computers that is well-connected to the Internet and is available for use by nearby mobile devices	Dew computing is an on-premises computer software-hardware organization paradigm in the cloud computing environment where the on-premises computer provides functionality that is independent of cloud services and is also collaborative with cloud services	Edge computing refers to the enabling technologies allowing computation to be performed at the edge of the network, on downstream data on behalf of cloud services and upstream data on behalf of IoT services. Here we define "edge" as any computing and network resources along the path between data sources and cloud data centers	Fog computing is a scenario where a huge number of heterogeneous ubiquitous and decentralised devices communicate and potentially cooperate among them and with the network to perform storage and processing tasks without the intervention of third-parties. Users leasing part of their devices to host these services get incentives for doing so
Principals	Puts small-scale cloud data centers at the edge of the Internet; it is close to a mobile device but not on the mobile device	Collaborates with cloud service when online, and provides basic services when offline	Pushes applications, data, and services away from central servers to the edge of a network	Extends cloud computing and services to devices such as routers, routing switches, multiplexers, and so on
Sample App	Akamai Cloudlets [1]	Dropbox [5]	AWS's Lambda@Edge [2]	SONM [20]
Choice Suggestions	Those interested in improving mobile services	Those interested in the design of novice distributed applications	Those interested in infrastructure design, such as smart home & Smart city, or interested in cloud offloading for improved efficiency	Those related to IoT research or IoT industry

5 Conclusion

In this paper, we briefly introduced the origins, definitions, basic principles, and applications of cloudlet, dew computing, edge computing, and fog computing; such introduction is not simply a compilation of materials; it involves extensive exploration and careful selection. We compared these features and defined post-cloud computing as an umbrella concept that covers computing models that extend cloud computing and work together with cloud computing. From these discussions, we can see that these computing models are quite different. The essential differences among them are not in their definitions that claim their coverage because definitions can be easily updated, expanded, and interpreted in different ways. The essential values of these computing models exist in their built-in principles, architectures, styles, and philosophy. Similar to programming languages, although each programming language has full computing power of a Turing Machine, each language has its own style, strength, and characteristics. People won't accept the idea that using one programming language to replace all other programming languages. These computing models will work together with cloud computing to provide different frameworks, paradigms, guidelines, and architectures to researchers and developers in the post-cloud era.

References

1. Akamai: Akamai cloudlets. https://cloudlets.akamai.com/
2. Amazon: Lambda@edge. online. https://aws.amazon.com/lambda/edge/
3. Ananthanarayanan, G., et al.: Real-time video analytics: the killer app for edge computing. Computer **50**(10), 58–67 (2017)
4. Bonomi, F., Milito, R., Zhu, J., Addepalli, S.: Fog computing and its role in the Internet of Things. In: Proceedings of the First Edition of the MCC Workshop on Mobile Cloud Computing MCC 2012, pp. 13–16. ACM, New York (2012). https://doi.org/10.1145/2342509.2342513
5. Dropbox: Dropbox, February 2014. https://www.dropbox.com/
6. Bonomi, F.: Connected vehicles, the Internet of Things, and fog computing, September 2011. https://www.sigmobile.org/mobicom/2011/vanet2011/program.html
7. Ananthanarayanan, G., Bahl, V., Wolman, A.: Edge computing, October 2008. https://www.microsoft.com/en-us/research/project/edge-computing/
8. Garcia Lopez, P., et al.: Edge-centric computing: vision and challenges. SIGCOMM Comput. Commun. Rev. **45**(5), 37–42 (2015). https://doi.org/10.1145/2831347.2831354
9. Gardner, D.: Get ready for the post-cloud world. Datamation, July 2017. https://www.datamation.com/cloud-computing/get-ready-for-the-post-cloud-world.html
10. Ibrahim, S., Jin, H., Cheng, B., Cao, H., Wu, S., Qi, L.: CLOUDLET: towards mapreduce implementation on virtual machines. In: Proceedings of the 18th ACM International Symposium on High Performance Distributed Computing, HPDC 2009, Garching, Germany, 11–13 June 2009, pp. 65–66 (2009). https://doi.org/10.1145/1551609.1551624
11. White, J.: Microsoft Azure enables a new wave of edge computing. here's how, September 2018. https://azure.microsoft.com/en-us/blog/microsoft-azure-enables-a-new-wave-of-edge-computing-here-s-how/
12. Pan, Y., Thulasiraman, P., Wang, Y.: Overview of cloudlet, fog computing, edge computing, and dew computing. In: The 3rd International Workshop on Dew Computing. Toronto, Canada, October 2018. preprint
13. Pu, Q., et al.: Low latency geo-distributed data analytics. SIGCOMM Comput. Commun. Rev. **45**(4), 421–434 (2015). https://doi.org/10.1145/2829988.2787505
14. Rabinovich, M., Xiao, Z., Aggarwal, A.: Computing on the edge: a platform for replicating Internet applications. In: Douglis, F., Davison, B.D. (eds.) Web Content Caching and Distribution, pp. 57–77. Springer, Dordrecht (2004). https://doi.org/10.1007/1-4020-2258-1_4
15. Ren, J., Pan, Y., Goscinski, A., Beyah, R.A.: Edge computing for the internet of things. IEEE Netw. **32**(1), 6–7 (2018)
16. Satyanarayanan, M.: The emergence of edge computing. Computer **50**(1), 30–39 (2017)
17. Satyanarayanan, M., Bahl, P., Caceres, R., Davies, N.: The case for VM-based cloudlets in mobile computing. IEEE Pervasive Comput. **8**(4), 14–23 (2009)
18. Shi, W., Cao, J., Zhang, Q., Li, Y., Xu, L.: Edge computing: vision and challenges. IEEE Internet Things J. **3**(5), 637–646 (2016)

19. Skala, K., Davidovic, D., Afgan, E., Sovic, I., Sojat, Z.: Scalable distributed computing hierarchy: cloud, fog and dew computing. Open J. Cloud Comput. (OJCC) **2**(1), 16–24 (2015)
20. SONM: Decentralized fog computing platform. https://sonm.com/
21. Thulasiraman, P., Wang, Y.: Post-cloud computing and its varieties. In: The 4th International Workshop on Dew Computing. Online Conference, November 2019. preprint
22. Vaquero, L.M., Rodero-Merino, L.: Finding your way in the fog: towards a comprehensive definition of fog computing. SIGCOMM Comput. Commun. Rev. **44**(5), 27–32 (2014). https://doi.org/10.1145/2677046.2677052
23. Wang, Y.: Cloud-dew architecture. Int. J. Cloud Comput. **4**(3), 199–210 (2015)
24. Wang, Y.: Post-cloud computing models: from cloud to CDEF. Research Gate, November 2018. https://doi.org/10.13140/RG.2.2.34150.47688. preprint
25. Wang, Y.: What is post-cloud computing? ResearchGate, November 2018. https://doi.org/10.13140/RG.2.2.31568.35843. preprint
26. Wang, Y.: A blockchain system with lightweight full node based on dew computing. Internet Things **9**, 100184 (2020). https://doi.org/10.1016/j.iot.2020.100184
27. Wang, Y., Pan, Y.: Cloud-dew architecture : realizing the potential of distributed database systems in unreliable networks. In: Proceedings of the 21st International Conference on Parallel and Distributed Processing Techniques and Applications (PDPTA 2015) Las Vegas, USA, pp. 85–89, July 2015
28. Wang, Y.: Definition and categorization of dew computing. Open J. Cloud Comput. (OJCC) **3**(1), 1–7 (2016)
29. Zhou, Y.Z., Zhang, D.: Near-end cloud computing: opportunities and challenges in the post-cloud computing era. Chin. J. Comput. **41**(25), 1–24 (2018). online publishing, in Chinese, abstract in English
30. Zhou, Y.Z., Zhang, D., Xiong, N.: Post-cloud computing paradigms: a survey and comparison. Tsinghua Sci. Technol. **22**(6), 714–732 (2017)

Wise Toolkit: Enabling Microservice-Based System Performance Experiments

Rodrigo Alves Lima[1]($\boxtimes$), Joshua Kimball[1], João E. Ferreira[2], and Calton Pu[1]

[1] Georgia Institute of Technology, Atlanta, USA
{ral3,jmkimball,calton.pu}@cc.gatech.edu
[2] University of São Paulo, São Paulo, Brazil
jef@ime.usp.br

Abstract. In this paper, we present the Wise toolkit for microservice-based system performance experiments. Wise comprises a microservice-based application benchmark with controllable workload generation; milliScope, a set of system resource and event monitoring tools; and WED-Make, a workflow language and code generation tool for the construction and execution of system experiments with automatic provenance collection. We also show a running example reproducing the experimental verification of the millibottleneck theory of performance bugs to illustrate how we have used Wise for the performance study of microservice-based benchmark applications in the cloud.

1 Introduction

Public cloud providers (e.g., Amazon Web Services) sell computing resources in a "pay-as-you-go" model that can only be profitable under high utilization; likewise, for their customers, high utilization is essential to maximize the return on investment. Therefore, virtualization technologies play a key role in the field of cloud computing, with physical hosts being typically shared by multiple virtual machines (VMs) and many containers running on top of each VM.

Virtualized systems are more susceptible to resource contention, hence making the performance of cloud applications less predictable [11]. Furthermore, the widespread adoption of virtualization technologies has spurred the trend of splitting large programs comprising the functionalities of entire applications into loosely-coupled microservices, whose inherently large number of synchronous calls makes performance even less predictable. For example, a well-known performance predictability problem is the long tail latency of web-facing applications, where a small number of requests take seconds to return while the majority return within a few tens of milliseconds [5].

Long tail latency has been reported to be bad for businesses (Amazon found that every increase of 100 ms in page loading time is correlated to roughly 1% loss in sales [15]; similarly, Google found that a 500 ms additional delay to return search results could hurt revenues by up to 20% [14]) so companies want to reduce

Q. Zhang et al. (Eds.): CLOUD 2020, LNCS 12403, pp. 152–163, 2020.
https://doi.org/10.1007/978-3-030-59635-4_11

their response time long tails to the 99.9th percentiles and above [5,6]. However, this is a puzzling problem: requests with very long response time (VLRT) can start to happen when none of the system resources seem close to saturation (e.g., 40% average CPU utilization) and its cause may not be related to the requests themselves (i.e., different requests with the exact same parameter values may have VLRT or not) [20].

In previous work, so-called *millibottlenecks* were shown to be a cause of the long tail latency. According to the *millibottleneck theory of performance bugs* [20], transient resource bottlenecks in the order of milliseconds (millibottlenecks) can propagate through a distributed system using RPC-style communication (e.g., through queue overflows) and have their effects amplified (e.g., by the retransmission of dropped TCP packets), causing severe performance bugs [22,27].

Detecting millibottlenecks is particularly hard due to their very short lifespan: according to the Sampling Theorem, phenomena with the duration of a fraction of a second are not detectable by observation tools with sampling periods of multiple seconds or minutes, which is the typical configuration of many cloud monitoring tools [20]. Also, studying the propagation of millibottlenecks through a distributed system requires logging all messages exchanged between servers, with their arrival and departure timestamps, for each request – a level of detail that is not usually found in native server logs [16].

The study of the causes, propagation mechanisms, and amplification effects of millibottlenecks thus represents a research challenge with potentially high financial impact. In this paper, we present the Wise toolkit for microservice-based system performance experiments. In summary, Wise comprises (1) a microservice-based application benchmark with tunable workload generation; (2) milliScope [16], a set of system resource and event monitoring tools; and (3) WED-Make [17], a workflow language and code generation tool for the construction and execution of system experiments. We also present an illustrative example of how we have used Wise to reproduce the experimental verification of the millibottleneck theory of performance bugs, showing how its components fit together in the experiment workflow.

In Sect. 2, we present the microblog application benchmark we have mostly used for the performance study of microservice-based applications in the cloud. Then, in Sect. 3, we present milliScope, a set of fine-grained system resource and highly-detailed event monitoring tools with low overhead. Next, we show how we have used WED-Make to construct and execute our experiment workflows in Sect. 4. In Sect. 5, we present an illustrative example of the millibottleneck theory of performance bugs. Finally, we present related work in Sect. 6 and summarize our conclusions in Sect. 7.

2   The Microblog Application Benchmark

Microservice-based applications have an inherently large number of synchronous calls between servers that make performance study more challenging. Most experiments conducted with the Wise toolkit use an application benchmark that simulates requests to a Twitter-like microblog website. As shown in Fig. 1, this application benchmark comprises a client, an Apache HTTP server [25], Thrift microservices [1], workers to process asynchronous jobs, and a PostgreSQL [19] database server.

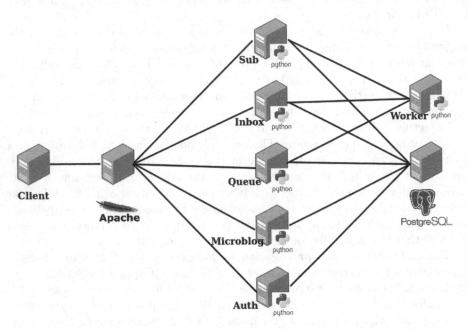

Fig. 1. Architecture of the microblog application benchmark that is part of Wise.

The client generates HTTP requests simulating user interactions such as creating and endorsing posts, subscribing to other users, viewing personal inboxes, viewing recent posts, etc. These requests first arrive at the Apache HTTP server and are processed by a Flask application [8] that sends requests to five Thrift microservices:

- *auth*: Handle user registration and authentication.
- *queue*: Enqueue and dequeue objects. It is used to offload jobs that can be processed asynchronously.
- *microblog*: Implement the microblog functionalities, like creating and viewing posts.
- *sub*: Manage user subscriptions.
- *inbox*: Push and fetch objects from named inboxes.

To keep latencies low, these microservices offload jobs with high processing times (e.g., pushing a post to the inboxes of its author's subscribers) to the queue so they can be asynchronously processed by workers.

2.1   Servers Configuration

Studying performance of distributed systems usually requires analyzing the saturation level of each server through the calculation of its queue lengths. Therefore, this application benchmark has configuration parameters to set the number of processes and threads of the servers, as well as the size of their connection pools.

For the experiment analyzed in Sect. 5, we configured the servers as follows:

```
# Apache/mod_wsgi configuration.
readonly APACHE_PROCESSES=8
readonly APACHE_THREADSPERPROCESS=5
# Postgres configuration.
readonly POSTGRES_MAXCONNECTIONS=100
# Workers configuration.
readonly NUM_WORKERS=32
# Microservices configuration.
AUTH_THREADPOOLSIZE=16
INBOX_THREADPOOLSIZE=16
QUEUE_THREADPOOLSIZE=16
SUB_THREADPOOLSIZE=16
MICROBLOG_THREADPOOLSIZE=16
```

32 workers process jobs offloaded to the queue, microservices are set to have 16 threads, the Apache server is set to have 8 processes with 5 threads per process, and the PostgreSQL server is set to handle at most 100 transactions at a time.

2.2   Workload Configuration

Furthermore, we have identified millibottlenecks that cause VLRT requests in different hardware resources (e.g, CPU, disk I/O) and also due to the anti-synchrony between workload bursts and DVFS clock rate adjustments [20,26]. Therefore, this application benchmark's workload is tunable, with fine-grained controls over its size (e.g., number of concurrent client sessions), characteristics (e.g., frequency of each user interaction, which allows stressing specific servers and hardware resources), and burstiness (e.g., intermittent variations in the number of requests per second).

The workload is configured declaratively. A workload comprises one or more groups of clients that simulate user interactions with this microblog application. The delay associated with these interactions (uniform or Gaussian distribution) and the probability of transitioning between interactions (stochastic model) are declared in YAML files for each group of clients.

For the experiment analyzed in Sect. 5, action *sign_up* to register new users was configured as follows for its single group of clients:

```
- action: sign_up
  delayDistribution:
    type: gaussian
    mean: 5.0
    sd: 1
  transitionWeights:
    create_post: .25
    view_recent_posts: .75
```

Action *sign_up* has a delay with Gaussian distribution whose mean is 5 s and standard deviation is 1. After signing up, a client session has a 25% probability of creating a post and a 75% probability of viewing recent posts.

Client groups are also configured in a YAML file. The single group of clients of the experiment analyzed in Sect. 5 was configured as follows:

```
- sessionConfig: {{WISEHOME}}/experiment/conf/session.yml
  noConcurrentSessions: 150
  startTime: 0
  endTime: 360
  rampUpDuration: 15
  rampDownDuration: 15
  burstiness:
    - speedUpFactor: 2.0
      startTime: 60
      endTime: 90
```

There are 150 client sessions, which are started at the beginning of the experiment and finished after 360 s. Ramping up these client sessions take 15 s and ramping them down takes 15 s as well. Actions are speed up by a factor of 2 (*speedUpFactor: 2*) between 60 and 90 s after the experiment started, thus cutting their latencies by half.

3   System Resource and Event Monitoring with MilliScope

Finding correlations between millibottlenecks and interesting events like server queue overflows and VLRT requests are essential to the study of performance bugs in microservice-based applications. However, it is not possible to detect millibottlenecks using resource monitoring tools with sampling intervals in the order of seconds or minutes – the typical configuration of many cloud monitoring tools [16]. Furthermore, the study of millibottleneck propagation requires logging all messages exchanged between servers, with their arrival and departure timestamps, for each request – a level of detail that is not usually found in native server logs [16].

milliScope [16] is a set of system resource and event monitoring tools suitable for the study of performance bugs in microservice-based applications.

The resource monitoring component of milliScope contains open-source tools like sar [24] and Collectl [3] to monitor resources like CPU, memory, and disk I/O with low-overhead and fine granularity. For the experiment analyzed in Sect. 5, we chose to monitor CPU, memory, and disk using Collectl at intervals of 50 ms.

To monitor interesting system events, Wise adopted a system-based specialization approach that is independent of any server software. Specifically, we patched the Linux Kernel 4.15 to make its syscall table visible and writable to Linux Kernel Modules (LKMs). In this way, a LKM can set pointers to its own specialized syscalls. When called, such a specialized syscall could then create a log entry containing the current timestamp and arguments of interest. These log entries can be stored in a buffer and read from the special /proc filesystem (regularly or at the end of the experiment). For the experiment analyzed in Sect. 5, syscalls *connect*, *sendto*, and *recvfrom* were specialized with LKMs.

The excerpt below shows log entries resulting from the execution of the specialized *sendto* syscall, where each row represents an invocation of that syscall. The columns give timestamp, IDs of the corresponding user-level process and thread, and the socket file descriptor.

```
TS,PID,TID,SOCK_FD
1581967233336111,765,767,6
1581967233339232,765,796,8
1581967233339330,765,795,10
1581967233339924,765,796,8
```

Log entries resulting from the execution of the specialized *connect* syscall are shown below. In addition to the columns present in the log entries produced by the specialized *sendto* syscall, these have the port to which the socket is connected to (in this example, port 5432 represents the PostgreSQL database server).

```
TS,PID,TID,SOCK_FD,PORT
1581967121048310,765,778,6,5432
1581967121155318,765,779,5,5432
1581967121194899,765,780,4,5432
1581967121299137,765,781,6,5432
```

By aggregating log entries from these 3 resulting log files, we can reconstruct a request: a pair (PID, SOCK_FD) is unique at any point in time and represents a socket. Therefore, starting from a *connect* log entry, we look for log entries with the same pair (PID, SOCK_FD) and higher timestamp (TS) in the *sendto* and *recvfrom* log files, until that socket is reused (i.e., until there is a log entry in the *connect* log file with the same pair of PID and SOCK_FD).

For the experiment analyzed in Sect. 5, we calculate the response times of each request between servers by calculating the difference between the timestamps of the last log entry of that request (most likely a *recvfrom* log entry) and the first log entry of that request (the *connect* log entry). Furthermore, we used the port number that the request is connected to for calculating the queue length of each server.

4   Experiment Workflow Construction and Execution with WED-Make

Manually recreating experiment environments is an intricate, error-prone, and time-consuming task, especially of microservice-based experiments with a diverse and large set of servers: ensuring the correct execution of benchmarks usually demands more than simply releasing their software, scripts, and data – it is also necessary to satisfy their hidden and implicit dependencies, as shown in Table 1 [17].

Table 1. Common dependencies of application benchmarks.

Dependency Type	Example
Filesystem	Experiment artifacts location
Hardware	CPU features like DVFS
Cloud infrastructure	Hostname convention
Software	Installed libraries
Workload	Burstiness level

The basic workflow of a system experiment comprises:

1. Provisioning computing resources
2. Installing software
3. Configuring software and hardware (System, servers, and applications)
4. Starting servers and monitors
5. Executing benchmark
6. Collecting, parsing, and storing log data

Wise leverages the WED-Make [17] language for the construction of experiment workflows. WED-Make has embedded Bash code and the execution of so-called *WED-Makefiles* (workflow specifications in WED-Make) is driven by declared dependencies themselves, guaranteeing their satisfaction, making it appropriate for the specification of system experiment workflows.

Furthermore, provenance collection is integral to the study of past experiments [4], although not a feature of scripts commonly used for the automation of experiment workflows. In Wise, a code generation tool translates a WED-Makefile to SQL commands that create a database table and stored procedures to manage the workflow execution [17]. The columns and rows of this table represent, respectively, the Bash variables used in the WED-Makefile and workflow execution instances. In this way, provenance data (e.g., configuration parameters, location of resulting log data) are automatically stored in a relational database, enabling sophisticated analysis of past experiment executions.

5   Illustrative Example of the Millibottleneck Theory of Performance Bugs

For this experiment, we provisioned c8220 machines in CloudLab [2], a scientific cloud provider, with OpenStack installed. As an overview of the hardware and software used, each server runs in its own virtual machine with 4 virtual CPUs and 8 GB of RAM. As shown in Sect. 3, these VMs run Ubuntu 18.04 LTS with a patched Linux 4.15 kernel and the Linux Kernel Modules from milliScope that specialize syscalls *connect*, *sendto*, and *recvfrom*; also, each server runs the Collectl performance monitoring tool, version 4.3.1, with a sampling interval of 50 ms. The web server runs Apache HTTP server version 2.4 with a mod_wsgi adapter for the Flask application. The microservices are implemented in Python 3 using the Apache Thrift library version 0.13. The database runs PostgreSQL 10. The configuration of servers was presented in Sect. 2, and we also set the system parameter SOMAXCONN, which gives the maximum size of a listening socket backlog, to 64.

As shown in Sect. 2, the workload was configured to have a single group of 150 clients generating a bursty workload. Fig. 2a shows the number of requests per second with a peak close to 60. The CPU utilization graph of the database server depicted in Fig. 2b shows millibottlenecks, and the transient spikes in the data written to the database server disk in Fig. 2c is another indication of resource contention. Also, PostgreSQL database server was configured to process at most 100 transactions concurrently and, with the SOMAXCONN system parameter set to 64, the database server could not had accepted and be processing more than 164 connections at the same time. When such a limit is reached, TCP packets are dropped and have to be retransmitted. The graph depicted in Fig. 2d shows the queue length of the database server with a time window of 25 ms, where that limit is reached many times. As expected, the long-tail latency problem can be observed in the distribution of response times shown in Fig. 2e, and the point-in-time response time graph depicted in Fig. 2f shows exactly when the VLRT requests happen.

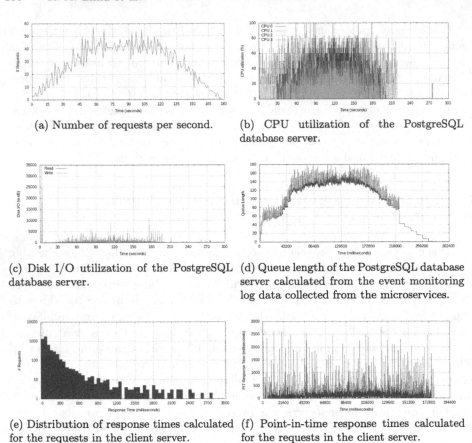

(a) Number of requests per second.

(b) CPU utilization of the PostgreSQL database server.

(c) Disk I/O utilization of the PostgreSQL database server.

(d) Queue length of the PostgreSQL database server calculated from the event monitoring log data collected from the microservices.

(e) Distribution of response times calculated for the requests in the client server.

(f) Point-in-time response times calculated for the requests in the client server.

Fig. 2. System performance analysis with Wise.

6   Related Work

Most of our past experiments ran RUBBoS [21], an n-tier system benchmark. More recently, microservice-based benchmark applications have been published and we highlight TrainTicket [28], a benchmark application simulating a railway ticketing, and the DeathStarBench [9], a suite of six cloud and edge microservice-based applications.

Many other approaches have been proposed for monitoring events in distributed systems. We highlight Dapper [23], a production-ready distributed tracing tool that uses sampling to reduce overhead, and the software-based specialization of previous releases of milliScope [16], which extended native server logs to contain unique message identifiers to idenitify request boundaries.

WED-Make is based on the WED-flow model [7]. Another workflow execution engine based on WED-flow is called WED-SQL [18], which also translates its own language to SQL commands. Another approach to generate code for configurable benchmark executions is based on templates and we highlight Mulini

[13]. DevOps configuration tools have also been used for the orchestration of system experiments, as in the Popper convention [12].

7 Conclusions

This paper presents a running example showing how Wise components fit together in a workflow that starts with the benchmark servers and workload configuration and finishes with the experiment metadata stored in a relational database, with automatic collection of provenance. The challenges and technical details behind system resource and event monitoring, experiment workflow automation and provenance, and the study of a microservice-based system performance experiment were presented, as well as how we address them with Wise. Finally, we showed an illustrative example of millibottlenecks causing the long tail latency problem in a microservice-based application benchmark.

This first Wise release has had practical impact as it is being used by several of our undergraduate and graduate students for course projects on the performance study of microservice-based applications in the cloud. For upcoming releases, we plan to build a more complex benchmark application, with a higher number of microservices and dependencies between them. Consequently, the log data analysis will become more complex, likely demanding an automated approach [10].

Acknowledgements. This research has been partially funded by National Science Foundation by CISEís SAVI/RCN (1402266, 1550379), CNS (1421561), CRISP (1541074), SaTC (1564097) programs, an REU supplement (1545173), and gifts, grants, or contracts from Fujitsu, HP, Intel, and Georgia Tech Foundation through the John P. Imlay, Jr. Chair endowment. Any opinions, findings, and conclusions or recommendations expressed in this material are those of the author(s) and do not necessarily reflect the views of the National Science Foundation or other funding agencies and companies mentioned above.

References

1. Apache Thrift. https://thrift.apache.org/. Accessed 05 Mar 2020
2. CloudLab Scientific Cloud Infrastructure. https://cloudlab.us/. Accessed 05 Mar 2020
3. Collectl Performance Monitoring Tool. http://collectl.sourceforge.net/. Accessed 05 Mar 2020
4. Davidson, S.B., Freire, J.: Provenance and scientific workflows: challenges and opportunities. In: Proceedings of the 2008 ACM SIGMOD International Conference on Management of Data, pp. 1345–1350 (2008)
5. Dean, J.: The tail at scale. Commun. ACM **56**(2), 74–80 (2013)
6. DeCandia, G., et al.: Dynamo: amazon's highly available key-value store. ACM SIGOPS Operating Syst. Rev. **41**(6), 205–220 (2007)
7. Ferreira, J.E., et al.: Transactional recovery support for robust exception handling in business process services. In: 2012 IEEE 19th International Conference on Web Services, pp. 303–310. IEEE (2012)

8. Flask. https://palletsprojects.com/p/flask/. Accessed 05 Mar 2020
9. Gan, Y., et al.: An open-source benchmark suite for microservices and their hardware-software implications for cloud & edge systems. In: Proceedings of the Twenty-Fourth International Conference on Architectural Support for Programming Languages and Operating Systems, pp. 3–18 (2019)
10. Gan, Y., et al.: Seer: leveraging big data to navigate the complexity of performance debugging in cloud microservices. In: Proceedings of the Twenty- Fourth International Conference on Architectural Support for Programming Languages and Operating Systems, pp. 19–33 (2019)
11. Gregg, B.: Systems Performance: Enterprise and the Cloud. Pearson Education (2013)
12. Jimenez, I., et al.: Popper: making reproducible systems performance evaluation practical. In: UC Santa Cruz School of Engineering, Technical report UCSC-SOE-16-10 (2016)
13. Jung, G., Pu, C., Swint, G.: Mulini: an automated staging framework for QoS of distributed multi-tier applications. In: Proceedings of the 2007 Workshop on Automating Service Quality: Held at the International Conference on Automated Software Engineering (ASE), pp. 10–15. ACM (2007)
14. Kohavi, R., Henne, R.M., Sommerfield, D.: Practical guide to controlled experiments on the web: listen to your customers not to the hippo. In: Proceedings of the 13th ACM SIGKDD International Conference on Knowledge Discovery and Data Mining, pp. 959–967 (2007)
15. Kohavi, R.: Online experiments: lessons learned. Computer **40**(9), 103–105 (2007)
16. Lai, C.A., et al.: milliScope: a fine-grained monitoring framework for performance debugging of n-tier Web services. In: 2017 IEEE 37th International Conference on Distributed Computing Systems (ICDCS), pp. 92–102. IEEE (2017)
17. Lima, R.A., Kimball, J., Ferreira, J.E., Pu, C.: Systematic construction, execution, and reproduction of complex performance benchmarks. In: Da Silva, D., Wang, Q., Zhang, L.-J. (eds.) CLOUD 2019. LNCS, vol. 11513, pp. 26–37. Springer, Cham (2019). https://doi.org/10.1007/978-3-030-23502-4_3
18. Padilha, B., Roberto, R.L., Schwerz, A.L., Pu, C., Ferreira, J.E.: WED-SQL: an intermediate declarative language for PAIS execution. In: Jin, H., Wang, Q., Zhang, L.-J. (eds.) ICWS 2018. LNCS, vol. 10966, pp. 407–421. Springer, Cham (2018). https://doi.org/10.1007/978-3-319-94289-6_26
19. PostgreSQL. https://www.postgresql.org/. Accessed 05 Mar 2020
20. Pu, C., et al.: The millibottleneck theory of performance bugs, and its experimental verification. In: 2017 IEEE 37th International Conference on Distributed Computing Systems (ICDCS), pp. 1919–1926. IEEE (2017)
21. RUBBoS Benchmark. http://jmob.ow2.org/rubbos.html. Accessed 05 Mar 2020
22. Shan, H., Wang, Q., Pu, C.: Tail attacks on web applications. In: Proceedings of the 2017 ACM SIGSAC Conference on Computer and Communications Security, pp. 1725–1739 (2017)
23. Sigelman, B.H., et al.: Dapper, a large-scale distributed systems tracing infrastructure (2010)
24. sysstat: Performance Monitoring Tools for Linux. https://github.com/sysstat/sysstat. Accessed 05 Mar 2020
25. The Apache HTTP Server Project. https://httpd.apache.org/. Accessed 05 Mar 2020
26. Wang, Q., et al.: Lightning in the cloud: A study of very short bottlenecks on n-tier web application performance. In: Proceedings of USENIX Conference on Timely Results in Operating Systems (2014)

27. Zhang, S., et al.: Tail amplification in n-tier systems: a study of transient cross-resource contention attacks. In: 2019 IEEE 39th International Conference on Distributed Computing Systems (ICDCS), pp. 1527–1538. IEEE.(2019)
28. Zhou, X., et al.: Poster: benchmarking microservice systems for software engineering research. In: 2018 IEEE/ACM 40th International Conference on Software Engineering: Companion (ICSE-Companion), pp. 323–324. IEEE (2018)

Abstracting Containerisation and Orchestration for Cloud-Native Applications

José Ghislain Quenum$^{(\boxtimes)}$ and Gervasius Ishuuwa

Namibia University of Science and Technology, Windhoek, Namibia
jquenum@nust.na, gishuuwa@gmail.com

Abstract. Developing cloud-native applications demands a radical shift from the way we design and build traditional applications. Application designers usually divide their business logic into several business functions, each developed according to a microservices architectural style and packaged in containers. Throughout the stages of cloud-native application development (development, testing, staging and production), container orchestration helps coordinate the execution environment. Thanks to the increasing popularity of cloud-native applications, there has been a growing interest in container and orchestration technologies recently. However, despite their closeness, these two inter-related technologies are supported by different toolsets and specification formalisms, with minimal portability between them and usually a disregard for the best practices. This paper presents `velo`, a domain-specific language (DSL) that unifies containerisation and orchestration concepts. `velo` has two components: (1) a specification language that supports an abstract description of containerisation and orchestration for a complex application; and (2) a transpiler, a source-to-source compiler into concrete container manifest and orchestration description.

Keywords: Containerisation · Orchestration · Domain-specific language · Transpiler

1 Introduction and Background

The growth in complexity of cloud-native applications, together with other factors, led to the introduction of *microservices* as an architectural style. More often these microservices are packaged in application containers to make them *portable, scalable, modular, flexible* and *isolated* from the rest of the application. In the past, several techniques, including virtual machines, have been used to distribute and isolate various components of a complex application [1,11,14]. However, application containers prove to be a more efficient approach thanks to the level of isolation they proffer (e.g., lower starting time and resource optimisation) [6,10,21]. When the number of related services for an application

Q. Zhang et al. (Eds.): CLOUD 2020, LNCS 12403, pp. 164–180, 2020.
https://doi.org/10.1007/978-3-030-59635-4_12

increases drastically, the management of the life cycle of the containers hosting these services, the provisioning of their resources, load balancing, security and network configuration become challenging. A standard solution to this is to introduce an *orchestrator*. The latter provides a better way to manage related distributed services across varied infrastructure using methods that can guarantee predictability, scalability and high availability. Application containerisation and orchestration have risen as two inter-related technologies. Thanks to their early success, new tools are emerging to support application containerisation and orchestration [1, 10]. These tools include `Docker` and `Rkt` for containers and `Kubernetes`, `Docker Compose`, `Docker Swarm` and `Marathon` for orchestrators.

These emerging tools still present several gaps for application containerisation and orchestration. First, the formalism used to specify the desired state of the system both for containerisation and orchestration varies from one tool to another. As such, the lack of high-level abstraction as well as unifying underlying concepts hinders complex application containerisation and orchestration. By way of illustration, consider a software development team adopting different containerisation and orchestration tools/technologies for the various stages an application goes through (development, testing, production). Specifying the desired state in a similar formalism for containerisation and then for orchestration for that application, and then adequately translating them for specific container and orchestration tools at each stage is currently not feasible. Furthermore, for a separate team to reuse the same application using different container and orchestration tools will require the second team to rewrite the same desired state of containerisation and orchestration for their tools. In short, the increase in flexibility of application development and deployment using containerisation and orchestration is matched with the increase in complexity through many moving parts.

The second gap we identified through our analysis is the lack of portability and interoperability between container or orchestration tools. New trends in software development are to write code that can be shipped instantly [19], and thus reduce the release cycle. The lack of interoperability and portability between various container or orchestration tools then introduces a bottleneck, since the same desired state will be re-written in the system only due to a change of tool. The last gap we identified is the lack of best practice enforcement in container and orchestrator specifications. Because currently, no standard governs the specification of a container or an orchestrator, only best practices can help guard against imperfect container and orchestrator specifications.

We argue that a substantial variation between containerisation or orchestration technologies is not a challenge per se. Instead, in our view, the real challenge comes from the lack of portability from one tool to another. Indeed, with different types of container tools diverging from one another, comes the looming effect of proprietary standards which introduces the risk of vendor lock-in [12]. As such, the promise containers have been touted for, i.e. provide an abstraction layer that localises applications within the container, and then port it to other computing environments, is threatened by these competing standards and formats [12]. In this paper, we present `velo`, a tool to abstract and unify the desired state specification for both containerisation and orchestration of a cloud-native application using one single declarative specification formalism. Although we presented the limitations for containerisation separately from orchestration, we advocate in our approach for unifying their specification in our quest for abstraction. `velo` has two components: (1) a domain-specific language (DSL) where we express abstract specification for containerisation and orchestration desired state; (2) a transpiler, a source-to-source compiler that translates the abstract specification into a concrete container and orchestrator. In the remainder of the paper, we discuss the related work in Sect. 2. In Sect. 3, we present the syntax of the DSL and provide a semi-formal interpretation of the underlying concepts. In Sect. 4, we discuss the compilation process in `velo` and further illustrate it in Sect. 5. Finally, we conclude the paper in Sect. 6 and highlight future directions.

2   Related Work

In [17], Peinl et al. survey a variety of containerisation tools for services in the cloud that are not cloud-aware or cloud-native. Their work focuses more on addressing the various requirements, including communication of containers across hosts and migration of containers to different hosts for multi-container applications.

Goncalves et al. present the first DSL explicitly designed to describe cloud entities, CloudML [9], introduced in the context of Distributed Clouds. CloudML fulfils three requirements: (i) representation of physical and virtual resources as well as their state; (ii) representation of services provided; and (iii) representation of developers' requirements. Building on CloudML, Ferry et al. introduce CloudMF [7], which aims at supporting provisioning and deployment of applications in multiple cloud runtime and design time. CloudMF observes a separation of concerns as well as provider independence and reusability and abstraction.

To enable the creation of portable cloud applications and the automation of their deployment and management, Topology and Orchestration for Cloud Applications (TOCSA) [4] models application components, their relations, and management in a portable, standardized, machine-readable format. Tobias et al. [3] introduce OpenTOSCA, an open-source runtime environment for the TOCSA description, which is responsible for deployment and management. It processes the cloud service archives, runs plans and also manages the deployment states. Although TOCSA looks similar to `velo`, the latter centres its efforts towards unification of descriptions through abstraction.

On the other hand, Quint and Kratzke [18] prototyped a DSL that enables to describe cloud-native applications being transferable at runtime without downtime. This work mainly focuses on the deployment and execution of cloud-native applications in a multi-cloud environment. The early results show a model that allows various services in different clouds to be moved around without interrupting the overall execution of the complex application.

The related work discussed here, although focusing on containerisation and orchestration, does not address the challenge of the growing diversity of tooling and configuration specification languages for these two inter-related concepts. In this research, we introduce an abstraction mechanism that does not prohibit the diversity of tooling but maintains consistency around the existing tools.

3   The Velo DSL

3.1   The Syntax

velo combines and relates concepts used for containerisation and orchestration. We assume that the infrastructure involves a cluster of machines (physical or virtual machines). Two concepts form the pillar of the DSL: (1) a container, a specific space within the infrastructure where processes corresponding to the services (or applications) can be executed, and (2) a *virtual bag*, a subset of the infrastructure to run containers. A virtual bag represents a coherent unit containing one or several containers. It could translate to the notion of a *pod* in Kubernetes, specified as a *Pod* **kind** or as a *Deployment* or *Service* as prescribed by the best practices. We further distinguish between two types of virtual bags; a virtual bag that can host a *single* container is called svbag, while one that can host multiple containers, called mvbag. The rationale behind this distinction is that there might only be a need for a lightweight deployment. In that case, the orchestration still provides services such as scalability and monitoring.

velo is designed to be used in two modes: *light* and *rich*. In a rich mode, all the parameters (health check, scheduling, storage, etc.) required to run the containerisation and orchestration of an application are provided in the specification file. In a light mode, these parameters are omitted from the specification file and re-introduced during compilation.

The following BNF [13,23] production rules summarise the syntax of a virtual bag. The metadata of a virtual bag includes its *identifier*, the number of expected *instances*, the *network* endpoints it has access to, the *users* who can authenticate to it, and its *version* number. *Labels*, when they are used, provide identifiers for entity names in the setup. Finally, a container has its *metadata*, the *image* it should be built from, *labels*, *resources*, *network* ports and protocols and a logical *volume* for data access and persistence. Inside the image of a container, there may be labels and commands, the actual instructions to be executed inside the container.

$$
\begin{aligned}
\langle velo\text{-}app\rangle &::= \langle velo\_metadata^*\rangle \ \langle orchestration\rangle \\
\langle velo\_metadata^*\rangle &::= \langle author\rangle \mid \langle title\rangle \\
\langle author\rangle &::= \text{'author'} \ \langle string\rangle \\
\langle title\rangle &::= \text{'title'} \ \langle string\rangle \\
\langle orchestration\rangle &::= \langle vbag\rangle \\
\langle vbag\rangle &::= \langle svbag\rangle \mid \langle mvbag+\rangle \\
\langle svbag\rangle &::= \langle v\_metadata^*\rangle \ \langle labels?\rangle \ \langle container\rangle \\
\langle mvbag\rangle &::= \langle v\_metadata^*\rangle \ \langle labels?\rangle \ \langle container+\rangle \\
\langle v\_metadata\rangle &::= \langle id\rangle \mid \langle inst\rangle \mid \langle nets\rangle \mid \langle auth\rangle \mid \langle version\rangle \\
\langle labels\rangle &::= \langle label+\rangle \\
\langle label\rangle &::= \langle label\_name\rangle \ \text{'='} \ \langle string\rangle \\
\langle label\_name\rangle &::= \langle string\rangle \\
\langle container\rangle &::= \langle c\_metadata^*\rangle\langle image\rangle\langle labels?\rangle\langle resources?\rangle \\
 & \qquad \langle network\rangle\langle volume\rangle \\
\langle c\_metadata\rangle &::= \langle name\rangle \mid \langle policy\rangle \mid \langle auth\rangle \\
\langle policy\rangle &::= \text{'restart'} \ \text{'='} \ \langle policy\_val\rangle \\
\langle policy\_val\rangle &::= \text{'always'} \mid \text{'on-failure'} \mid \text{'no'} \mid \text{'unless-stopped'} \\
\langle image\rangle &::= \langle labels?\rangle \ \langle commands\rangle
\end{aligned}
$$

3.2 Illustration

Consider a travel application consisting of four microservices: *UI Service, Car Reservation Service, Hotel Reservation Service* and *Flight Reservation Service*. Each of the last three services has a data store connected to it (i.e., polyglot

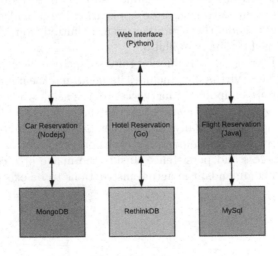

Fig. 1. Travel app

persistence). Fig. 1 depicts the interconnection between services. The TOML [22][1] in Listing 1.1 presents the light[2] abstract specification of both containerisation and orchestration for the application using velo. In this scenario, we package each component in its container. Thus, we use a mvbag with six containers.

Lines 3–6 define the *identifier* (id), number of *instances* (instances) and *network* characteristics (networks) of the virtual bag. Other attributes include matchExpressions, user and mvbag.labels (lines 7–9). matchExpressions is a grouping mechanism which groups containers according to the specified expression. user denotes the user account from which the application will be running. mvbag.labels assign labels to the virtual bag; it can be used as an identity mechanism.

Lines 15–144 define the various containers. For example, the *UI Service* (a *Web Interface*) is defined on lines 15–32. It shows the image (mvbag.containers.image) the container is an instance of, the various instructions (mvbag.containers.image.commands) to run in the container and the labels (mvbag.containers.labels) available in the container to access resources outside. mvbag.containers.networks is used to open ports for the containers. Finally, velo supports ephemeral volumes, which are defined at the container or virtual bag level. The definition must include the name, mount − path and the access right (i.e., read − only or not). This pattern is repeated for the rest of the containers in the application with some slight variation.

```
1    author = "John Doe john@example.com"
2    [mvBag]
3    id = "travel−web−app"
4    instances = 2
5    networks = ["Net1","Net2"]
6    matchExpressions = [["app","In","travel−web−app"],[ "environment","In","production"]]
7
8    user = "gervasius"
9    version = "0.1"
10
11   [[mvBag.labels]]
12   App = "travel−web−app"
13   Environment ="production"
14
15   [[mvBag.containers]]
16   name = "web−interface"
17
18     [mvBag.containers.image]
19     forcePull = true
20     id = "ubuntu:16.04"
21
22       [[mvBag.containers.image.commands]]
23       runShell = ["install","−y", "git core"]
24       run = "apt−get install −y python−pip"
25
26       [[mvBag.containers.image.commands]]
27       runShell = ["git","clone", "https://git.logicpp.net/app/python−app.git"]
28       run = "python app/python−app.py"
29
30     [[mvBag.containers.labels]]
31     tier = "front−end"
32     App = "booking−web−app"
33
34   [[mvBag.containers]]
35   name = "car−reservation"
36
37     [mvBag.containers.image]
38     forcePull = true
39     id = "nginx:1.15.8−alpine"
40
41       [[mvBag.containers.image.commands]]
```

---

[1] A minimal configuration file format compatible with YAML.

[2] The corresponding rich specification is accessible at https://github.com/joques/velo-spec.git.

```
42    workdir = "/usr/src/app"
43    #copy package.json
44    run = "npm install"
45    copy = ["./package.json","/release"]
46    entrypoint = ["sh", "run.sh"]
47
48    [[mvBag.containers.labels]]
49    tier = "back-end"
50    App = "travel-web-app"
51
52  [[mvBag.containers]]
53  name = "hotel-reservation"
54
55    [mvBag.containers.image]
56    forcePull = true
57    id = "golang:1.12.0-alpine3.9"
58
59      [[mvBag.containers.image.commands]]
60      workdir = "/usr/src/app"
61      copy = [".","/app"]
62
63      [[mvBag.containers.image.commands]]
64      #we run go build to compile the binary
65      run = "go build -o main ."
66
67    [[mvBag.containers.labels]]
68    tier = "back-end"
69    App = "travel-web-app"
70
71  [[mvBag.containers]]
72  name = "flight-reservation"
73
74    [mvBag.containers.image]
75    forcePull = true
76    id = "openjdk:8-jdk-alpine"
77
78      [[mvBag.containers.image.commands]]
79      workdir = "/usr/src/app"
80      copy = ["./application.jar", "/app"]
81      entrypoint = ["/usr/bin/java",""]
82
83      [[mvBag.containers.image.commands]]
84      runShell = ["-jar", "/usr/src/app/application.jar"]
85
86    [[mvBag.containers.labels]]
87    tier = "back-end"
88    App = "travel-web-app"
89
90    [[mvBag.containers]]
91  name = "mongoDB"
92
93    [mvBag.containers.image]
94    forcePull = true
95    id = "ubuntu:10.4"
96
97      [[mvBag.containers.image.commands]]
98      workdir = "/data"
99      run = "apt-get install -y mongodb-org"
100
101      [[mvBag.containers.image.commands]]
102      runShell = ["mongod"]
103
104    [[mvBag.containers.labels]]
105    tier = "storage"
106    App = "travel-web-app"
107
108    [[mvBag.containers]]
109  name = "RethinkDB"
110
111    [mvBag.containers.image]
112    forcePull = true
113    id = "ubuntu:10.4"
114
115      [[mvBag.containers.image.commands]]
116      workdir = "/data"
117      run = "apt-get install -y rethinkdb python-pip"
118
119      [[mvBag.containers.image.commands]]
120      # Install python driver for rethinkdb
121      runShell = ["pip","install","rethinkdb"]
122
123    [[mvBag.containers.labels]]
124    tier = "storage"
125    App = "travel-web-app"
126
127  [[mvBag.containers]]
128  name = "MySql"
129
130    [mvBag.containers.image]
131    forcePull = true
```

```
132    id = "ubuntu:10.4"
133
134        [[mvBag.containers.image.commands]]
135        workdir = "/data"
136        run = "apt−get install −y mysql−server"
137
138        [[mvBag.containers.image.commands]]
139        runShell = ["mysqld_safe"]
140
141        [[mvBag.containers.labels]]
142        tier = "storage"
143        App = "travel−web−app"
144
```

Listing 1.1. Travel App Specification – Light

3.3   Interpretation

The reader should note that the actual technologies being used for both containerisation and orchestration have their semantics. In this section, we discuss an interpretation of the concepts defined earlier as a means to express the desired state of containerisation and orchestration. Let $\mathcal{H}_i$ denote a host (a physical or a virtual machine). Let $\mathbb{C}$ denote a cluster of hosts $\mathcal{H}_0, \ldots, \mathcal{H}_n$; $\mathbb{C} = \{\mathcal{H}_0, \ldots, \mathcal{H}_n\}$. A virtual bag v is a tuple consisting of a configuration cn_v and a collection of containers running within the bag; $\mathsf{v} = \langle cn_\mathsf{v}, \{c_0, c_1, \ldots, c_\ell\}\rangle$. As well, a container c_i is a tuple of configurations, cn_{c_i}, the image the container is built upon, im_{c_i} and finally the processes running within the container; $c_i = \langle cn_{c_i}, im_{c_i}, \{\mathsf{p}_0, \mathsf{p}_1, \ldots, \mathsf{p}_k\}\rangle$. The reader should note that the configurations of both a virtual bag and a container encompass all the attributes used to describe these concepts. As well, the processes making up a container do not include the processes involved in the inner workings of the container. Rather, they include the processes corresponding to the tools and applications running under the container.

We introduce three predicates *execute*, *run* and *completed* using Linear Temporal Logic (LTL) [2] to interpret the behaviour of containerisation and orchestration. *execute* denotes the behaviour of a virtual bag (a subset of $\mathbb{C}$) during the execution. Given a virtual bag $\mathsf{v}_j = \langle cn_{\mathsf{v}_j}, \{c_0, c_1, \ldots, c_m\}\rangle$, (1) defines the *execute* predicate. It requires two conditions *always* to be met: (1) the configurations of the virtual bag must be enforced, and (2) every container orchestrated by the virtual bag must keep running until it completes.

$$execute(\mathsf{v}_j) \models \Box((enforce(cn_{\mathsf{v}_j}))\land$$
$$(\forall c_i \in orchestrated\_by(\mathsf{v}_j) \cdot run(c_i) \; U \; completed(c_i))) \tag{1}$$

As for the *run* predicate (see (2)), given a container c_i, the image of the container must first be instantiated, followed immediately by the enforcement of the configuration and the execution of the processes within c_i.

$$run(c_i) \models (inst\_image(im_{c_i}) \land (\circ(enforce(cn_{c_i})$$
$$\land (\forall \mathsf{p}_\ell \in hosted\_by(c_i) \cdot \Diamond(exec\_proc(\mathsf{p}_\ell)))))) \tag{2}$$

Finally, when c_i completes, all processes created and hosted by the container are *done*.

$$completed(c_i) \models \Box(\forall \mathsf{p}_\ell \in hosted\_by(c_i) \cdot done(\mathsf{p}_\ell)) \tag{3}$$

4   Transpiler

4.1   Mechanism

The purpose of our compilation is to transform the **abstract** specification of the desired state of an application deployment, both regarding containerisation and orchestration, into a **concrete** specification for a given containerisation or orchestration technology, and thus the configuration language that technology supports. `velo` currently supports `Kubernetes`, `Docker Compose` and `Mesos Marathon` as target orchestration technology/tool and `Docker` for containerisation (see Fig. 2).

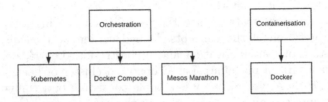

Fig. 2. Containerisation and orchestration tools

The grammar presented in Sect. 3.1 has been defined[3] in `antlr` [15,16] and implemented it in `GoLang` [5]. `antlr` is an *adaptive* LL parser [20] that distinguishes three compilation phases: *lexical analysis* (lexer), *parsing* and *tree walking*. The compiler first uses the lexer to analyse the input file (our specification in `TOML` format). The lexer groups the characters from the input file into a stream of tokens. The parser then parses the stream and generates the parse tree. Rather than using the parse tree, we generate an abstract syntax tree (AST), a finite, directed, labelled tree, where each node represents a language construct and its children represent components of the construct. Based on the generated AST, the compiler will then generate the specification file for the selected container and orchestration tools as discussed earlier. The various compilation phases include a `lexer`, a `parser` and a `transpiler` in both a target container and an orchestrator.

The final step, the generation of the target specification file, requires the traversal of the AST. By default, `antlr` provides a *visitor* pattern [8] for tree traversal. However, we opted to implement a *listener* pattern to automate the call for each specific module whenever an event related to the listener occurs. Furthermore, `antlr` checks by default the input against the grammar syntax. If there are any inconsistencies, the corresponding error information is printed in the console, and the string is returned as recognised by `antlr`. In reality, `antlr` replaces the unrecognised nodes with 'undefined'. In our compiler, however, we introduce a more customised error handling approach by overriding

---

[3] A full description of the grammar is accessible at https://github.com/joques/velo-spec.git.

`antlr`'s default error listener. We throw a syntax error exception for any syntax error encountered and save the exception information to a log file and then print all useful information (e.g., the line and column number in the input file causing the error) to the console. This assists the user in addressing the syntax error correctly and restart the process. Finally, in order to save users time during the debugging process, all errors are reported to the user during each compilation round.

To run the compiler, one invokes the `Go` program and passes the path to the `TOML` abstract specification (option −f) as well as which specific container and orchestrator(s) to generate (options −doc, −kub, −com and −mar to be set to true or false). We designed the compiler to automatically detect whether we are in light or rich specification mode. In the former case, the user is prompted to provide the missing information.

4.2 Illustration

Below we present the generated **Docker** manifests Listing 1.2 to 1.8 and **Kubernetes** orchestration description Listing 1.9 after applying our transpiler against Listing 1.1 for the travel application presented in Sect. 3.2. As this illustration demonstrates, from one single abstract specification of the desired state of the deployment, one can now automatically produce both orchestration and containerisation specifications. Moreover, the process can be reiterated for other containerisation and orchestration[4] tools.

```
1  FROM ubuntu:16.04
2  LABEL maintainer = "John Doe john@example.com"
3  LABEL description = "web-interface"
4  LABEL version = "0.1"
5  RUN [install ,-y ,git core ]
6  RUN install python-pip
7  RUN [git ,clone ,https://git.logicpp.net/app/python-app.git ]
8  RUN python app/python-app.py
9  VOLUME bookingFolder /docker_storage/booking
```

Listing 1.2. Dockerfile for the Web UI Service

```
1  FROM node:10
2  LABEL maintainer = "John Doe john@example.com"
3  LABEL description = "car-reservation"
4  LABEL version = "0.1"
5  EXPOSE 8080
6  WORKDIR /usr/src/app
7  RUN npm install
8  COPY ./package.json /release
9  ENTRYPOINT [sh ,run.sh]
```

Listing 1.3. Dockerfile for Car Reservation Service

```
1  FROM golang:1.12.0-alpine3.9
2  LABEL maintainer = "John Doe john@example.com"
3  LABEL description = "hotel-reservation"
4  LABEL version = "0.1"
5  EXPOSE 8081
6  WORKDIR /usr/src/app
7  COPY . /app
8  RUN go build -o main .
```

Listing 1.4. Dockerfile for Hotel Reservation Service

---

[4] The generated **Marathon Mesos** and **Docker Compose** files can be found at https://github.com/joques/velo-spec.git.

```
1  FROM openjdk:8-jdk-alpine
2  LABEL maintainer = "John Doe john@example.com"
3  LABEL description = "flight-reservation"
4  LABEL version = "0.1"
5  EXPOSE 8888
6  WORKDIR /usr/src/app
7  COPY ./application.jar /app
8  ENTRYPOINT [/usr/bin/java , ,]
9  RUN  [-jar ,/usr/src/app/application.jar ]
10 VOLUME configFolder /var/lib/config-repo
```

Listing 1.5. Dockerfile for Flight Reservation Service

```
1  FROM ubuntu:10.4
2  LABEL maintainer = "John Doe john@example.com"
3  LABEL description = "mongoDB"
4  LABEL version = "0.1"
5  EXPOSE 27017
6  EXPOSE 28017
7  WORKDIR /data
8  RUN apt-get install -y mongodb-org
9  RUN  [mongod]
10 VOLUME dataFolder /data
```

Listing 1.6. Dockerfile for MongoDB

```
1  FROM ubuntu:10.4
2  LABEL maintainer = "John Doe john@example.com"
3  LABEL description = "RethinkDB"
4  LABEL version = "0.1"
5  EXPOSE 8080
6  EXPOSE 28015
7  EXPOSE 29015
8  WORKDIR /data
9  RUN apt-get install -y rethinkdb python-pip
10 RUN  [pip ,install ,rethinkdb ]
11 VOLUME dataFolder /data
```

Listing 1.7. Dockerfile for RethinkDB

```
1  FROM ubuntu:10.4
2  LABEL maintainer = "John Doe john@example.com"
3  LABEL description = "MySql"
4  LABEL version = "0.1"
5  EXPOSE 3306
6  WORKDIR /data
7  RUN apt-get install -y mysql-server
8  RUN  [mysqld_safe]
9  VOLUME dataFolder /etc/mysql
```

Listing 1.8. Dockerfile for MySql

```
1  apiVersion: v1
2  kind: Deployment
3  metadata:
4    name: travel-web-app
5    labels:
6    - App: travel-web-app
7    - Environment: production
8  spec:
9    replicas: "2"
10   selector:
11     matchExpressions: [{key: app, operator: In, values: [ travel-web-app]}, {
         key: environment,
12          operator: In, values: [ production ]}]
13   template:
14     metadata:
15       name: travel-web-app
16       labels:
17       - App: travel-web-app
18       - Environment: production
19     containers:
20     - name: web-interface
```

```
21      image: ubuntu:16.04
22      restartPolicy: Always
23      volumeMounts:
24      - name: bookingFolder
25        mountPath: /docker_storage/booking
26      resources:
27        limits:
28        - cpu: "4"
29          memory: "32"
30   - name: car− reservation
31     image: node:10
32     restartPolicy: OnFailure
33     ports:
34     - containerPort: "8080"
35   - name: hotel− reservation
36     image: golang:1.12.0− alpine3 .9
37     restartPolicy: OnFailure
38     ports:
39     - containerPort: "8081"
40   - name: flight − reservation
41     image: openjdk:8−jdk−alpine
42     restartPolicy: OnFailure
43     ports:
44     - containerPort: "8888"
45     volumeMounts:
46     - name: configFolder
47       mountPath: /var/lib/ config −repo
48   - name: mongoDB
49     image: ubuntu:10.4
50     restartPolicy: OnFailure
51     ports:
52     - containerPort: "27017"
53     - containerPort: "28017"
54     volumeMounts:
55     - name: dataFolder
56       mountPath: /data
57   - name: RethinkDB
58     image: ubuntu:10.4
59     restartPolicy: OnFailure
60     ports:
61     - containerPort: "8080"
62     - containerPort: "28015"
63     - containerPort: "29015"
64     volumeMounts:
65     - name: dataFolder
66       mountPath: /data
67   - name: MySql
68     image: ubuntu:10.4
69     restartPolicy: OnFailure
70     ports:
71     - containerPort: "3306"
72     volumeMounts:
73     - name: dataFolder
74       mountPath: /etc/mysql
```

Listing 1.9. Orchestration for Kubernetes

Thus far, we have demonstrated that the transpiler in velo can automatically generate syntactically correct container manifest and orchestration specification. To further demonstrate that the execution of the generated files yields the expected behaviour, we set up a cluster of three virtual machines, each machine running on CentOS Linux (release 7.5.1884 (Core)) OS. We installed Kubernetes on the cluster and deployed the generated files (Listing 1.2 to 1.9). Then, we monitored the execution of the application and more particularly, the behaviour of both **Docker** and **Kubernetes**. Figure 3b is a snapshot of the dashboard of all containers being orchestrated. The details of the actual processes or services being containerised are in Fig. 3a. Our observation, while monitoring the execution through the dashboard, reveals an equivalence with an execution that would follow from a manual configuration.

(a) List of Docker containers.

(b) Minikube Dashboard.

Fig. 3. Application monitoring

5   Evaluation

We evaluate the transpiler in two ways: (1) the ability of the *lexer* and the *parser* to distinguish between correct and wrong syntax, and (2) the correctness of the generated AST. In the first case, we used Go testing framework[5] to write and execute several test cases. Each test case consists of input/output pairs of rules. The input can be single or multiple lines arranged in a file whose path is provided, while the output can be only success or failure, an AST, or some text output which could be a rule's template return value. In our example, we use four input files, lines 15–18 in Listing 1.10[6]. The results are summarised in Table 1. All tests pass because they generate the correct type of output. Moreover, although the

---

[5] https://golang.org/pkg/testing/.
[6] The files used for testing are accessible at https://github.com/joques/velo-spec.git.

code coverage proves to be a small percentage in each example, we make sure that each example focuses on a different scenario.

```go
package main

import (
"testing"
"../parser"
"./utils"
"github.com/antlr/antlr4/runtime/Go/antlr"
)

func TestGrammar(t *testing.T) {
    tables := []struct {
        filePath string
        isValid  bool
    }{
        {"../input/sample-svbag-rich.toml", true},
        {"../input/sample-mvbag-rich.toml", true},
        {"../input/sample-simple-error.toml", false},
        {"../input/sample-empty.toml", false},
    }
    for _, table := range tables {
        errorListiner := utils.NewVeloErrorListener()
        input, _ := antlr.NewFileStream(table.filePath)
        lexer := parser.NewVeloLexer(input)
        stream := antlr.NewCommonTokenStream(lexer, 0)
        p := parser.NewVeloParser(stream)
        p.RemoveErrorListeners()
        p.AddErrorListener(errorListiner)
        tree := p.Velo()
        antlr.ParseTreeWalkerDefault.Walk(NewVeloListener(), tree)
        if len(errorListiner.Errors) > 0 && table.isValid {
            t.Errorf("Grammar was incorrect for %s , got: %t, expected: %t.", table.filePath, table.isValid,
!table.isValid)
        }
        if len(errorListiner.Errors) == 0 && !table.isValid {
            t.Errorf("Grammar was incorrect for %s , got: %t, expected: %t.", table.filePath, !table.isValid,
table.isValid)
        }
    }
}
```

Listing 1.10. Grammar test

Table 1. Results for syntax testing

Test case	Code coverage	Test result	Time
sample-svbag-rich.toml	29.3%	**PASS**	0.024 s
sample-mvbag-rich.toml	29.8%	**PASS**	0.028 s
sample-simple-error.toml	20.4%	**PASS**	0.028 s
sample-empty.toml	1.1%	**PASS**	0.008 s

In the second case, we use a JSON representation of the AST to verify that the produced AST corresponds to the expected one. Each *terminal* node is converted into a JSON array that can contain other JSON objects. Each *non-terminal* node is converted into a JSON object that has two properties: *type*, which contains the integer value mapping to the type of token; while *text* contains the actual value of the token specified in the input file. We used JUnit 5[7] testing framework to write and execute our test cases. We compare the expected JSON to the one generated from compilation using the built-in assertion mechanism. As depicted in Table 2, the first two tests pass while the AST generated from the last test failed.

---

[7] https://junit.org/junit5/.

Table 2. Results for compiler testing

Test case	Code coverage	Test result	Time
sample-svbag-rich.toml	29.3%	**PASS**	0.193 s
sample-mvbag-rich.toml	29.8%	**PASS**	0.2 s
sample-simple-error.toml	20.4%	**FAIL**	0.224 s

6 Conclusion

In this paper, we addressed the growing diversity in application containerisation and orchestration. These are two interrelated deployment and execution technologies which embrace different tools with no interoperability and portability between their specification languages. As a solution, we introduced velo, a unifying DSL that abstracts containerisation and orchestration in complex applications, including cloud-native applications. velo has two components: (1) a language that helps specify an abstract desired state of the deployment in terms of containerisation and orchestration, and (2) a source-to-source compiler that automatically generates concrete target container and orchestration specifications. The velo DSL offers two specification modes. In the *rich* mode, the user can specify every single detail of the desired state of the orchestration and containerisation. In the *light* mode, all of the unnecessary details are removed, allowing the user to provide them during the compilation. In this paper, we discussed both the DSL and the compiler and illustrated them using a real-world example.

The benefit of velo is that in one single abstract specification, both containerisation and orchestration concepts are defined and then automatically generated for concrete tools and environments. This allows a high level of flexibility for a developer team while maintaining a consistent core. It embraces the growing diversity around cloud application deployment, particularly regarding orchestration and containerisation. Finally, it enables us to enforce the best practices for each of these technologies.

In the future, we wish to extend the range of target tools, particularly for containerisation. Moreover, although the compiler can distinguish between rich and light specifications, we wish to make the language even leaner. For example, currently, whenever the RUN command in a container refers to a tool, it goes without saying that the latter should be automatically installed first and foremost. By the same token, whenever tools need to be installed an upgrade of the underlying OS distribution might be required before the installation. All these optimization rules will then be incorporated in the transpiler. Finally, we wish to make the compiler smarter by introducing richer heuristics, particularly with regards to the best practices that can be followed during the compilation.

References

1. de Alfonso, C., Calatrava, A., Moltó, G.: Container-based virtual elastic clusters. J. Syst. Softw. **127**, 1–11 (2017)
2. Babenyshev, S., Rybakov, V.: Linear temporal logic LTL: basis for admissible rules. J. Logic Comput., pp. 157–177. (2011). https://doi.org/10.1093/logcom/exq020
3. Binz, T., Breitenbücher, U., Haupt, F., Kopp, O., Leymann, F., Nowak, A., Wagner, S.: OpenTOSCA – a runtime for TOSCA-based cloud applications. In: Basu, S., Pautasso, C., Zhang, L., Fu, X. (eds.) ICSOC 2013. LNCS, vol. 8274, pp. 692–695. Springer, Heidelberg (2013). https://doi.org/10.1007/978-3-642-45005-1_62
4. Binz, T., Breitenbücher, U., Kopp, O., Leymann, F.: TOSCA: portable automated deployment and management of cloud applications. In: Bouguettaya, A., Sheng, Q., Daniel, F. (eds.) Advanced Web Services, pp. 527–549. Springer, New York. https://doi.org/10.1007/978-1-4614-7535-4_22
5. Donovan, A.A., Kernighan, B.W.: The Go Programming Language, 1st edn. Addison-Wesley Professional, Boston (2015)
6. Felter, W., Ferreira, A., Rajamony, R., Rubio, J.: An updated performance comparison of virtual machines and linux containers. In: 2015 IEEE International Symposium on Performance Analysis of Systems and Software, ISPASS 2015, Philadelphia, PA, USA, 29–31 March 2015, pp. 171–172 (2015). https://doi.org/10.1109/ISPASS.2015.7095802
7. Ferry, N., Chauvel, F., Rossini, A., Morin, B., Solberg, A.: Managing multi-cloud systems with cloudMF. In: Proceedings of the Second Nordic Symposium on Cloud Computing & Internet Technologies, pp. 38–45. ACM (2013)
8. Gamma, E., Helm, R., Johnson, R., Vlissides, J.: Design Patterns: Elements of Reusable Object-oriented Software. Addison-Wesley Longman Publishing Co., Inc., Boston (1995)
9. Goncalves, G., et al.: Cloudml: an integrated language for resource, service and request description for d-clouds. In: 2011 IEEE Third International Conference on Cloud Computing Technology and Science, pp. 399–406. IEEE (2011)
10. Kratzke, N.: About microservices, containers and their underestimated impact on network performance. CoRR abs/1710.04049 (2017)
11. Kratzke, N.: Smuggling multi-cloud support into cloud-native applications using elastic container platforms. In: CLOSER, pp. 29–42 (2017)
12. Linthicum, D.S.: Moving to autonomous and self-migrating containers for cloud applications. IEEE Cloud Comput. **3**(6), 6–9 (2016)
13. McCracken, D.D., Reilly, E.D.: Backus-naur form (BNF). In: Encyclopedia of Computer Science, pp. 129–131. John Wiley and Sons Ltd., Chichester, UK (2003). http://dl.acm.org/citation.cfm?id=1074100.1074155
14. Pahl, C., Brogi, A., Soldani, J., Jamshidi, P.: Cloud container technologies: a state-of-the-art review. IEEE Trans. Cloud Comput. 1 (2017). https://doi.org/10.1109/TCC.2017.2702586
15. Parr, T.J., Quong, R.W.: ANTLR: a predicated-LL(k) parser generator. Softw. Pract. Exper. **25**(7), 789–810 (1995). https://doi.org/10.1002/spe.4380250705
16. Parr, T.P., Fisher, K.: LL(*): the foundation of the ANTLR parser generator. In: PLDI, pp. 425–436. ACM (2011)
17. Peinl, R., Holzschuher, F., Pfitzer, F.: Docker cluster management for the cloud-survey results and own solution. J. Grid Comput. **14**(2), 265–282 (2016)
18. Quint, P., Kratzke, N.: Towards a lightweight multi-cloud DSL for elastic and transferable cloud-native applications. In: CLOSER, pp. 400–408. SciTePress (2018)

19. Rodríguez, P., et al.: Continuous deployment of software intensive products and services: a systematic mappingstudy. J. Syst. Softw. **123**, 263–291 (2017). https://doi.org/10.1016/j.jss.2015.12.015. http://www.sciencedirect.com/science/article/pii/S0164121215002812

20. Sippu, S., Soisalon-Soininen, E.: On LL(k) parsing. Inf. Control **53**(3), 141–164 (1982). https://doi.org/10.1016/S0019-9958(82)91016-6. http://www.science direct.com/science/article/pii/S0019995882910166

21. Soltesz, S., Pötzl, H., Fiuczynski, M.E., Bavier, A., Peterson, L.: Container-based operating system virtualization: a scalable, high-performance alternative to hypervisors. SIGOPS Oper. Syst. Rev. **41**(3), 275–287 (2007). https://doi.org/10.1145/1272998.1273025. http://doi.acm.org/10.1145/1272998.1273025

22. TOML. https://github.com/toml-lang/toml. Accessed 8 June 2019

23. Zaytsev, V.: BNF was here: what have we done about the unnecessary diversity of notation for syntactic definitions. In: Proceedings of the 27th Annual ACM Symposium on Applied Computing SAC 2012, pp. 1910–1915. ACM, New York (2012). https://doi.org/10.1145/2245276.2232090. http://doi.acm.org/10.1145/2245276.2232090

Toward a Decentralized Service Marketplace: The Interplay Between Blockchain and Algebraic Service Composition

Chen Qian[1] and Wenjing Zhu[2(✉)]

[1] School of Computer Science and Technology,
Donghua University, Shanghai, China
`chen.qian@dhu.edu.cn`
[2] Institute of Scientific and Technical Information of Shanghai,
Shanghai Library, Shanghai, China
`wjzhu@libnet.sh.cn`

Abstract. Service marketplaces are supposed to guarantee an open platform for sellers and customers of cloud services. But their potentials cannot be fully released, due to the widely known shortcomings including but not limited to central power of authority, data privacy, lack of customization, rigid and complex trading procedure. We argue that decentralized marketplaces, although not mature, are the most promising solution to address these issues. In this paper, we present our work in progress, which is oriented toward a blockchain-enabled marketplace for sharing services at different levels of granularity in a flexible and trustworthy manner.

1 Introduction

Over the past decade, cloud technologies have been developed at an unprecedented speed, whilst cloud-based applications have increasingly penetrated all areas of industry, e.g., E-commerce [1] and intelligent manufacturing [2]. Cloud services allow companies and individuals to focus on their core business and researches whilst gain the benefits from software resources that are managed by third parties at remote locations. Thus, a service marketplace providing rapid, flexible and trusted outsourcing of computing services is in demand.

Conventional services are developed and deployed in the form of monolithic computation units, in which all the code is interwoven into one large piece [3]. As a result, the monolith hinders the scalability and efficiency of client applications, especially when the number of participant services is increased. To address the issue, Function-as-a-Service (FaaS) is proposed, by means of structuring a *serverless architecture* that decomposes software applications into fine-grained functions [4]. Such functions are further invoked remotely at runtime. Therefore, our proposed marketplace is FaaS oriented.

© Springer Nature Switzerland AG 2020
Q. Zhang et al. (Eds.): CLOUD 2020, LNCS 12403, pp. 181–198, 2020.
https://doi.org/10.1007/978-3-030-59635-4_13

On the other hand, most of the cloud services are offered in a centralized manner. Figure 1(a) demonstrates a centralized marketplace, in which off-the-shelf functions are gathered by a service provider, and further remotely invoked by clients. During the transaction process, there is no direct communication between third parties and clients. However, in many cases, customers demand more specific functions with strategic flexibility for ad hoc domains. Furthermore, they want to keep cost transparent and lower the risk of investment. Likewise, sellers also have concerns about the security in the trade, e.g., the privacy of their algorithms and data. Hence, we establish a decentralized market governed by blockchain.

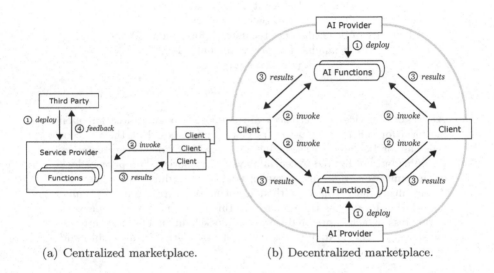

(a) Centralized marketplace.　　　　(b) Decentralized marketplace.

Fig. 1. Main entities and interactions in marketplaces.

Blockchain used to be defined as a distributed ledger for recording unalterable transactions of any digital asset [5]. With the integration of *smart contract*, it has evolved to *blockchain 2.0*, which refers to a programmable distributed trust infrastructure that enables the decentralization of markets more generally [6]. Undoubtedly, it becomes the most promising technology to create a decentralized service marketplace. Figure 1(b) expresses such a marketplace, which is essentially a peer-to-peer (P2P) network. The interconnected users share resources among each other without the usage of a centralized service provider. The blockchain plays an important role in our marketplace. Its usages include but not limit to (i) identifying every stakeholder in the open market by digital ID; (ii) monitoring supply chains that every service can be traced back to its original owner; (iii) depositing every transaction after the smart contract is executed; and (iv) protecting the copyrights by verification of contents. The details will be discussed below.

In this paper, we integrate a novel service composition model, namely BOX-MAN, with blockchain technology, with the purpose of establishing a decentralized service marketplace. In Sect. 3, we explain the research motivation by an example. In Sect. 4, we introduce BOX-MAN service model, including its structure, semantics and composition mechanism. Then, in Sect. 5, we demonstrate the prototype of our decentralized marketplace in terms of a platform based on the integration of BOX-MAN model and blockchain. Section 7 discusses the advantages of BOX-MAN, along with the proposed decentralized service marketplace. The final section makes a conclusion and looks forward to the future work.

2 Related Work

2.1 Serverless Computing

The concept of serverless computing originally refers to P2P software [7]. In the cloud era, serverless computing refers to an execution model that allows software engineers focus on their core business by developing and deploying code into production without concerning the server. Notably, the serverless solutions are in effect server-hidden, i.e., the physical servers are still adopted, but scaling planning and maintenance operations are hidden from the user [8].

Most of the cloud providers offer databases and underlying storage services for serverless computing. Moreover, many providers establish a platform offering function-as-a-service (FaaS), such as *AWS Lambda* and *Google Cloud Functions* [9]. These platforms usually support edge computing, so code segments can be executed closer to the location where they are needed [10].

Serverless computing has several advantages, as listed below [11]:

- **Cost.** Comparing to renting or purchasing servers, serverless computing is much cheaper, due to the clients do not need to pay for underutilization or idle time.
- **Scalability.** Adding or updating computation resources is no longer relying on developers. Instead, the cloud provider is responsible for scaling the capacity to the demand.
- **Productivity.** Traditional software engineering has many concerns, such as multi-threading processes or dependencies between modules. Serverless computing requires less programming knowledge.

2.2 Blockchain

Blockchain is one of the most promising technologies in the future, because it has the abilities of (i) encouraging data sharing, (ii) optimizing business processes, (iii) reducing operating costs, (iv) improving collaboration efficiency and (v) building trustworthy systems. At present, blockchain has been adopted in many industry domains, such as supply chains, intellectual property protection, digital voting, medical recordkeeping and so forth [12].

Blockchain has several advantages, as listed below [13]:

- **Decentralization.** Blockchain does not contain a central data hub. Instead, it deposits data across a P2P network. Hence, the blockchain eliminates a number of risks caused by centralized points of vulnerability and failure. For example, if a node in the network is hacked, we can still restore the data through other nodes.
- **Transparency.** All data on the blockchain is public, i.e., any user can access any data stored on the blockchain.
- **Traceability.** In blockchain, the history of transaction is deposited in the blocks, which are connected one after another. Therefore, every transaction can be traced.
- **Self-governing.** Blockchain is organized and managed by every node, since every transaction must be validated and confirmed via consensus. Thus, blockchain upholds a trustworthy system.

Since the second generation of blockchain, users can achieve agreements among parties through *smart contracts*. Simply put, smart contracts can be considered as electronic contracts that can be partially or fully executed or enforced without human interaction [14]. It is worth noting that a smart contract cannot be modified or withdrew after it is deployed on the blockchain.

2.3   Service Marketplace

At present, there are many *cloud service providers* (CSPs) on the market, but most of them just peddle their software frameworks as development tools that allow developers to build and launch their own applications, or issue some very common APIs such as map or weather forecast. Simply put, what these CSPs sell are more of commodity products than services [15]. In fact, a service is largely a piece of commodity product, e.g.., a well-trained neural network, which is acquired by customers to fill the placeholder in their own applications. Only a few of CSPs provides vendor-dedicated marketplaces.

Unfortunately, limitations still exist in current vendor-dedicated marketplaces. Because services are more complex to understand than ready-to-go products, CSPs can just label the services and let customers search what they want by a set of keywords. As a consequence, it is inevitable that for every acquisition customers spend a lot of time and effort interacting with the service provider [16]. Moreover, customers are not allowed to systematically compare all available services across different service providers, especially when CSPs want to promote their own services.

It becomes obvious that a decentralized service marketplace is the most promising solution to improve the effectiveness and efficiency of service acquisition.

3   Motivating Example

Deep learning has been increasingly applied in various specialties in medicine [17], such as radiology, imaging and disease diagnosis. A practical intelligent healthcare application usually consists of several well-trained deep learning models, each of which is a multi-layer neural network that processes medical data in a hierarchical fashion. Thereby, it becomes obvious that AI algorithms and datasets are crucially important in intelligent healthcare. However, some medical domains are close enough to share parts of the functional requirement, along with similar (even identical) datasets. Hence, during the development of an intelligent medical application, we can take advantage of reusing AI functions from existing ones. In this section, we use an example to demonstrate our research motivation.

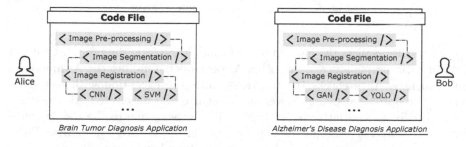

Fig. 2. Two AI applications containing same functions.

Figure 2 shows that Alice plans to develop an AI-based application for brain tumor diagnosis, whereas Bob already implemented an Alzheimer's disease diagnosis application. Both applications require user to upload the brain MRI scans for pre-processing, segmentation and registration, with the aim of obtaining the normalized information for further analysis. Apparently, Alice can save time and computing resource if she reuses some functions of Bob's software. But, here is the problem: Bob's post-trained AI model is formed as a monolithic code file, in which the couplings between code segments would hinder the extraction and reuse of required functions. Thus, the first task of our research is to investigate a reuse mechanism for intelligent applications.

Notwithstanding, let us assume the reuse issues are addressed. Now, Alice sends a query about a particular AI function in the network. Four strangers, namely Bob, Charlie, Dave and Eve, respond and claim to have the functions conforming with the requirement. Unfortunately, Alice can only afford one function among them. In order to pick up the most suitable AI function, she need to make a comparison before the trade.

As Fig. 3(a) shows, Alice tries to solves the problem by sending the test data to all four strangers. Ideally, she will receive four test results for comparison. However, Fig. 1(a) illustrates the risks possibly happening in the procedure. For example, Charlie's function is not actually fit, so it returns invalid result; while Dave forges the result to make sure that he can win the contract, and Eve somehow does not respond at all. As a consequence, Alice perhaps choose Charlie or Dave, even though only Bob gives back the valid and honest result.

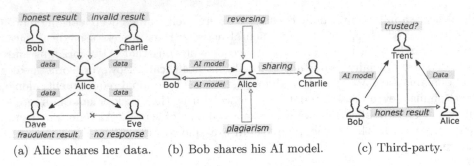

(a) Alice shares her data.   (b) Bob shares his AI model.   (c) Third-party.

Fig. 3. Sharing strategies in marketplace.

Now, Alice realizes the flaws in her solution. Therefore, she proposes a work-around with reverse process, i.e., other AI developers send her the AI functions. Subsequently, Alice checks the functions, runs the execution with test data, selects the optimized one and eventually returns the unselected AI functions. Undoubtedly, her initiative is not accepted by others, due to the risk is transferred to them. For example, as depicted in Fig. 3(b), Alice can analyze Bob's code via reverse engineering, and refactor the function in her own way, which in essence is plagiarism. Moreover, Alice can share Bob's AI function or her refactored function to others, which severely violates Bob's intellectual property rights.

The lesson from the previous try-outs is that direct trades between buyers and sellers are not safe. Thus, Alice and Bob decide to introduce *centralized management*. As Fig. 3(c) shows, Trent plays a role as a trusted third-party, who receives test data from Alice and AI function from Bob, respectively. Then, Trent can perform the testing and return the result to both Alice and Bob. However, this method is not flawless because Trent can be the loophole. He can easily gather tremendous information in the network, and misuse them without supervision.

The blockchain technology gives us a glimmer of hope to address the issues in our motivating example. For instance, every transaction can be recorded in the decentralized database, whereas every trader's behavior can be constrained by smart contracts. However, keeping using tangling and scattering code within disorganized systems as shown in Fig. 2 does not help. In order to unlock the full potential of blockchain, we need a platform that promotes understanding, communication and negotiation between all stakeholders, captures early decisions about the system designs, and supports large-scale adoption with flexibility and complexity considerations.

4   BOX-MAN

In this section, we put forward a service composition model, called BOX-MAN (Blockchain-Oriented X-MAN), which is inspired by X-MAN component model and its extensions [18–20]. In our proposed platform, we adopt BOX-MAN to design and implement systems, as well as to establish the smart contracts. In addition, BOX-MAN can be used for content verification. Figure 4 illustrates the BOX-MAN constructs which we further describe below.

The BOX-MAN model defines two types of services: *atomic* or *composite*, and three kinds of connectors: *composition, adaptation* and *parallel* connector. An atomic service encapsulates a set of methods in the form of an input-output function with a purpose that different services can access. A composite service consists of sub-services (atomic or composite) composed by exogenous composition connectors, which coordinate control flows between sub-services from the outside. Therefore, services are unaware they are part of a larger piece of behavior.

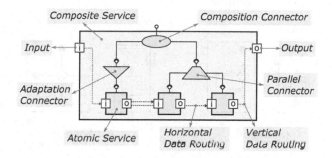

Fig. 4. BOX-MAN: Service models.

Notably, BOX-MAN model defines *algebraic service composition* [21, 22]. This idea is enlightened by algebra where functions are composed hierarchically into a new function of the same type. Hereby we utilize a composition connector as an operator to hierarchically compose multiple sub-services into a bigger service, while the resulting service can be further composed with other services, yielding a more complex one.

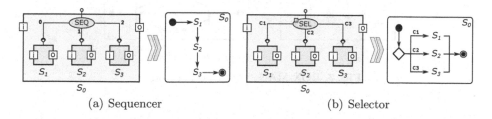

(a) Sequencer   (b) Selector

Fig. 5. BOX-MAN: Composition connectors.

There are two types of composition connectors: *sequencer* and *selector*. The former defines sequencing, while the latte defines branching. For example, in

Fig. 5(a)[1], S_0 is a composite service composed by S_1, S_2 and S_3. The execution order of sub-services is defined by numbers in ascending order. Therefore, when S_0 is invoked, virtually sub-services S_1, S_2 and S_3 are executed one after another. Similarly, in Fig. 5(b), the control flow of S_0 is coordinated by a selector with conditions. So, when S_0 is invoked, only one sub-service should be executed (or none if no condition is satisfied) according to the parameter received by the selector.

Unlike the composition connectors, the adaptation connectors do not compose services. Instead, they are applied to individual services with the aim of adapting the received controls. As Fig. 6(a) and 6(b) show respectively, a *guard* connector allows control to reach a service only if the condition is satisfied, while a *loop* connector repeats control to a component a fixed number of times until the condition is no longer fulfilled.

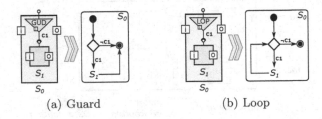

(a) Guard   (b) Loop

Fig. 6. BOX-MAN: Adaptation connectors.

Except for the composition and adaptation connectors, BOX-MAN additionally defines a parallel connector to handle the parallel invocation of sub-services. As shown in Fig. 7, when S_0 is invoked, all its sub-services are executed simultaneously.

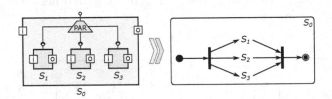

Fig. 7. BOX-MAN: Parallel connectors.

While the exogenous connectors coordinate the control flows, the *data channels* coordinate the data flows. After a composite service is structured, we need to add data channels between services in order to define the direction of each data

---

[1] For the simplicity, we omit all the data channels in the following figures, except Fig. 11. We show partial data channels in Fig. 11.

flow. Such a channel links the *input* and *output* of services. Figure 4 demonstrates two types of data channels in the composite service: *horizontal data routing* and *vertical data routing* [23]. The former is between two individual services, which indicates a service passes the outcome data to another. The latter is data propagation between the services and its sub-services, which illustrates the data received by the composite service is passed to the first invoked sub-service, whereas the outcome data of last invoked sub-service becomes the output of the composite service.

In the next section, we present an example that shows how to use the BOX-MAN composition semantic to construct services on our platform and related smart contracts of the blockchain.

5   The Proposed Platform

We hereby present an example of a blockchain-based platform using BOX-MAN for service trading.

In Sect. 3, we discuss that an intelligent application is usually composed by several AI services, such as Bob's Alzheimer's disease diagnosis application in Fig. 2. Because of the algebraic nature of BOX-MAN, such an AI application can be designed and implemented in the form of an algebraic service composition. For example, as depicted in Fig. 8, Eve develops an application with five accessible services, which consists of three atomic services (A_1, A_2 and A_3) and two composite ones (S_E and S_0). Notably, S_E is a composition of A_2 and A_3, while S_0 is a composition of A_1 and S_E. As a result, Eve can share the five services (or their functional specifications) on the platform without exposing the encapsulated code.

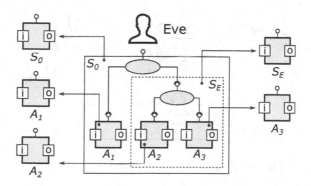

Fig. 8. Eve shares five AI services.

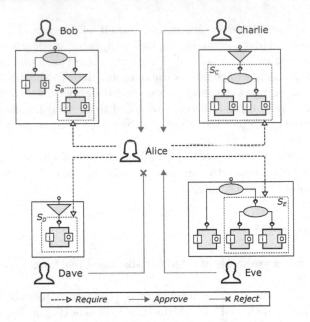

Fig. 9. Step 1: Alice asks for the AI services she desires.

Now, Alice desires an AI service of image registration for brain MRI, as we mention in Sect. 3. Then, she starts to search the appropriate services, and eventually finds out four potential results: S_B, S_C, S_D and S_E. As Fig. 9 illustrates, Alice makes requests to Bob, Charlie, Dave and Eve, respectively. Dave rejects her proposal, whereas others approve.

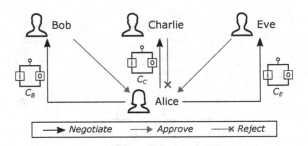

Fig. 10. Step 2: Alice negotiates with others.

After that, Alice negotiates conditions with Bob, Charlie and Eve, respectively. For instance, if Alice makes a decision to accept Bob's AI service, she may pay Bob some credits for it. Such a deal is realized by programming encapsulated in a BOX-MAN service, which is further adopted in the smart contract deployed at the platform layer. In Fig. 10, the negotiation between Alice and

Charlie breaks down, but Bob and Eve approve their conditions, i.e., C_B and C_E are implemented and deployed at Bob's and Eve's nodes, respectively.

The next step is crucial. Alice must establish a fair mechanism in order to choose the optimized service out of Bob's and Eve's AI services (S_B and S_E). Figure 11 demonstrates a smart contract by means of a distributed BOX-MAN composite service. In this case, Alice sends the same set of test data to S_B and S_E simultaneously for execution. Subsequently, two sets of actual results, as well as a set of expected result, are automatically sent to S_J. The main functions of S_J are (i) respectively investigating how many predictions in the actual results are correct, and (ii) determining the better service according to the accuracies. After that, the decision will be passed to the selector. Finally, if S_B is the winner, contract C_B will be executed, and *vice versa*.

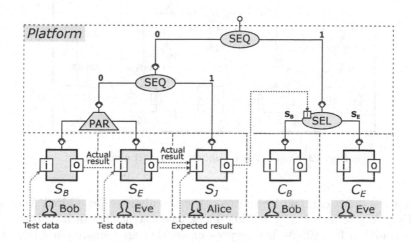

Fig. 11. Step 3: Alice constructs her own AI service.

It is worth noting that our smart contracts are distributed systems, whose sub-services are located on different networked nodes. For instance, in Fig. 11, S_B and C_B are deployed in Bob's node, as well as S_E and C_E in Eve's node and S_J in Alice's node. The rest of the contract, i.e., the connectors, are deployed in the platform layer. Therefore, our smart contract not only keeps the deal alive, but also protect the stakeholders' rights, as listed below:

1. For Alice, it reduces the risk of data breach. Only Bob and Eve, who sincerely want to close the deal, get the test data. Notably, neither of them can access the expected result. On the other hand, Alice does not need to worry about being cheated.
2. For other stakeholders, it prevents their AI algorithms and code from falling into the wrong hands all along. The computation unit is encapsulated in an AI service, which is deployed in local node only.

3. For Bob and Eve, they do not concern if Alice violates the contract, because she has no authority to interfere the smart contract in the run-time or modify the negotiated conditions deployed in other nodes.
4. Although the platform coordinate the activities defined in the smart contract, it does not handle any data or code. Simply put, no matter who manages the platform, the administrator knows less than anyone in the deal.

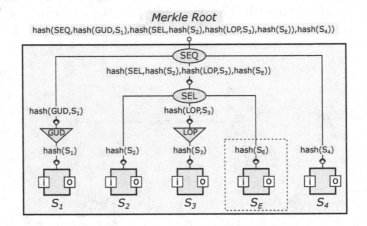

Fig. 12. Step 4: Alice publishes a smart contract.

After the smart contract is executed, Alice finally gets her desired AI service from Eve. So, she uses it as a building block to construct her own AI service, as demonstrated in Fig. 12. We hereby present another area where our BOX-MAN model could potentially bring advantages. Blockchain has been widely considered suitable for copyright protection, due to the digitized assets can be stored in a distributed database for good [24]. However, in order to verify content in a large body of data in a efficient and secure manner, blockchain introduces *Merkle trees* as one of its fundamental parts [25]. As a matter of fact, Our BOX-MAN model is a tree structure of services, which can be converted to an n-ary Merkle tree [26]. Figure 12 also expresses the Merkle tree of Alice's new AI service. Each of these leaf services (S_1 to S_4, S_B) is hashed using some hash function. Then each group of nodes and the connector are recursively hashed until reaching the root node, which is a hash of all nodes below it. Eventually, the resulting tree has one *Merkle root*, three *Merkle nodes* and five *Merkle leaves*, as shown in Fig. 13. Notably, this Merkle tree will be verified, if Alice pushes her AI services onto the markets.

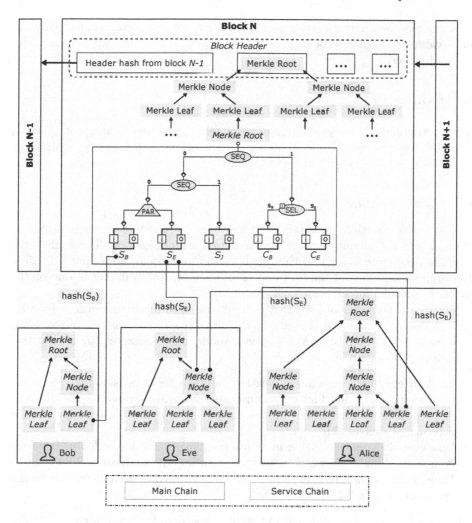

Fig. 13. Step 5: Using blockchain to record transactions.

It becomes obvious that each smart contract can be converted to an n-ary Merkle tree, due to it is also constructed by BOX-MAN. Hence, we design a *multi-chain* structure for our platform. As Fig. 13 demonstrates, the multi-chain consists of two blockchains, namely *main chain* and *service chain*. In the main chain, each of the blocks contains a unique header, and each such block is identified by its block header hash individually. The Merkle root in the header contains all of the hashed transactions in the form of Merkle leaves, each of which is another Merkle root that represents an executed smart contract. Notably, the services involved in a smart contract are hashed and stored in the leaves. The service chain essentially is a distributed database that stores the information related to every service provided by every stakeholder. Therefore, services scattering across the smart contracts and applications are connected via the identical hash values. As a direct consequence, any user can trace back any service to its original owner.

6   Evaluation

This section provides an evaluation of our algebraic and hierarchical composition model via several quality attributes, i.e., low coupling, testability, scalability, reusability, maintainability and evolvability.

6.1   Low Coupling

In software evaluation, *coupling* is a term used to measure the degree of connection and the amount of interaction between modules [27]. The higher the coupling, the more likely it is that changes to the inside of a module will effect the original behavior of another one [28]. Thereby, low coupling is one of the ultimate pursuits for software engineering.

There are six levels of coupling, as enumerated in increasing order of malignity [29]: *data coupling, stamp coupling, control coupling, common coupling* and *content coupling*. Our BOX-MAN service model only generates the loosest two couplings in a system:

1. In data coupling, the communication between services is limited, i.e., via scalar parameters, in which only simple arguments are allowed to pass directly, e.g., variable and array. The passed data is always used for an invocation or a return of control [30].
2. Likewise, the communication in stamp coupling is also limited. But it passes composite data item, which usually is a entire data structure. Thus, sometimes a data structure may contain pieces of data that are unnecessary to the recipient module [31].

The coupling has a huge impact on testability, scalability, reusability, maintainability and evolvability.

6.2   Testability

Testability refers to the effort and time required to validate the software against its requirement. Thus, a system with better testability can be validated faster and easier [32]. However, perform testing in a serverless environment is never a simple task. An application using FaaS indicates that local code and foreign code are tangling together. It is difficult to run such an application locally, unless the local environment can fully simulate the cloud environment [33].

Although the problem cannot be tackled once for all, we do facilitate the testability of systems build by BOX-MAN service model. Firstly, such a system is completely modularized with low coupling, which means every behavior implemented in the local environment can be examined in isolation by means of unit testing. Secondly, the control flows are coordinated by the exogenous connectors, i.e., outside of the services, which implies we can verify the system behavior through a statechart directly derived by following the control flows, without take the services (local and remote) into account.

6.3 Scalability

Scalability is a term that frequently appears in a variety of computer science domains. Hence, we must explicitly understand the scalability needed to be evaluated in the scope of FaaS. In order to avoid the ambiguity, we hereby define the scalability from two different aspects.

From the perspective of software engineering, scalability is a fundamental quality referring to the impact of code expansion [34]. In other words, the scalability of BOX-MAN denotes the effectiveness of BOX-MAN when used on differently sized problems. As presented in Sect. 4 and 5, BOX-MAN provides outstanding mechanisms for partitioning, composition and visibility control, which result in great scalability [35]. For example, the mammography reading system constructed in Fig. 11 can be regarded as another BOX-MAN service, which can be composed with other services, such as a *mammography report generator*, to create a *breast cancer auxiliary diagnosis application*, which can be further composed again for a very large software.

On the other hand, scalability in the context of cloud computing describes the capability of a system to increase its throughput under an increased load, e.g., creating more service instances [36]. As a matter of fact, comparing to the traditional monolithic models, FaaS achieves much better scalability. A monolithic model encapsulates all its functionalities into a single process, and scales by replicating the entire monolith. Contrariwise, current FaaS models put implemented functionalities into separate services, and replicate the desired services for scaling. Apparently, in FaaS, only services with higher demand will be scaled, while the monolithic models anyhow waste resources.

Our BOX-MAN model make a further improvement on scalability. Except the advantages brought by general FaaS models, BOX-MAN also has a superb tailorability, which is another way of assessing scalability [35]. For example, we can directly instantiate the sub-services of a BOX-MAN composite service, and use them for new compositions.

6.4 Evolvability

Evolution of software is inevitable in industry, due to the changing requirements must be satisfied during the life cycle. Thus, the cost of application mainly depends on the evolution in long term.

Apparently, in a BOX-MAN composite service, we can easily replace any sub-service with a new one, or change a connector without touching any sub-service. But, if service owner want to modify a service after it is sold, the service owner must obtain the consent of all buyers, otherwise the evolved service becomes illegitimate, i.e., any buyer has the right to forbid it from being deposited to the blockchain. In that case, the service owner has to create a new one instead.

7 Discussion and Conclusion

In this paper, we discuss a novel decentralized service marketplace from a technical aspect. Simply put, what we focus on is the underlying infrastructure (which is constructed by BOX-MAN service composition model) and the safe exchange mechanism (which is designed on the basis of BOX-MAN model as well), instead of the financial activities occurred in the course of transactions. In fact, the functions of monetary transactions are realized in the form of BOX-MAN services, and embedded in the smart contract, e.g., C_B and C_E in Fig. 11.

In order to elaborate our work, we use well-trained AI models in services to exemplify our idea in Sect. 3 and 5. It is worth noting that our platform undoubtedly supports the services of pre-trained AI models as well. For instance, Alice could delegate the training task to Bob and Dave, respectively, and choose the better one. Moreover, to protect her own right, Alice can delegate the training task and verification task to different people, all she needs to do is designing a bit more complex smart contract.

Another potential advantage of the proposed platform is easy-to-use, even for user who knows few about computer science. As we present in Fig. 5, 6 and 7, each kind of connectors has a fixed semantic that can form a statement. Hence, a smart contract can be efficiently drafted if the underlying logic is determined. But, we hope to make it easier to use, by leveraging the power of AI technology. We are working on automated BOX-MAN construction for intelligent contract using natural language inputs.

In the future, we plan to implement an integrated development environment (IDE) for developing our BOX-MAN service and the multi-chain. The subsequent plan is to evaluate our research in an industrial setting. Furthermore, we will keep investigating the convergence of cloud computing and blockchain technology.

Acknowledgments. This work has been supported by the Initial Research Funds for Young Teachers of Donghua University, the National Key R&D Program of China under Grant 2019YFE0190500 and Shanghai Engineering Research Center on Big Data Management System.

References

1. Cai, H., Zhang, K., Wang, M., Li, J., Sun, L., Mao, X.: Customer centric cloud service model and a case study on commerce as a service. In: 2019 IEEE International Conference on Cloud Computing, pp. 57–64. IEEE (2009)
2. Li, B., Hou, B., Yu, W., Lu, X., Yang, C.: Applications of artificial intelligence in intelligent manufacturing: a review. Front. Inf. Technol. Electron. Eng. **18**(1), 86–96 (2017). https://doi.org/10.1631/FITEE.1601885

improve the effect of the POI recommendation, we usually utilize time factor or social information to enhance the recommendation performance of the model.

2.1 Recommendation with Temporal Influence

POI recommendation is time-aware [6]. For example, the user may prefer to go to the restaurant at noon while go to the bar at night. And users' check-ins will be usually near the office on weekdays and close to entertainment venues on weekends. Therefore, the POI recommendation is closely related to the time. Users' preferences affect the performance of the recommendation at different time periods.

Gao et al. [6] first proposed the recommendation of LBSNs exploring temporal effects. It assumed that the user had similar behavior preference in the adjacent time slots, and they developed a regularized nonnegative matrix factorization model to establish the optimization objective. Yuan et al. [7] added the time factor into the collaborative recommendation model, and smoothed the sparse data in the current time slot by using the user's check-ins in other similar time slots. Yuan et al. [8] carried on the POI recommendation by using temporal exponential function, and proposed the GTAG method based on graph. Zhang et al. [9] proposed a time-aware successive POI recommendation and established a temporal regularization term by using the similarity of adjacent time slot. Yao et al. [10] proposed the POI recommendation of temporal matching in POI popularity and user activity regularity, and established the recommendation model by combining the heterogeneous of human activities and the POI popularity of check-ins varying with the time, which is based on GPS trajectory data set.

2.2 Recommendation with Social Influence

Social influence also plays an important role in POI recommendation [11]. The utilizing of social relationships among users can solve the cold start problem of the recommendation system to a certain extent. Ye et al. [5] made use of the similarity between different users to recommend. Jamali et al. [11] first proposed the social matrix factorization (SocialMF), which assumed that the user's check-in behavior is influenced by his friends. Further, they established a recommendation model by adding the trust relationship among friends into matrix factorization. Ma et al. [12] utilized the trust relationship of friends and combined with the probability matrix factorization to recommend. Most of the existing works only focused on measuring the impact of direct friends on users, without considering other users' impact on target users.

3 Preliminaries

3.1 Problem Description

Definition 1 (a time-aware new POI recommendation): Let $U = \{u_1, u_2, \dots u_m\}$ be the set of users, $L = \{l_1, l_2, \dots l_n\}$ be the set of POIs' locations and $T = \{t_1, t_2, \dots t_q\}$ be the set of timestamps. Where m, n, q are the numbers of users, POIs and timestamps, respectively. For a given user u ($u \in U$), according to his (or her) history check-ins (u, t, *l*) (a user *u* visit location *l* at time *t*), we aim to recommend top *N* unvisited POIs in the future, which is called a time-aware new POI recommendation. Here, $l \in L$, $t \in T$.

Definition 2 (TPR-TF Model): It is a time-aware recommendation model based on tensor factorization, and it can make use of the interaction influences between different latent vectors to construct a functional relationship, which is called TPR-TF model.

Define the score function *f*, which maps each check-in (*u*, *t*, *l*) in tensor to a real value. We aim to get a score, which can express the possible score of user *u* visiting POI *l* at time *t*. The function *f* is defined as follows:

$$f(u, t, l) = U_u^T \cdot L_l + T_t^T \cdot L_l + U_u^T \cdot T_t \tag{1}$$

Where $U_u, L_l, T_t \in R^K$ are latent vectors of user *u*, location *l*, timestamps *t* respectively. The dimensionality of the latent vectors is denoted as *K*. The inner product of U_u and L_l represents the interactive influence between user and location. The inner product of T_t and L_l represents the interactive influence between time and location. The inner product of U_u and T_t represents the interactive influence between user and time. The key notations are shown in Table 1.

Table 1. Notations

Notation	Description
U, T, L	The sets of users, timestamps, POIs' locations
D	The set of all check-ins, $D = \{di = (u, t, l)|(u, t, l) \in U \times T \times L\}$, d_i the *i*th check-in of user *u* visiting POI *l* at time *t*
U_u, L_l, T_t	The latent vectors of user *u*, location *l*, timestamps *t*
f(*u*, *t*, *l*)	The score function *f*, which is the possible score of user *u* visiting POI *l* at time *t*
$w_{i,j}^s, w_{i,j}^c, w_{i,j}$	The similarity between user *i* and *j* based on their common friends, the similarity between user *i* and *j* based on common check-ins, the mean of the similarity between user *i* and *j* based on common friends and common check-ins
A(*i*), *A*(*j*)	The set of all POI locations visited by user *i* and user *j* respectively
$l_i >_{u,t} l_j$	For $l_i, l_j \in L$, the order that user u visits POI l_i but not l_j at time *t*
$L_{soc\text{-}fri}$, $L_{soc\text{-}undirect\text{-}fri}$	The social influence regularization term of direct friendship, the social influence regularization term potential friendship
$\theta, \gamma, \lambda, \mu$	The parameter set, the learn rate, coefficient of regularization term, the coefficient of friendship's regularization term

3.2 Temporal Dynamic Segmentation Algorithm (Time Dynamic Partition Algorithm Based on Hierarchical Cluster)

In this paper, we proposed a temporal dynamic segmentation algorithm based on the hierarchical clustering. The details are shown in Algorithm 1.

Algorithm 1: Time Dynamic Segmentation Algorithm based on Hierarchical Clustering

---

Input: $D = \{d_i = (u,t,l) | (u,t,l) \in U \times T \times L\}$, ns

Output: TS

1: $TS = \phi$

2: **for each** $d_i \in D$ **do**

3:　　$TS = TS \cup \{(d_i.time, d_i.time, d_i.time)\}$;

4: end for

5: while $|TS| > ns$ do

6: $\min_{dist} = +\infty$

7: for each $s_i \in TS$ do

8:　　**for each** $s_j \in TS$ where $j > i$ **do**

9:　　　**if** $|s_i.avg - s_j.avg| < \min_{dist}$ **then**

10.　　　　$\min_{dist} = |s_i.avg - s_j.avg|$; $s_a = s_i, s_b = s_j$;

11:　　　end if

12:　　end for

13:　end for

14: $TS = TS - \{s_a, s_b\}$;

15 $s_c = (\min(s_a.start, s_b.start), \max(s_a.end, s_b.end), (s_a.avg + s_b.avg) / 2)$;

16: $TS = TS \cup \{s_c\}$;

17: end while

18: **return** TS

The input of Algorithm 1 is the set D of all check-in records and the number of segments ns, where d_i is the i-th check-in record (u, t, l) and $d_i.time$ represents the visiting time of the i-th check-in record. The output is the set of d_i time segments dynamically segmentation $TS = \{s_1, s_2, ..., s_{ns}\}$, where $s_1 = (start, end, avg)$ is the first segment of the dynamic segmentation, $s_1.start, s_1.end, s_1.avg$ is the starting time of the first segment, $s_1.end$ is the end time of the first segment, $s_1.avg$ is the average time of all check-in records in this segment. The basic flow of the algorithm is as follows: Initially, the TS set are empty (line1), and then each record d_i in the set D is preprocessed. All records are placed in the collection TS in the form of ($start, end, avg$), which is the element of TS, and each subsegment takes the average time segment as the time of the current segment. When the number of elements in the set TS is greater than ns, the two intervals with the smallest average time interval in TS are merged (line 5–17) until all records are merged into ns segments. Where s_a and s_b are the subsegments with the smallest average time interval found (line 7–13), they are removed from the set TS and then are merged into a new segment s_c into TS. Meanwhile, we record the first and last time of the new segment and update the average time (line 14–15), and finally merge the newly time segment into the original set TS.

3.3 The Influence of Social Relationships

In social networks, associated users tend to have similar interests, and users are more likely to accept the advice from friends [13, 14]. However, due to the cold start and data sparse problems of social networks, only using direct friends influence on target users is not enough to have a better result. At the same time, there is a social relationship that is generally followed in social networks. Friends of friends may be friends in the future, friends of friends also have an impact on the user [15].

Based on the above facts, we establish two kinds of social influence regularization terms for POI recommendation: the regularization term of the influence of direct friendship and the influence of potential friendship (that is, the influence of friends of friends). At the same time, it based on such a fact in the social network: If a user is far away from other users in a social network, the user's influence on the target user is likely to be weaker. Therefore, we only consider the users' influence within two hops here. The establishment of regularization term of friendship not only prevents the over-fitting of the recommendation model, but also indicates an interactive relationship between the user and his friends, which ultimately ensures that the user and his (or her) friends are more similar. We use the method of adding the regularization term of the influence of social relationships into objective function, and integrate the influence of social relationships into the recommendation model.

The Social Influence Regularization Term of Direct Friendship
Definition 3 (Direct friendship): In the friendship network, a social relationship between the user and the other user are directly connected. We use the similarity of the latent vectors of user i and his (or her) direct friend j to define the social influence regularization term of direct friendship:

$$L_{soc-fri} = \sum_{i \in U} \left\| U_i - \frac{1}{\sum_{j \in F(i)} w_{i,j}} * \sum_{j \in F(i)} w_{i,j} U_j \right\|_F^2 \tag{2}$$

Where U_i and U_j represent the latent vectors of user i and user j respectively, U is the set of all users, and $F(i)$ is the set of direct friends of the user i. $\|X\|_F^2$ is the Frobenius norm of a matrix X, that is, $\|X\|_F^2 = \sum_{i=1}^m \sum_{j=1}^n |x_{i,j}|^2$. w_{ij} is the result of the similarity measure between the user i and user j. We will discuss it in the following two cases.

(1) The similarity measure based on common friends

When user i is a friendship with user j and both have a common friend q, the similarity measure among friends can be defined by cosine similarity.

$$w_{i,j}^s = \frac{\sum_{q=1}^{|U|} F_{i,q} F_{j,q}}{\sqrt{\sum_{q=1}^{|U|} (F_{i,q})^2} \sqrt{\sum_{q=1}^{|U|} (F_{j,q})^2}} \tag{3}$$

F is an friendship matrix with its entry $F_{i,q} = 1$ (or $F_{j,q} = 1$), if the user i (or user j) and user q are friend, otherwise, $F_{i,q} = 0$ (or $F_{j,q} = 0$).

(2) The similarity measure based on common check-ins

When user i and j are friends but have no common friends between them, the similarity between friends is 0, which means the influence between friends is invalid. However, in fact that the user i and user j may not only interact with each other, but also cannot be ignored. Therefore, we use the ratio of two users with the common check-in locations to solve the problem. We use the Jaccard coefficient to define the similarity based on common check-ins:

$$w_{i,j}^c = \frac{A(i) \cap A(j)}{A(i) \cup A(j)} \tag{4}$$

Where $A(i)$, $A(j)$ represent the sets of all POI locations visited by user i and user j respectively. Based on the above two cases, we use the mean value to define the similarity between user i and its friend j based on common friends and common check-ins.

$$w_{i,j} = \frac{1}{2} * w_{i,j}^s + \frac{1}{2} * w_{i,j}^c \tag{5}$$

The Social Influence Regularization Term of Potential Friendship
Definition 4 (potential friendship): In the social network, a social relationship between the user and the other user are indirectly connected, which has two hop paths to connect social friend. For users i, his (or her) friend j's friend g may be a friendship with user i in the future. That is, g has an impact on i, and g is considered a potential friend of user i. We use the similarity of the latent vector of user i and potential friend g to define the social influence regularization term of potential friendship:

$$L_{soc-undirect-fri} = \sum_{i \in U} \left\| U_i - \frac{1}{\sum_{g \in H(i)} w_{i,g}} * \sum_{g \in H(i)} w_{i,g} U_g \right\|_F^2 \tag{6}$$

Where $H(i)$ is the set of the user i's two-hop neighbors, where $w_{i,g}$ is the average of the similarity measure between user i and his (or her) two-hop friend g based on common friends and common check-ins.

4 Model Inference and Learning

4.1 Model Inference

Based on the idea of BPR method [16, 17], we make the model inference by using the ranking order of the check-in possibility under the experience hypothesis. We suppose the order $l_i >_{u,t} l_j$, which means at time t, user u visits POI l_i not l_j. Here, we suppose the checked-in POI l_i is higher than the unchecked-in POI l_j, or the number of checked-in POI l_i more than checked-in POI l_j. Similarly, given $\forall\ l_i, l_j, l_k \in L$, if we have $l_i >_{u,t} l_k, l_k >_{u,t} l_j$, there must be $l_i >_{u,t} l_j$.

According to the definition of f function, there must be $f(u, t, l_i) > f(u, t, l_j)$. Therefore, for the scoring function f, we learn the model parameters by minimizing the negative log likelihood of all the pair orders. We also assume that users and their history check-ins are independent, then we can estimate the model using maximum a posterior (MAP):

$$
\begin{aligned}
\arg\max_{\theta} p(\theta | l_i > {}_{u,t} l_j) &= \arg\max_{\theta} p(\theta | f(u, t, l_i) > f(u, t, l_j)) \\
&= \arg\max_{\theta} \frac{p((f(u, t, l_i) > f(u, t, l_j)) \cap \theta)}{p(f(u, t, l_i) > f(u, t, l_j))} \\
&\propto \arg\max_{\theta} p(f(u, t, l_i) > f(u, t, l_j) | \theta) * P(\theta)
\end{aligned}
\tag{7}
$$

For $f(u, t, l_i) - f(u, t, l_j)$ in Eq. (7), we use the logistic function $g(x)$ to define by $p(x > 0) = g(x) = 1/e^{-x}$, then we have $p(f(u, t, l_i) > f(u, t, l_j) | \theta) = g(f(u, t, l_i) - f(u, t, l_j)) = (1 + e^{-(f(u,t,li)-f(u,t,lj))})^{-1}$, where θ represents the parameter set of U_u, L_l, T_t and $p(\theta)$ is prior probability. Furthermore, by applying Gaussian prior model, we assume the parameters $\theta \sim N(0, \sigma^2)$. The optimization objective is further adjusted to:

$$
\begin{aligned}
&\arg\max_{\theta} \prod_{(u,t,l) \subset U \times T \times L} g(f(u, t, l_i) - f(u, t, l_j)) * p(\theta) \\
&= \arg\max_{\theta} \ln(\prod_{(u,t,l) \subset U \times T \times L} g(f(u, t, l_i) - f(u, t, l_j)) * p(\theta)) \\
&= \arg\min_{\theta} \sum_{(u,t,l) \subset U \times T \times L} -\ln g(f(u, t, l_i) - f(u, t, l_j)) + \lambda \|\theta\|_F^2
\end{aligned}
\tag{8}
$$

Here, λ is regularization term coefficient corresponding to U_u, L_l, T_t. Combining the influences of temporal factor and social relationships, the optimization objective of time-aware POI recommendation is defined as:

$$
L = \arg\min_{\theta} \sum_{(u,t,l) \subset U \times T \times L} -\ln g(f(u, t, l_i) - f(u, t, l_j)) + \lambda \|\theta\|_F^2 + \mu(L_{soc-fri} + L_{soc-undirect-fri})
\tag{9}
$$

Where μ is the coefficient of friendship's regularization term.

4.2 Model Learning

In this paper, the stochastic gradient descent (SGD) method is used to learn the parameters of the model. Compared with the popular BPR method, it is to randomly select a user in training data and randomly to select the location l_i that has been visited by the user. And then, location l_j that has never been visited in training data is selected to compare with l_i. Unlike the existing BPR method, our method is performed for each user as follows: Firstly, we calculate the distribution of the frequency of the check-ins that has been actually visited by the user; Secondly, we randomly select the POI location l_i to be visited according to the ratio of frequency distribution. If it is greater, its probability of being chosen is greater and vice versa. Finally, we randomly select a new location l_j that the user has not visited in the current time segment to compare with l_i. And then we deal with the next time segment, and so on. The model parameter update process is as follows:

$$\theta = \theta - \gamma \left(\frac{\partial}{\partial \theta} (\ln g(f(u, t, l_i) - f(u, t, l_j))) + \lambda \|\theta\|_F^2 + \mu(L_{soc-fri} + L_{soc-undirect-fri}) \right)$$

$$(10)$$

Where γ is the step length (learning rate). The process of derivation is as follows:

$$\frac{\partial L}{\partial U_u} = \frac{-1}{g(f(u,t,l_i)-f(u,t,l_j))} * \frac{e^{-(f(u,t,l_i)-f(u,t,l_j))}}{(1+e^{-(f(u,t,l_i)-f(u,t,l_j))})^2} * (L_i - L_j)$$
$$+ 2\mu\left(U_u - \frac{1}{\sum_{j\in F(u)} w_{u,j}} \sum_{j\in F(u)} w_{u,j}U_j\right)$$
$$+ 2\mu\left(U_u - \frac{1}{\sum_{g\in H(u)} w_{u,g}} \sum_{g\in H(u)} w_{u,g}U_g\right) + 2\lambda U_u \qquad (11)$$

$$\frac{\partial L}{\partial L_i} = \frac{-1}{g(f(u, t, l_i) - f(u, t, l_j))} * \frac{e^{-(f(u,t,l_i)-f(u,t,l_j))}}{(1 + e^{-(f(u,t,l_i)-f(u,t,l_j))})^2} * (U_u + T_t) + 2\lambda L_i$$

$$(12)$$

$$\frac{\partial L}{\partial L_j} = \frac{-1}{g(f(u, t, l_i) - f(u, t, l_j))} * \frac{e^{-(f(u,t,l_i)-f(u,t,l_j))}}{(1 + e^{-(f(u,t,l_i)-f(u,t,l_j))})^2} * (-1)(U_u + T_t) + 2\lambda L_j \quad (13)$$

$$\frac{\partial L}{\partial T_t} = \frac{-1}{g(f(u, t, l_i) - f(u, t, l_j))} * \frac{e^{-(f(u,t,l_i)-f(u,t,l_j))}}{(1 + e^{-(f(u,t,l_i)-f(u,t,l_j))})^2} * (L_i - L_j) + 2\lambda T_t$$

$$(14)$$

$$\theta \leftarrow \theta - \gamma \frac{\partial L}{\partial \theta} \qquad (15)$$

5 Experimental

5.1 Experimental Setting

Data Description
In this paper, we select two real LBSNs datasets of Gowalla and Brightkite to verify the performance of our model. Gowalla is a mobile internet application service based on location-based social networking. Users can share POIs with each other to find the locations of interest. The datasets collected a total of 6442890 check-in records from February 2009 to October 2010, where the friendship included 196491 nodes and 950327 edges. In Brightkite, users check in and share POI location via SMS or APP.

The dataset contains many kinds of information, such as friendship, user's check-in time, location of POI. Among them, there are 58228 nodes and 214078 edges, including 4491143 check-ins from April 2008 to October 2010. Each check-in in two datasets includes user ID, time stamp, POI ID and the longitude and latitude of the POI. The whole dataset is split into three parts: training (70%), validation (10%), testing (20%). The statistical results of the two datasets are shown in Table 2.

Table 2. Statistics of two datasets

Category	Gowalla	Brightkite
Number of users	26287	24227
Number of POIs	11640	43592
Number of check-ins	1104464	3260809

Evaluation Metrics

We use two metrics to evaluate the performance of the recommendation system: Precision and Recall. In order to evaluate the effectiveness of the recommendation results, the precision and recall of the top N recommendations results were represented by P@N and R@N respectively.

The State-of-the-Art POI Recommendation Models

BRP [16]: It is the first method put forward by using the idea of ranking order to setup optimization objectives for POI recommendation. It has excellent performance for recommendation with implicit feedback.

RegPMF [18]: The POI recommendation model was established by using the similarity among friends.

UTE+SE [7]: The combination of temporal enhancement and spatial popularity enhancement is used to establish a hybrid POI recommendation model.

GTAG-BPP [8]: It is a POI recommendation using time and other related information.

Rank-GeoFM [19]: It is a POI recommendation based on ranking method by using temporal information and geographical information.

USGT [20]: It is also a time-aware POI recommendation.

5.2 Experimental Result

Parameter Settings

To get the best tuning results of the model, under the two datasets, we conduct a great number of experiments on the performance of TPR-TF model under different parameter settings. The step length is set to 0.004. The performance is optimal when the regularization term coefficient $\lambda = 0.0003$, and the friendship regularization term coefficient $\mu = 0.0001$. we set shared parameters on the two datasets as follows: we can gain the optimal result in our experiment for 5000 iterations when the dimensionality of latent vectors $k = 40$, $\gamma = 0.004$, $\lambda = 0.0003$, $\mu = 0.0001$.

The Performance Comparisons with Other Models

Figure 1 is a comparison of the performance of the TPR-TF model with the-state-of-the-art models. Based on analysis of the experimental results, we conclude as follows:

(1) The performance of TPR-TF model is better than other methods. P@5 of TPR-TF model on Gowalla and Brightkite is 11.71% and 17.60%, and R@5 is 30.09% and 72.67%, respectively.

(2) The TPR-TF model is similar to the models of BPR and Rank-GeoFM, all of which are based on the ranking order method to build the optimization objective for model learning.

(3) The TPR-TF model is superior to RegPMF from the perspective of the influence of social relationship. Although the RegPMF model also adds social relationship into the matrix factorization, it only considers the influence of the neighbors on the target users, without considering the influence of potential friends, so the performance is slightly worse. The P@5 of TPR-TF is superior to the RegPMF model by 378% and 351% respectively on Gowalla and Brightkite dataset.

(4) As a time-aware POI recommendation, our TPR-TF model is better than the USGT, GTAG-BPP, and UTE+SE models. Among several models, USGT has the highest precision. The TPR-TF model is still 50.89% and 54.79% higher than the USGT model on two datasets, in term of P@5. At the same time, the USGT model mainly emphasizes different recommendations between weekdays and weekends. The GTAG-BPP model is a POI recommendation at a specified time. Although the influence of geographic information is added into the recommendation system, the effect is much weaker than that of TPR-TF.

The Effect of Different Temporal Segmentations Methods on TPR-TF
For a time-aware POI recommendation, the result is different at different time. The recommendation system needs to divide the time segmentations to acquire users' behavioral preferences for time, by exploiting user's check-ins at different time periods. Existing

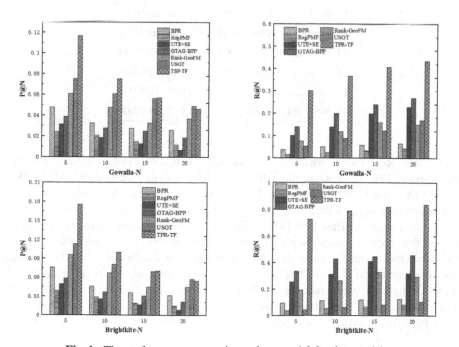

Fig. 1. The performance comparison of our model & other models.

methods usually divided identical temporal segmentation empirically. In this paper, we propose a dynamic temporal segmentation algorithm based on hierarchical clustering, which is more reasonable for time division. At the same time, the algorithm is also suitable for POI recommendation with arbitrary time granularity. Table 3 and Table 4 respectively compare the results of manual temporal segmentation with temporal dynamic segmentation under the division of 4 and 8 segments.

Table 3. Statistical results of time segmentation in Gowalla ($ns = 4$)

Category	Empirical	Dynamic
T1	00:00–06:00	00:08:55–06:57:60
T2	06:00–12:00	06:57:60–13:24:03
T3	12:00–18:00	13:24:03–19:00:01
T4	18:00–00:00	19:00:01–00:08:55

Table 4. Statistical results of time segmentation in Gowalla ($ns = 8$)

Category	Empirical	Dynamic
T1-Weekday	00:00–06:00	00:04:40–05:36:15
T2-Weekday	06:00–12:00	05:36:15–10:41:59
T3-Weekday	12:00–18:00	10:41:59–16:16:48
T4-Weekday	18:00–00:00	16:16:48–00:04:40
T5-Weekend	00:00–06:00	04:02:08–07:48:44
T6-Weekend	06:00–12:00	07:48:44–12:43:10
T7-Weekend	12:00–18:00	12:43:10–16:13:57
T8-Weekend	18:00–00:00	16:13:57–04:02:08

In the TPR-TF model, we adopt the temporal dynamic segmentation method. Different from the TPR-TF-manual, the TPR-TF model can dynamically divide all check-in records by time. From Table 3 and Table 4, we can see that the temporal dynamic segmentation does not significantly change the empirically temporal segmentation, but the result is more accurate than before. Figure 2 is a comparison of the recommendation performance of the two segmentation methods on the two datasets when $ns = 8$. The experimental results show that the performance of the model using the temporal dynamic segmentation (TPR-TF) is better than the empirically temporal segmentation (TPR-TF-manual), which fully demonstrates the effectiveness of the temporal dynamic segmentation method based on hierarchical clustering. In Gowalla, the method of temporal dynamic segmentation can reach 11.71% and 7.54% respectively, in terms of $P@5$

and $P@10$, which is 3.54% and 2.34% higher than the method of the empirically temporal segmentation. Similarly, in Brightkite, the former can reach 17.60% and 9.98% respectively, in terms of $P@5$ and $P@10$, which is 2.92% and 1.98% higher than the latter.

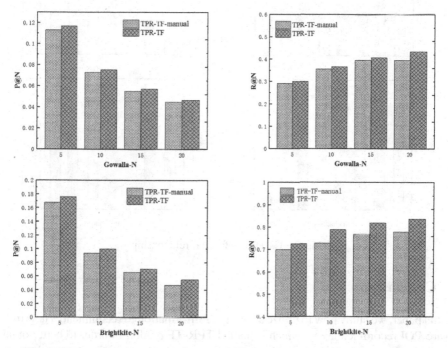

Fig. 2. The performance comparison on different temporal segmentations ($ns = 8$)

The Effect of Social Relationship on TPR-TF

Figure 3 is the performance comparison of three cases in two datasets: no friendship influence (TPR-TF without friends), the influence of direct friendship (TPR-TF with dir-friends), the influence of direct and potential friendships (TPR-TF model in this paper).

Figure 3 are the precision and recall for top N on Gowalla dataset and Brightkite dataset, respectively. The $P@5$ of TPR-TF without friends is 11.06% and 16.61% respectively in Gowalla and Brightkite, respectively, 5.55% and 5.63% lower than TPR-TF. It shows that the influence of social relationship is not negligible for POI recommendation. At the same time, the performance of the common influences of potential friendship and direct friendship (TPR-TF) is slightly higher than the model performance of TPR-TF with dir-friends, indicating that the influence of potential friendship plays a positive role in the POI recommendation.

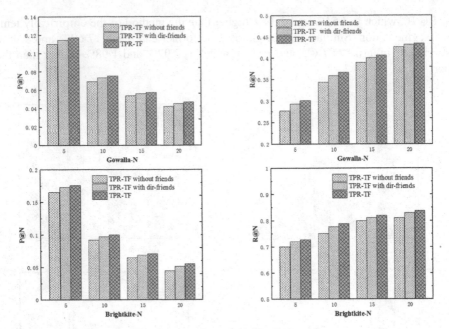

Fig. 3. The effect of social relationship

6 Conclusions

In this paper, we study how to utilize a variety of information to recommend a new time-aware POI recommendation, which is named TPR-TF model. In order to better obtain user behaviors preferences at different time, a time dynamic segmentation algorithm based on hierarchical clustering is designed, which is more reasonable than empirically temporal segmentation. To improve the performance of POI recommendation, we propose two kinds of social relationships, including direct friendship and potential friendship. Moreover, to learn the parameters of the TPR-TF model more accurately, we use the random gradient descent method to solve the model parameters. Finally, we use the interactive influences among users, POIs and time to establish a time-aware POI recommendation model based on tensor factorization. The experiments on the two real datasets show that: (1) the TPR-TF model is superior the state-of-the-art models, and (2) the application of temporal dynamic segmentation, social relationship and selecting the POIs can further improve the performance of POI recommendation.

References

1. Guo, L., Wen, Y., Liu, F.: Location perspective-based neighborhood-aware POI recommendation in location-based social networks. Soft Comput. **23**, 11935–11945 (2019). https://doi.org/10.1007/s00500-018-03748-9
2. He, J., Li, X., Liao, L., et al.: Next point-of-interest recommendation via a category-aware listwise Bayesian personalized ranking. J. Comput. Sci. **28**, 206–216 (2018)

3. Huang, H., Dong, Y., Tang, J., et al.: Will triadic closure strengthen ties in social networks. ACM Trans. Knowl. Discov. Data **12**(3), 1–25 (2018)
4. Shu-Dong, L., Xiang-Wu, M.: Recommender systems in location-based social networks. Chin. J. Comput. **38**, 322–336 (2015)
5. Ye, M., Liu, X., Lee, W., et al.: Exploring social influence for recommendation: a generative model approach. In: International ACM SIGIR Conference on Research and Development in Information Retrieval 2012, pp. 671–680 (2012)
6. Gao, H., Tang, J., Hu, X., et al.: Exploring temporal effects for location recommendation on location-based social networks. In: Conference on Recommender Systems 2013, pp. 93–100 (2013)
7. Yuan, Q., Cong, G., Ma, Z., et al.: Time-aware point-of-interest recommendation. In: International ACM SIGIR Conference on Research and Development in Information Retrieval 2013, pp. 363–372 (2013)
8. Yuan, Q., Cong, G., Sun, A., et al.: Graph-based point-of-interest recommendation with geographical and temporal influences. In: Conference on Information and Knowledge Management 2014, pp. 659–668 (2014)
9. Zhang, W., Wang, J.: Location and time aware social collaborative retrieval for new successive point-of-interest recommendation. In: Conference on Information and Knowledge Management 2015, pp. 1221–1230 (2015)
10. Yao, Z., Fu, Y., Liu, B., et al.: POI recommendation: a temporal matching between poi popularity and user regularity. In: International Conference on Data Mining 2016, Barcelona, pp. 549–558 (2016)
11. Jamali, M., Ester, M.: A matrix factorization technique with trust propagation for recommendation in social networks. In: Conference on Recommender Systems 2010, pp. 135–142 (2010)
12. Hao, M.A., Zhou, T.C., Lyu, M.R., et al.: Improving recommender systems by incorporating social contextual information. ACM Trans. Inf. Syst. **29**(2), 77–100 (2011)
13. Bin, C., Gu, T., Sun, Y., Chang, L.: A personalized POI route recommendation system based on heterogeneous tourism data and sequential pattern mining. Multimed. Tools Appl. **78**(24), 35135–35156 (2019). https://doi.org/10.1007/s11042-019-08096-w
14. Wu, L., Sun, P., Hong, R., et al.: SocialGCN: An Efficient Graph Convolutional Network based Model for Social Recommendation. https://arxiv.org/abs/1811.02815v2, July 2019
15. Guo, J., Zhang, W., Fan, W., et al.: Combining geographical and social influences with deep learning for personalized point-of-interest recommendation. J. Manag. Inf. Syst. **35**(4), 1121–1153 (2018)
16. Rendle, S., Freudenthaler, C., Gantner, Z., et al.: BPR: Bayesian personalized ranking from implicit feedback. In: Uncertainty in Artificial Intelligence 2009, Montreal, pp. 452–461 (2009)
17. Li, H., Diao, X., Cao, J., et al.: Tag-aware recommendation based on Bayesian personalized ranking and feature mapping. Intell. Data Anal. **23**(3), 641–659 (2019)
18. Ma, H., Zhou, D., Liu, C., et al.: Recommender systems with social regularization. In: Web Search and Data Mining 2011, pp. 287–296 (2011)
19. Li, X., Cong, G., Li, X., et al.: Rank-GeoFM: a ranking based geographical factorization method for point of interest recommendation. In: International ACM SIGIR Conference on Research and Development in Information Retrieval 2015, pp. 433–442 (2015)
20. Hosseini, S., Li, L.T.: Point-of-interest recommendation using temporal orientations of users and locations. In: Navathe, S., Wu, W., Shekhar, S., Du, X., Wang, X., Xiong, H. (eds.) DASFAA 2016. LNCS, vol. 9642, pp. 330–347. Springer, Cham (2016). https://doi.org/10.1007/978-3-319-32025-0_21

Manage Storage Resources Efficiently Using Predictive Analytics

Gazanfur Ali Mohammed[✉] [iD]

Cisco Systems, San Jose, CA, USA
mgazanfu@cisco.com

Abstract. Univariate time series forecasting can be used to dynamically tune the resource allocation for databases. It is vital that relational databases have adequate storage for archive logs since lack of space can cause the database to hang, while overallocation can reduce the efficiency of utilization. Most of the time, storage is allocated for the peak usage and kept for the duration of its lifecycle. This paper presents a conceptual model that uses predictive analysis to dynamically scale the storage allocation for archive logs generated by databases. The framework presented in this paper includes an exploratory data analysis on archive logs data and compares the accuracy of various statistical models, such as autoregressive integrated moving average (ARIMA); Holt damped trend; Holt linear trend; and Mean, Naïve, and Seasonal Naive models. It also suggests the best model suited for each database and provides a forecast of storage usage. These predictions can be used as input in other automated systems to automatically provision the storage or repurpose unused storage as needed.

Keywords: Database · Archive logs · Storage · Forecast · Predictive analytics

1 Introduction

Relational databases such as Oracle store all the data changes in a set of files called "redo logs" for transaction recovery, in the event of a system crash. The circular usage of these files allows the first file to be overwritten with new changes, once all files are used. Redo log files need to be archived and retained for a longer time to recover from data corruption or disasters. For example, in a situation where a database is corrupted at 11:00 am, and the last backup was created at 2:00 am, that backup needs to be restored. Then, all the archived redo logs that were generated between 2:00 am and 11:00 am need to be applied, in order to recover the database up to that point in time.

Database transaction volume and archive redo generation are correlated: a high transaction volume generates high archive redo logs. Depending on the database transaction volume, the storage required for archive logs may increase up to a few terabytes per day for a database. Moreover, the total storage consumption by archive redo logs could be high in an environment where hundreds of databases are operational.

Based on business functionality, the transaction volume of each database varies throughout the year. For example, retail store applications and databases may have higher

© Springer Nature Switzerland AG 2020
Q. Zhang et al. (Eds.): CLOUD 2020, LNCS 12403, pp. 214–225, 2020.
https://doi.org/10.1007/978-3-030-59635-4_15

transaction volumes during holiday seasons; airline applications and their databases may receive higher transactions seasonally and consume more archive redo log storage during those periods.

Based on the statistical analytics on historical data, it is possible to forecast the storage usage for the near term and plan for its efficient utilization for archived redo logs. This paper provides a conceptual model that uses predictive analytics to analyze the historical data, apply statistical models, and provide a forecast for archive storage usage for near-to mid-term. The forecasted data can be visualized using the standalone application or can be fed to a broader ecosystem that either procures more storage or repurposes it. It was found that the use of forecasting algorithms leads to significant cost reductions in both under-provisioning and over-provisioning, which is of great importance to the industry that provides cloud computing [1].

The content of the paper is organized as follows: 2. Literature Review; 3. Key Building Blocks; 4. Methodology; 5. Results and Discussions; 6. Conclusions.

2 Literature Review

Statistical, artificial intelligence, and hybrid models exist for time series forecasting. Based on the dataset, input variables, and objective of the prediction, we need to choose the right model that fits the requirements. Predictive analytics have been extensively used in finance, healthcare, manufacturing, and services domains.

Cuong et al. [2] presented a data schema that is suitable for keeping forecasting data in a table as a part of a relational database or as a portable file. They also showed how to implement various algorithms for accuracy evaluation based on the data structures proposed.

Hiroyuki [3] discussed the architecture of long-term hierarchical storage systems in order to preserve digital contents and proposed a modified file-moving algorithm with access frequency and format translations. Additionally, Mukund et al. [4] proposed a data-driven algorithm to predict the throughput bottlenecks in a production system based on the active periods of the machines.

Calvimontes et al. [5] sustained that, in a period with general demand, data can be decomposed into deterministic patterns and random fluctuations. While it is impossible to predict random fluctuations in demand, deterministic patterns can, in theory, be learned or approximated by corresponding forecasting models.

Kavya and Arumugam [6] compared the different predictive analytics techniques used in various fields. Also, Ronnachai et al. [7] concluded that the relationship between inputs and output has more effect on the model accuracy than the number of variables to generate the model. Further, these authors found out that the univariate time series model that determines inputs to relate with output has more accurate estimation and detects a movement of data better than the multivariate time series modeling that has inputs not related to output.

Ina et al. [8] demonstrated the effectiveness of the functional link artificial neural network model for seasonal time series forecasting, using unprocessed raw data. The traditional statistical models eliminate the effect of trend and seasonality from a time series before making a future forecast. This kind of preprocessing increases the computational cost and may even degrade the forecasting accuracy.

Moraes et al. [9] proposed a new methodology to reduce the number of inputs keeping an acceptable value of the estimation error; more inputs do not necessarily mean more accuracy. The longer the forecast horizon is, the fewer inputs are needed to keep prediction errors acceptable.

The calculation of the second input variable is done by the following Equation:

$$dn(T) = d(\tau) - \langle d(t)|d(t - m)\rangle \|d(t - m)\|2d(T - m)$$

where *dn(T)* is the normal vector, *d(t)* is the demand projection, *d(t − m)* is the first input, *m* is the number of sample lags between the first input and the value to be estimated, and $\langle \cdot|\cdot \rangle$ is the scalar product between the arguments.

Then Yang Syu et al. [10] forecasted the quality of service in cloud applications using genetic programming and concluded that the genetic programming machine learning technique gives better results than the traditional forecasting approaches.

3 Key Building Blocks

Not having enough storage for archive logs can cause a database to hang while over-allocating the storage, and not using it efficiently can affect the overall cost. It is very important to have storage for its maximum usage when needed and repurpose it where it is underutilized. Predicting archive log generation for each database enables the elasticity mechanism to increase or decrease the storage allocations on demand. In this section, discussion is about databases; however, the same methodology can be applied to other applications where storage usage varies significantly. These data are univariate time series data (Fig. 1).

3.1 Data Collection

The database stores the archive log details in metadata views for 45 days. In order to achieve ideal accuracy in forecast data, we use three years of archive log data that include patterns and seasonality for training the statistical models. The archive log data have to be pulled from each database and stored in a central repository for data aggregation, transformation, analysis, and forecasting. The MongoDB or MySQL database would be a good choice for the repository. These data play a crucial role for the rest of the process.

3.2 Definition of the DB Profile

Each database has its own attributes and requirements. Specific attributes and requirements of the database have to be collected and stored in a flat file in a key-value format. *Profile* is used in various stages of the workflow, and, based on attributes and criteria, necessary action is taken. Databases are classified into multiple categories, such as production, non-production, critical, and non-critical. Each category has different thresholds for alerts, archive log purging and retention, and database recovery service-level agreement. All this information is stored in *Profile* (Table 1).

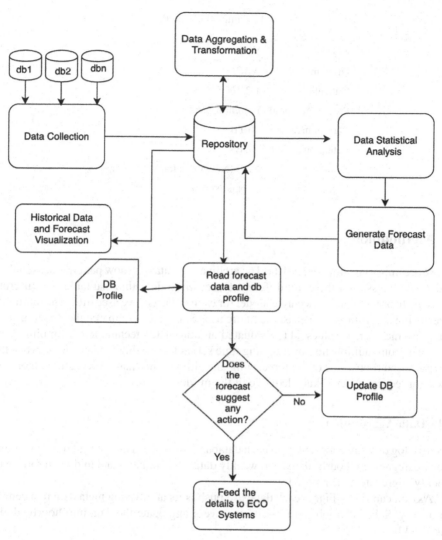

Fig. 1. Overview flow diagram of the proposed system

3.3 Feeding the Forecast Data into Echo Systems

Echo systems use forecast and profile data to initiate the necessary actions. In addition to taking necessary action to use the archive log storage efficiently, it also provides insights into data patterns, periodic fluctuations, and seasonality. Echo systems have a completely independent mechanism to fulfill the outcomes of the forecast decision. Java and Python are used to build this framework.

Table 1. Sample DB profile

Key	Value
DB name	ABC
Criticality	1/2/3/4/5
Prod or non-prod	Prod/non-prod
Max archive size	20 TB
Retention period	7 days
Storage type	NAS (Network-attached storage)
Last action	Expand/shrink

4   Methodology

These are univariate time series data. The archive log datasets show patterns, seasonality, and randomness, and there are different forecasting algorithms suitable for different datasets. In order to find an accurate model for each database, we used different automatic forecasting algorithms to forecast the future usage, and then compared their accuracy by verifying mean error values. [11] Evaluated an automated technique of combining the forecasts from multiple non-overlapping time series forecasting methods to improve the accuracy and robustness of the forecasting algorithm. Automatic forecasting algorithm does not require experts' knowledge to fit the model.

4.1   Data Aggregation

Archive log data are collected from each database, store them in a central repository, and then aggregate into hourly, daily, and weekly datasets. For near- and mid-term forecasts, weekly aggregate data are used.

As you can see in Fig. 2, each database pushes its archive log meta data to a central repository. Scheduled jobs on repository servers aggregate the data into hourly, daily, and weekly.

4.2   Data Exploration

Before venturing into any advanced analysis of the data using statistical, machine learning, and algorithmic techniques, it is essential to perform basic data exploration to study the basic characteristics of a dataset [12].

These are univariate time series data and do not contain data points at periodic intervals. As an archive log file is created, a new data point is generated. We used mean, variance, and standard deviation for numerical metrics, and histogram and plots for data visualization.

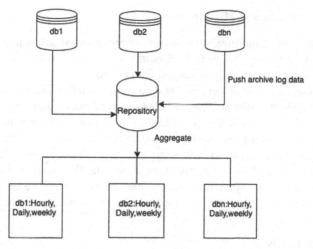

Fig. 2. Data collection and aggregation

The histogram in Fig. 3 shows that the data are not distributed normally and have peaks and lows. The plot in Fig. 4 shows a random variance in data.

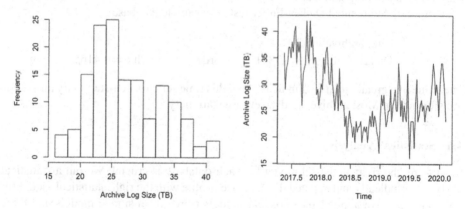

Fig. 3. Histogram of archive log data   **Fig. 4.** Raw archive log data

4.3 Training and Testing Datasets

When choosing models, it is common practice to separate the available data into two portions, namely training and test data, where the training data are used to estimate any parameters of a forecasting method and the test data are used to evaluate its accuracy [13]. The archive log dataset is split into 80:20, where 80% is to train and 20% is to test. Using the training dataset, we trained various statistical models and tested their fitted values against test data. Every statistical model uses a different methodology to forecast the data, and different models best suit different scenarios.

4.4 Handling Outliers and Missing Data

The presence of outliers and missing data can corrupt a statistical analysis and lead to wrong results. Archive logs are generated based on transactional activity that can be dynamic; there are no periodically generated data points.

In this analysis, we used all seven-days data, even though fewer transactions occur on the weekend and on public holidays. Except during a planned or unplanned outage, archive log data always persist. For some reason, if any database does not generate an archive log for an hour, the monitoring script triggers a redo log switch that causes archive log data to be created. An hourly aggregate may have missing data; however, this occurs very rarely in daily or weekly aggregated data. We used standard techniques to impute the missing data with either mean value or last observed value. R's tsoutliers () and tsclean () functions from the forecast package can be used to replace the outliers.

4.5 Data Stationarity

It is important to know if the data have the same statistical properties (e.g., variance, mean, and autocorrelation) throughout the time series. If the data are non-stationary, they can be transformed into stationary using various techniques, such as de-trending and differencing. We used the augmented Dickey-Fuller test [14] to determine if a dataset was stationary or non-stationary:

Output of Augmented Dickey-Fuller test on a sample database

data: archivelog.db1
Dickey-Fuller = -2.3841, Lag order = 5, p-value = 0.4165

The value of p greater than 0.05 indicates that this time series is non-stationary and needs transformation. Most archive log datasets are stationary.

4.6 Statistical Analysis

Identifying the right statistical model for each database is crucial. We ran a statistical analysis periodically and updated the database profile with the right statistical model for each database. We applied six statistical models (three from simple models and three from advanced models) to identify the right model for each database. We used mean, naïve, and seasonal naïve from simple models, and autoregressive integrated moving average (ARIMA), Holt linear trend, and Holt damping trend from advanced models.

An ARIMA model is a generalization of an autoregressive moving average (ARMA) model. Both of these models are fitted to time series data either to better understand the data or to predict future points in the series [15]. The database profile is updated with the best-fitted model, so subsequent execution can use the same model without the need to re-evaluate. However, it is important to re-evaluate the models periodically to include newly generated data in the model selection.

4.7 Forecasting the Archive Log Data

We checked the mean absolute error (MAE) and the root mean squared error (RMSE) values for each model and picked the model with least values. This can be further verified with a residual analysis, a Shapiro-Wilk normality test, and an ACF test (Fig. 5).

```
 1:     Function forecast_db_archivelog_storage_usage()
 2:         For database(i) in databases_list ;
 3:             Y <- timeseries data of database(i)
 4:             Ytrain <- eighty percent of (Y)
 5:             Ytest. <- twenty percent of(Y)
 6:
 7:                 meanm <- meanf(Ytrain, h=33)
 8:                 naivem <- naive(Ytrain,h=33
 9:                 driftm <- rwf(Ytrain, h=33 , drift = T)
10:                 holttrend = holt(Ytrain, h = 33)
11:                 holtdamped = holt(Ytrain, h = 33, damped = T)
12:                 arimafore = forecast(auto.arima(Ytrain), h = 33)
13:
14:                 M=accuracy(meanm,Ytest)
15:                 N=accuracy(naivem,Ytest)
16:                 D=accuracy(driftm,Ytest)
17:                 HL=accuracy(holttrend,Ytest)
18:                 HD=accuracy(holtdamped,Ytest)
19:                 A=accuracy(arimafore,Ytest)
20:
21:                 Database(i)_Model = min(MSE(M,N,D,HL,HD,A))
22:                 Database(i)_archivelog_forecast=forecast using Database(i)_Model
23:                 Update profile with Database(i)_Model
24:                 Store Database(i)_archive_forecast in repository
26:         for end
25:     End Function
```

Fig. 5. Functional flow of the archive log storage forecasting method

5 Results and Discussion

The accuracy of forecasts can only be determined by considering how well a model performs on new data that were not used when fitting the model [13]. R is used to perform all the statistical analysis and generate forecast data and graphs. Differencing a time series means, to subtract each data point in the series from its successor. It is commonly used to make a time series stationary. For most time series patterns, 1 or 2 differencing is necessary to make it a stationary series [16].

We used the differencing functionality to transform non-stationarity data into stationary data. The ndiffs function from the forecast package in R shows how many differencings are required to transform the dataset into stationary.

forecast::ndiffs(archivelog.db1, test = "adf")
forecast::ndiffs(archivelog.db1, test = "kpss")

Figure 6 shows the comparison of test data with fitted data using ARIMA; Holt linear trend; Holt damped trend; and mean, naïve, and seasonal naive methods for a database.

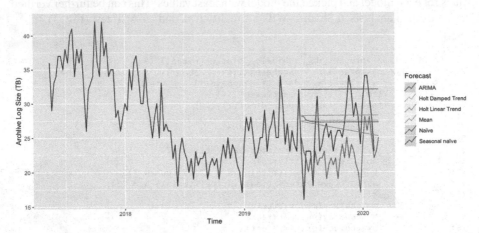

Fig. 6. Comparison of forecast from six different models

There are many algorithms are available for performing the prediction. The best algorithm has to be selected for the effective operation of the prediction for a given database [17]. We used MAE and RMSE values to pick the right model for each database. Additionally, we analyzed further using residuals to confirm that the chosen model is the right fit for the given dataset. Table 2 shows that the Holt's damped trend and the ARIMA model's MAE and RMSE values are very close.

Table 2. MAE and RMSE comparison

Forecast models	RMSE	MAE
Mean	4.526421	3.727273
Naïve	6.958753	5.939394
Seasonal naïve	6.620856	5.555185
Holt's linear	4.567357	3.616127
Holt's damped	4.291682	3.490582
ARIMA	4.359989	3.496993

Figure 7 shows the autocorrelation function (ACF) graph of residuals from the Holt's damped and ARIMA models. The Holt's damped model shows two lags above the threshold, and the ARIMA model shows one lag above the threshold, which indicates the ARIMA model may be a good fit for this dataset.

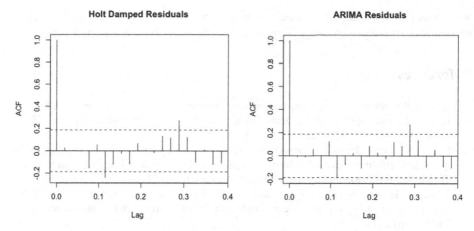

Fig. 7. ACF graph of residuals from Holt's damped and ARIMA models

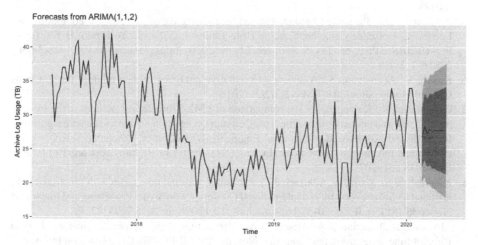

Fig. 8. Forecast of archive log space for a database

Figure 8 shows the forecasted low, mean, and high archive log space usage for a database. Based on database profile attributes, either the mean or high value can be used as a forecast for a database.

6 Conclusions

Whether it is a cloud platform or on-premises, it is essential to use an elasticity mechanism to utilize hardware resources efficiently. This paper proposes a conceptual model to use the storage allocated for database archive log files efficiently. We apply various statistical models on historical data, compare the forecast generated by multiple models with the test dataset, choose the best-fitted model for each database, and forecast the storage usage. This forecast data is fed into ecosystems that take necessary action to use the storage optimally. Additionally, this conceptual model can be used for various applications where storage usage is dynamic and changes significantly over periods.

References

1. Baldan, F.J., Ramirez-Gallego, S., Bergmeir, C., Herrera, F.: A forecasting methodology for workload forecasting in cloud systems. IEEE Trans. Cloud Comput. **6**(4), 929–941 (2018). https://doi.org/10.1109/TCC.2016.2586064
2. Cuong, S.V., Davydenko, A., Shcherbakov, M.: Data schemas for forecasting (with examples in R). In: 2018 International Conference on System Modeling & Advancement in Research Trends. IEEE (2018). https://doi.org/10.1109/sysmart.2018.8746985
3. Kawano, H.: Hierarchical storage systems and file formats for web archiving. In: 2011 21st International Conference on Systems Engineering. IEEE Press (2011). https://doi.org/10.1109/icseng.2011.46
4. Subramaniyam, M., et al.: A data-driven algorithm to predict throughput bottlenecks in a production system based on active periods of the machines. Comput. Ind. Eng. **125**, 533–544 (2018)
5. Calvimontes, J., Bürger, J.: Product demand forecasting based on reservoir computing. In: Leiras, A., González-Calderón, C.A., de Brito Junior, I., Villa, S., Yoshizaki, H.T.Y. (eds.) POMS 2018. SPBE, pp. 15–25. Springer, Cham (2020). https://doi.org/10.1007/978-3-030-23816-2_2
6. Kavya, V., Arumugam, S.: A review on predictive analytics in data mining. Int. J. Chaos Control Model. Simul. (IJCCMS) **5**(1/2/3) (2016)
7. Chuentawat, R., Kan-ngan, Y.: The comparison of PM2.5 forecasting methods in the form of multivariate and univariate time series based on support vector machine and genetic algorithm. In: 2018 15th Conference on Electrical Engineering/Electronics, Computer, Telecommunications and Information Technology (ECTI-CON). IEEE (2019). https://doi.org/10.1109/ecticon.2018.8619867
8. Khandelwal, I., Satija, U., Adhikari, R.: Forecasting seasonal time series with functional link, artificial neural network. In: 2nd International Conference on Signal Processing and Integrated Networks (SPIN). IEEE (2015). https://doi.org/10.1109/spin.2015.7095387
9. Moraes, L.A., Flauzino, R.A., Araújo, M.A., Batista, O.E.: Development of a methodology to forecast time series using few input variables. In: 2013 IEEE PES Conference on Innovative Smart Grid Technologies (ISGT Latin America). IEEE (2013). https://doi.org/10.1109/isgt-la.2013.6554376
10. Syu, Y., Fanjiang, Y.-Y., Kuo, J.-Y., Su, J.-L.: Quality of service timeseries forecasting for web services: a machine learning, genetic programming-based approach. In: 2016 Annual Conference on Information Science and Systems (CISS). IEEE (2016). https://doi.org/10.1109/ciss.2016.7460526
11. Shetty, J., Shobha, G.: An ensemble of automatic algorithms for forecasting resource utilization in cloud. In: 2016 Future Technologies Conference (FTC). IEEE (2017)
12. Kotu, V., Deshpande, B.: Data Science, 2nd edn. Morgan Kaufmann, Burlington (2018)
13. Hyndman, R.J., Athanasopoulos, G.: Forecasting: Principles and Practice. 2nd edn. OTexts, Melbourne, Australia. OTexts.com/fpp2 (2018). https://otexts.com/fpp2/accuracy.html. Section 3.4 Evaluating forecast accuracy
14. Holmes, E.E., Scheuerell, M.D., Ward, E.J.: Applied time series analysis for fisheries and environmental data (2020). https://nwfsc-timeseries.github.io/atsa-labs/sec-boxjenkins-aug-dickey-fuller.html

15. Autoregressive integrated moving average. https://en.wikipedia.org/wiki/Autoregressive_int egrated_moving_average. Accessed 2020
16. Prabhakaran, S.: Time Series Analysis. http://r-statistics.co/Time-Series-Analysis-With-R. html. Accessed 2020
17. Navya, R., Rashmi, R., Darshana, M.K., Shankar, G.: A predictive model for analyzing electric consumption patterns in solar photo voltaic micro grid. In: 2017 2nd International Conference on Computational Systems and Information Technology for Sustainable Solution (CSITSS). IEEE (2017)

Scalable Sketch-Based Sport Video Retrieval in the Cloud

Ihab Al Kabary$^{(\boxtimes)}$ and Heiko Schuldt

Department of Mathematics and Computer Science, University of Basel,
Basel, Switzerland
{ihab.alkabary,heiko.schuldt}@unibas.ch

Abstract. Content-based video retrieval in general and in sport videos in particular has attracted an increasing interest in the past few years, due to the growing interest in sports analytics. Especially sketch-based queries, enabling spatial search in video collections, are increasingly being demanded by coaches and analysts in team sports as an essential tool for game analysis. Although there has been great progress in the last years in the field of sketch-based retrieval in sports, most approaches focus on functional aspects and only consider just a very limited number of games. The problem is to scale these systems to allow for interactive video retrieval on a large game collection, beyond single games. In this paper, we show how *SportSense*, our sketch-based video retrieval system, can be deployed and scaled-out in the Cloud, allowing managers and analysts to interactively search for scenes of their choice within a large collection of games. In our evaluations, we show how the system can scale to a collection of the size of an entire season with response times that enable real-time analysis.

1 Introduction

Multimedia retrieval is concerned with the search for and the delivery of multimedia documents, such as images, video and/or audio. The need for effective, efficient, and intuitive retrieval algorithms has increased due to the ever-growing amount of multimedia documents being created. In the last decade, the proliferation of smart phones with built-in high resolution cameras, the increase in television content broadcasted over the Internet, together with the growing storage capacity, has led to an enormous increase in image, video and audio content.

This trend has also affected sports, both professional and leisure. Especially in professional team sports, the analysis of the performance of a club's own team and the qualitative and quantitative assessment of the strengths and weaknesses of opposing teams has become a major issue. Clubs are investing vast amounts of money in the infrastructure for data capturing (sensors, camera systems) in order to collect huge volumes of raw sensor data and video material, often in combination with curated datasets from commercial providers. It is then usually the task of dedicated video analysts to manually examine this content and select the most interesting events and corresponding video sequences, which are then made available to the coaches.

© Springer Nature Switzerland AG 2020
Q. Zhang et al. (Eds.): CLOUD 2020, LNCS 12403, pp. 226–241, 2020.
https://doi.org/10.1007/978-3-030-59635-4_16

Over the last years, we have been developing an innovative system, called *SportSense* [1–4], that allows coaches and analysts to search within a collection of sports videos based on many query types, including hand-drawn sketches [5,6]. While previous work has focused on novel query paradigms, this paper focuses on the scalability of the *SportSense* approach when being deployed in the Cloud. The contribution of this paper is twofold: First we show how the response time of *SportSense* can be reduced by applying both scale-in and scale-out using Cloud resources. Second, we show that *SportSense* can scale to large sports video collections, providing interactive response times for various types of queries in collections of at least the size of an entire season of games.

The remainder of this paper is structured as follows: Sect. 2 surveys related work. Section 3 showcases a scalable version of *SportSense* deployed in the Cloud. Section 4 presents the comprehensive evaluations that show how the system performs on a large video collection. Section 5 concludes.

2 Related Work

Retrieval in sports videos has gained increasing attention. Searching for scenes in team sport videos is a task that recurs very often in the daily activities of game analysis, coaches, broadcasters, and is even relevant for sports fans. In most cases, queries are formulated on the basis of specific motion characteristics the user remembers from the video. Most current sports video analysis or retrieval systems rely on extracting motion information of the ball, players and even the referees either manually, from broadcast videos, or from especially deployed on-the-field high definition (HD) cameras. Systems such as [7–9] rely on already recorded broadcast videos from which they extract motion trajectories. However, their main limitation lies in the fact that they can only extract what the camera and its recording angle has to offer. Hence, while a camera is showing two or three players in action, the motion activity on the rest of the field is ignored. In addition, it is very challenging to project the coordinates of the obtained trajectory on the sports field, so the retrieval process can only assist in retrieving motion flow trajectories of object(s) with respect to their locations within several sequential video frames, instead of retrieving motion based on movement on the field. These same limitations can be pointed out at the very early attempt at providing sketch-based motion queries with VideoQ [10].

On the other hand, academic research [11,12] and commercial products [13–17] have developed methods to capture and make use of the action on the entire field. This is done by deploying several on-the-field HD cameras which capture videos of the entire field and apply object detection and recognition techniques to extract tracking information of entities on the field. This approach allows for the automatic generation of a variety of information such as distance covered by players, heat maps of player positions, and even video summarizations of certain events. However, in certain situations, when players come too close to each other (e.g., after goal celebrations or corner kicks), they cannot be properly distinguished anymore. Weather conditions such as rain can also be a problem.

Novel light-weight wireless sensor devices dedicated for sports use [18,19] allow to acquire reliable and accurate position information without the need for sophisticated object detection and recognition. These sensor data serve as basis for the detection of events in the data streams they emit [20] that, in turn, can be linked to the video for retrieval purposes. Chalkboarding [21] uses a similar approach to *SportSense* for sketch-based retrieval in sports videos and also support aggregate queries. However, since [21] focuses on functional aspects, a comparison of the scalability with *SportSense* is difficult to achieve.

3   Scalable *SportSense*

SportSense [1–6] enables sketch-based motion queries in sport videos by harnessing information contained within an overlay of metadata that incorporates spatio-temporal information about various events within a game. Users can input their search queries using a variety of query types.

3.1   System Architecture

In order to enable sketch-based motion queries in video collections enriched with spatio-temporal metadata, three main components need to be supported: (i) the storage of the spatio-temporal data into efficient index structures; (ii) the formulation of the query from the user-drawn sketch using intuitive interfaces; (iii) the execution of the query against the stored spatio-temporal data with the application of similarity search techniques in order to retrieve an ordered list of fitting and partially fitting video snippets. An overview of the architecture of *SportSense* is depicted in Fig. 1.

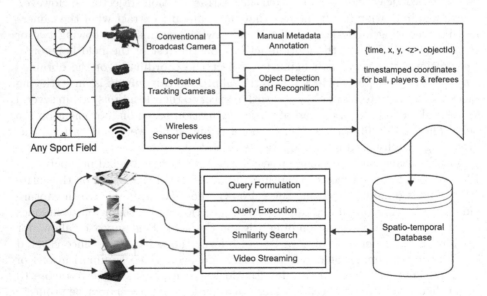

Fig. 1. SportSense architecture

The entire software stack of *SportSense* has been released under an open source license. It is available on GitHub under the GNU Affero General Public License v3.0 (https://github.com/sportsense).

3.2   Spatio-Temporal Input

The tracked spatio-temporal data originating from sport games are rather low-multidimensional. It contains time-stamped x, y field coordinates of the ball, players and the referees, and in some cases the ball has an additional z coordinate capturing its height: $record_i : (x_i, y_i, \langle z_i \rangle, time_i, objId_i)$. Thus, index structures that exist within spatio-temporal databases such as R*trees [22] and multi-layered grids [23] on top of B$^+$trees [24] are very useful for storage and retrieval. Listing 1 shows how to create a spatial index on a SQL Server table. Spatial indexes are vital for improving the response time of the spatial and spatio-temporal queries that are derived from the sketch-based queries in *Sport-Sense*.

Listing 1. SQL Server Spatial Index

```
CREATE SPATIAL INDEX [BallMotion_SpatialIndex]
ON [dbo].[BallMotion] ( [trackedPoint] )
USING GEOMETRY_AUTO_GRID
WITH (
   BOUNDING_BOX =(0,0,532,356), CELLS_PER_OBJECT = 64,
   PAD_INDEX = OFF, STATISTICS_NORECOMPUTE = OFF,
   SORT_IN_TEMPDB = OFF, DROP_EXISTING = OFF, ONLINE = OFF,
   ALLOW_ROW_LOCKS = ON, ALLOW_PAGE_LOCKS = ON ) ON [PRIMARY];
```

3.3   Spatial and Spatio-Temporal Motion Query Formulation

In what follows, we briefly survey the different query types we have developed for both pure spatial and spatio-temporal motion queries.

Pure Spatial Queries. Sketch-based spatial queries involve nding certain events happening within sports games by providing a sketch that encompasses where on the field the events have occurred, possibly constrained by filters restricting the time of the event or a particular team or player. For this, *Sport-Sense* allows a user to either exploit geometric shapes (circles or rectangles) or to draw a free-style closed sketch as spatial lter. As an example, Fig. 2a shows the spatial location of four shots on and off target. An example query provided by a user can be seen in Fig. 2b. It is worth mentioning that the three different inputs are depicted as overlay.

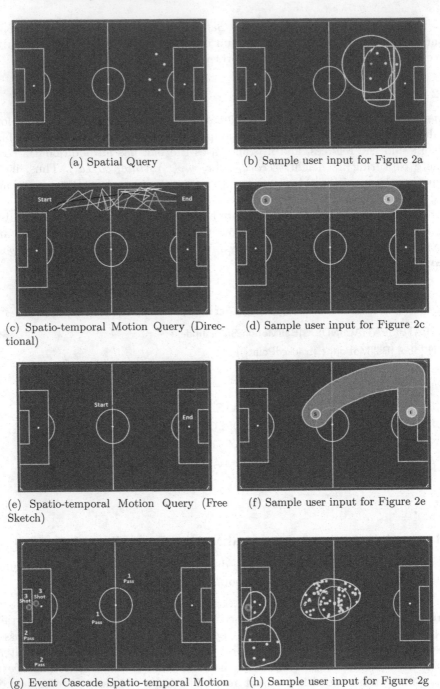

(a) Spatial Query

(b) Sample user input for Figure 2a

(c) Spatio-temporal Motion Query (Directional)

(d) Sample user input for Figure 2c

(e) Spatio-temporal Motion Query (Free Sketch)

(f) Sample user input for Figure 2e

(g) Event Cascade Spatio-temporal Motion Query

(h) Sample user input for Figure 2g

Fig. 2. Examples of query (right) and their results (left): (a+b) locations of attempts on goal; (c+d) motion paths on the left wing; (e+f) a specific attack originated from the midfield and ended with a cross-in; (g+h) two attacks starting with a pass, followed with a cross-in pass and ending with a goal attempt.

Fig. 3. Geometric buffer generated using Minkowski sum

Spatio-Temporal Motion Queries (Directional and Free Sketch). Spatio-temporal queries allow users to formulate a query that expresses the intended direction of play within a game or the required sequence of events that needs to be found in a video scene to qualify as a relevant item. *Directional* queries capture the direction of the flow of the ball or a player by drawing a line. This is done by pinpointing the start and end of the line, thus capturing the direction of play, then restricting or relaxing the tolerated distance from the line which acts as a white box filter where the motion is acceptable. *Free-style* sketches will be effective when searching for video scenes that include rapid change in direction of movement since a complex path instead of a line can be sketched.

For both these types of spatio-temporal motion queries, the buffering around the line or path is created using the Minkowski sum as shown in Fig. 3 to allow for this custom level of tolerated variance as shown in Fig. 4. For directional queries, Fig. 2c visualizes the ball motion of the twelve relevant videos scenes that are played by a team within the left side of the football field in one half of the game. Each motion path is represented using a different color. Figure 2d depicts a sample query. As for the free-style sketch queries, Fig. 2e illustrates a specific scene where the home team attacks from the center of the field, moves up to the left side of the field and makes a cross inside the penalty box. Figure 2f shows a sample query to search for this known video scene.

From the generated buffer boundary, sample boundary points (data type *Point* in spatial SQL) are chosen to construct the polygon (data type *Polygon*) to be used by the query. The following SQL code snippet in Listing 2 shows the formulation of a spatial query in SQL Server. The constructed polygon in the SQL syntax is generated using points obtained from the perimeter of the geometric buffer placed

Listing 2. SQL Server Express Spatial Query

```
SELECT trackedPoint, trackedTime FROM TrackedInfo
WHERE trackedPoint.STWithin(
geometry::STGeomFromText('POLYGON((453 32, 460 32,..,453 94,453 32))', 0)) = 1
ORDER BY trackedTime ASC;
```

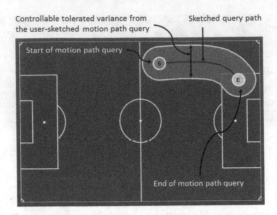

Fig. 4. Sample sketched-based motion path query on the field.

around the user-provided sketch query path created with the Minkowski sum. Not all points on the perimeter are needed to construct the polygon, just a sample that will give a sufficient approximation. The selection of a too large subset of perimeter points will render a perfect approximation of the polygon, however, it will increase the retrieval time of the spatial query. At the same time, a selection of a too small subset of perimeter points will give a very bad approximation despite the rapid retrieval time for the spatial query. We have empirically evaluated that selecting points that have a distance between 10 and 20 pixels is an adequate ratio as illustrated in Fig. 5. The order in which the points are selected from the geometric buffer perimeter is circular, either clockwise or anti-clockwise.

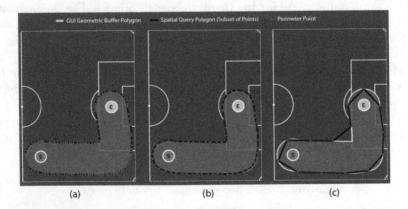

Fig. 5. The selected perimeter points (in red) give a proper approximate polygon (in black) of the polygon generated from the user-drawn sketch (in yellow) in cases (a) and (b), but not in (c) as the distance between points needed to select the approximation is too high. In case (a), the spatial query will take longer than in case (b) due to the large number of points used for the approximation. (Color figure online)

Chronological Event Cascade Queries. If a coach or a sports analyst wants to retrieve scenes that contain events in a particular sequence (e.g., a free-kick in the midfield, followed by a pass near the corner post, then a crossover inside the penalty box and finally a shot on goal), a new query type called *Event Cascade Query* is needed. It provides a way to formulate queries that capture events happening in chronological order. Figure 2g depicts two specific attacking scenes, forming two ordered sets of chronological series of three events (pass, cross-in pass, and shot on goal) originating from the mid-field, left side of the field and inside the penalty box, respectively. Figure 2h shows a sample query to search for known video scenes in a game. Hence, this type defines a query pipeline in which results are narrowed down at each phase until the desired results are reached; for this, users have to roughly remember at every single step where the events happened, and to correctly transform their 3D memory into a 2D sketch.

Reverse-Chronological Event Cascade Queries. The concept of *Reverse Chronological Queries* is inspired by the observation that when trying to recall a series of events happening within a game, usually the most important events tend to be easily remembered, in contrast to the events that lead to them. For example, a user can rather easily recall the field location of important goals or shots on target in a football game but might have problems recalling four or five events back that led to these specific events. The user starts by specifying a region containing locations of the final events like goals and shots on goal and the system then automatically suggest paths on how to proceed retrospectively by harnessing the indexed spatio-temporal data. This is obvious when viewing the subsequent steps in Fig. 6. The formulation of queries in reverse chronological order also avoids information overload, since important events tend to be selective and occur less frequently.

3.4   Query Execution

The output generated from queries such as those shown in Listing 2 acts only as phase one in a two phase solution. The second phase involves detecting separate motion segments from the set of points obtained in the first phase and computing how similar they are to the sketched motion query path provided by the user.

Motion Segment Extraction. A perfect motion flow or segment will be found if a motion starts and ends within the query region at its beginning and end, respectively, and does not leave this region in between. However, partially fitting motion paths can also be useful for the user. To detect both perfect and partially fitting matches, we loop sequentially on a chronologically-ordered list of all the returned motion points. A sliding window of two seconds is used to detect if there is discontinuity in a motion flow or not. Hence, if a motion flow starts in the query region and then temporarily moves out less than two seconds, it is still considered one logical motion flow (see Fig. 7). This coarsens the motion flows detected and generates more logical video snippets in the result set.

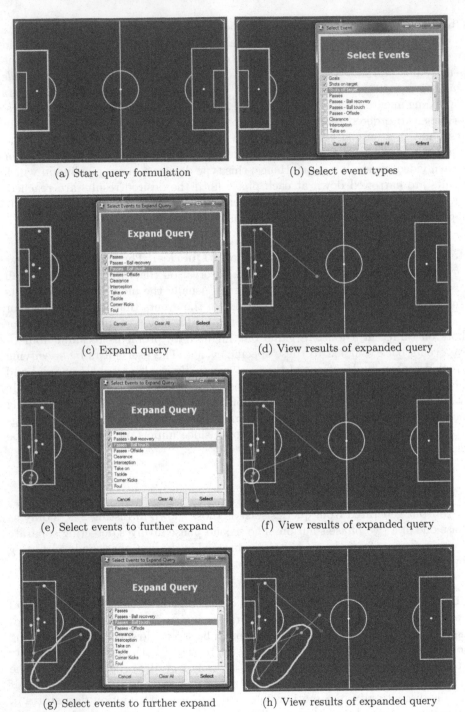

(a) Start query formulation

(b) Select event types

(c) Expand query

(d) View results of expanded query

(e) Select events to further expand

(f) View results of expanded query

(g) Select events to further expand

(h) View results of expanded query

Fig. 6. Example steps in the formulation of an *auto-suggest* reverse chronological event cascade query.

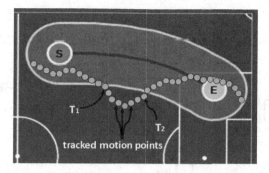

Fig. 7. Partially fitting motion flow retrieved as one flow if $T_2 - T_1 < 2$ s.

Motion Query Similarity Search. Retrieval of motion paths is based on the similarity between sketch and the trajectory retrieved from the database. If the motion is in the direction of the sketched path, the similarity score is incremented and if not, the score is penalized. We also increment the similarity score if the retrieved motion path originates at the start of the query and ends at the end of the query, in order to boost the similarity of motion paths that completely fulfil the requirements of the motion query. Finally, when motion paths have been found, the corresponding video snippets are extracted and synchronized with the start and end time of the matching motion flows and shown to the user.

3.5   Scaling-Up and Scaling-Out

Vertical scaling, also referred to as scaling-up, usually involves either using more powerful computing devices or more efficient software that makes use of more CPU cores. On the other hand, horizontal scaling, also referred to as scaling-out, involves adding more compute nodes to a distributed system to enable it to be more efficient and achieve a higher degree of scalability.

With horizontal scaling, it is always possible to add further to a distributed system in order to make intelligent use of the extra resources, for example by means of methods such as MapReduce [25]. In the case of *SportSense*, scaling the system to support hundreds of games requires horizontal scaling. An approach is to rely on commercial Cloud platforms such as Amazon AWS, Microsoft Azure or Google Cloud instead of investing in on-premise data centers as the latter would exceed the resources of sports clubs. An overview of the design for such a distributed version of *SportSense* is depicted in Fig. 8. Each compute node (right hand side) hosts a specific number of matches, and this breakdown of games among the compute nodes is known by the application triggering the search, referred to as SportSense Central. SportSense Central UI, which triggers the search process, will know from the user which game(s) the user wants to search in, maps these games to the related compute node(s) and then obtains the results, aggregates them if they are being retrieved from multiple nodes,

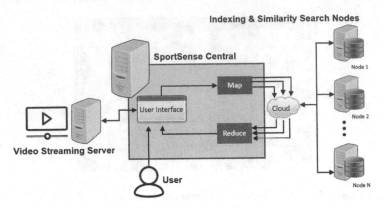

Fig. 8. Top-level design for Horizontally Scaling (Scaling-out) *SportSense*.

sorts them, and presents them to the user in the form of video snippets that are streamed upon request from the video streaming server.

4   Evaluation

In our evaluations, we focus on assessing how the responsiveness of *SportSense* changes for different Cloud deployments. For this, we analyze various scenarios covering spatial and spatio-temporal chronological and reverse-chronological queries. Note that we focus on measuring the response times of *SportSense*, since the precision and recall rates have been previously addressed in [1,6], and this effort to scale *SportSense* does not affect its effectiveness.

4.1   Deployment

For our evaluation, we use resources from the Amazon AWS Cloud, in particular several EC2 instance types in order to assess how scaling-out can benefit the system. Table 1 shows the main configuration settings of our experiments. For all EC2 instances, we used an Amazon Machine Image (AMI) that has Windows 2012 installed with SQL Server Express 2014. Note that it is very beneficial to place the EC2 compute instances within the same region to allows them to communicate using low-latency links and decrease retrieval time between compute nodes hosting the games and performing the similarity search, and the central node that aggregates the results, sort and presents them to the user. Users can remotely access the central node.

Table 1. AWS infrastructure configuration.

AWS component	Configuration
Elastic Compute Cloud (EC2)	T2.Small (1 vCPUs and 2 GB RAM)
	T2.Large (2 vCPUs and 8 GB RAM)
	C5.2XLarge (8 vCPUs and 16 GB RAM)
Amazon Machine Image (AMI)	WINDOWS_2012_SQL_SERVER_EXPRESS_2014
Firewall (Security Group)	Allow for MS SQL Remote Connections

4.2 Dataset

We created a dataset of 38 games, which is the typical total number of games a team plays in one season in most leagues consisting of 20 teams. However, since it is difficult to get access to (mainly commercial) datasets with spatio-temporal event data and accompanying videos, we have used three football games (one Premier League match of which the data was provided by Manchester City [26] and two friendly matches of the Swiss National Team where the data was provided by Opta [14]). In order to work with a collection of 38 matches, we have accordingly duplicated the available game data. The data in each game are in the form of discrete events (such as passes, corner-kicks, offsides, fouls, shots on goal, goals, etc.) stored in XML format, accompanied with (x, y, z) location information (relative to the field), the time of the event and players involved. In order to allow for the implementation of spatio-temporal motion queries, we transformed the discrete event dataset into a 5 fps (frames per second) dataset by interpolating location and time information between each two consecutive events. Every game has approximately 1,500 discrete events, with the 38 games having a total of 54,250 discrete events. These events were then transformed into a motion-query friendly dataset with > 1 million records.

4.3 Participants

Ten users with different sketching skills participated in the evaluation. When the evaluation sessions started, information was automatically logged during each session to assist in measuring the response times and avoid interrupting the user. Video snippets showing the known items that the users were to search for were shown for each user. The videos were repeated if users requested to see them again. Evaluation sessions were not time-boxed.

4.4 Evaluation Scenarios

In order to assess the efficiency of *SportSense*, we have compiled a characteristic mix of different query types relevant for searching for video scenes within football games. (i) a purely spatial query for retrieving locations of shots on goal originating from a specific area. (ii) spatio-temporal queries for finding attacking sprints done by player(s) and for retrieving specific attack(s) performed by a team by providing a chronological, or (iii) reverse chronological list of events and their approximate location. We categorized the sketch-based motion query scenarios mainly as either chronological or reverse-chronological spatio-temporal queries. Figures 2 and 6 show examples of these queries. Note that no filtering on specific games was performed to allow the queries to run against the entire dataset of 38 games.

4.5   Results

Initially, we needed to decide on the power of each node, and to accomplish this, we ran the evaluation with three AWS EC2 instance types: T2.Small, T2.Large and C5.2XLarge, which have the compute power outlined in Table 1. Each of the five compute nodes hosted data for a maximum of 8 games. The results in Table 2 show how the increased compute power of the EC2 instances leads to a drop in response times. This is especially evident with motion queries (see Fig. 2f) where the average response times decreased from 3.88 s to 2.77 s. We chose to proceed in the evaluations with EC2 instances of type C5.2XLarge, which are compute optimized but still balanced in terms of price and performance. AWS allows to go as high as C5d.metal which has 96 vCPU and 192 GB RAM. Details on the EC2 instance types can be seen on the AWS overview page [27].

The second part of the evaluations is concerned with the number of games each node can host. We evaluated four settings: having everything in one EC2 node, another setting with 5 nodes having a maximum of 8 games each, another

Table 2. Average response times for spatial, chronological, and reverse chronological spatio-temporal queries using difference EC2 Node Instance Types.

Query scenario	5× T2.Small	5× T2.Large	5× C5.2XLarge
Figure 2b Circular	0.03 s	0.03 s	0.02 s
Figure 2b Rectangular	0.02 s	0.02 s	0.02 s
Figure 2b Sketch	0.03 s	0.02 s	0.02 s
Figure 2d	1.97 s	1.92 s	1.47 s
Figure 2f	3.88 s	3.13 s	2.77 s
Chronological Phase (1) Figure 2h (Spatial SQL)	0.44 s	0.31 s	0.17 s
Chronological Phase (2) Figure 2h (Spatial SQL)	0.30 s	0.13 s	0.08 s
Chronological Phase (3) Figure 2h (Spatial SQL)	0.02 s	0.02 s	0.02 s
Reverse-Chron. Phase (1) Figure 6b (Spatial SQL)	0.02 s	0.02 s	0.02 s
Reverse-Chron. Phase (2) Figure 6c (Classic SQL)	2.47 s	0.92 s	0.89 s
Reverse-Chron. Phase (3) Figure 6e (Classic SQL)	0.62 s	0.31 s	0.26 s
Reverse-Chron. Phase (4) Figure 6g (Classic SQL)	0.39 s	0.11 s	0.12 s

Table 3. Average response times using 1, 5, 8 and 13 nodes (EC2: C5.2XLarge)

Query Scenario	All-in-one	5 Nodes	8 Nodes	13 Nodes
Figure 2b Circular	0.04 s	0.02 s	0.02 s	0.02 s
Figure 2b Rectangular	0.03 s	0.02 s	0.02 s	0.02 s
Figure 2b Sketch	0.03 s	0.02 s	0.02 s	0.02 s
Figure 2d	2.66 s	1.47 s	1.06 s	0.72 s
Figure 2f	5.26 s	2.77 s	1.89 s	1.08 s
Chronological Phase (1) Fig. 2h (Spatial SQL)	1.83 s	0.17 s	0.12 s	0.15 s
Chronological Phase (2) Fig. 2h (Spatial SQL)	0.11 s	0.08 s	0.11 s	0.14 s
Chronological Phase (3) Fig. 2h (Spatial SQL)	0.02 s	0.02 s	0.02 s	0.12 s
Rev.-Chron. Phase (1) Fig. 6b (Spatial SQL)	0.03 s	0.02 s	0.02 s	0.02 s
Rev.-Chron. Phase (2) Fig. 6c (Classic SQL)	0.82 s	0.89 s	1.03 s	0.97 s
Rev.-Chron. Phase (3) Fig. 6e (Classic SQL)	0.20 s	0.26 s	0.28 s	0.21 s
Rev.-Chron. Phase (4) Fig. 6g (Classic SQL)	0.19 s	0.22 s	0.11 s	0.09 s

setting with 8 nodes having a maximum of 5 games each, and finally, a setting with 13 nodes, each having a maximum of 3 games. Examining Table 3, we can clearly see a trend showing the drop in response time as we increase the number of compute nodes. Again, if we focus on the most compute expensive motion query such as shown in Fig. 2f, we observe a drop from 5.26 s, with an all-in-one setting, to 1.08 s with 13 compute nodes. Another observation is that the pure spatial queries did not benefit as much from the distributed Cloud computing environment, but that was expected since they are not as computationally expensive as the spatio-temporal queries. Overall, we managed to decrease the response times of the most compute extensive queries to around a second which results in a very responsive video retrieval system.

5 Conclusion

In this paper, we have showcased how we enabled *SportSense*, our system for sports video retrieval, to scale-up and scale-out and allow users to interactively search for video scenes of game plays of their choice within a large collection of games using novel sketch-based queries. To accomplish this, we leveraged the Cloud. Our evaluations have shown that searching within a full-season of games for a team is responsive and interactive and meets the needs of game analysts, as we managed to decrease the response times of the most compute extensive queries to around one second. In our current work, we are extending *SportSense* to other types of sports, in particular ice hockey, by adding query support for the specifics of these disciplines (such as an analysis of box play and shifts in ice hockey).

References

1. Al Kabary, I., Schuldt, H.: Towards sketch-based motion queries in sports videos. In: 2013 IEEE International Symposium on Multimedia (ISM), December 2013
2. Kabary, I.A., Schuldt, H.: Using hand gestures for specifying motion queries in sketch-based video retrieval. In: de Rijke, M., et al. (eds.) ECIR 2014. LNCS, vol. 8416, pp. 733–736. Springer, Cham (2014). https://doi.org/10.1007/978-3-319-06028-6_84
3. Probst, L., et al.: SportSense: user interface for sketch-based spatio-temporal team sports video scene retrieval. In: Proceedings of the IUI 2018 Workshop on User Interfaces for Spatial and Temporal Data Analysis, Tokyo, Japan, March 2018
4. Seidenschwarz, P., Jonsson, A., Rauschenbach, F., Rumo, M., Probst, L., Schuldt, H.: Combining qualitative and quantitative analysis in football with sportsense. In: Proceedings of the ACM Workshop on Multimedia Content Analysis in Sports, France, October 2019
5. Al Kabary, I., Schuldt, H.: SportSense: using motion queries to find scenes in sports videos. In: Proceedings of the CIKM 2013, San Francisco, CA, USA. ACM, October 2013
6. Al Kabary, I., Schuldt, H.: Enhancing sketch-based sport video retrieval by suggesting relevant motion paths. In: Proceedings of the 37th International ACM SIGIR Conference, Gold Coast, QLD, Australia. ACM (2014)
7. Ballan, L., Bertini, M., Bimbo, A.D., Nunziati, W.: Soccer players identification based on visual local features. In: Proceedings of the 6th ACM CIVR Conference, July 2007
8. Fleischman, M., Roy, D.: Unsupervised content-based indexing of sports video. In: Proceedings of the 9th ACM International Workshop on Multimedia Information Retrieval, Augsburg, Germany, pp. 87–94. ACM, September 2007
9. Su, C., Liao, H., Tyan, H., Lin, C., Chen, D., Fan, K.: Motion flow-based video retrieval. IEEE Trans. Multimedia **9**, 1193–1201 (2007)
10. Chang, S.F., Chen, W., Meng, H., Sundaram, H., Zhong, D.: A fully automated content-based video search engine supporting spatiotemporal queries. IEEE Trans. Circ. Syst. Video Technol. **8**, 602–615 (1998)
11. Shitrit, H.B., Berclaz, J., Fleuret, F., Fua, P.: Tracking multiple people under global appearance constraints. In: International Conference on Computer Vision (ICCV), Barcelona, Spain. IEEE, November 2011
12. Wilhelm, P., et al.: An integrated monitoring and analysis system for performance data of indoor sport activities. In: 10th Australasian Conference on Mathematics and Computers in Sport, Darwin, Australia, July 2010
13. Interplay Sports. www.interplay-sports.com. Accessed Mar 2020
14. OptaSportsPro. www.optasportspro.com. Accessed Mar 2020
15. Panasonic Ultra Wide Angle Camera. www.newatlas.com/panasonic-ultra-wide-camera-system/28826/. Accessed Mar 2020
16. Stats Perform. www.statsperform.com. Accessed Mar 2020
17. TracAB. https://chyronhego.com/products/sports-tracking/tracab-optical-tracking. Accessed Mar 2020
18. Adidas Runtastic. www.runtastic.com. Accessed Mar 2020
19. ZXY. www.zxy.no. Accessed Mar 2020
20. Probst, L., Brix, F., Schuldt, H., Rumo, M.: Real-time football analysis with streamteam. In: Proceedings of the 11th ACM International Conference on Distributed and Event-based Systems, Barcelona, Spain. ACM, June 2017

21. Sha, L., Lucey, P., Yue, Y., Carr, P., Rohlf, C., Matthews, I.A.: Chalkboarding: a new spatiotemporal query paradigm for sports play retrieval. In: 21st International Conference on Intelligent User Interfaces, Sonoma, CA, USA, March 2016
22. Beckmann, N., Kriegel, H.P., Schneider, R., Seeger, B.: The R*-tree: an efficient and robust access method for points and rectangles. In: Proceedings of the ACM SIGMOD Conference on Management of Data, Atlantic City, NJ, USA, May 1990
23. Fang, Y., Friedman, M., Nair, G., Rys, M., Schmid, A.E.: Spatial indexing in microsoft SQL server 2008. In: Proceedings of the ACM SIGMOD Conference on Management of Data, Vancouver, BC, Canada, pp. 1207–1216. ACM, June 2008
24. Comer, D.: Ubiquitous B-tree. ACM Comput. Surv. **11**, 121–137 (1979)
25. Dean, J., Ghemawat, S.: MapReduce: simplified data processing on large clusters. Commun. ACM **51**, 107–113 (2008)
26. Manchester City Football Club. www.mcfc.co.uk. Accessed Mar 2020
27. Amazon EC2. https://aws.amazon.com/ec2/instance-types/. Accessed Mar 2020

Capestor: A Service Mesh-Based Capacity Estimation Framework for Cloud Applications

Lun Meng[1], Yao Sun[2], and Shudong Zhang[3](✉)

[1] Nanjing Institute of Big Date, Jinling Institute of Technology, Nanjing 211169, China
m_l_01@163.com
[2] College of Public Administration, Hohai University, Nanjing 210098, China
suny216@jit.edu.cn
[3] Information Engineering College, Capital Normal University, Beijing 100048, China
zsd@cnu.edu.cn

Abstract. Due to complex deployment configurations and dynamic application logics in cloud computing, microservice architectures are widely used to divide cloud applications into multiple independent microservices communicating with each other through APIs that are not associated with languages and platforms. However, a large amount of various microservices make it difficult for operators to predict the performance of microservices and then estimate cloud applications' capacity. This paper proposes a capacity estimation framework called as Capestor for cloud applications based on a service mesh. Capestor employs a service mesh to place target microservices in isolated containers, simulates workloads, and collect monitoring data related with performance metrics and physical resources. Then, Capestor employs an ElasticNet regression model to correlate resources and performance, and estimates the capacity of each microservice to plan fine-grained flexible expansion. Finally, we evaluate Capestor with a typical microservice based application. The experimental results show that Capestor can estimate the capacity of microservices, and guarantee performance for applications with a low prediction error rate.

Keywords: Cloud applications · Microservices · Cloud computing · Capacity plan

1 Introduction

Cloud computing has been widely used in industries, which provides shared physical resources to users in the form of virtual machines or containers. The customers of cloud services can easily access shared computing, storage, network and other physical resources through Internet. The physical servers of a cloud data center are managed and maintained by cloud service providers. Cloud customers only pay for the actual usage cost, regardless of the maintenance and operations of physical devices. Due to the differences in physical device configurations, VM types, and running applications in cloud computing, the expected performance of services often deviates from the expected performance significantly [1]. Thus, establishing cloud applications' performance is

Q. Zhang et al. (Eds.): CLOUD 2020, LNCS 12403, pp. 242–249, 2020.
https://doi.org/10.1007/978-3-030-59635-4_17

necessary for scheduling physical resources to guarantee the quality of service (QoS). Workloads is the key factor affecting the performance metrics of interactive applications. If the concurrency number of workloads exceeds a certain value, the QoS (e.g., response time, throughput) of an application will significantly degrade. For example, the response time of processing requests exceeds the defined expected value. Therefore, we use the concurrency number that can satisfy the constraint of response time to represent the capacity of a cloud application. We determine the value with stress test by gradually increasing the concurrency number of workloads till the response time exceeds the pre-defined expected value [2]. Estimating the capacity of a cloud application is one of key technologies to the dynamic and flexible scaling for improving resource utilization.

Due to complex deployment configurations and dynamic application logics in cloud computing, microservice technologies are widely employed to divide applications into multiple independent microservices communicating with each other through APIs that are not associated with languages and platforms, and these microservices cooperate to implement a cloud application [3]. Each microservice can be independently deployed, scheduled and monitored, and thus a cloud application can start, stop or expand specific microservices without operating all the parts of the cloud application to simplify the procedure of developing and operating a complex cloud application. The microservice architecture widely used in many fields in recent years provides the high flexibility for the management of cloud applications. Large-scale microservices are usually deployed in cloud computing platforms sharing physical resources. Operators often improve cloud applications' performance by expanding the capacity of specific microservices deployed in VMs or containers with cloud management systems, e.g., Kubernetes, Mesos. This paper defines the capacity of a microservice as "the maximum request rate" that is the number of processed requests per second by a microservice within the pre-defined expected response time [4]. The metric that is maximum request rate can be used to effectively estimate the performance bottleneck, which is the key microservices causing cloud applications' performance degradation. Thus, operators can adaptively increase the number of specific microservices' replicas to improve the cloud application's overall performance.

This paper proposes a service mesh-based capacity estimation framework called as Capestor for cloud applications based on a service mesh. Capestor employs a service mesh to place target microservices in isolated containers, simulates workloads, collects monitoring data related with performance and resources, employs an ElasticNet regression model to correlate resource metrics and performance metrics, and then estimates the capacity of each microservice to plan fine-grained flexible expansion. Finally, we evaluate Capestor with a typical microservice-based application.

2   Related Work

The methods of capacity estimation for applications often model an application's performance, forecast workloads, detect performance bottleneck, and then allocate resources for the bottleneck. Performance modelling is the key to accurately identify applications' performance bottlenecks and effectively improve the applications' performance. However, it is difficult for existing technologies to model the performance of cloud applications with various virtual resources and deployment configurations. Ref. [5] proposed a

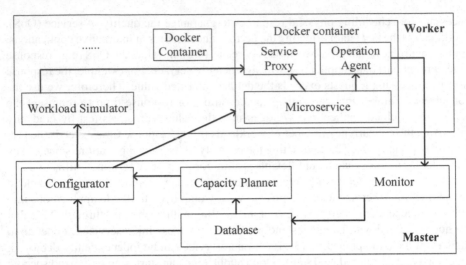

Fig. 1. Capestor system architecture

performance model to detect bottleneck and predict performance for multi-layer applications. Ref. [6] proposed suggestions for performance optimization based on identifying potential resource bottlenecks. Ref. [7] automatically detected the abnormal performance of web applications deployed in PaaS (Platform-as-a-service) cloud computing. However, these existing methods are often only applicable for applications with a few layers and a limited scale, and require further manual interpretation and analysis. Thus, they are difficult to cope with large-scale and diverse microservice-based applications in cloud computing with complex deployment environments [8].

3 Capestor

3.1 Design

We design the service mesh-based capacity estimation framework called as Capestor for microservice-based interactive cloud applications as follows. Service mesh is a low–latency infrastructure designed to handle network-based communication among microservices, which provides service discovery, load balancing, observability and traceability [10]. We employ the service mesh to provide a service proxy for transparently tracing microservices. Capestor provides restful APIs for operators to set configuration parameters and simulate workloads by calling the APIs, and then estimates microservices' capacity to suggest the suitable number of microservices' replicas. Capestor deploys microservices in a cluster, generates workloads, collects monitoring data, models microservices' performance, and then plans microservices' capacity. As shown in Fig. 1, Capestor with a microservice architecture is composed of a master node and many worker nodes. The master node includes a monitor module collecting monitoring data from worker nodes and recording the monitoring data in a database, a configurator module setting the cluster, and a capacity planner module estimating microservices' capacity.

A worker node has deployed containers with microservices and a workload simulator. A container has a service proxy to monitor requests and responses and an operation agent to collect resource metrics. We introduce these modules in detail as follows.

Microservice Container. Capestor deploys target microservices in containers as independent deployment environment to isolated them from each other.

Service Proxy. Capestor deploys a service mesh that is Istio to forward requests and responses by installing a service proxy for each microservice regardless of dependent microservices, when the container is instantiated. Each microservice is deployed in a container, and a proxy is established in a container for each microservice. The proxy's URL of each microservice as an environment variable is passed to all the microservices of a cloud application. Then, every request can be intercepted, and the response can be responded by the service proxy that collects all received and sent monitoring data to model the performance of a single microservice with little or no changes to the original application.

Operation Agent. Capestor deploys an agent in the container to manage the container with configurations (e.g., Yaml file, microservice name, Restful API), and monitors physical resources utilized by each microservice.

Workload Generator. Capestor employs JMeter to linearly generate increasing workloads in a specific deployment configuration after microservices are deployed in the container cluster, and collects resources and performance related metrics. When the response time exceeds the pre-defined expected threshold, the collected data with workloads' characteristics (e.g., request type, concurrency number) are persisted in the database to represent the capacity of a specific microservice. We repeat the above process of simulating workloads and collecting monitoring data in different deployment configurations, and incrementally train the model by increasing samples till the accuracy of the trained model is no longer significantly improved.

Capacity Planner. Capestor constructs an ElasticNet regression-based performance model in a certain deployment configuration to estimate the number of microservices' replicas. We train the regression model [9] with collected monitoring data in the previous tests to model the correlations between physical resources (e.g., virtual CPU, memory, network) and performance metrics (i.e., maximum request rate). Compared with other regression models (e.g., support vector regression, simple linear regression, polynomial regression), the ElasticNet regression has a higher accuracy and can converge in a short time interval. We employ the model to predict the capacity of a microservice in a specific deployment configuration, and then determine the number of required microservice replicas for processing requests. We employ the ElasticNet regression to model the performance of a microservice, where the input is a multi-dimension vector representing workloads and configurations, and the output is microservice's capacity that is the maximum request rate.

Configurator. Capestor employs Yaml files to configure microservices (e.g., replica number, resource limit), packages microservices in containers for deployment, and creates corresponding containers as containers.

3.2 Implementation

Capestor packages the microservices of the cloud application as Docker container images with Yaml files, deploys them in the container cluster, simulates workloads automatically according to pre-defined scripts, collects monitoring data with the service proxies and operation agents, establishes an ElasticNet regression based performance model of each microservice according to the collected monitoring data, estimates the capacity of each microservice based on the established performance model, and then suggests the number of microservice replicas. Customers only need to select a cloud application, set the parameters of Capestor with restful APIs, and write a workloads simulation script. Capestor estimates microservices' capacity in detail as follows:

- The microservice container module initializes a cluster with Kubernetes, runs the images packaging microservices as containers, and sets configurations (e.g., the number of pod replicas constraint, physical resources constraint);
- The service proxy for the microservice is initialized by Istio, when the container starts;
- The operation agent employs JMeter to simulate linearly increasing workloads, and employs Prometheus to collect microservices' monitoring data of workloads, performance metrics and physical resources;
- The capacity planner establishes a performance model based on an ElasticNet regression model, where deployment configurations and physical resources are input, and the maximum request rate is output. Then, it predicts a microservice's capacity in a specific development configuration, and plans the number of the microservice's replicas.

4 Evaluation

4.1 Setting

The experimental deployment environment includes two physical hosts, including a master node to manage the cluster and estimate every microservice's performance capacity, and a worker node to deploy microservices in containers, simulate workloads and collect monitoring data. Each host is configured with Intel(R) Core(TM) i7-8558U CPU@1.8 GHZ, 32 GB RAM memory, 1 TB disk, and 1000 Mbps network. The operating system that is Ubuntu 18.04.4 Server (64-bit) installed in each host runs Docker CE 19.03.01 to deploy microservices, and runs Kubernetes 1.18 to manage a Docker cluster and schedule Docker containers.

We validate Capestor with a typical microservice-based application Sock-Shop, which simulates an e-commerce website selling socks to demonstrate and test microservices [11]. We select five typical microservices from Sock-Shop, i.e., Users, Catalogue, Payment, Fronted and Distributor. Users is to manage customers' information; Catalogue is a database access microservice to query sock information stored in the backend database MongoDB; Payment is to pay for purchased socks; Frontend is a Web access microservice receiving customers' requests and sending corresponding strings; Distributor receives customers' requests and assigns them to the backend microservices

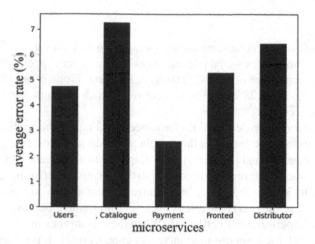

Fig. 2. Capacity prediction accuracy

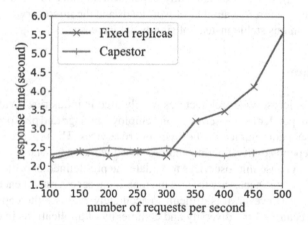

Fig. 3. Overall performance comparison

including Users, Catalogue and Frontend. After receiving responses from all the processed microservices, the Distributor summarizes them as a response, and then sends it back to customers.

We generate workloads with different ratio of request types. The resource utilization caused by workloads linearly increases. The simulation starts with a single request, and then the number of requests linearly increases. These microservices are accessed 15 times per minute. We evaluate the performance of Sock-Shop with the response time of 85% requests processed within a given time interval. We define the expected QoS threshold of response time as 2.5 s per request.

5   Results

For capacity prediction accuracy, we use the average error rate to evaluate the accuracy by comparing the actual and expected microservices' performance capacity. Figure 2 shows that the average error rates of Users, Catalogue, Payment, Frontend and Distributor are 4.72%, 7.26%, 2.57%, 5.28%, 6.43%, respectively, which presents that Capestor has a high prediction accuracy.

For guaranteeing microservices' performance, we compare the application's performance with Capestor. We first start three replicas for each microservice in the experiment without Capestor, and then we employ Capestor to adaptively adjust the number of different microservices' replicas according to the monitored performance metrics and workloads. Figure 3 shows that when the concurrency number of workloads is below 300, the response time of the two applications does not differ much, because the application does not reach the performance bottleneck. When the concurrency number of workloads is greater than 300, the response time increases exponentially in the experiment without Capestor, because Catalogue microservice has become the performance bottleneck. Meanwhile, as Capestor can dynamically expand the number of Catalogue's replicas according to the concurrency number of workloads and the microservice's capacity, the response time remains stable instead of significant increase.

6   Conclusion

In recent years, microservice architectures widely used in industries divide applications into multiple independent microservices, and employ language and platform independent APIs to implement communication between microservices. The resource utilization of a microservice depends on its function and processed workloads. The sudden increase of workloads should cause microservices to violate the pre-defined expected performance metrics. Therefore, it is necessary to limit the maximum access rate of each microservice to guarantee QoS. However, it is difficult to accurately evaluate the capability of each microservice, because of the diversity and complexity of applications in cloud computing. This paper proposes a service mesh-based capacity estimation framework called as Capestor for cloud applications. The target microservice is first placed in a container, the workloads are generated, and the monitoring data of performance metrics and resource metrics are collected. The correlations between deployment configurations, physical resources and performance metrics are established with an ElasticNet regression model, and then the capacity of each microservice is evaluated to assist fine-grained flexible expansion. Capestor is deployed in a container cluster to schedule a typical microservice-based application that is Sock-Shop. The experimental results show that Capestor has low prediction error rate, and can effectively guarantees applications' performance.

Acknowledgment. This work is supported by National Key R&D Program of China (2018YFB1402900).

References

1. Samreen, F., Elkhatib, Y., Rowe, M., Blair, G.S.: Daleel: simplifying cloud instance selection using machine learning. In: IEEE/IFIP Network Operations and Management Symposium, pp. 557–563. IEEE Press, Piscataway (2016). https://doi.org/10.1109/noms.2016.7502858
2. Beyer, B., Murphy, N.R., Rensin, D.K., Kawahara, K., Thorne, S.: The Site Reliability Workbook: Practical Ways to Implement SRE, 1st edn. O'Reilly Media, Farnham (2018)
3. Newman, S.: Building Microservices, 1st edn. OReilly Media, Sebastopol (2015)
4. Casale, G., Ningfang, M., Smirni, E.: Model-driven system capacity planning under workload burstiness. IEEE Trans. Comput. **59**(1), 66–80 (2010). https://doi.org/10.1109/TC.2009.135
5. Urgaonkar, B., Shenoy, P., Chandra, A., Goyal, P.: Dynamic provisioning of multi-tier internet applications. In: The 2nd International Conference on Autonomic Computing, pp. 217–228. IEEE Press, Piscataway (2005). https://doi.org/10.1109/icac.2005.27
6. Leymann, F., Breitenbücher, U., Wagner, S., Wettinger, J.: Native cloud applications: why monolithic virtualization is not their foundation. In: Helfert, M., Ferguson, D., Méndez Muñoz, V., Cardoso, J. (eds.) CLOSER 2016. CCIS, vol. 740, pp. 16–40. Springer, Cham (2017). https://doi.org/10.1007/978-3-319-62594-2_2
7. Jayathilaka, H., Krintz, C., Wolski, R.: Performance monitoring and root cause analysis for cloud-hosted web applications. In: The 26th International Conference on World Wide Web, pp. 469–478. ACM Press, New York, NY. https://doi.org/10.1145/3038912.3052649
8. Wang, Q., Kanemasa, Y., Li, J., Jayasinghe D., Shimizu, T., Matsubara, M., Kawaba, M., Pu C.: Detecting transient bottlenecks in n-tier applications through fine-grained analysis. In: the 33rd International Conference on Distributed Computing Systems, pp. 31–40. IEEE Press, Piscataway, NJ (2013). https://doi.org/10.1109/icdcs.2013.17
9. Hastie, T., Tibshirani, R., Friedman, J.: The Elements of Statistical Learning. Springer, Heidelberg (2017)
10. Hastie, T., Tibshirani, R., Friedman, J.: The Elements of Statistical Learning. Springer, Heidelberg (2017). https://doi.org/10.1007/978-0-387-84858-7
11. Nginx, Inc.: What Is a Service Mesh? https://www.nginx.com/blog/what-is-a-service-mesh/
12. Weaveworks, Inc.: Sock Shop: A Microservices Demo Application. https://microservices-demo.github.io/

Cardinality Based Rate Limiting System for Time-Series Data

Sudeep Kumar$^{(\boxtimes)}$ and Deepak Kumar Vasthimal

eBay Inc., 2025 Hamilton Avenue, San Jose, CA 95125, USA
{sudekumar,dvasthimal}@ebay.com

Abstract. Massive monitoring systems that require high availability and performance for both ingestion and retrieval of data are often encountered with rogue streams of data having a high cardinality. The management of such high cardinality data sets for time-series data and a performance sensitive system is challenging. The challenges primarily arise as the time-series data sets, typically needs to be loaded onto a limited memory space before results can be returned to the client. This affects the number of incoming queries that can be supported simultaneously. Too many time-series can potentially degraded read performance and thereby affect user experience. Our proposed rate-limiting system described herein seeks to address a key availability issue on a high-volume, time-series system by using a dynamic cardinality computation in combination with a central assessment service to detect and block high cardinality data streams. As a result of this technical improvement, anomalous logging behavior is detected quickly, affected tenants are notified, and hardware resources are used optimally.

Keywords: Cloud computing · Hyperlog · Cardinality · Time-series · Micro-services · Rate-limiting · Metrics

1 Introduction

A time-series is a series of data points indexed (or listed or graphed) in time order. Most commonly, a time series [1] is a sequence taken at successive equally spaced points in time.

For Ex: "Customer A" logs a time-series which can be represented as cpu.utilization ["host" = 'host1', "region" = 'prod'] 1562532547 80

- 'cpu.utilization' is a metric name
- "host" = 'host1', "region" = 'prod' are dimension K, V value pair
- 1562532547 is epoc source timestamp
- 80 is the value of the metric at a given timestamp.

Supported by eBay Inc. San Jose, California, USA.

Q. Zhang et al. (Eds.): CLOUD 2020, LNCS 12403, pp. 250–260, 2020.
https://doi.org/10.1007/978-3-030-59635-4_18

Cardinality broadly refers to unique data values (or unique time-series) contained in a data set group. High cardinality implies, that group contains a large percentage of totally unique values. Low cardinality implies that the group contains many repeated elements.

Time-series data tends to be paired with metadata (also referred to as "tags") that describes the data. Often this primary time-series data or the metadata is indexed [6] for faster query performance through data filters. The cardinality [2] of a time-series dataset is typically defined by the cross-product of the cardinality [2] of each individual indexed column.

Systems that contain multiple indexed columns, each with a large number of unique values, the cardinality of such cross-product can get really large and fall under "high-cardinality."

The rest of this paper is organized as follows. Section 2 outlines the architecture and high level design. Section 3 proposes a novel solution to avoid cardinality explosion using cardinality based rate limiting. The section also goes on to describe sequencing steps. Section 4 provides details of tenants that are blacklisted due to cardinality explosion. Section 5 describes future work of integrating proposed solution into Kubernetes for ease of deployment and self-healing. Finally, Section 6 concludes the paper describing the importance of proposed architecture on availability of eBay massively parallel and scalable metric platform.

2   Architecture and Design

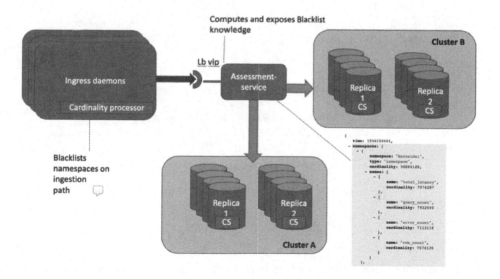

Fig. 1. System architecture

The Figure in 1 illustrates high level design and architecture of the system. Cardinality server(s) (annotated as CS), runs within each instance of the time series database. The server intercepts all metrics signals that a replica shard receives and computes cardinality using HyperLogLog (HLL) at namespace (customer or tenant) and at for each metric identified by its name. This information is periodically polled by a central assessment service which applies pre-configured threshold based rules on cardinality limits. Based on these policies either a namespace or its associated metric is marked as blacklisted. Once a metric or tenant is blacklisted, additional metric values are ignored at ingestion. A snapshot of blacklisted information is shown in the Fig. 1. Ingress daemon are stateless application which listen on a distributed streaming platform powered by Apache Kafka for all incoming metric signals. This application uses blacklisting provided by assessment service to block incoming namespaces or its associated metrics on hot path.

```
{
    "hostname": "ms-nsn-0-3",
    "startime": 1562515200,
    "endtime": 1562533400,
    "count": 5244571,
    "namespaces": [{
        "namespace": "dbmon-benchmark",
        "count": 832567,
        "names": [{
            "name": "db_AverageQueryTime",
            "count": 411636
        }, {
            "name": "db_Waits",
            "count": 410377
        }, {
            "name": "database_totalWaits",
            "count": 5268
        }, {
            "name": "database_averageHighWaterWaiters",
            "count": 5249
        }],
        "metric_count": 4
    }]
}
```

Fig. 2. Sample structure

Time series data tends to be paired with metadata [9] (sometimes called "tags") that describes incoming data points. The primary time series data or the metadata [6] is indexed for faster query performance, so that one can quickly find the values that match all of the specified tags. The cardinality of a time series data set is typically defined by the cross product of the cardinality of each individual indexed column. For example for a set of candies of 10 colors with 5 categories (plain, peanut, almond, dark, and vanilla), the cardinality of such a set is $10 \times 5 = 50$ or sum permutations of candies. The underlying storage system must have correct indices that would then allow it to efficiently retrieve all blue and crispy candies (which are objectively the best). A time series data set with multiple indexed columns, each with a large number of unique values, the cardinality of that cross-product can get really large and termed as "high-cardinality".

Cardinality typically affects time-series in following manner:

- In a high-speed ingestion/indexing time series [1] system, the total memory footprint [12] is directly proportional to the number of active time-series it can handle.
- Data series with high cardinality can adversely affect the read service level agreements (SLAs), as there are far more unique data points that need to be retrieved or rendered on a graph. This provides for a bad user experience. Many times having so many data points rendered on a graph panel is not very useful for a visual representation of that data.

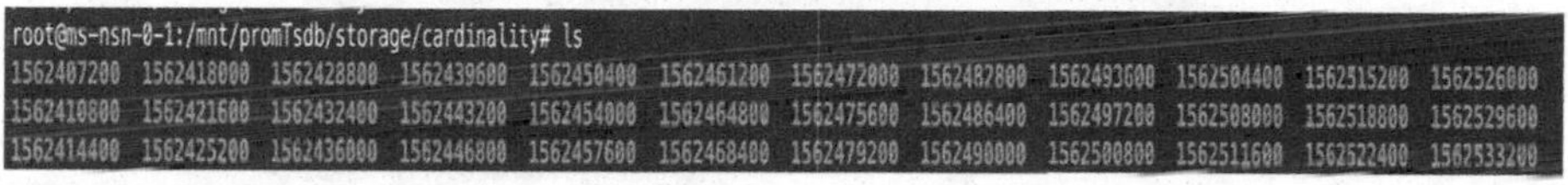

Fig. 3. HLL blocks

There are multiple mechanisms available today to compute the overall cardinality of a time series data that are provided by various Open source libraries. Most of the libraries use HyperLogLog [4] (HLL, or its variant HLL++) to compute the cardinality on a data set. The basis of the HyperLogLog [4] algorithm, is the observation that the cardinality of a multiset of uniformly distributed random numbers can be estimated by computing the maximum number of leading zeros in the binary representation of each number in the set. On a data set with maximum number of leading zeros observed is n, an estimate for the number of distinct elements in the set is 2n. In the HyperLogLog [4] algorithm, a hash function is applied to each element in the original multiset to obtain a multiset of uniformly distributed random numbers with the same cardinality as the original multiset. The cardinality of this randomly distributed set can then be estimated using the algorithm above. The simple estimate of cardinality obtained using the algorithm above has the disadvantage of a large variance. In the 'HyperLogLog' [4] algorithm, the variance is minimized by splitting the multiset into numerous subsets, calculating the maximum number of leading zeros in the numbers in each of these subsets, and using a harmonic mean to combine these estimates for each subset into an estimate of the cardinality of the whole set.

3   Solution

The proposed solution attempts to reduce cardinality explosion or slow poisoning (where cardinality of time series increases slowly over a period of time) done by non-compliant tenants by performing cardinality based rate limiting [12]. Rate limiting is performed on ingestion source (which receives time-series data in a system) based on centralized cardinality computation for a tenant on its logged [8] time series signals using custom threshold based cardinality policies across all available times-series underlying infrastructure.

```
<?xmlversion="1.0"
encoding="UTF-8"?>
            <profiles>
                <profile>
                    <namespace>dbmon-benchmark</namespace>
                    <threshold>1000000</threshold>
                    <metrics>
                        <name>query_count</name>
                        <threshold>1000000</threshold>
                    </metrics>
                </profile>
                <profile>
                    <namespace>netmon</namespace>
                    <threshold>1000000</threshold>
                    <metrics>
                        <name>ping</name>
                        <threshold>1000000</threshold>
                    </metrics>
                </profile>
            </profiles>
```

Fig. 4. Policy definition

The proposed solution listed has following features.

- Quota management is against cardinality at a tenant level and additionally at a metric level within a tenant. Such quota management allows multi-tenant support for time series data on shared infrastructure.
- Metrics with high cardinality are identified with ease and blacklisted for a given customer. This avoids a blanket level blacklisting for the entire tenant. For instance, consider a production code roll-out done by a customer where it introduced a new metric. However, since the metric was logged incorrectly it leads to a cardinality explosion against that metric name. In such cases, if the cardinality for that metric breaches a certain threshold only that metric is blacklisted instead of blacklisting the entire customer profile.
- Custom rules for cardinality quota is possible, where a specific customer requires high cardinality support for multiple metrics or a specific metric. Both of these proposals are supported and implemented.

- Controlling the cardinality allows the system to better predict read performance throughout. For example, the maximum time of read queries are clearly determined. (since all queries will return data for only time-series within their cardinality limits as they were rate limited during ingestion)
- Users are notified in real time, about cardinality threshold breaches both against individual metric or tenant during metric ingestion.
- Today, many metric storages have scalability challenges when it comes to supporting huge cardinality data sets [10]. This problem is generally alleviated by horizontal scaling of shards to a cluster (total cardinality/number of unique time-series per shard). This is clearly not enough as more infrastructure is required as cardinality continues to grow for a tenant. There needs to be a way to compute cardinality quota for tenants based on their logging across all clusters or underlying infrastructure where their time-series is stored. This is currently not available in any systems out in the industry. Also, cardinality computation should allow us to blacklist certain tenants when they go over the time-series quota to prevent any underlying storage stability issues. The blacklisting would mean feeding the cardinality threshold breach information back to ingestion source which is lacking in the time series system today. The system should only blacklisting certain offending metrics in tenant space.

```
                ← → C ⟳   ⓘ Not Secure   assessment-service.sherlock-storage.svc.23 tess.io 8089/blacklist

{
    time: 1562457601,
  - namespaces: [
      - {
            namespace: "recs",
            type: "name",
            cardinality: 5823693,
          - names: [
              - {
                    name: "algo_execution_duration_seconds",
                    cardinality: 2363397
                },
              - {
                    name: "algo_execution_duration_seconds_count",
                    cardinality: 1132420
                },
              - {
                    name: "algo_execution_duration_seconds_sum",
                    cardinality: 1127671
                }
            ]
        },
      - {
            namespace: "nodejs",
            type: "name",
            cardinality: 745681,
          - names: [
              - {
                    name: "http_request_duration_ms",
                    cardinality: 502731
                }
            ]
        }
    ]
}
```

Fig. 5. BlackList namespaces with cardinality

3.1 Sequencing Steps

The following steps are performed for every incoming metric signal into ingress daemons as described in Fig. 1

- A hash of incoming metric signal is computed and written to shard (replica) on metric store by ingress daemon locally.
- Incoming data time series signals are then intercepted and passed on to the light weight cardinality module on every time series database process in the back end.
- Cardinality module (CS) computes cardinality at two levels (tenant and metric) by creating separate HLLs per customer (hereafter referred to as a namespace) and at namespace + metric name (hereafter referred to a name level) The computation is done at (namespace, HLL) and (namespace, name, HLL)
- This information is exposed on each cardinality server (CS) by a REST service using HTTP(s) '$hostname:8091/admin/cardinality' as shown in Fig. 2.

The cardinality information depicts the start from where cardinality is computed to its endpoints. The REST service can optionally take in custom query parameters. 'namespaces[]-namespaces-count' depicts the cardinality on the time series database (TSDB) instance for a customer and 'namespaces[]-namespaces-names[]-¿count' which cardinality of top K metric names within the namespace. The HLLs per (namespace) and (namespace, name) are persisted in local TSDB instances at a specified location '/mnt/promTsdb/storage/cardinality' every hour, in HLL blocks as shown in Fig. 3.

- The HLL blocks are mergeable over time and it will used to determine cardinality history for a (namespace) and (namespace,name) combination.
- A central "assessment-service" (AS) described in Fig. 1 discovers all the Prometheus TSDB shards [5]. The discovery mechanism can be either static or dynamic. The assessment service is topology or infrastructure aware. This implies that the service is aware of the location of TSDB instances (or shards) that houses replica for a given column.
- Assessment service invokes the REST service at "$hostname:8091/admin/cardinality" on every TSDB instances. The maximum cardinality number are computed across replicas of a given shard. Assesment service performs a sum total of the cardinality grouped by tenant and metric name. Cardinality is computed at both tenant level and top-K metric names within a tenant.
- The central service exposes blacklisted information shown in Fig. 5, at a REST endpoint "blacklist". This provides capability to source ingestion layer to either drop all incoming metrics for a tenant or specific metrics within a tenant quota. This information can be additionally persisted to ensure stateful cardinality information.

A tenant or a metric is blacklisted based on cardinality quota rules. As shown in Fig. 4, 'profiles-)profile[]-) namespace-) threshold' depicts customer or tenant cardinality quota and 'profiles-) profile[]-) namespace-) metrics[]-) threshold' is custom overridden quota for a metric within a tenant space.

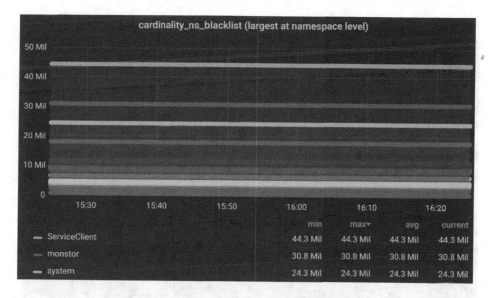

Fig. 6. Blacklisted tenants

Ingress daemons showin in Fig. 1 feeds off the "blacklist" endpoint exposed by assessment service and blacklists any future time. Series for a (namespace) and (namespace, name) based on the cardinality list and rules.

The running cardinality context or quota is reset at the end of day (or custom time interval), further to which all signals are allowed until they breach the cardinality policy rules again (they get blacklisted on breach of quota).

4 Evaluation

The graph in Fig. 6 depicts reporting on tenants that either blacklisted or one of their associated metrics is blacklisted. The threshold alerts are configured on tenants identified by namespace, when they breach 80% of the allowed cardinality limits.

The graph in Fig. 7 depicts total cardinality seen per shard per day. This is a important measure to determine the rate of cardinality growth on a daily basis. The shards within the time series database based on internal benchmarks can support 20 million unique series per day. System administrators are notified by alerts when a shard reaches near this limit. This allows for resizing, capacity planing of the storage cluster to support growth in time series data.

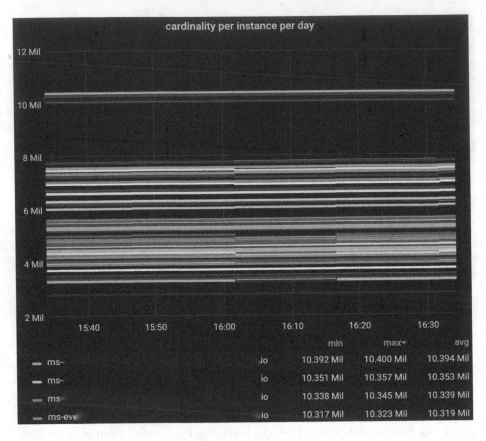

Fig. 7. Cardinality per instance per day

5   Future Work

The entire platform is running on virtual machines and will be migrated to Kubernetes [13] that allows to containerize and orchestrate the deployment for centralized assessment service. Additionally, rules can be configured as custom resource definitions which will be propagated to entire infrastructure on any change. Any subscriber, such as assessment service will be notified on these changes and would have blacklisting information. Also, in the current systemdoes not account for historic cardinality information. In future, the system can use 'Bollinger Bands' [14] to compute moving average of cardinality information. The blacklist can be further enhanced by computing threshold over standard deviations on upper and lower bands.

6   Conclusion

The proposed system outlined in this paper uses custom cardinality rules, has helped to scale underlying monitoring platform and support ingestion of approximately five million metrics per second without any outages. Extensive benchmarking have been performed to see the overhead on including cardinality server on timeseries database and time to detect a rogue namespace or its associated metric. On a 50 node TSDB database, the system can handle approximately 8–10 million metrics per second with a footprint of 10% of CPU on database and 400 MB of memory. The solution was extremely efficient in finding slow poisoning use-cases.

Availability of metric [11] platform depends on proposed system. In many cases, it was observed that corrupt tenants can cause substantial damage to underlying infrastructure and metric platform. Extensive monitoring and alerting built around proposed system provides visibility into cardinality trends for customer data volumes. Cardinality trends has been used as an input in predicting future infrastructure scaling needs of metric platform.

Acknowledgement. This work has been performed with support of eBay Inc. The views expressed are those of the authors and do not necessarily represent eBay Inc. eBay Inc. or any of its subsidiaries is not liable for any use that may be made of any of the information contained herein.

References

1. Korenberg, M.J., Paarmann, L.D.: Orthogonal approaches to time-series analysis and system identification. IEEE Signal Process. Mag. 8(3), 29–43 (1991)
2. Zheng, Y., Li, M.: ZOE: fast cardinality estimation for large-scale RFID systems. In: 2013 Proceedings IEEE INFOCOM, Turin (2013)
3. Vasthimal, D.K., Kumar, S., Somani, M.: Near real-time tracking at scale. In: IEEE 7th International Symposium on Cloud and Service Computing (SC2). Kanazawa 2017, pp. 241–244 (2017)
4. Chabchoub, Y., Hebrail, G.: Sliding hyperloglog: estimating cardinality in a data stream over a sliding window. In: 2010 IEEE International Conference on Data Mining Workshops, NSW, Sydney (2010)
5. Prometheus TSDB. https://github.com/prometheus/tsdb
6. Sellisa, T.K.: Intelligent caching and indexing techniques for relational database systems. Information Systems, Elsevier (1988)
7. Bennett, J.M., Bauer, M.A., Kinchlea, D.: Characteristics of files in NFS environments. In: Proceedings of the ACM SIGSMALL/PC Symposium on Small Systems, Toronto, Ontario, Candada (1991)
8. V, D.K., Shah, R.R., Philip, A.: Centralized log management for pepper. In: 2011 IEEE Third International Conference on Cloud Computing Technology and Science, Athens, 2011, pp. 1–3 (2011)
9. Han, H., Giles, C.L., Manavoglu, E., Zha, H., Zhang, Z., Fox, E.A.: Automatic document metadata extraction using support vector machines. In: 2003 Joint Conference on Digital Libraries, 2003. Proceedings., Houston, TX, USA (2003)

10. Vasthimal, D.: Robust and Resilient migration of data processing systems to public hadoop grid. In: 2018 IEEE/ACM International Conference on Utility and Cloud Computing Companion (UCC Companion), Zurich, 2018, pp. 21–23 (2018)
11. Gupta, D., et al.: Difference engine: harnessing memory redundancy in virtual machines. Commun. ACM **53**(10), 85–93 (2010)
12. Raghavan, B., Vishwanath, K., Ramabhadran, S., Yocum, K., Snoeren, A.: Cloud Control with Distributed Rate Limiting. In: SIGCOMM (2007)
13. Hightower, K., Burns, B., Beda, J.: Kubernetes: Up and Running: Dive Into the Future of Infrastructure, 2nd edn. O'Reilly Media, Sebastopol (2019)
14. Ngan, H.Y.T., Pang, G.K.H.: Novel method for patterned fabric inspection using Bollinger bands. Opt. Eng. **45**(8), 087202 (2006)

Bioinf-PHP: Bioinformatics Pipeline for Protein Homology and Phylogeny

Michael Zhou[1(✉)] and Yongsheng Bai[2(✉)]

[1] Skyline High School, 2552 N Maple Rd, Ann Arbor, MI 48103, USA
2021zhoumichaelh@aaps.k12.mi.us
[2] Next-Gen Intelligent Science Training, Ann Arbor, MI 48105, USA
bioinformaticsresearchtomorrow@gmail.com

Abstract. Catalase is a special category of enzyme that plays a critical role in regulating the level of harmful hydrogen peroxide in cells. There are three main families of these proteins: Typical Catalases, Catalase-Peroxidases (katG), and Manganese Catalases. In order to uncover potential evolutionary relationships between these enzymes, we have developed a bioinformatics pipeline named *Bioinf-PHP* to search for protein homology and phylogeny, and to compare these three families at the functional level based on sequence similarity. Protein motif analysis of the sequences featured in the pipeline were conducted using the MEME algorithm. The top three significant motifs were reported for all of the catalase sequences. The *Bioinf-PHP* pipeline also runs BLASTP to search for homology between bacteria catalase and yeast protein sequences. The neighbor-joining phylogenetic tree was constructed with *Saccharomyces cerevisiae* to infer evolutionary relationships as a test example. The structural similarities between orthologous sequences provided further evidence of functional similarity.

Keywords: Homology · Bioinformatics pipeline · Catalase · Sequence analysis · Multiple sequence analysis

1 Introduction

Hydrogen peroxide is a by-product of cell metabolism, and can turn into hydroxyl radicals, which are harmful to DNA and proteins in the cell. Catalases are some of the most important enzymes because they regulate harmful hydrogen peroxide levels in cells, thus preventing the formation of dangerous hydroxyl radicals.

Catalase is present in almost all living organisms (including bacteria and human beings) whose cells undergo an oxidation reaction. The study of catalase reactions can be traced back to early 1920s [1]. RedoxiBase [2] serves as the central protein sequence repository for all known oxido-reductase superfamilies, making it an ideal data source for homology studies.

There are three main families of these proteins: mono-functional, haem-containing typical Catalases, bi-functional haem-containing Catalase-Peroxidases

© Springer Nature Switzerland AG 2020
Q. Zhang et al. (Eds.): CLOUD 2020, LNCS 12403, pp. 261–269, 2020.
https://doi.org/10.1007/978-3-030-59635-4_19

(katG), and non-haem Manganese Catalases [3]. Different catalase classes play similar roles in their biological context, although they do not share much similarity at the sequence level. In this study, we are trying to advance computational methods for sequence analysis and examine whether catalases are likely to be conserved across species.

We focus on the development of our new bioinformatics pipeline using catalase sequences found in bacteria as a pioneer study, although the pipeline could be used to process protein sequences from a variety of different species. We chose the *Saccharomyces cerevisiae*(Baker's yeast)[4] as the outgroup protein for multiple sequence analysis and phylogenetic tree construction because *Saccharomyces cerevisiae* serves as an excellent outgroup to construct phylogenetic trees, as well as being a well-studied eukaryotic organism. We would like to understand the homology between bacteria catalases and *Saccharomyces cerevisiae*.

2   Materials and Methods

2.1   Pipeline Workflow

In order to automate the sequence analysis steps, we have built an open-source Bioinformatics pipeline for Protein Homology and Phylogeny(*Bioinf-PHP*). The workflow of the pipeline is shown in Fig. 1.

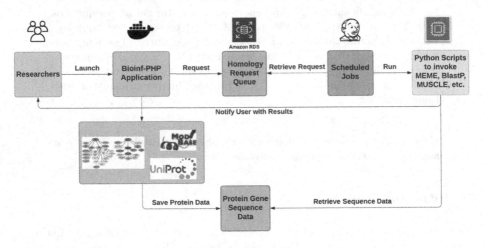

Fig. 1. Workflow of *Bioinf-PHP*

The pipeline contains a Django web application with the gene/protein sequence data stored in a database. The user can make protein/gene homology and phylogeny analysis requests inside the web application. We use Jenkins scheduler server to arrange multiple Python scripts to run on scheduled time intervals, for tasks such as motif analysis, protein database lookup, multiple sequence analysis, phylogenetic tree generation, etc. The Bioinformatics tools and databases adopted by the pipeline are listed in Table 1.

Table 1. Bioinformatics tools and databases adopted in *Bioinf-PHP*

Tools/Databases	Output/Function
RedoxiBase	protein sequences
UniProt [5]	protein lookup
SWISS-MODEL [6]/ModBase [7]	3D structure lookup
MEME [8]	Motif Analysis
BLASTP [9]	Homology analysis with target protein (e.g. yeast)
MUSCLE [10]	Multiple Sequence Alignment and Phylogenetic Tree reconstruction

2.2 Obtaining Catalase Sequences

RedOxibase is a database dedicated to peroxidases and other oxidoreductase super families. It contains protein sequences for over 1000 organisms across many NCBI taxonomies. In this research, we analyzed catalase protein sequences within the Bacteria SuperKingdom, and Bacteroidetes/Chlorobi Phylum.

2.3 Motif Analysis

The user can pick a protein class type within the pipeline interface, and submit a request for Multiple Expectation maximization for Motif Elicitation (MEME)[8] analysis. The backend web server will run MEME script accordingly based on the request details and with the configuration settings shown in Table 2.

Table 2. MEME Configuration parameters

Option	Setting
Motif Site Distribution	zero or one occurrence per sequence (zoops)
Number of Motifs	3
Minimum width of Motif	6
Maximum width of Motif	30
Maximum allowed dataset size	1000000
Print no status messages to terminal	on

The pipeline generates MEME results in HTML format, along with individual motif log image files. Those files will be compressed and send to the requester's email address as a .zip file attachment.

2.4 Protein Blast Analysis

The NCBI BLASTP [9] algorithm is often used to compare query protein sequences of interest against database sequences. Since *Saccharomyces cerevisiae* is a well-studied eukaryotic organism that serves as an outgroup for bacteria in our phylogeny analysis, we examined sequence similarities between Catalase/-Catalase Peroxidase sequences and *Saccharomyces cerevisiae* sequences.

Since the NCBI [11] BLAST web service API does not let the user specify the target sequence set, we have to run the BLASTP algorithm locally, which brings us two advantages: the running speed is faster than when running on a remote server, and one can specify to search the customized database (in our case, it is the yeast sequence database) for input sequences.

We installed the latest release version of NCBI BLAST+ suite [9] on our web server. Our Python script uses Biopython [13] code interface to construct a BLASTP command line string with Expectation value set to be 1e-05, and output results set to tabular format.

2.5   Multiple Sequence Alignment

MUSCLE [10] is one of the most widely used multiple sequence alignment softwares. We obtained a list of the sequence data from all catalases and catalase-peroxidases for bacteria species, as well as yeast catalases, cytochrome c peroxidase(CCP), peroxisomal catalase(catalase A) and cytosolic catalase (catalase T), which are encoded by the CTA1 and CTT1 genes respectively. We used the MUSCLE algorithm for creating multiple alignment of protein sequences, and constructed phylogenetic trees to show the history of catalase family evolution.

Table 3 shows the command line arguments of running MUSCLE for multiple sequence alignment and Neighbor-Joining tree [16] in PHYLIP [17] format:

Table 3. MUSCLE Scripts Command lines

Name	Command
Multiple Sequence Alignment	muscle −in <input_protein_fasta_file.faa> −fastaout <output_fasta_file.afa> −htmlout <output_HTML_file.afa>
Neighbor-Joining tree	muscle −maketree −in <output_HTML_file.afa> −out <output_phylogenetic_tree.phy> −cluster neighborjoining

2.6   Protein 3D Structure Lookup

Based on the catalase protein names, our pipeline queries these sequences against UniProt web URLs [5] to retrieve mapped protein in UniProt knowledge base (UniProtKB).

Not all catalase proteins could be found or mapped in UniProt. For the mapped proteins, the pipeline code parses the UniProt protein page to retrieve functional information (i.e. Biological Process, Molecular Function and Cellular Component information based on Gene Ontology(GO)), and also structure information by following the listed SWISS-MODEL Repository links and ModBase links, if any.

3   Results and Discussion

We used protein sequences for bacteria catalase to evaluate our pipeline.

3.1   Catalase Sequences

The Bacteroidetes/Chlorobi category within RedoxiBase contains 44 organisms and 105 sequences. We downloaded all 105 sequences in FASTA format. There are 12 sequences of typical Catalases, 33 sequences of Catalase peroxidases, and 2 sequences of Manganese Catalases. Due to the small sample size of the Managanese Catalase data set, we focus our analysis only on the typical Catalase and Catalase-Peroxidase categories.

3.2   Motif Analysis

We ran the MEME program with the following settings: motif number = 3, and motif width is between 6 and 30 (Table 2). The MEME results for typical catalase and Catalase peroxidase sequences are shown side by side in Fig. 2.

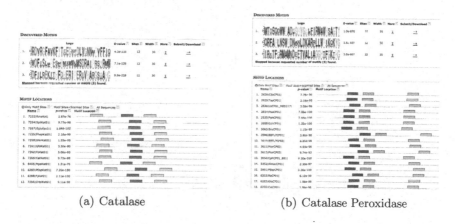

(a) Catalase   (b) Catalase Peroxidase

Fig. 2. MEME motifs for Catalase and Catalase Peroxidases

All sequences within both the mono-functional catalase and catalase peroxidase categories contain three well-aligned conserved motifs but from two different sets, with significant p-values. Those two types of heme enzyme demonstrate high catalase activities; however, these protein sequences contain very little similarities, and there are no overlapping motifs found between mono-functional catalase and catalase peroxidase categories, which suggests that different motifs might serve similar critical catalase functions for these enzymes.

3.3   Motif Homology

BLASTP results show that all Catalase sequences show statistically significant similarity with *Saccharomyces cerevisiae* peroxisomal catalase A (CTA1), and *Saccharomyces cerevisiae* cytosolic catalase T(CTT1). Both CTA1 and CTT1 play a role in protection from oxidative damage by hydrogen peroxide.

On the other hand, all catalase peroxidase sequences are homologous to *Saccharomyces cerevisiae* cytochrome-c peroxidase (CCP), the first heme enzyme to have its crystallographic structure determined. Therefore, it serves an important role in heme protein reactivity study.

3.4   Catalase Phylogeny

The Phylogenetics tree results (Fig. 3) confirmed that Catalase T and Catalase A from the yeast family are more closely related to the catalase proteins for bacteria than to the CCP peroxidase protein.

Fig. 3. Phylogenetic tree consists of 12 catalase sequences (Red), 33 catalase-peroxidase sequences(Blue), and 3 yeast sequences(Green), based on Neighbor-Joining tree generated from MUSCLE multiple sequence alignment results (Color figure online)

3.5   Catalase Protein Structures

With a search for known 3D Protein structures within ModBase and SWISS-MODEL, we have located 3D structure results for 8 Catalases and 8 Catalase-Peroxidases. Table 4 provides an overview of the 3D Protein structure search results. At the time of this study, ModBase contains Template(e.g. 3ewn, 3gra, 3mgk) based calculation for only catalase protein sequences, while SWISS-MODEL repository contains modeling for 8 Catalase-Peroxidase proteins.

Table 4. Known 3D Structures of 8 Typical Catalases and 8 Catalase-Peroxidase (KatG) based on ModBase and SWISS-MODEL

Name	Class	UniProt ID	ModBase ID	SWISS-MODEL ID
CatKat01	Catalase	A3UA09	3ewn	
CHpiKat01	Catalase	C7PGE8	3gra	
DferKat01	Catalase	C6VVN3	3ewn	
FbKat01	Catalase	C6X255	3mgk	
FjKat01	Catalase	A5FF54	3mgk	
GfoKat01	Catalase	A0M4R4	3ewn	
PEspKat01	Catalase	A6EG61	3ewn	
PhepKat01	Catalase	C6Y413	3gra	
CchCP01	Catalase peroxidase	Q3ATL6		Q3ATL6
CphCP01_BS1	Catalase peroxidase	B3EKE9		B3EKE9
CphCP01_DSM266	Catalase peroxidase	A1BEI1		A1BEI1
FjCP01_UW101	Catalase peroxidase	A5FD11		A5FD11
GfoCP01	Catalase peroxidase	A0LZM9		A0LZM9
PaeCP01	Catalase peroxidase	B4S3B3		B4S3B3
PphCP01	Catalase peroxidase	B4SAT7		B4SAT7
SruCP01	Catalase peroxidase	Q2RZX7		Q2RZX7

3.6   Cloud Computing Benefits

The *Bioinf-PHP* source code is hosted on GitHub (https://github.com/mzhou08/bioinformatics_pipeline) as open-source software. Since the application is packaged as a docker image, others will be able to run the application with identical system settings on any machine or cloud service with Docker support. We welcome the community to make contributions and improve the application.

We compared the system performance metrics in three deployment environments. The average results taken from 5 trials are listed in Table 5. The cloud environment, even with the low tier of Amazon EC2 instance, still offers performance advantages over other on-prem deployments.

Table 5. Performance Metrics Comparison among three deployment environments: (1) AWS Linux 2 AMI (t2.micro) + PostgreSQL AWS RDS; (http://www.bioinformaticspipeline.net:8000) (2) On-Prem Ubuntu Server + PostgreSQL AWS RDS (http://jdbbioinformatics.science) (3) localhost + PostgreSQL on MacOS

Deploy Type	App Load Time (ms)	Average Query Time (ms)
1	8.72	12.77
2	13.61	42.93
3	24.00	50.12

4   Conclusions and Future Plans

We have developed a web-based bioinformatics pipeline, *Bioinf-PHP*, that enables researchers to upload protein sequence data to perform subsequent homology and phylogeny analysis. We have used the publicly available bacteria catalase sequences to test our pipeline and identified motifs and construct phylogeny tree of catalase proteins with yeast proteins. We believe our tool is useful for automating multiple steps of homology analysis. Although the current work focuses on protein sequence analysis for prokaryotic organisms, our pipeline can also accept sequences for eukaryotic organisms as input.

We will explore the Amazon Elastic Container Service (ECS) to deploy more containerized applications at scale, and to schedule long-running batch jobs.

References

1. Morgulis, S.: A Study of the catalase reaction. J. Biological Chem. (1921)
2. Savelli, B., et al.: RedoxiBase: a database for ROS homeostasis regulated proteins. Redox Biol. **26**, 101247 (2019)
3. Zamocky, M., Furtmuller, P.G., Obinger C.: Evolution of catalases from bacteria to humans. Antioxid Redox Signal 1527–1548 (2008)
4. Izawa, S., Inoue, Y., Kimura, A: Importance of catalase in the adaptive response to hydrogen peroxide: analysis of acatalasaemic Saccharomyces cerevisiae. Biochem. J. **320** 61–67 (1996)
5. The UniProt Consortium: UniProt: a worldwide hub of protein knowledge. Nucleic Acids Res. **47**, 506–515 (2019)
6. Waterhouse, A., et al.: SWISS-MODEL: homology modelling of protein structures and complexes. Nucleic Acids Res. **46**(W1), 296–303 (2018)
7. Pieper, U., et al.: MODBASE, a database of annotated comparative protein structure models and associated resources. Nucleic Acids Res. **42**, 336–346 (2014)
8. Bailey, T., Elkan, C.: Fitting a mixture model by expectation maximization to discover motifs in biopolymers. In: Proceedings of the Second International Conference on Intelligent Systems for Molecular Biology, pp. 28–36, AAAI Press, Menlo Park, California (1994)
9. Camacho, C., Coulouris, G., Avagyan, V.: BLAST+: architecture and applications. BMC Bioinform. **10**, 421 (2009)

10. Edgar, R.C.: MUSCLE: multiple sequence alignment with high accuracy and high throughput. Nucleic Acids Res. **32**(5), 1792–1797 (2004)
11. National Center for Biotechnology Information. http://www.ncbi.nlm.nih.gov. Last Accessed 4 Feb 2020
12. Letunic, I., Bork, P.: Interactive Tree Of Life(iTOL) v4: recent updates and new developments. Nucleic Acids **47**(W1), 256–259 (2019)
13. Cock, P., et al.: Biopython: freely available Python tools for computational molecular biology and bioinformatics. Bioinformatics **25**(11), 1422–1423 (2009)
14. Chen C., Huang H., Wu C.H. Protein Bioinformatics Databases and Resources. In: Wu, C., Arighi, C., Ross, K. (eds.) Protein Bioinformatics. Methods in Molecular Biology 2017, vol. 1558. Humana Press, New York, NY (2017)
15. Author, F., Author, S.: Title of a proceedings paper. In: CONFERENCE 2016, LNCS, vol. 9999, pp. 1–13. Springer, Heidelberg (2016). https://doi.org/10.10007/1234567890
16. Saitou, N., Nei, M.: The neighbor-joining method: a new method for reconstructing phylogenetic trees. Molecular Biol. Evol. **4**(4), 406–425 (1987)
17. Felsenstein, J.: PHYLIP - Phylogeny inference package (Version 3.2). Quarterly Rev. Biol. **64**(4), 164–166 (1989)

Online Tutoring Through a Cloud-Based Virtual Tutoring Center

Xiaolin Hu$^{(\boxtimes)}$, Sai D. Tabdil, Manisha Achhe, Yi Pan, and Anu G. Bourgeois

Georgia State University, Atlanta, GA 30303, USA
xhu@gsu.edu

Abstract. Online tutoring has gained popularity in recent years, which allows students to get tutoring service from tutors in an online, virtual environment. To support effective online tutoring, an integrated online tutoring system is essential. This paper presents a cloud-based virtual tutoring center that supports online tutoring for college students to complement the tutoring service of physical tutoring centers on a campus. We present the overall architecture of the virtual tutoring center system and show preliminary results of using the virtual tutoring center to provide online tutoring for computer science students.

Keywords: Online tutoring · Virtual tutoring center · Cloud computing

1 Introduction

Advances of cloud computing have had major impacts on education, and will continue to influence how educational services are delivered. Examples of cloud computing-enabled educational services are abundant. Cloud computing is one of the key technologies that support Massive Open Online Courses (MOOCs) [1], which represent a new way of delivering classes to students. Cloud computing also makes it possible to set up *virtual computer labs* (see, e.g., [2, 3]), where students carry out labs on virtualized resources remotely through the Internet. These examples motivate developers to explore new ways of using cloud computing to support educational services.

Online tutoring refers to the process for students to get help from tutors in an online, virtual environment. It has grown in importance in recent years and many online tutoring websites have been launched to connect students with tutors through the Internet. As more and more students take online courses and engage in various forms of online learning, it is essential to incorporate technologies and resources to adapt and meet the needs of these students. Online tutoring allows students who cannot make it to campus to receive assistance, without being constrained by the boundaries of the campus. This advantage makes it a great candidate to support the growing trend of online learning. Previous works have studied several issues related to online tutoring, including best practices for online tutoring [4], and effectiveness of online tutoring for college Math courses [5]. The work of [6] studied the role of the tutor in online learning and suggests that online tutors need to have both technical competence and online interaction skills.

© Springer Nature Switzerland AG 2020
Q. Zhang et al. (Eds.): CLOUD 2020, LNCS 12403, pp. 270–277, 2020.
https://doi.org/10.1007/978-3-030-59635-4_20

To support effective online tutoring, an integrated online tutoring system is important. There are strong interests in the industry to support online tutoring in recent years. Websites such as Skooli, Udemy, Tutorroom.net, and Wyzant provide platforms to allow tutors and students to pair with each other and interact. These platforms focus on open and dynamic online tutoring spaces as they target all users on the Internet. Tools such as Skype and Google Hangouts are also commonly used for online tutoring [7]. Nevertheless, none of these platforms and tools are designed to support online tutoring in a college environment that mimics the physical tutoring centers in college campuses. In this paper, we present a cloud-based virtual tutoring center that supports online tutoring in a college setting and show preliminary results. The virtual tutoring center is installed in a private cloud environment maintained by the Computer Science department at Georgia State University.

2   A Virtual Tutoring Center (VTC) System

An effective VTC system needs to support several essential functions of online tutoring, including managing online tutoring sessions and users and recording data, and providing an engaging platform to support tutor-student interactions. To support tutor-student interaction, we leverage an open source video conferencing system *BigBlueButton* (https:// bigbluebutton.org/) and integrate it as part of our VTC system. BigBlueButton offers many of the features that are important for real time tutor-student interaction, including audio and video call, presentation with extended whiteboard capabilities, public and private chat, shared notes, and desktop sharing. In a previous work [8], we developed a collaborative virtual computer lab tool that integrates an early version of BigBlue-Button implemented in Flash. The Flash-based BigBlueButton needs web browsers to have Flash support in order to use the system. This often requires students to install Flash on their computers and thus deters students from using the system. To make the VTC system easily accessible for an open group of students, we develop the VTC system using the newer version of BigBlueButton implemented in HTML5. Since HTML5 is supported by all modern web browsers, students can access the system without the need of installing any extra software. The HTML5-based BigBlueButton also brings the advantage of working with mobile devices, and thus makes the VTC accessible through mobile devices.

Figure 1 shows the software architecture of the VTC system, which includes four subsystems: 1) Users, 2) VTC Management subsystem, 3) BigBlueButton (denoted as BBB) HTML5 clients, and 4) BigBlueButton server. Below we describe each of these subsystems.

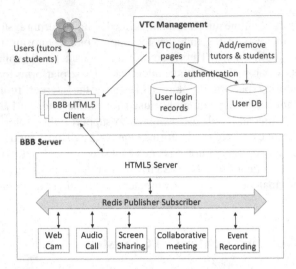

Fig. 1. Architecture of the virtual tutoring center system

2.1 Users

Users are participants of the virtual tutoring center. There are two types of users: students and tutors. Students ask questions and tutors help students. Due to the different roles of tutors and students, they access the VTC in different ways and have different functions available to them. Students enter a tutoring session in the role of *viewer*. As viewers, they can join the video conference, share their webcam, raise their hand, and chat with others. Tutors enter the tutoring session in the role of *moderator*. As moderators, they may mute/unmute others, eject any user from the session, and make any user the current presenter. The presenter can upload slides, control the presentation, and share their desktop. In the current implementation, an online tutoring session can have one tutor and multiple students. Future implementations will support multiple tutors and students, so that students can choose specific tutors for help, and each tutor will interact with their students in a separate breakout room.

2.2 VTC Management

The VTC Management subsystem is in charge of managing the tutoring sessions as well as managing the users and data. This includes providing an interface to start/stop a tutoring session, providing login webpages for users, adding/removing users, and storing data related to the tutoring sessions. Typically, a tutor needs to start a tutoring session so students can join, and end the session after finishing the tutoring. Our implementation also allows a tutoring session to be started in the beginning of a semester and remain open until the end of the semester. With this implementation, students can log in at any time, while tutors are available only in the publically announced tutoring hours. A major function of the VTC management subsystem is to provide a web portal for students to log in to the system to use the online tutoring service. As an example, Fig. 2 shows the web portal for the CS virtual tutoring center that we implemented in Spring 2020. As can be seen, students need to provide their campus IDs to log in to the system. They also need to select the course for their tutoring questions. A different web portal is provided for tutors to log in that allows the VTC to differentiate tutors from students and assign them different roles.

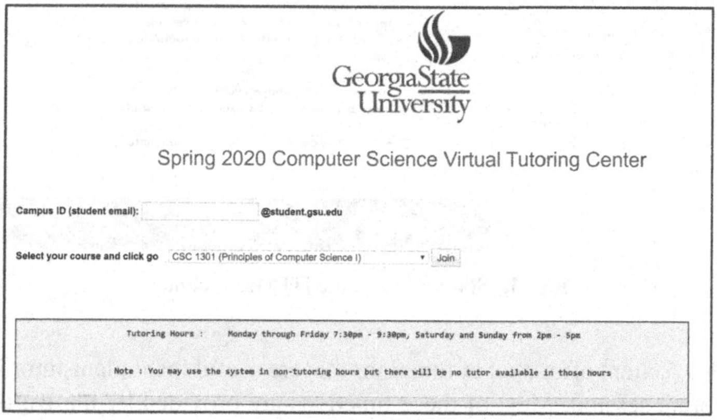

Fig. 2. Web portal for students to use the VTC

The VTC management subsystem is also responsible for user management and data storing. User management handles adding/removing users (tutors and students), as well as supporting the authentication procedure. An administrator (e.g., a faculty) can add/remove tutors and students, whose information is stored in a user database. This user database is checked by the authentication procedure when users try to log in to the system. Data storing deals with storing all the login records in a central database. Each record includes user ID, login date and time, and the course name selected by the student during login. This information is useful for analyzing the usage of the VTC.

2.3 BigBlueButton HTML5 Client

The BigBlueButton HTML5 client is a single-page web application that allows users to interact in a virtual touring session. The HTML5 client is launched after a user clicks the *Join* button on the login page (see Fig. 2) and passes the authentication. It connects with the BigBlueButton server to provide the video conferencing service needed for the tutoring session. Both tutors and students use the HTML5 client to enter the conference. Tutors are identified by displaying the tutor role behind their names. Figure 3 shows a screenshot of the HTML5 client after logging in to the system. The client window is roughly divided into three regions. The left region lists all the users (there is one tutor and one student in the Fig. 3 example). It also displays the *public chat* and *shared notes* icons. The middle region shows the public chat messages or shared notes depending on which icon is clicked by a user. The right region is the presentation/whiteboard window. It also allows a user to enable/disable audio and video, and for the user who is the presenter to share his/her desktop if needed.

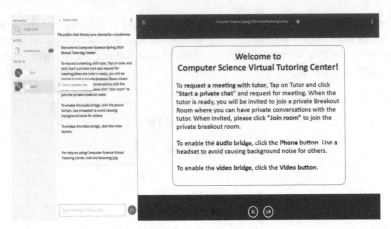

Fig. 3. Screenshot of the HTML5 client

The HTML5 client offer a set of functions that are useful for student-tutor interaction during a tutoring session. Most of these functions are provided by the BigBlueButton system, including: 1) video and audio conference; 2) public and private chat; 3) shared notes among multiple users; 4) uploading and presenting slides; 5) whiteboard capabilities such as drawing, adding notation, and zooming; 6) desktop sharing; 7) setting up and joining breakout rooms; and 8) conference recording. Furthermore, to facilitate student-tutor interaction in a multi-student environment, we developed a waiting list feature. A student can see how many other students are waiting to talk to the tutor, add himself/herself to the waiting list, and withdraw from the waiting list if needed.

2.4 BigBlueButton Server

The BigBlueButton Server is the back-end software that enables all the video conferencing functions described above. The server runs on Ubuntu 16.04 64-bit and can be installed either from source code or from Ubuntu packages. In our implementation, we install the BigBlueButton server on an Ubuntu instance in a private cloud environment maintained by the department. This configuration allows us to store all the data within the private cloud while allowing students to access the system from the Internet.

An important component of the BigBlueButton Server is the HTML5 server (see Fig. 1), which is responsible for communicating with the HTML5 clients, and for keeping the state of each client consistent with the server. The HTML5 server maintains a database containing information about all meetings on the server as well as each client connected to the meetings. All clients subscribe to the published collections on the server, and updates on the server side are automatically pushed to clients. Within the BigBlueButton Server, Redis Publisher-Subscriber is used to provides a communication channel between different modules/applications running on the server. These functional modules include Web Cam, Audio Call, Screen Sharing, Collaborative Meeting, and Event Recording as illustrated in Fig. 1. Note that the BigBlueButton server can support users connecting from either a Flash or HTML5 client. But in this work we are only interested in the HTML5 clients.

3   Setting up the CS Virtual Tutoring Center

The Georgia State University Computer Science (CS) department offers free tutoring to core 1000-, 2000-, and 3000-level courses in each semester through a *physical* tutoring center on campus. Students need to go to the tutoring rooms in order to get the tutoring service. In Fall 2019, the tutoring hours of the physical tutoring center were Monday - Thursday from 10 am–5 pm, Friday 10 am–3 pm. In each time slot of the tutoring hours, two or three tutors (recruited senior or junior undergraduate students) were assigned to help answer students' questions. To supplement the physical tutoring service, we launched the CS virtual tutoring center in the middle of the Fall 2019 semester, which offers free tutoring service to students similar as what the physical tutoring center does. Students access the tutoring service through URL http://cstutoring. cs.gsu.edu/ (see Fig. 2). The tutoring hours were Monday - Friday, 7:30 pm–9:30 pm, Sunday 3 pm–5 pm. Two students were recruited to work as tutors for the virtual tutoring center. They were assigned different tutoring days so that each day had only one tutor. Since the virtual tutoring center was launched in the middle of the semester, a publicity message was sent to all students through the CS undergraduate listserv. Another message was sent to faculty to encourage them to mention the service in their classes.

4   Results and Analysis

We collected the student login data for the virtual tutoring center from October 14, 2019 (when the VTC was launched) to December 15, 2019 (when the Fall semester ended). Figure 4 shows the weekly user data in the 9 weeks of the period, where the top figure shows the number of users in all the hours of a week and the bottom figure shows the number of users only in the tutoring hours. The week 11/25-12/01 is the Thanksgiving holiday week and there was no tutoring service provided in that week.

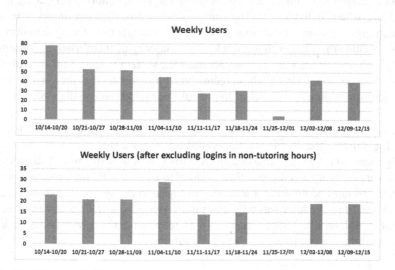

Fig. 4. Weekly Users: (**top**) all logins; (**bottom**) after excluding logins in non-tutoring hours

Comparing Fig. 4 (top) and Fig. 4 (bottom) we can see that in each week there were a considerable number of students logged in to the system during non-tutoring hours. This was especially true for the first week when the system was launched, when many students tried the system in non-tutoring hours. To show the usage of the tutoring service, we exclude all the logins in the non-tutoring hours and will analyze only the tutoring-hour data in the rest of this paper. Figure 4 (bottom) shows that on average there were about 20 students using the tutoring service in each week. Each week has 6 tutoring sessions (see Sect. 3). This means each session had about 3 student visitors. This number is consistent with what the tutors reported to us.

Figure 5 shows the number of users broken down based on different days of the week. We can see that Monday had the most users and other days (including Sunday) had about the same number of users. Note that the Monday-Friday tutoring hours are in the night, which is different from the tutoring hours of the physical tutoring center. This data shows that the night and weekend virtual tutoring service is used by students and complements the physical tutoring service.

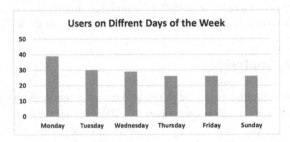

Fig. 5. Users on different days of the week

Figure 6 shows the number of times of using the virtual tutoring service by individual students, where individual students are represented by IDs not linked to their real identifications. The figure shows that a total of 77 students used the system during the 8 weeks (exclude the Thanksgiving week). The majority of them used the system only once. Nevertheless, there were 17 students used the system at least 3 times, with two of them using the system 9 times. These recurrent users indicate that the system is useful for a group of students as otherwise they would not return to use the system multiple times.

The two tutors also reported other useful information that are not reflected in the student login data. First, it was often observed that several students would log in to the VTC together and asked the same questions. This is probably due to that fact that those students were studying together and then decided to join the VTC for the same questions. Second, it was not uncommon for a student to log in to the system and then leave right away as he/she saw the tutor was busy helping other students. This behavior is different from that in a physical tutoring center. How to make students stay or come back in an online environment is an interesting topic for future work.

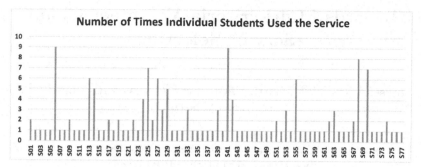

Fig. 6. Number of times individual students used the service

5   Conclusion

This paper presents a cloud-based virtual tutoring center that supports online tutoring in a college environment. We present the overall architecture of the system and describe how we set up a virtual tutoring center for students in Fall 2019. Preliminary results show that the virtual tutoring center is useful to students and complements the physical tutoring center on campus. Future work includes adding more functions to the system and using the system for more comprehensive evaluation.

Acknowledgement. The work is partially supported by the National Science Foundation under award: DUE-1712384.

References

1. Kaplan, A.M., Haenlein, M.: Higher education and the digital revolution: about MOOCs, SPOCs, social media, and the Cookie Monster. Bus. Horiz. **59**(4), 441–450 (2016)
2. Averitt, S., et al.: The virtual computing laboratory. In: Proceedings of the International Conference on Virtual Computing Initiative, pp. 1–16. IBM Corporation, Research Triangle Park, NC (2007)
3. Xu, L., Huang, D., Tsai, W.T.: V-Lab: a cloud-based virtual laboratory platform for hands-on networking courses. In: Proceedings of the 17th Annual Conference on ACM ITiCSE, pp. 256–261 (2012)
4. Turrentine, P., MacDonald, L.: Tutoring online: increasing effectiveness with best practices. NADE Digest **2**(2), 9–18 (2006)
5. Farrar, C.H., Rooney, J., Markham, B.: Online Tutoring Data as a Guide to Student Pathways, White Paper. https://www.achievingthedream.org/resource/17370/online-tutoring-data-as-a-guide-to-student-pathways-tutorcom. Accessed 01 Mar 2020
6. O'Hare, S.: The role of the tutor in online learning. In: Williams, G., Statham, P., Brown, N., Cleland, B. (eds.) Changing Demands, Changing Directions. Proceedings ASCILITE Hobart 2011, pp. 909–918 (2011)
7. Online tutoring in 2016: a research study, White Paper. https://blog.withcoach.com/online-tutoring-in-2016-a-research-study-51d60cdd711f. Accessed 01 Mar 2020
8. Hu, X., Le, H., Bourgeois, A., Pan, Y.: Collaborative learning in cloud-based virtual computer labs. In: Proceedings of the Frontiers in Education 2018, FIE 2018 (2018)

Towards Multi-criteria Volunteer Cloud Service Selection

Yousef Alsenani[1](✉), Garth V. Crosby[2](✉), Khaled R. Ahmed[1](✉),
and Tomas Velasco[3](✉)

[1] School of Computing,
Southern Illinois University at Carbondale, Carbondale, USA
{yalsenani,khaled.ahmed}@siu.edu
[2] Texas A&M University, College Station, USA
gvcrosby@tamu.edu
[3] School of Applied Engineering and Technology,
Southern Illinois University at Carbondale, Carbondale, USA
velasco@siu.edu

Abstract. Volunteer cloud computing (VCC) have recently been introduced to provide low-cost computational resources to support the demands of the next generation IoT applications. The vital process of VCC is to provide on demand resource provisioning and allocation in response to resource failures, behavior of volunteers (donors, users) and dynamically changing workloads. Most existing work addresses each of these factors (reliability, trust, and load) independently. Finding the most reliable machine (e.g., the lowest hardware failure rate) does not guarantee that the machine is trustworthy or not loaded, and vice versa. To address these problems, this research proposed a model to select volunteer node (VN) based on three criteria: the trustworthiness of the volunteer, the reliability of the node, and the resource load. We use three different models to estimate the three factors. We used exponential distribution reliability to estimate the reliability of VN and neural network to predict VN resource usages. In addition, we propose a new version of the beta function to estimate trustworthiness. Then we apply multiple regression to weigh each factor and decide which factor will be most effective for preventing task failure. Finally, a VN is selected based on multiple criteria decision analysis.

1 Introduction

Volunteer cloud computing (VCC) [1,16] utilizes spare personal computer resources (referred to as volunteer nodes) owned by individuals and organizations rather than relying on dedicated data centers. Although VCC shares similar technology with traditional cloud computing in using a virtualization layer and with desktop grid computing in utilizing spare resources, VCC has unique technical challenges. Reliability and trustworthiness are two challenging technical issues for any unreliable system. Crashes dropped connections, and the behavior of volunteer nodes (VNs) can result in task failure on VCC systems,

Q. Zhang et al. (Eds.): CLOUD 2020, LNCS 12403, pp. 278–286, 2020.
https://doi.org/10.1007/978-3-030-59635-4_21

while a heavily loaded system (heavily loaded machines) can affect task performance. To address these problems, we need to evaluate these three factors (reliability, trust, and load). There exists extensive research that addresses each of the three factors independently [2,9,11,12]. In this paper we propose a framework, which includes different stages to find the best suitable node, using three different models to estimate the three factors. We estimate the reliability of a VN via exponential distribution reliability, and in some cases, the parameters for the exponential distribution can be estimated using probability plotting. Then we predict resource (CPU and memory) usage with an artificial neural network (ANN). Next, we expand the concept of trustworthiness in VCCs and develop two new metrics: (a) trustworthiness based on the priority of the task, called *loyalty*, and (b) trustworthiness affected by behavioral change. To estimate the trustworthiness, we exploit a new version of the beta function. Finally, we use multiple criteria decision analysis to select a VN.

2 Motivation

Regardless of whether VCC systems offer an economical alternative to the cloud computing environment, the present dedicated cloud systems may not be appropriate for some IoT application scenarios, such as (a) dispersed data-intensive services (big data) and (b) scenarios in which research groups would like to execute distributed tasks. In these cases, a VCC model is an appropriate and affordable solution [1]. Although volunteer clouds share many similarities with traditional clouds and desktop grid computing models, they have several essentially different issues, such as resource availability and volatility, volunteer hosts, and diverse workloads. VCC resource management needs to proactively consider methods for effective and efficient management of resources. Simply finding the most reliable VN (e.g., with the lowest hardware failure rate) does not guarantee that the node is trustworthy or not heavily loaded. For example, a malicious donor might have reliable hardware, a trusted donor might have incapable VN with a high failure rate, and a reliable and trusted VN can become heavily loaded when a task is added to it.

3 Related Work

There is intensive research in each domain of trust, reliability, and resource load in distributed systems. However, each of these factors was investigated independently. To the best of our knowledge, the idea of combining this three-factor to evaluate node selection is new. In trust research work, in [2] evaluate the trust in unreliable and federated cloud respectively, while in [14] the authors exploit Beta distribution to evaluate the resource in volunteer cloud environment. In Reliability work in [9] proposed a Proactive fault-tolerance technique for cloud federation environment. In [10] The author evaluates the node selection by the combination of two metrics the reliability of resources and the capacity. There is some research that combines reliability and resource load factors to enhance system performance [12]. In volunteer cloud computing there are a few numbers of research that evaluate task scheduling [4,5,7]. The authors in [1] propose a system to run big data applications over the volunteer cloud. However, the work doesn't considers the node's failure neither the security issues in the placement technique. To this end, we propose a framework that is suitable and tackles the three factors that impact the solution quality from the perspective of a variety of requirements; such as meeting SLAs and QoSs.

4   Framework

The management server in VCC is responsible to distribute cloud user service request (task) or set of tasks to a single volunteer node r_j or a set of volunteer nodes where $j \in [1, 2, \ldots, p]$, and p is number of volunteer node. In our framework, volunteer node process is based on three criteria: the trustworthiness of the volunteer, the reliability of the node, and the resource load. While we can model each of these criteria independently, it is important to know which of the criteria will have a significant impact on system performance. Therefore, we exploit multiple regression to measure the weight of each factor, and a VN is then selected using multiple criteria decision analysis. In the following subsections, we discuss how we model and weigh each of these criteria and then present the VN selection method.

4.1   Modeling Trust

Assume that server S has assigned task to volunteer node r. Then the task outcome for r that S can observe is summarized by a binary variable, x, where $x = 1$ if task succeeded and $x = 0$ if task failed. At any time t, the history of observed task outcomes for r is recorded in the 2-tuple $\Re^t = (\gamma_p(x)^t, \gamma_n(x)^t)$, where x is the set of observed task outcomes, the value of the function $\gamma_p(x)^t$ is the number of successful tasks, and the value of $\gamma_n(x)^t$ is the number of unsuccessful tasks. The obligation of a volunteer node r to successfully complete tasks is controlled by its behavior [3]. The behavior of r, denoted as B_r, is modeled as the probability that $x = 1$, in other words, the probability that r will successfully complete the task, and it is defined as $B_r = p[x = 1]$, with $B_r \in [0, 1]$. After many interactions, we can monitor the behavior of node r by calculating B_r. In statistics, we cannot assume that we have all information and complete knowledge. However, we can exploit the expectation value. Thus, we define trustworthiness τ_r at time t as the expected value of B_r given the number of task outcomes as $\tau_r = E[B_r | x^{1:t}]$, where $x^{1:t}$ is the set of task outcomes from time 1 to the assessment time t. The expected value of a continuous random variable depends on the probability density function that is utilized to shape the probability that the variable will have a certain value. To this end, the framework estimates the trustworthiness of a VN by using the beta distribution. The Beta system uses the standard *beta* distribution, which works well with prior expectations. In our case, when a new volunteer node joins the system, not much information has been disclosed. The *beta* distribution is a two-parameter distribution that is commonly used in trust models. Several platforms and domains such as peer-to-peer (P2P) networks, wireless sensor networks (WSNs), and grid and cloud computing also exploit a *beta* distribution. This distribution is adaptable, with a robust foundation in probability theory. While alternative methods, for instance, Machine Learning, may deliver more accurate results; there are a number of known issues, such as cold start problems and elongated prediction times due to the small samples which are obtained from newer nodes.

Beta Distribution. The beta distribution gives the pdf $prob(x|\alpha,\beta)$ for a value x on the interval (0,1); it can be expressed using the gamma function, Γ, as follows:

$$Beta(\alpha,\beta): \; prob(x|\alpha,\beta) = \frac{\Gamma(\alpha)\,\Gamma(\beta)}{\Gamma(\alpha+\beta)}x^{\alpha-1}(1-x)^{\beta-1}, \tag{1}$$

where $0 \leqslant x \leqslant 1, \alpha > 0$, and $\beta > 0$, with the restriction that the probability variable $x \neq 0$ if $\alpha < 1$. The expected value for the beta distribution is defined as $E(x) = \frac{\alpha}{\alpha+\beta}$.

We model trustworthiness based on the direct interactions between the server and a VN. This is unlike P2P networks, which rely on direct interactions between nodes for the reputations of nodes evaluated by the network. In the next subsections, we introduce the concept of *loyalty* and behavior change.

Trustworthiness by Priority of Task. In this subsection, we address

Limitation 1. *Trustworthiness is evaluated irrespective of the priority of tasks.*

Existing trust models [3,7] assign higher trust scores to VN that complete more lower priority-sensitive tasks (more batch tasks) in shorter periods of time. Additionally, lower trust scores are assigned to VNs that complete more high-priority or performance-sensitive tasks if these require more time to complete. Moreover, these trust models assign identical probabilities of success to VNs solely based on the resources' trust scores. However, untrusted resources with highly sensitive tasks should have reduced probabilities of success. Moreover, VNs with the same rate of success receive identical trust scores, regardless of the individual characteristics of the successfully completed tasks, and failure across a range of sensitive and high-priority tasks would dominate the effectiveness of trust scores for distinguishing between untrusted and trusted nodes.

Loyalty is therefore a mechanism that clusters direct task outcomes into different levels. In what follows, we show how to rank the feedback from VNs with respect to the different priorities. First, we calculate the number of successful high-priority tasks outcomes, t_{high}^{succ}, as follows:

$$t_{high}^{succ} = \sum_{i=1}^{N} x_i * \omega_h, \tag{2}$$

where x_i in this case, are the successful high priority tasks outcomes and N is the total number of successful high-priority tasks and ω_h is a constant weight. We follow the same technique for medium–priority tasks as $t_{med}^{succ} = \sum_{i=1}^{N} x_i * \omega_m$, and low-priority tasks as $t_{low}^{succ} = \sum_{i=1}^{N} x_i * \omega_l$. Where ω_m and ω_l are the constant weights for medium- and low-priority tasks outcomes. Then we can compute the function $\gamma_p(x)$ for these successful computations as follows:

$$\gamma_p(x) = t_{high}^{succ} + t_{med}^{succ} + t_{low}^{succ}. \tag{3}$$

We follow the same procedure to compute $\gamma_n(x)$, which represents the negative feedback for unsuccessful tasks as $\gamma_n(x) = t_{high}^{unsucc} + t_{med}^{unsucc} + t_{low}^{unsucc}$

Updating the Shape Parameter. The logic of the loyalty that we have implemented in this technique is adaptive to heterogeneity and different priorities of tasks. Therefore, we use the beta function parameters α and β to represent the numbers of successful and unsuccessful outcomes, which depend on the levels of loyalty $\gamma_p(x)$ and $\gamma_n(x)$ for volunteer node r_j , as follows:

$$\alpha_j = \gamma_{pj}(x)^{1:t} + \frac{1}{p-1} \sum_{i=1,i\neq j}^{p} \alpha_i \tag{4}$$

$$\beta_j = \gamma_{nj}(x)^{1:t} + \frac{1}{p-1} \sum_{i=1,i\neq j}^{p} \beta_i \tag{5}$$

where $\gamma_{pj}(x)^{1:t}, \gamma_{nj}(x)^{1:t}$ is the successful and unsuccessful tasks from time 1 to the assessment time t for volunteer node r_j. The second part of the above equation calculate the average value of both parameters α_i, β_i from all other volunteer node and sets this value as the prior knowledge, where p is number of VN. This is different from work in the literature that initializes α and β with 1 because there is no prior knowledge. We believe that it is fair to have a new VN that has just joined the system begin with the average trust score that all resources have thus far obtained. Finally, we estimate the trustworthiness of node r with the expected value of a random variable according to the beta distribution $Beta(\alpha, \beta)$:

$$\tau_{r_j} = E[B_{r_j}|\alpha_j, \beta_j] = \frac{\alpha_j}{\alpha_j + \beta_j}. \tag{6}$$

Trustworthiness Affected by Behavioral Change. In this subsection, we address

Limitation 2. *The updates of trustworthiness do not consider VNs' behavioral changes.*

The framework considers the influence of past task outcomes and behavioral changes over time in the dynamic and constrained infrastructure. Behavior detection is beneficial for two reasons. First, some volunteer node aims to improve their trust scores (e.g., those who had a bad start), and second, some nodes may have recently begun to act maliciously. Behavior detection aims to minimize task failures by not assigning tasks to nodes whose behavior has recently changed for the worse. Therefore, we propose behavior detection that utilizes a method for detecting change points. To detect a change in behavior, we use the pruned exact linear time (PELT) method to search for changepoints [15]. The most common approach for finding multiple change points is

$$\min_{\kappa, z} \left\{ \sum_{i=1}^{\kappa+1} \left[-\ell(x_{z_{i-1}:z_i}) \right] + \lambda f(k) \right\},$$ (7)

where κ is the number of change points at positions $z_{1:\kappa} = (z_1, \ldots, z_\kappa)$. The formula can be cast in terms of minimizing a function of k and z of the following form as $CPT = \sum_{i=1}^{k+1} \left[\mathcal{C}(y_{(z_{i-1}+1):z_i}) \right] + \lambda f(k)$,

where $\lambda f(k)$ is a penalty to protect against overfitting, such as a threshold cost or a multiple change-point version, and $\mathcal{C}$ is a function of the cost for a segment. After finding the most optimal change point (assume this change point is z), our trust value considers the history of observations after this change point.

4.2 Modeling Reliability

VCC runs over non-dedicated VNs. The high failure rate for VNs has a major impact on the system performance [12]. Therefore, it is necessary to estimate the reliability of these nodes. There are different continuous probability distributions that could model the reliability of each of these nodes, and taking into account the electronic nature of their components. Where all node failure events are independent and may happen randomly, we exploit the commonly used probability distribution named Exponential Distribution [13]. The reliability function equation for the Exponential distribution is presented as in the following Eq. (8):

$$R(t) = e^{-\lambda \cdot t},$$ (8)

In order to estimate the parameter λ in the equation above, the procedure is to convert the reliability function equation into a line equation and use regression analysis procedures to estimate λ. In order to make this conversion, first, the natural logarithm is applied on both sides of this equation yielding as $ln[R(t)] = -\lambda \cdot t$

Next, let $y = ln[R(t)]$, $a = 0$, and $b = \lambda \cdot t$, which results in the following linear equation as, $y = a + bt$.

4.3 Modeling the Resource Load

The performance of tasks is detrimentally impacted when a VN is heavily loaded and might cause task failure. Therefore, the framework considers the resource load to be an important factor that has a significant impact on the system. We use an ANN to predict the resource load; ANNs are a powerful model that extracts the complex relationship between input and output factors, which helps to predict the output after the training phase. We aim to predict the CPU and memory load, where the input is the sliding window means of the CPU and memory load ratios, denoted as $cload(t - i)$ and $mload(t - i)$, where i is the number of sliding windows, and the capacity of the CPU and memory are denoted as cc and mc. The hidden layer and output layer use log-sigmoid and pure linear functions, respectively, and a two-layer, feed-forward ANN is employed for prediction.

4.4 Modeling the Weights

After estimating the three factors (reliability, load, and trustworthiness), we need to determine which of these has more significance for task failure. Thus, we use multiple regression to find the weight or significance of these factors, which are the independent variables for the multiple regression $y = b_0 + b_1 X_1 * b_2 X_2 ... b_i X_n$, where y, b, X, and n represent the dependent variable, the coefficient, the independent variables, and the number of independent variables, respectively. To do this, we first need to find the actual failure rate for the task at time interval t as the dependent variable, and the estimated reliability $R(t)$, trustworthiness $\tau(t)$, and load $l(t)$ values as the independent variables, as follows:

$$fail_{rate} = b_0 + b_1 R(t) + b_2 \tau(t) + b_3 l(t) \tag{9}$$

The multiple regression will then return the weight for each factor, which we can use for the final step as described in the next section.

4.5 Multiple Criteria Decision Analysis

In this section, we discuss how to combine the three factors. In multiple criteria decision analysis, we have criteria $g_1, g_2, ..., g_i$, alternatives, and the assigned weight for each criteria discussed in Sect. 4.4. In our context, the factors reliability, load, and trustworthiness are the criteria, and the available VNs are the alternatives. The goal is to select the best alternatives by evaluating these alternatives over the criteria. To this end, we use the PROMETHEE model [8], which is based on pairwise comparisons of the alternatives. The preference of one alternative over another is modeled as a function of the difference $(g_i, P_i(a, b))$, named generalized criterion where a and b are the two alternatives. The model uses a generalized criterion and determines the aggregated preference indices. This provides insights into the extent to which one option is preferable to an alternative option. Using these indices the model ranks alternatives in the form of the net outranking flow and computes how each VN stacks up against the alternatives. The option that has the highest outranking flow represents the best option. Having completed the ranking process, the model finds the VN that has achieved the highest net outranking flow.

4.6   Preliminary Results

We plan to implement the proposed framework on a large scale infrastructure computing system such as GENI.[1], and compare the framework with existing systems [1,4]. However, we are on a theoretical stage, thus in this paper we only test the resource load factor on the Google cluster usage trace [6], before we move to the real system. The trace consists of 29 days, we divided the data into two-part. The first part, the modeling (from day 1 to 27), is used to train the resource usage for a volunteer host. The second part is to validate the resource usage (day 27 to day 29). As a final figure, we utilized the first 27-day period, which covers approximately 640 h of the Google trace data. Then, to validate the accuracy of the framework, we calculated the average resource usage that were observed in the next 5 h, i.e., hours 641–645 (next five hours–short prediction), and we calculated the average resource usage on day 28 (next day prediction) and on days 28 and 29 (next 2 days–long prediction). The mean squared error value (MSE) for 100 machines for all predictions cases: (a) short ·prediction is 0.008, (b) next day prediction is 0.009, and (c) the long prediction is 0.008, which is very low and shows the ANN is an appropriate model. We are working on evaluating the other factors, but we do not have the complete result to discuss on the paper.

5   Conclusion and Future Work

VCC runs over nondedicated infrastructures. Reliability and trust are the most important technical challenges that can result in task failure in these kinds of environments. The load or workload can also impact task performance. In this paper, our framework, which is comprised of different phases to select suitable VNs. The PROMETHEE model is suitable to find the most suitable VN while considering load, trust, and reliability. Overall, despite the significant work remaining to be done, we believe that our framework is sufficiently trusted and reliable to facilitate most of the main challenge required to host IoT a general application on volunteer cloud. As future work, we plan to implement the proposed framework on a large scale infrastructure computing system and evaluate the framework to test its feasibility to host IoT and general applications.

References

1. Rezgui, A., et al.: CloudFinder: a system for processing big data workloads on volunteered federated clouds. IEEE Trans. Big Data **6**, 347–358 (2017)
2. Mashayekhy, L., et al.: A trust-aware mechanism for cloud federation formation. IEEE Trans. Cloud Comput. (2019)
3. Teacy, W.L., Patel, J., Jennings, N.R., Luck, M.: TRAVOS: trust and reputation in the context of inaccurate information sources. Auton. Agents Multi-Agent Syst. **12**(2), 183–198 (2006). https://doi.org/10.1007/s10458-006-5952-x

---

[1] https://www.geni.net.

4. Sebastio, S., et al.: A holistic approach for collaborative workload execution in volunteer clouds. ACM Trans. Model. Comput. Simul. (TOMACS) **28**(2), 1–27 (2018)
5. Sebastio, S., et al.: Optimal distributed task scheduling in volunteer clouds. Comput. Oper. Res. **81**, 231–246 (2017)
6. Reiss, C., et al.: Google cluster-usage traces: format+ schema. Google Inc., White Paper, pp. 1–14 (2011)
7. McGilvary, G.A., et al.: Ad hoc cloud computing. In: 2015 IEEE 8th International Conference on Cloud Computing (CLOUD), pp. 1063–1068. IEEE (2015)
8. Mareschal, B.: Aide a la Decision Multicritere: Developpements Recents des Methodes PROMETHEE. Cahiers du Centre d'Etudes en Recherche Operationelle, pp. 175–241 (1987)
9. Ray, B., et al.: Proactive fault-tolerance technique to enhance reliability of cloud service in cloud federation environment. IEEE Trans. Cloud Comput. (2020)
10. Fu, S.: Failure-aware resource management for high-availability computing clusters with distributed virtual machines. J. Parallel Distrib. Comput. **70**(4), 384–393 (2010)
11. Chen, R., et al.: Trust management for SOA-based IoT and its application to service composition. IEEE Trans. Serv. Comput. **9**(3), 482–495 (2016)
12. Alsenani, Y., et al.: ReMot reputation and resource-based model to estimate the reliability of the host machines in volunteer cloud environment. In: 2018 IEEE 6th International Conference on Future Internet of Things and Cloud (FiCloud), pp. 63–70. IEEE (2018)
13. Wang, X., Yeo, C.S., Buyya, R., Su, J.: Optimizing the makespan and reliability for workflow applications with reputation and a look-ahead genetic algorithm. Future Gener. Comput. Syst. **27**(8), 1124–1134 (2011)
14. Alsenani, Y., et al.: SaRa: a stochastic model to estimate reliability of edge resources in volunteer cloud. In: Accepted to the IEEE International Conference on Edge Computing (EDGE). IEEE (2018)
15. Killick, R., et al.: Optimal detection of changepoints with a linear computational cost. J. Am. Stat. Assoc. **107**(500), 1590–1598 (2012)
16. Alsenani, Y.S., et al.: ProTrust: a probabilistic trust framework for volunteer cloud computing. IEEE Access **8**, 135059–135074 (2020)

ZTIMM: A Zero-Trust-Based Identity Management Model for Volunteer Cloud Computing

Abdullah Albuali[✉], Tessema Mengistu, and Dunren Che

School of computing, Southern Illinois University at Carbondale, 1230 Lincoln Drive,
Engineering A319, Mail Code 4511, Carbondale, IL 62901, USA
{abdullah.albuali,tessema.mengistu,dche}@siu.edu

Abstract. The availability of efficient, affordable, green computing alternatives for emerging paradigms, such as edge, mobile, and volunteer cloud computing, is growing. But these models are plagued by security issues, such as in volunteer cloud computing, where trust among entities is nonexistent. This paper presents a zero-trust model that assumes no trust for any volunteer node and always verifies using a server-client model. This paper proposes an adaptive behavior evaluation model that estimates each VN's trust score. Therefore, tasks are assigned to the most trusted VN in the system. A series of trust-aware mechanisms to handle VN's life cycle is also presented.

1 Introduction

With the emergence of computing paradigms such as edge/fog, volunteer cloud (e.g. cuCloud [1,2,7]), and mobile cloud computing, the rise of efficient, low-cost, green computing infrastructures is more promising. However, dealing with heterogeneous, unreliable, non-dedicated hosts is a major challenge. Around 2 billion devices are connected to the Internet, most of which are underused, leading to enormous wasted capacity (e.g. CPU cycles, storage spaces). Using that spare capacity for volunteer cloud computing has produced encouraging results [1]. Virtual machines (VMs), scheduling algorithms, and volunteer resource management on volunteer nodes (VNs), which are "donated" by participating volunteers, have enabled volunteer cloud computing systems to complement expensive data-center cloud infrastructures [2,3]. Volunteer computing resources can also be used in edge computing [4]. However, trust and security remain a roadblock and require further study.

Showing the importance of online security, cyberattacks are increasingly sophisticated, large-scale, and costly. For example, about 81% of data breaches are caused by weak or reused passwords, and 40% originate from authorized users accessing unauthorized systems. In cloud systems, unauthorized access is the second highest security threat (55% of such threats), the first being misconfiguration of cloud platforms. Such threats have far-reaching consequences for industry and individuals. According to a 2018 survey [5], around 80% of 400

Q. Zhang et al. (Eds.): CLOUD 2020, LNCS 12403, pp. 287–294, 2020.
https://doi.org/10.1007/978-3-030-59635-4_22

organizations migrated their data or applications from public to private clouds due to increased concerns about the security and privacy requirements of their organizations and cloud providers.

With the growing scope of these threats in mind, it is vital to make cloud computing safer and more secure. In fact, trust in a cloud service is strongly tied to security and reliability. A major concern in volunteer cloud computing, in general, comes from the anonymous and ad hoc nature of VNs in such a system. Beside, the high churn rate of VNs joining and leaving threatens the security and reliability of services. To accomplish these goals, one must take into account its components. In volunteer cloud computing, there are three modules with different trust concerns: volunteer cloud management system, VN, and volunteer cloud customer. A major challenge is how to ensure trust between these actors and their relationship to each other [9]. For example, researchers need to create a best-fit trust management and computing model that facilitates trust between the volunteer cloud management system and VNs. Likewise, they should examine the degree to which there is constant confidence between VNs and the VMs deployed to them. Due to the complexity of this area, this paper focused on trust evaluation between the volunteer cloud management system and participating VNs using direct trust.

The proposed model aims to replace traditional perimeter-based security (trust, but verify) with a new zero-trust mindset (trust no one, and *always* verify) to help meet the Service Level Agreement (SLA) and Quality of Service Assurance (QoS) for volunteer cloud computing [6]. This paper's contribution is two-fold:

1. It introduces a zero-trust identity management model (ZTIMM) to select and allow only the most trusted VNs to join a system and execute tasks. The model uses adaptive behavior evaluation contexts based on authentication scores, risk rates, and reliability and availability prediction values. To the best of the researchers' knowledge, this is the first published work to combine three factors to evaluate VN selection in volunteer cloud computing.
2. It develops a series of trust-aware mechanisms to handle each VN's life cycle from membership, execute user tasks on VNs, prevent the admission of untrusted VNs, and blocklist misbehaving and untrustworthy VNs. Any VN in the blocklist that does not exceed the limited consecutive number of entering penalty periods can rejoin the service after finishing its penalty period. We believe that this is the first work to propose a way to allow VNs to rejoin the service after finishing a penalty period.

The rest of the paper is organized as follows. Section 2 reviews the proposed trust model in detail. Section 3 concludes the study and offers avenues for future research.

2 Proposed Trust Model

This study proposes a zero-trust identity management model (ZTIMM) for the volunteer cloud paradigm to ensure only trusted VNs join the system and execute tasks. As shown in Fig. 1, the ZTIMM consists of a pool of VNs that would like to join the volunteer cloud management system as hosts. Those VNs are controlled by *Member Controller* (MC) agent which is a software that installed on each VN. Thus, it aims to securely monitor the resource usage at VN, encrypt all communications between server and VN, and assist monitoring mechanisms of the ZTIMM based on the historical demand of resources and behavior of VN [7]. Each VN will continue to be assessed, entire its life cycle, based on an authentication score, risk rate, and reliability and availability prediction value to detect any malicious or suspicious VNs. Based on these scores, a VN is granted access if deemed suitable, reverified if it is suspicious, or blocked if declared malicious. This model is further described below.

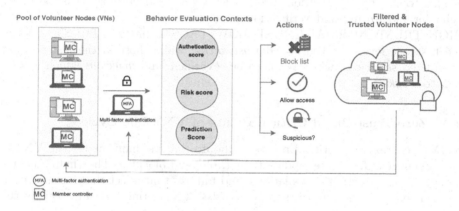

Fig. 1. ZTIMM model

2.1   Basic Concepts of VN Life Cycle

To efficiently monitor the VN life cycle in volunteer cloud computing, there is a need to understand the stages of a VN's life cycle and corresponding security concerns. A reward and penalty system is also needed, based on the trust levels of a VN.

VN Life Cycle. Each VN goes through a series of life-cycle stages in terms of joining a volunteer cloud computing. These consist of *non-exit*, *active*, *inactive*, and *deleted* as listed and explained in Table 1. To monitor these stages, the volunteer cloud management system needs an efficient monitoring mechanism. This mechanism ensures the volunteer cloud management system accepts and retains only authenticated, well-behaving, and reliable VNs.

Table 1. VN life cycle

Stage	Description
Non-exit	Volunteer cloud management system creates a new VN's identity
Active	Either executing task or in idle mode
Inactive	VN is either blocked or needs to be reverified
Deleted	Volunteer cloud management system drops VN from the system

VN Trust Level. Setting of trust levels to categorize VNs depends on user requirements. More levels afford more precision, but with a zero-trust model, we needed to classify VNs without overburdening a cloud network with too many behavior monitoring and verification procedures. Thus, we chose four levels: HIGH TRUST, NORMAL TRUST, LOW TRUST, and NO TRUST. VNs in the first two levels are considered *trustworthy*, while those in the last two are considered *suspicious*, which needs to be reverified, and *malicious* which will be sent to *blocklist*.

2.2   Zero-Trust-Based Critical Points of VN's Life Cycle

ZTIMM contains five critical points as monitoring mechanisms for the VN life cycle: join, rejoin, execute, update trust table, and blocklist. They help ZTIMM detect malicious activities, violations, and failures that affect the trust scores of less trusted VNs and reward the most trusted VNs during their life cycle in the system.

Join Volunteer Cloud Computing. When a VN tries to join the system, the *"non-exist"* stage, its identity must be validated the first time using a username and password. Since this is a zero-trust model, a list of strong authentication techniques is used as an additional step, such as multi-factor authentication (MFA), which might contain an authentication code [8]. Hence, the VN is authenticated by the trust manager, which is a component that calculates the trust score of each joined VN. The resource manager, which is responsible of managing VNs and their requests, has the VN send basic resource information (e.g. CPU, RAM) and the VN device's information (e.g. domain, IP, MAC address) to the trust manager through the membership controller (MC) agent that resides on each VN. The VN's resource information coupled with its trust score is then stored in an encrypted database with NORMAL TRUST as the default trust level for stage *active*. At this stage, the VN is now ready to host VMs.

Rejoin. A VN usually requests to rejoin because it left the system intentionally or a request was rejected by the server due to a failure in verifying the VN's identity and trustworthiness. After the VN's login information is checked, the trust manager needs to check the last final trust score of the VN in the trust table with its corresponding trust level and whether the VN's stage was set to *inactive*. Based on this data, it decides whether to accept that VN, ask for advanced authentication steps mentioned earlier, or send it to the blocklist if it exceeds the limit on verification attempts.

Execute Task. Once a VN is ranked based on its trust score, the scheduler and resource manager assign it tasks based on that score. When a task is completed, not completed, or rejected by the VN, the trust manager rewards or penalizes the VN. This mechanism of evaluation and its calculation is explained in the next section.

Update Trust Table. The trust manager checks the trust table to ensure it is updated and ready to be used. Since volunteer cloud computing is voluntary and has a high rate of churn, ZTIMM uses dual validation:

1. A *FrontLineTimeRate* is used to indicate how long the available information from the VNs (CPU, Memory, etc.) is valid without further updates [1]. If the last updated available information is less than or equal to 15 min, the system keeps that VN *active*. If not, the resource manager sends a request to the membership controller to have the VN update its available information and send the results back to the trust manager. If the VN does not respond to the resource manager, that VN will be in a *critical situation* and must be reverified by the trust manager, as explained below.
2. A *CriticalTimeRate* indicates how long the resource manager waits for a response before taking further actions. If the waiting response time passes *CriticalTimeRate*, in addition to setting the VN's node stage to *inactive* and downgrading its trust score, the trust manager will need to reverify the VN's legitimacy using a strong authentication technique. Eq.(1) explains the concept:

$$CID_{vi} = \begin{cases} 1 & \text{for response time} \leq \textit{Twait}, \\ 0 & \text{for response time} > \textit{Twait} \end{cases} \quad (1)$$

where, ID_{vi} is the identity parameter of the VN with two values: 1 to keep the VN in the system or 0 to reverify the VN's legitimacy. *Twait* is the duration of time the resource manager waits for a VN's response. Exceeded maximum number of login attempts

Blocklist. Any VN will be sent to blocklist if its trust level falls into *NO TRUST* and its life cycle stage is *inactive* due to different malicious acts are done by such VN that is previously calculated by ZTIMM. For example, such a VN exceeded the maximum number of login attempts within an allowed time slot. The blocklist includes a list of penalty levels, as shown in Table 2, and is categorized into flags, where the first violation is noted as the first flag, the second earns a second flag, and so on. Unlike related systems that do not allow blocked VNs to rejoin [9], ZTIMM imposes violation flags in the form of classification to reduce attacks against the network, and as a punishment for the violators while continuing to encourage them to return to the volunteer cloud system after the penalty duration is over. Notice that a VN could be allowed to reset its violation score to zero after it passes a certain period without any new flags. Besides, it could be permanently blocked if it exceeds the maximum number of flags within a limited time.

Table 2. VN Blocklist Levels

Violation	Penalty duration
1st flag	24 h
2nd flag	48 h
3th flag	72 h
4th flag	Permanent

2.3 Adaptive Behavior Evaluation Contexts

Behavior evaluation contexts help ZTIMM detect which VNs have NO TRUST, which have HIGH TRUST, and which fall somewhere between. A VN's trust score is calculated using authentication score, risk rate, and reliability and availability prediction value:

Authentication Score (A_{vi})

$$A_{vi} = X_p/X_t \tag{2}$$

Where, x_p is the number of passing multi-factor authentication challenges and X_t is the total number of joining requests, and $0 \leq A_{vi} \leq 1$

Examining Eq. (2), consider a VN that tries to join the system. Every time it gets an authentication code match, the value X_t, X_p is increased by 1 and it is granted access. If a VN fails to match an encrypted authentication code, X_p gets zero points while X_t increases by 1. In case VN exceeding its rate limit to logon, a VN is added to the blocklist.

Risk rate (S_{vi}) works as a second phase of monitoring VNs after they successfully logon. The risk rate of a VN is calculated using average of incomplete tasks, average of rejected tasks, and average of rejoin requests.

$$Svi = \left(\frac{\text{total incomplete tasks}}{\text{total assigned tasks}}\right)\omega_1 + \left(\frac{\text{total rejected tasks}}{\text{total assigned tasks}}\right)\omega_2 + \left(\frac{\text{rate of rejoin requests}}{periodoftime}\right)\omega_3 \tag{3}$$

Where $\omega_1, \omega_2,$ andω_3 are constant weights, and the period of time is set by the trust manager. In Eq. (3), consider a VN that has committed many suspicious acts within 24 h, such as passing 24 h in idle mode with no task assigned, or the number of rejoin requests to the system is unusually high. The more *Svi* events occur, the higher the VN's risk score likely is.

Reliability and Availability Score Using Prediction Technique R(t). In volunteer cloud environments, trust is strongly related to the reliability of the VNs that host the cloud services. In our previous work [2], we developed a Semi-Markov technique that predicts the reliability of a VN, called Reliability Profile, for a duration t in the future. A VN can be in 5 different states and its Reliability Profile is calculated if it is in States 1 and 2 using Eq. (4). We used the Reliability Profile as a factor in the trust score calculation, as shown in Eq. (5).

$$R(t) = \sum_{j=1}^{2} \Phi_{j1} + \lambda \sum_{i=1}^{2} \Phi_{i2} \tag{4}$$

Where λ **is penalty coefficient and** $0 \leq \lambda \leq 1$

Calculating Trust Score of Each VN. To calculate the most trusted VN, we used the three previously mentioned techniques to calculate the final score $S(t)$ by combining Eqs. (2), (3), and (4) as follows:

$$S(t) = (\frac{A_{vi} + R(t)}{Svi}) \tag{5}$$

Where S(t) is a suitable final score for a VN. Note that the higher the risk score, the less trusted a VN could be, and the higher the authentication score and availability prediction values, the more highly trusted a VN could be. In this work, every VN passes through ZTIMM to calculate its trust score at zero-trust-aware critical points (i.e., join, rejoin, execute, update, and blocklist) of the VN's life cycle by using the three behavior evaluation factors: authentication score, risk rate, and reliability and availability prediction value. These factors help ZTIMM determine *Trust Level* of each VN, store in the database, and use only trusted VNs, reverify suspicious ones, and blocklist malicious ones. As a result, this stored list of VNs will assist the decision-making scheduling algorithm to choose the most trusted VN, accordingly.

3   Conclusion and Future Work

There is a growing need to manage volunteer nodes (VNs) that participate in emerging paradigms, such as volunteer cloud computing. We propose a zero-trust identity management model (ZTIMM) to calculate the trust score of VNs inside volunteer cloud computing networks. Our future plans include a full evaluation of the proposed model, working on five trust aware-based algorithms to manage the VN life cycle, datasets to test ZTIMM, and a real opportunistic cloud system, called cuCloud, we developed in our lab to obtain experimental results.

References

1. Mengistu, T., Alahmadi, A., Albuali, A., Alsenani, Y., Che, D.: A "no data center" solution to cloud computing. In: 10th IEEE International Conference on Cloud Computing, pp. 714–717 (2017)
2. Mengistu, T.M., Che, Alahmadi, A., Lu, S.: Semi-Markov process based reliability and availability prediction for volunteer cloud systems. In: 11th IEEE International Conference on Cloud Computing, IEEE CLOUD 2018 (2018)
3. McGilvary, G.A., Barker, A., Atkinson, M.: Ad Hoc cloud computing. In: 2015 IEEE 8th International Conference on Cloud Computing, pp. 1063–1068, New York (2015)
4. Mengistu, T.M., Albuali, A., Alahmadi, A., Che, D.: Volunteer cloud as an edge computing enabler. In: Zhang, T., Wei, J., Zhang, L.-J. (eds.) EDGE 2019. LNCS, vol. 11520, pp. 76–84. Springer, Cham (2019). https://doi.org/10.1007/978-3-030-23374-7_6
5. IDC's 2018 Cloud and AIAdoption Survey (2018). www.idc.com/getdoc.jsp?containerId=US44185818/
6. Kindervag, J.: No more chewy centers: introducing the zero trust model of information security. Forrester Research (2010)
7. Mengistu, T.M., Alahmadi, A.M., Alsenani, Y., Albuali, A., Che, D.: cuCloud: volunteer computing as a service (VCaaS) system. In: Luo, M., Zhang, L.-J. (eds.) CLOUD 2018. LNCS, vol. 10967, pp. 251–264. Springer, Cham (2018). https://doi.org/10.1007/978-3-319-94295-7_17
8. Indu, I., Rubesh Anand, P.M., Bhaskar, V.: Identity and access management in cloud environment: mechanisms and challenges. Eng. Sci. Technol. Int. J. **21**(4), 574–588 (2018)
9. Mohsenzadeh, A., et al.: A new trust evaluation algorithm between cloud entities based on fuzzy mathematics. Int. J. Fuzzy Syst. **18**, 1–14 (2016)

Author Index

Printed in the United States
By Bookmasters